PRAISE FOR
Clementine

"Winston Churchill kept nothing from Clementine. 'You know,' he informed FDR, 'I tell Clemmie everything.' Purnell has delivered an astute, pacey account of a woman who hardly ever emerged from the shadows. It is a sharp analysis of what it meant to be a politician's wife and shows how much we can learn about Winston Churchill from his wife and marriage."
—*The Wall Street Journal*

"Engrossing . . . Clementine Churchill became her husband's essential confidante and adviser, vetting his speeches, smoothing over his faux pas, dealing with his constituents. . . . Purnell's book is the first formal biography of a woman who has heretofore been relegated to the sidelines."
—*The New York Times*

"An acute and sympathetic biography which brings Clementine Churchill out of the shade into which her illustrious and domineering husband has cast her and shows how key she was to his success. Sonia Purnell makes us ask how Clementine endured life with Winston, and provides the answers."
—Margaret MacMillan, author of *Paris 1919* and
The War That Ended Peace

"Thorough and engaging . . . Purnell's extensive and insightful biography offers a much welcome portrait of Clementine Churchill, a woman whose remarkable life has long been overshadowed by her famous husband."
—*The Washington Post*

"In this wonderful book Sonia Purnell has at long last given Clementine Churchill the biography she deserves. Sensitive yet clear-eyed, *Clementine* tells the fascinating story of a complex woman struggling to maintain her own identity while serving as the conscience and principal adviser to one of the most important figures in history. Purnell succeeds brilliantly at an almost impossible task: providing fresh and thought-provoking insights into Winston Churchill in the course of examining his complicated marriage. I was enthralled all the way through."
—Lynne Olson, bestselling author of
Citizens of London and *Those Angry Days*

"An excellent book . . . Both scrupulous and fair-minded, Sonia Purnell has done her subject proud in this eye-opening and engrossing account of the strong-willed and ambitious woman without whom Winston Churchill's political career would have been a washout."
—Miranda Seymour, *The Telegraph* (UK)

"It seems extraordinary that no one has given this remarkable woman proper biographical treatment before. . . . She sacrificed her children and her health in the greater service of her husband, but she also kept him buoyant. This book is a salutary reminder that the Churchills were always a team."
—*The Times* (London)

"Sonia Purnell has restored Clementine Churchill to her rightful place in history. Behind every great man there is a great woman—and this was especially true of Winston Churchill. *Clementine* is a fascinating portrait of a highly complex woman who only ever showed a brave and elegant face to the world. At last, thanks to Sonia Purnell's excellent book, we see her true nature."
—Amanda Foreman, author of *A World on Fire* and *Georgina: Duchess of Devonshire*

"Until this biography, Clementine's influence had been completely overlooked and undervalued by Winston's biographers. Clementine was a complicated, mercurial figure, and Purnell does a wonderful job painting a full picture of a woman who was an excellent wife, a mediocre at best mother, and privy to some of the most profound moments of the modern era."
—Jessica Grose, in Lena Dunham's *Lenny Letter*

"A fascinating and well-written account of a woman who played a key role in many pivotal moments of early-twentieth-century British and world politics."
—*Minneapolis Star-Tribune*

"Fascinating . . . this book may leave you thinking Clementine is one of the most underrated, complex women in British history."   —*The Daily Beast*

"The extensive research shines a deserved spotlight on Britain's first lady through wartime and beyond."   —*Fort Worth Star-Telegram*

"A probing, well-researched, and wise biography."   —*The Washington Times*

"Sonia Purnell's fine biography . . . brings out of the shadows this formidable woman who was much more than strictly a spouse."   —*Newsday*

"At last Sonia Purnell has given us the first political biography of Clementine Churchill, a woman of power and progressive vision. Although she was her husband's best guide and most astute advisor during the worst of times, her essential role is generally unacknowledged. Boldly written and illuminating, this is a generative restoration of a fascinating woman who transcended family grief and marital agonies to lead her husband and the nation with grace, commitment, and persistence."
—Blanche Wiesen Cook, author of *Eleanor Roosevelt*

"Compellingly readable . . . Sonia Purnell's biography of Winston's wife Clementine brings her out from behind the shadow cast by the Great Man. She became her husband's wise counselor, discreetly offering sound advice, rewriting his speeches, toning down his foolish or angry letters, preventing him from making certain terrible political mistakes. . . . Her wheeling and dealing was done behind a veil of gracious femininity." —*The Independent* (London)

"Eye-opening . . . A bold biography of a bold woman; at last Purnell has put Clementine Churchill at the center of her own extraordinary story, rather than in the shadow of her husband's." —*The Mail on Sunday* (UK)

"In our own era of sturdy individualism, it is remarkable to read of Clementine's resolve to subordinate her own desires and her children's happiness to her husband's cause. . . . An intriguing study of a character both deeply flawed and, in her way, magnificent." —*Evening Standard*

"A sharply drawn, absorbing portrait of Churchill's elegant, strong-willed wife, who was also his adviser, supporter, protector, and manager . . . Purnell argues persuasively for Clementine's importance to history: she functioned as her husband's astute political strategist; insisted that he consider her feminist views; vetted his speeches; and campaigned for his successes. . . . A riveting, illuminating life of a remarkable woman." —*Kirkus Reviews* (starred review)

"This exemplary biography illustrates how Clementine's intelligence, hard work, and perseverance in often difficult circumstances made her every bit a match for her remarkable, intimidating husband, and a fascinating figure in her own right." —*Publishers Weekly* (starred review)

"Purnell does a remarkable job of proving that Clementine had a large impact on Winston's life. . . . He seems to have known immediately upon meeting her that she would be the one who could support his great ambitions and moderate his mood swings and gambling. . . . She edited his writing, advised him on political decisions, and volunteered in many ways throughout both world wars. Her significance, in many ways, can be compared to that of Eleanor Roosevelt." —*Library Journal*

ABOUT THE AUTHOR

Sonia Purnell is a biographer and journalist who has worked at *The Economist*, *The Telegraph* (UK), and *The Sunday Times* (London). Her first book, *Just Boris*, a candid portrait of London mayor and Brexit champion Boris Johnson, was longlisted for The Orwell Prize. *Clementine*, published as *First Lady: The Life and Wars of Clementine Churchill* in the UK, was chosen as a Book of the Year by *The Telegraph* (UK) and *The Independent* (London) and was shortlisted for the Plutarch Award.

Clementine

THE LIFE OF
MRS. WINSTON CHURCHILL

Sonia Purnell

PENGUIN BOOKS

PENGUIN BOOKS
An imprint of Penguin Random House LLC
375 Hudson Street
New York, New York 10014
penguin.com

First published in the United States of America by Viking Penguin, an imprint of Penguin
Random House LLC, 2015
Published in Penguin Books 2016

First published in Great Britain under the title *First Lady: The Life and Wars of Clementine Churchill*
by Aurum Press Ltd.

THE LIBRARY OF CONGRESS HAS CATALOGED THE HARDCOVER EDITION AS FOLLOWS:

Names: Purnell, Sonia, author.
Title: Clementine : the life of Mrs. Winston Churchill / Sonia Purnell.
Description: New York : Viking, [2015]
| Includes bibliographical references and index.
Identifiers: LCCN 2015373202 | ISBN 9780525429777 (hc.) | ISBN 9780143128915 (pbk.)
Subjects: LCSH: Churchill, Clementine, 1885–1977. | Churchill, Winston,
1874–1965—Marriage. | Prime ministers' spouses—Great Britain—
Biography. | Prime ministers—Great Britain—Biography. | Churchill,
Clementine, 1885–1977.| Churchill, Winston, 1874–1965. |
Marriage. | Prime ministers. | Prime ministers' spouses. | Great Britain.
Classification: LCC DA566.9.C48 P87 2015 | DDC 941.08/092 B—dc23

Printed in the United States of America
1 3 5 7 9 10 8 6 4 2

For Jon, Laurie, and Joe

With all my love

I send this token, but how little can it express my gratitude to you for making my life & any work I have done possible, and for giving me so much happiness in a world of accident & storm.

Winston to Clementine, on their fortieth wedding anniversary,
September 12, 1948, Cap d'Antibes

Contents

Introduction

L ate in the evening of Monday, June 5, 1944, Clementine Churchill walked past the Royal Marine guards into the Downing Street Map Room wearing an elegant silk housecoat over her nightdress. Still fully made up, she looked immaculate and, as always, serene. Around her the atmosphere was palpably tense, even frayed. She glanced at the team of grave-faced "plotters" busily tracking troops, trucks and ships on their charts. Then she cast her eyes over the long central table, whose phones never stopped ringing, to the far corner, where, as expected, she spotted her husband, shoulders hunched, face cast in agonized brooding. She went to him as she knew she must, for no one else—no aide, no general, no friend, however loyal—could help him now.

Clementine Churchill was one of a tiny group privy to the months of top secret preparations for the next morning's monumental endeavor. Fully apprised of the risks involved in what would be the largest seaborne invasion in history, she knew the unthinkable price of failure: millions of people and a vast swath of Europe would remain under Nazi tyranny, their hopes of salvation dashed. She also knew the ghosts that haunted Winston that night, the thousands of men he had sent to their deaths in the Dardanelles campaign of the First World War. She alone had sustained him through that disaster and the horrors of his time serving in the trenches on the Western Front.

Churchill had delayed the D-day operation for as long as he could to ensure the greatest chance of success, but now British, American and Canadian troops would in a few hours attempt to take a heavily fortified coastline defended by men who were widely regarded as the world's best soldiers. Huge convoys were already moving through the darkness toward their battle stations off the coast of Normandy. Earlier that evening, Winston and Clementine had discussed the prospects of the gambit's success, at length and alone, over a candlelit dinner. No doubt he had poured out his fears and she had sought, as so many times before, to stiffen his resolve. In the end, the command to proceed had been given.

Looking up now as she approached, Winston turned to his wife and said, "Do you realise that by the time you wake up in the morning twenty thousand men may have been killed?"[1]

To the outside world Winston Churchill showed neither doubt nor weakness. Since he had declared to the world in June 1940 that Britain would "never surrender," his was the voice of defiance, strength and valor. Even Stalin, one of his fiercest critics, was to concede that he could think of no other instance in history when the future of the world had so depended on the courage of a single man.[2] What enabled this extraordinary figure to stand up to Hitler when others all around him were crumbling? How did he find in himself the strength to command men to go to their certain deaths? How could an ailing heavy drinker and cigar smoker well into his sixties manage to carry such a burden for five long years, cementing an unlikely coalition of allies that not only saved Britain but ultimately defeated the Axis powers?

Churchill's conviction, his doctor Lord Moran observed while tending him through the war, began "in his own bedroom." This national savior and global legend was in some ways a man like any other. He was not an emotional island devoid of need, as so many historians have depicted him. His resolve drew on someone else's. In fact, Winston's upbringing and temperament made him almost vampiric in his hunger for the love and energy of others. Violet Asquith, who adored him all her life, noted that he was "armed to the teeth for life's encounter" but "also strangely vulnerable" and in want of "protection."[3]

Only one person was able and willing to provide that "protection" whatever the challenge, as she showed on that critical June night in 1944. Yet Clementine's role as Winston's wife, closest adviser and greatest influence was overlooked for much of her life, and has been largely forgotten in the decades since.

Neither mousy nor subservient, as many assume her to have been, Clementine Churchill was so much more than an extension of her husband. Like him, she relentlessly privileged the national interest above her health and family; her list of extramarital achievements would put many present-day government ministers, speechwriters, charity chiefs, ambassadors, activists, spin doctors, MPs and hospital managers to shame. Unlike Winston, she was capable of great empathy, and she had a surer grasp of the importance of public image. In her trendsetting sense of style she was a precursor to Jackie Onassis—with her leopard-skin coats and colorful chiffon turbans—and her skills as a hostess played a crucial role in binding America to the cause of supporting Britain. For all this and more, she was honored by three British monarchs, and by the Soviet Union. Just surviving, let alone shaping, what must surely count as one of the twentieth century's most challenging marriages should surely be a notable triumph in itself.

Winston once claimed that after their wedding they had simply "lived happily ever after." That is stretching the truth. There was never a break from the "whirl of haste, excitement and perpetual crisis"[4] that surrounded them. She could not even talk to him in the bathroom without on occasion finding members of the cabinet in there, half-hidden by the steam. Nor were their exchanges always gentle. They argued frequently, often epically, and it was not for nothing that he sometimes referred to her as "She-whose-commands-must-be-obeyed."[5] An opinionated figure in her own right, she was unafraid to reprimand him for his "odious"[6] behavior, or to oppose privately his more noxious political beliefs; gradually she altered his

Victorian outlook with what he called her "pinko" ideas and her support for women's rights. But however furiously they might have disagreed, she loved him and reveled in her union with a man so "exciting" and "famous." For his part, he simply doted and depended on her.

Throughout the first three decades of their marriage, Winston and Clementine were united by a common project: making him prime minister. When that goal was achieved, their aim changed and became survival itself. In peacetime, despite her misgivings about his refusal to give up politics, they were jointly dedicated to his legacy. Not only did they weather repeated public and personal humiliation together, they overcame the bitterest of personal tragedies and survived the all-but-intolerable strains of being at the center of two world wars. In so doing they forged one of the most important partnerships in history. The question is not just what she did for him, but what could he have done without her?

Even so, this formidable woman has virtually no public presence in popular history. While Churchill is understandably one of the most analyzed figures of all time, the preternaturally private Clementine has remained overlooked and unexplained. She is so elusive that views differ on such basic questions as the color of her eyes (gray, blue or hazel-brown?[7]) and hair (ash-blond, brown or red?[8]). Many people think Winston's wife was the "American one," when in fact it was his mother, Jennie, who came from the US. Consult certain biographies of Winston Churchill and she features as barely more than a passing acquaintance. The index of Nigel Knight's *Churchill: The Greatest Briton Unmasked*, for instance, contains not one single reference to Clementine. Other biographers, such as Richard Hough, author of *Winston and Clementine: The Triumph and Tragedies of the Churchills*, go so far as to claim that she was a "nuisance" who added to rather than reduced the pressures on her husband.

It is certainly true that Clementine was sometimes rigid and unforgiving, but in these traditionally minded, one-sided accounts Winston's own testament to what she meant to him has been conveniently underplayed or misconstrued. So have the perspectives of the many generals, politicians, ambassadors, civil servants and assistants who worked closely with them both and became her fervent admirers. Even Lord Beaverbrook, the buccaneering newspaper magnate who was for a long time her most loathed personal enemy, became in the end a devoted fan. It is ironic and telling that many of these incidental observers are far better known than she.

Today we are fascinated by the deeds and dress of our contemporary First Ladies, on both sides of the Atlantic. In a different era Clementine largely, if not wholly, escaped such media scrutiny. She hardly courted the press on her own account—though she was a skillful operator on behalf of her chosen causes. Yet she was more powerful and in some ways more progressive than many of her modern successors. The struggles she endured still resonate—not least her grueling inner turmoil, which Winston found so difficult to understand. It is high time for a fresh appraisal of the woman behind this great but erratic man, one that will allow her contribution to be duly recognized.

The only existing account of Clementine's life—an admirable book by the Churchills' daughter Mary Soames—was, although later revised, first published nearly forty years ago. It understandably treats its subject from the family's viewpoint, with conspicuous gaps in the story. Since then many revealing papers—such as the Pamela Harriman collections at the Library of Congress in Washington, DC—have been released or have come to light for the first time, and several former staff have opened up about their experiences. What fascinates over and over again is the strength of the impression Clementine made on so many people, including allies from Russia, Canada, Australia and America, as well as those who witnessed her in action closer to home. Some contemporaries recorded a "physical shock" on meeting her for the first time. Who would have guessed that she laughed louder than Winston? That she was taller than him and decidedly more athletic? That he cried more than she did and owned more hats? That the camera never quite captured her startling beauty and that she could, like a princess, lift a room merely by entering it? Or that she was not the paradigm of upper-class matronliness but the surprising product of a broken home, a suburban grammar school and a lascivious mother, and that one of her most formative years was spent in and around the fish market at Dieppe?

This is not a history of the war, or a study of Winston Churchill from an alternative vantage point, although oft-neglected aspects of his character do come to the fore. It is, instead, a portrait of a shy girl from a racy background who was related to Britain's most glamorous aristocratic family (in more ways than one) but was looked down upon by her own mother and disdained by the dominant political dynasty of her day. It is the story of someone who feared casinos and bailiffs, and struggled to bond with her children. It is an attempt to recover the memory of a woman who married a man variously described as "the largest human being of our times" and "the stuff of which tyrants are made." (That he never became one is in no small part thanks to her.) Even before 1940 Clementine's life was packed with drama, heartache and endurance. But, colorful and troubled as her life had been thus far, all of that was merely a lengthy and exhaustive apprenticeship for her critical role as First Lady during her country's "death fight" for survival.

Before Clementine Britain had known merely the "politician's wife": opinionated, perhaps, but rarely directly involved in government business. And today we have much the same: women glossed up for the cameras on set-piece occasions, thin, smiling and silent. Her immediate successors—Violet Attlee in 1945 and Clarissa Eden in 1955—were of markedly lesser ambition and failed to pick up her baton. Clarissa, Anthony Eden's wife, was glamorous, younger, more intellectual and arguably more modern than Clementine (her aunt by marriage), but she lacked a populist touch and admits she was never even briefed on government business, and lacked "the gumption to ask." She said: "I can't believe how passive and hopeless I was."[9] Clementine's postwar successor, Violet Attlee, was "jealous" of the time taken up by her husband's job[10] and Harold Wilson's wife, Mary, was at first so overawed at being the prime minister's spouse that she would be physically sick every morning.[11] Cherie Blair, probably the prime ministerial consort most involved in her husband's role since Clementine, explained the universal predicament thus: "There is no job description for the Prime Minister's spouse because there is no job. But there is a unique position that provides for each holder an opportunity and a challenge."[12] How interesting that a woman born into the Victorian age, who never went to university, had five children and could not vote until her thirties, should have grasped that opportunity and challenge with greater ambition and success than any of those who have come since.

The case can be made that no other president or prime minister's wife has played such a pivotal role in her husband's government. It was arguably greater than that of even the greatest of American First Ladies, Clementine's direct contemporary Eleanor Roosevelt. This appears all the more remarkable in light of how poorly defined and resourced the position at 10 Downing Street is in comparison with that of American First Ladies. From the very earliest days of the Union the wife of the US president has enjoyed a status that, albeit not enshrined in the Constitution itself, provides an official platform for public work and influence, backed by the heavily staffed Office of the First Lady. Clementine had no official staff, role model or guide-book. She in effect invented her wartime role from scratch, and eventually persuaded an initially reluctant government to help her.

She never sought glory for her achievements and rarely received it. She was in fact genuinely astonished when noticed at all. Curiously, it was often visiting Americans who were most observant of the scale of her contribution during the war. The US ambassador Gil Winant was intensely moved when he accompanied her on a tour of bombed-out streets during the Blitz. As she talked to people left with little more than piles of rubble, he noticed the "great appreciation" she stirred in middle-aged women, who seemed inspired and uplifted by her presence. Marveling at the "deep" and "significant" looks of empathy that "flashed between her and these mothers of England," he was puzzled as to why the newspapers and indeed the British government made so little of what she did.[13] Clementine's huge mailbag at the time was full of letters from people who were grateful for her help, people who viewed her as their champion. But while others, such as the queen, have been loudly and widely hailed for their war work, her part in the story seems to have been lost.

"If the future breeds historians of understanding," Winant wrote shortly after the return of peace, Clementine's "service to Great Britain" will finally be "given the full measure [it] deserves." This book attempts to do just that.

CHAPTER ONE

The Level of Events

1885–1908

F ear defined Clementine Hozier's earliest memory. Having been
deposited by her nurse at the foot of her parents' bed, she saw her
"lovely and gay" mother, Lady Blanche, stretch out her arms toward
her. Clementine yearned for her mother's embrace yet she froze on
the spot at the sight of her father slumbering at her mother's side. "I
was frightened of him," she explained much later.[1] By then the damage had been done. Clementine was never to gain a secure place in
her mother's affections nor would she conquer her trepidation of the
forbidding Colonel Henry Hozier, who, she came to believe, was not
her father anyway. For all the fortitude she would show in adulthood,
her instinctive insecurity never left her.

The Hoziers were living on Grosvenor Street, in central London,
a far cry from the romantically haunted Cortachy Castle, in the Scottish Highlands, where Lady Blanche had grown up. Clementine's
mother was the eldest daughter of the tenth Earl of Airlie, whose
ancient Scottish lineage was enlivened by castle burnings and Jaco-
bite uprisings. Her seraphic face belied her own rebellious spirit, and
her parents, their family fortunes much reduced by the earl's gambling losses, had been keen to marry her off. They were thus relieved
when in 1878, at the age of twenty-five, she became engaged to Colonel Hozier, even though he was fourteen years her senior and only
come-lately gentry of limited means.

Lady Blanche's mother, also called Blanche, was a Stanley of Alderley, a tribe of assertive and erudite English matriarchs who com-

bined radical Liberal views with upper-class condescension. They thought new clothes, fires in the bedroom and—above all—jam the epitome of excessive indulgence. Champions of female education, the Stanley women had cofounded Girton College in Cambridge in 1869. No less formidably clever than these eminent forebears, the elder Blanche had later mixed with the likes of the novelist William Makepeace Thackeray, the Tory prime minister Benjamin Disraeli, his bitter Liberal rival William Gladstone, and John Ruskin, the art critic, designer and social thinker. She had made her ineffectual husband switch the family political allegiance from Conservative to Liberal and was equally forceful with her tearful granddaughter Clementine, who was not her favorite. It was evidently unfitting for a girl of *Stanley* blood to show her emotions.

Hozier's family made its money in brewing, gaining entrance to society thanks to the profits of industry rather than the privilege of birth. Although his elder brother became the first Lord Newlands and Henry himself received a knighthood in 1903 for his innovative work at Lloyd's of London after a distinguished career in the army, the Hoziers remained essentially *nouveau*: middle-class stock who earned their own living.

In the eyes of many in the City, Henry was a "flamboyant" personality, but the Lloyd's archives suggest a darker nature. He had graduated top of his class from Army Staff College and was decorated with the Iron Cross by Emperor Wilhelm I when serving as assistant military attaché to the Prussian forces during the Austro-Prussian War of 1866, and this and his service in Abyssinia and China appear to have gone to his head. His colleagues at Lloyd's thought he was a "born autocrat" with an "excessive love of power" and an absence of humor. He also apparently suffered from an "excessive" fondness for spending the corporation's money. An internal investigation in 1902 revealed that his business methods, while productive, were of "doubtful ethics." Some of his soi-disant successes were, in truth, exaggerated or unfounded, and after he challenged one persistent critic to a duel in 1906, his reputation inside the upper echelons of Lloyd's never quite recovered.[2] Clementine was probably unaware of these stains on his character, admitting in a booklet she wrote for her own children, entitled "My Early Life," that she knew very little about her father's existence outside the home.

The earl considered his son-in-law a "bounder," and Lady Blanche soon discovered to her horror that her husband's previous career giving orders in the army had led him to expect the same unquestioning obedience at home. Far from liberating her from parental control, marriage to the splenetic and vengeful Henry proved even more restrictive. Before her wedding, Lady Blanche had assumed that she would become a notable political hostess in her own right. After leaving the military in 1874 Hozier had briefly dabbled in public life—standing unsuccessfully in 1885 as the Liberal Unionist candidate for Woolwich and helping to pioneer the idea of an intelligence service—but he had not the remotest interest in hosting his wife's freewheeling aristo friends. Nor did he want children. Lady Blanche decided that she would take the matter into her own hands if he refused to oblige her. It was not helpful that Hozier was frequently away on business and unfaithful himself. Sexy, bored and lonely, Lady Blanche saw no reason not to shop around for a worthy mate of her own.

Five years after her wedding day, on April 15, 1883, she gave birth to her first child, Kitty. Two years later, on April Fools' Day, Clementine (rhyming with *mean*, not *mine*) was born in haste on the drawing room floor. The twins—Nellie and William (Bill)—came three years later. It is now thought that none of the four children was Hozier's and that there may in fact have been more than one biological father. Although it was not unusual for upper-class couples in the late nineteenth century to take lovers, the custom was to wait until an heir had been born before playing the field. Discretion was also expected. Lady Blanche ignored all the rules to such an extent that there were rumors of altercations between rivals. Indeed, she is reputed to have juggled up to ten lovers at once—a feat of athletic organization that she was pleased to advertise quite widely.

Clementine had no knowledge of all this as a child, and the family has only in recent years publicly acknowledged the question marks over her paternity. Doubts were, however, well aired by others during her lifetime. Lady Blanche's own, albeit inconsistent, confessions to friends suggest that Clementine was in fact a Mitford. Her handsome and generous brother-in-law, the first Baron Redesdale, Bertie Mitford, was certainly a favored amour. Photographs of Clementine and Bertie—particularly in profile—suggest remarkable similarities, not least their fine aquiline noses. Perhaps it was as a tribute to her sister's forbearance in sharing her husband in this way that Lady Blanche named her second daughter after her. Bertie's legitimate son David went on to father the six renowned Mitford sisters: the novelist Nancy, the Nazi supporters Unity and Diana (whose brother Tom shared their fascist sympathies), the Communist Decca and Debo, later Duchess of Devonshire, and Pamela, who largely escaped public scrutiny.

Besides Mitford, the other prime candidate is Bay Middleton, an avid theatergoer of great charm and private melancholy. He later broke his neck steeplechasing but was a frequent visitor to Lady Blanche during the years when she conceived her two eldest daughters. She dropped hints to notable gossips that he was the one, although some have since suggested that this was a fig leaf for her sister's sake. Such was the complexity of Lady Blanche's sex life that we shall probably never know the truth. Clementine's daughter Mary Soames found it "difficult to take a dogmatic view," saying, *"Je n'y ai pas tenue la chandelle."*[3]

The excitable younger Mitfords relished their great-aunt's racy reputation, but the rest of Lady Blanche's family thought her "mad." London's more respectable drawing rooms were similarly scandalized by the public uncertainty over the Hozier children's paternity, with the result that Lady Blanche was regularly snubbed. Meanwhile, her children were cared for by a succession of grumpy maids and governesses who vented their frustration by swishing their wards' bare legs with a cane. The one kindly soul in those early years was sixteen-year-old Mademoiselle Elise Aeschimann, a Swiss governess who arrived when Clementine was three. She thought the infant girl starved of attention and took to carrying her around everywhere, despite Lady Blanche's admonitions not to spoil her. Mademoiselle

Aeschimann started Clementine and Kitty on their lessons, especially French, and though she stayed only two years her warmheartedness made a lasting impression. Clementine later went to visit her in Switzerland and even helped her financially when she fell on hard times in old age.

Clementine remained an anxious child, however, and was tormented by a perfectionist streak. According to her daughter Mary she had a "most sensitive conscience, and suffered untold miseries if the immaculate white of her lace-edged pinafore was marred by spot or stain."[4] She took endless pains to form the neatest handwriting, a trait that led the adult Clementine to describe her younger self as a "detestable little prig."[5] Her principal emotional crutch was a large black pet poodle called Carlo, which devotedly listened to her troubles until it was tragically killed under the wheels of a train. Clementine had been ordered to leave the dog behind at the family's new home, a country house outside Alyth in Scotland, but Carlo had pursued her to the station and tried to jump on board. "I do not remember getting over this," she told her children many years later.[6] Such emotional neediness—and a continuing fear of adults—earned her much maternal scorn. Kitty, by contrast, was puckish, pretty, shared her mother's extroverted flamboyance and won Lady Blanche's effusive love. Unsurprisingly, she became accustomed to getting her way—even once threatening to burn down the house to stop a governess from reporting her latest misdeed. Lady Blanche's devoted preference for her firstborn was brazen and consistent.

In autumn 1891, Hozier sued for divorce and the two elder girls became "helpless hostages" in a bitter battle over custody and financial support. Clementine was just six when she and Kitty were wrested from their mother and sent to live with their father and his sister, the spinster Aunt Mary, who believed children benefited greatly from being whipped. Hozier found the girls an inconvenience, so he parceled them off to a governess in the Hertfordshire town of Berkhamsted. Rosa Stevenson advanced her charges little academically but both girls observed her fastidious housekeeping, including the two hours spent every day polishing the oil lamps:

"They burnt as bright and clear as stars," Clementine remembered fondly.[7] She also recalled the delicious sausages, "although the slices were too thin and too few."

Sadly, Aunt Mary considered Mrs. Stevenson too soft and uprooted the girls again, this time dispatching them to a "horrible, severe"[8] boarding school in Edinburgh. The odor of yesterday's haddock and the crumbs on the floor offended Clementine, and like her sister she felt desperately homesick.

Hozier finally relented and allowed Lady Blanche to extract her unhappy daughters and whisk them back to her rented house in Bayswater, a district then known among the smart set as the West London "wildlands." Waiting for them there were the four-year-old twins Bill and Nellie, who, after a year apart from their elder siblings, no longer recognized them. Hozier came for tea on a couple of occasions but his awkward visits were not a success and soon stopped altogether. Once the divorce was finalized, almost all of his financial support dried up. Lady Blanche may have had her children back, but she was now dependent on her own cash-strapped family for handouts.

Over the following eight years, Lady Blanche and her brood led a peripatetic existence, moving from one set of furnished lodgings to another. In part this was out of financial necessity, to keep one step ahead of her creditors, but the constant roaming also suited her capricious nature. She ensured every new home was elegant and fresh, with snowy white dimity furniture covers (always two sets so they could be kept spotlessly clean) and fine muslin curtains on the windows. Clementine was enraptured by her mother's ability to spin comfort out of the least promising circumstances, writing in "My Early Life": "She had very simple but distinguished taste and you could never mistake a house or room in which she had lived for anyone else's in the world." Lady Blanche's exalted standards even inspired a new verb: to "hozier" became synonymous among her daughters' friends with to "tidy away." Unfortunately the cost of such stylish homemaking pushed the family ever further into debt.

In an effort to earn her keep, Lady Blanche, who was an excellent cook, wrote culinary articles for the newspapers, but she sometimes found herself too bored or distracted to put food on the table for her own offspring. She was frequently absent (presumably with one of her many lovers) but if her children sometimes wanted for maternal attention they rarely went short of instruction. Their mother employed full-time French- or German-speaking governesses and other teachers were brought in as required. The only, rigidly observed, omission from their education was arithmetic, which Lady Blanche deemed "unseemly" for girls.

Around 1898, when Clementine was thirteen, Lady Blanche decamped from London for rooms near the railway station at Seaford, just east of the English Channel port of Newhaven. There she lived with her dogs Fifinne and Gubbins on the first floor at 9 Pelham Place, a modest gray terrace house, while Clementine, Kitty, Nellie, Bill and their "feather-headed" governess stayed at number 11. Lady Blanche refused to muzzle her dogs, in contravention of strict new antirabies laws, and was once summoned to the magistrates' court in Lewes. Although she emerged from the trial with the desired "not guilty" verdict, perhaps due to the fact that one member of the bench was a personal friend, Clementine was troubled by her mother's being "not very law-abiding."9

This rackety existence could not have been in starker contrast to the four weeks the children spent every summer with their grandmother in the historic splendor of Airlie Castle. Here Lady Blanche's mother, the Dowager Countess of Airlie, kept an unblinking vigil against any hint of a lack of gratitude—a subject upon which she had written an essay—insisting on the need to instill this virtue in young children as "otherwise they grow up louts."10 She believed in fasting to "awaken the gifts of the Spirit" and loathed unladylike pursuits. Lady Blanche allowed Kitty and Clementine to play croquet (a practice that would later prove extremely useful) but only behind the gardener's cottage, out of Grannie's sight. She may have had a fiery temperament but her natural rebelliousness provoked her to give her daughters what were then unusual freedoms. Not only did she hire bicycles for them back in Seaford (with their being too expensive to buy), she allowed them to play bicycle polo on the rough grass opposite their lodgings too. Another beloved, unfeminine pastime was cricket, at which Clementine would in time become a decent player. She was also taught locally to play a creditable game of golf.

By now Clementine and Kitty were quite different: the former plain and awkward; the latter pretty and flirty—albeit impudent and ruthless as well. Clementine stood in her boisterous sister's shadow but never showed any jealousy. In fact she found Kitty a comfort in a bewildering world. The star relied on a devoted supporting act, and while this role was far from easy it was nonetheless one in which Clementine came to excel. Like Lady Blanche, she was "dazzled" by her sister. Kitty, meanwhile, shared her younger sibling's "unspoken contempt" for their mother's "violent, ungovernable partiality." "You mustn't mind it," she would counsel Clementine. "She can't help it."[11]

Clementine's plight won sympathy from at least one of Lady Blanche's friends—Mary Paget, a tenderhearted woman who often invited the girl to stay at her nearby home, West Wantley. Clementine adored the sixteenth-century manor with its ducks, chickens and boating lake, and envied the Pagets their stable family life. She considered Mary, who was her only real childhood friend, to be the most beautiful woman in the world. In truth, Mary was handsome but plump, and sometimes her stays would burst open while she was gardening. She pinned false gray hair into her rather sparse bun and it would habitually fall out among the flower beds.

Clementine's fondness for this generous woman made her return to Seaford all the more wrenching at the end of the golden weeks spent in her care. Many tears would be shed, and noticing Clementine's reddened eyes, Lady Blanche once angrily accused her of loving Mary Paget more than her. To which Clementine rashly replied: "Of course I do."[12] The Wantley trips were stopped.

With no real home or father, scant money and precious little maternal love, it is perhaps unsurprising that on the cusp of her adolescence Clementine entered an emotionally religious phase. She yearned for respectability and certainty, and in November 1898, she was confirmed in Kirriemuir Church, near Lady Blanche's family seat, watched by her mother, grandmother and Mary Paget. Her piety became so fervent that on one occasion, after listening to a sermon on charity, she donated a pendant given to her by a relative, only to be admonished for giving away such a valuable gift and compelled to ask for its return.

By the summer of 1899 Lady Blanche was deeply in debt. Hozier had failed to provide even the meager allowance he had agreed to following the divorce, but governesses still had to be paid, and then there were the annual fees for Bill's education at Summer Fields preparatory school in Oxford. Lady Blanche wanted him to benefit from the sort of schooling expected of the grandson of an earl, but her mother's help extended only so far, and lawyers instructed to pursue Hozier by her brother Lord Airlie had drawn a blank. Lady Blanche's financial straits had been worsened by illness. Over the spring months she had suffered from quinsy, a nasty complication of tonsillitis involving abscesses on the throat. In the age before antibiotics, it was a serious condition and she was laid low, finding it difficult to swallow. She was hardly in a fit state to up sticks once again, yet in the last week of July, out of the blue, the children were told they had just hours to pack all their possessions as the next morning they were moving to France.

Lady Blanche had long suspected that Hozier might try to snatch back Kitty and Clementine and it appears she suddenly had reason to suspect a strike was imminent. It was this fear that had motivated her curious decision to move to Seaford, as the town lay a mere five hours across the English Channel from their destination, Dieppe. Such was the haste of their departure that she had no time to plan what they would do once they reached France. Family lore has it that she chose where to go on arrival with the toss of a coin. What we do know is that she hailed a cab for Puys and, upon spotting an attractive farm, La Ferme des Colombiers, along the way, ordered the driver to stop so that she might ask the owners if they had spare rooms. Luck was on her side and the family stayed there for the next two months, enjoying an idyllic summer of swimming and picnics. Clementine was living out of a suitcase once again.

In the autumn Lady Blanche moved her brood into town, renting a modest redbrick house at 49 rue du Faubourg de la Barre in Dieppe itself, where she hoped to enroll the girls in the school at the Convent of the Immaculate Conception. Already an adept French speaker, Clementine adjusted well to her new setting, but she was keenly aware of her outsider status. When the nuns and other girls sided against the British following the outbreak of the Second Boer War in October 1899, she and Kitty played truant in protest, idling away the morning forlornly on the beach. Nonetheless, she enjoyed her surroundings. Much of her time was spent outdoors, and she became more athletic and confident, displaying a competitive streak on the hockey field, where she broke her stick during a particularly fierce bout with an opposing center-forward.

Lady Blanche made the best of her exile. She relished Dieppe's bohemian lifestyle, which attracted foreign writers and artists such as Oscar Wilde, Max Beerbohm and Walter Sickert. She also enjoyed the casino, quickly becoming a regular. Needless to say, she lost money she did not have, and to Clementine's shame, the family was forced to ask for credit in the local shops. She was learning all too young to deal with public humiliation, and it was difficult not to blame her mother for their plight. Here was the source of a lifelong puritan streak; her fear of gambling never left her—indeed, it would later come to haunt her in the most horrific fashion.

Clementine's acute discomfort was not shared by her mother. Still beautiful at forty-seven, Lady Blanche continued to walk proud. The Dieppois were intrigued by this titled lady who ignored the fashions of the day, replacing the customary hat perched on a bun with a stylish mantilla and long plait down her back. Nor did Lady Blanche's daughters escape her cut-price interpretation of *la mode*—when Kitty, Clementine and their younger sister, Nellie, went shopping in the markets they did so clothed in cheap gingham dresses.

Clementine was embarrassed by these deviations from upper-class norms but whatever their attire, the girls' beauty was making an impact. While Kitty was more striking, with her long dark hair and deep blue eyes, the slender, tall and fairer Clementine was finally beginning to blossom. The painter Walter Sickert, a frequent visitor, flirted with the older girl but he took Clementine more seriously. He once invited her to tea alone at his lodgings where he lived with Madame Augustine Villain, his mistress, model and landlady, and the acknowledged queen of the Dieppe fish market. Madame Villain had several children who looked uncannily like Sickert, but he also seems, to Clementine's horror, to have been involved with Lady Blanche. "She remembered terrible rows between her mother, Mr. Sickert and the fishwife," recalls Shelagh Montague Browne, who later worked for Clementine. "It was a ménage. The fishwife would be throwing things in the market in a jealous temper. Clementine thought it all *so* unseemly."

For all Sickert's reputation at the time as a figure of, at best, questionable morals known for his paintings of explicit nudes, Lady Blanche allowed her fourteen-year-old daughter to go unchaperoned to his house. (Later in life Clementine herself developed a poor opinion of Sickert, once telling Cecil Beaton, "He was, without doubt, the most selfish human being I've ever come across,"[13] and the crime writer Patricia Cornwell has recently suggested—though her thesis is much disputed—that he might even have been Jack the Ripper.) Following her mother's instructions, Clementine made her way up to Sickert's room. Finding him absent and the place a shambles, she followed her instincts and tidied up, throwing away the remains of a herring on the table. When Sickert returned, he angrily informed her that she had discarded the subject of his next painting. She was terrified at first but they soon sat down to chat over brioches and tepid cider. By the time she emerged, her intelligence and poise had won his admiration.

One snowy winter's night late in 1899, Lady Blanche's fears were confirmed. She was with Kitty, Clementine and Sickert in her sitting room, which looked directly out onto the street. The fire was lit but the curtains not yet drawn when Clementine noticed a strange male figure at the window. Before she could look again, her mother had grabbed her and Kitty and pushed them both onto the floor. The mysterious man stared and stared through the glass while they continued to lie prostrate out of sight. When he finally turned away, they heard the doorbell ring, but as Kitty rose to answer it her mother sharply pulled her back down. After an interminable wait, they heard the man walk away at last, and Lady Blanche revealed to the astonished girls that he was their father. She sent Kitty into the hall to see if he had left a letter.

Kitty returned with two, one for her, one for Clementine; they contained invitations from Hozier to dine and lunch with him in a private room at the Hôtel Royal on succeeding days. Clementine pleaded to be allowed not to go but her mother insisted they should; their trusty French maid Justine would accompany them to and from the hotel (although she would not be in attendance during the actual meals).

After Kitty's uneventful dinner, it was Clementine's turn for lunch. This time, Hozier tried to banish Justine from returning to collect her young mistress, insisting that he would escort his daughter home himself. Clementine directed an imploring look at her maid, begging her not to desert her, and during the meal of omelet and larks-en-brochette she was virtually speechless from anxiety. Hozier then delivered the dreaded news: she was to come to live with him, or rather with the whip-happy Aunt Mary.

Faced with this unthinkable prospect, Clementine exhibited a hitherto undetected determination and courage. While surreptitiously slipping on her gloves under the table, she announced calmly that her mother would refuse to allow her to leave Dieppe. The moment the faithful Justine returned for her, she rose from her chair and politely but firmly bade Hozier good-bye. In a fury, he suddenly barred her way, thrusting a gold coin into Justine's hand and pushing her violently out the door as he did so. Clementine was now trapped and alone with him once more, but when he moved to fetch a cigar, she valiantly seized her chance, flung the door open and ran full pelt toward Justine, who was waiting uncertainly outside. The two girls scrambled away as fast as they could on the icy pavements with Hozier, swearing angrily, in pursuit. Only once they neared the safety of the house did he finally give up and turn back.

The bank manager and the captain of the Dieppe–Newhaven steamer later confirmed that Hozier had been planning to kidnap Clementine and take her back to England that very afternoon. Her quick thinking had saved her. As her future husband would later put it, Lady Blanche's once timorous daughter had displayed an exceptional ability to "rise to the level of events."

Scarcely had one crisis passed before another came to test her. Just a few weeks later, in February 1900, Kitty contracted typhoid, probably from contaminated water. Clementine and Nellie were quickly sent away, making the long journey to relatives in Scotland alone. Fearing the effect on Kitty if she knew her sisters were leaving, Lady Blanche told them to say "good night" rather than "good-bye." The last they saw of Kitty, as they closed the door, was a silent and emaciated figure confined to bed.

With Bill already back at school in England, Lady Blanche was now free to pour all her energies into saving her sick child. She was helped by Sickert, who carried bucket after bucket of ice up to the girl's room in a bid to reduce her raging fever. But despite all her mother's efforts, Kitty died a month before her seventeenth birthday. Her body was taken back to England, where Lady Blanche pointedly chose to bury her beloved daughter at the Mitfords' home at Batsford rather than the family seat of Cortachy.

Clementine cut a lonely figure in the family now, for she was a young woman of nearly fifteen while the twins were three years younger and still children. Nor could her mother, who was never the same again, reach out to her. There was no enmity between them but their grief brought a further distancing. Clementine was never to know the full, undivided warmth of a mother's love and now she had lost the elder sibling who had understood and appreciated her. She became protective of her little sister, Nellie, but Lady Blanche also soon transferred her attentions to her youngest daughter, leaving Clementine out in the cold once more.

• • •

Their time in Dieppe was now over. Less than a year after leaving England, the family was uprooted yet again and returned to the picturesque suburban town of Berkhamsted, which offered cheap accommodation near a railway service to London and good inexpensive schools. They moved into an unpretentious Georgian terraced house on the high street, not far from where Clementine had stayed with Rosa Stevenson nine years earlier. She liked her new home, with its long narrow garden running up the hill at the back, and, despite the tragedy of losing Kitty, she was about to embark on what were probably the happiest and certainly the most settled years of her early life. Two months after her sister's death, Clementine started at the local grammar school, Berkhamsted School for Girls.

The experience was to change her outlook completely. Here she was fortunate to enjoy an education superior to that received by other aristocratic girls still tutored by governesses at home. A staff of clever, dedicated and often humorous female teachers quickly recognized her potential. Clementine was mixing with the largely friendly daughters of shopkeepers and doctors and both she and Nellie acclimatized quickly to all that provincial grammar school life entailed. Any awkwardness she might have felt in joining the school at fifteen, after her rackety aristocratic upbringing and with precious little formal schooling behind her, seems quickly to have dissipated. She had a particular fondness for her French teacher Mademoiselle Kroon, who would rouse daydreaming pupils with such lines as "Now, you fat bolster, wake up!" and she liked the company of her classmates. Indeed, she would seek them out again in later life, and would read the school magazine until her death. Seventy years after she left, Berkhamsted School was represented at her funeral.

On the family's return to England, Hozier asked to see Clementine once again. This time Lady Blanche accompanied her to his house in North Audley Street, London, but as she was taking leave of her daughter Hozier came to the door. He flew into a rage at the sight of his wife, leading to an ugly scene in the street and further mortification for Clementine. She had no way of knowing that this was the last time she would see this "strange, violent yet most compelling man."[14] Despite her fear of her ostensible father, she later came to regret that Hozier, who died in Panama in 1907 at the age of sixty-nine, a year before her wedding, would never meet her future husband.

Back in the safe and studious atmosphere of Berkhamsted School, Clementine continued to thrive. Starting in what would now be tenth grade, she was quickly promoted to senior French. Lady Blanche's aversion to the teaching of sums, however, accounted for a humiliating demotion to a lower year for math. While Nellie was relaxed about her studies—preferring to devote her energies to captaining the girls' cricket team—Clementine was highly competitive. Nearly half a century later, when she returned to give a speech on the school's Commemoration Day in 1947, she spoke of the joy her education had brought her. "I loved it," she told the girls. "I felt I was out in the world, and on my own, away from the fiddling little tasks of arranging the flowers, folding the newspapers and plumping up the cushions."

Prizes came quickly. In 1901, she won a solid silver medal for French presented by the French ambassador, and even Lady Blanche now recognized her daughter's potential. The following year she treated Clementine to a trip to Paris with a former governess, Mademoiselle Louise Henri. Having been told to stay as long as they could on £25, they eked out this sum by barely eating. They visited museums, lectures and art galleries and Mademoiselle Henri gave Clementine thrilling glimpses of another world, pointing out famous music hall artistes in the street. Sickert, who turned up out of the blue one evening, also took her to meet the painter Camille Pissarro, who lived in a garret, and then to dinner in an elegant house where everything was "exquisite"—the food, the furniture, the host's manners. Clementine lapped up every minute; she now thirsted for worldly knowledge and experience.

Encouraged by her headmistress Beatrice Harris, whose embrace of feminine independence and suffragist views would have an enduring influence on Clementine, she was secretly nursing dreams of academia. University for women was still a comparative novelty, but Miss Harris (who later described her former pupil to Winston as "one of the high lights of the school" and "a worthy helpmeet"[15]) was so confident of Clementine's chances that she offered to take her in over the holidays to continue her studies. This was going too far for Lady Blanche; she wanted her daughter to be well educated but not a bluestocking spinster. She rejected Miss Harris's generous offer and set about sabotaging Clementine's studious ambitions by diverting her into trivial traditionally feminine pursuits. Undeterred, Clementine crept up to the graveyard on the hill behind the house to study mathematics in secret, her books arranged across the flat tombstones. She was further spurred on in her studies by her great-aunt Maude Stanley, the sister of Lady Blanche's mother, who also introduced her to the exciting world of politics. A kindly intellectual spinster in her late sixties who took a great interest in the welfare of women and the poor, Maude considered Clementine a kindred spirit.

In the tussle over Clementine's future, however, Lady Blanche held the trump card. To stop this university nonsense once and for all she approached another relative, the wealthy Lady St. Helier, an aunt by marriage, and enlisted her help in launching Clementine into the world to which, by birth and upbringing, Lady Blanche deemed that she "properly" belonged. (Her own reputation and financial difficulties meant that she could do little to advance her daughter herself.)

Lady St. Helier—popularly known as Lady Santa Claus—loved to help the young. One of her beneficiaries, for whom she had pulled some strings in the British Army, was a certain Winston Churchill, the son of her American friend Lady Randolph Churchill, known to her closest friends as Jennie. Now here was a poor—and beautiful—female relation also in need of her support. Lady St. Helier invited Clementine to stay at her distinguished London mansion at 52 Portland Place, near Regent's Park, and bought her a gown. She took her to lavish balls and glittering dinners, where, no longer eclipsed by Kitty, Clementine was fêted for her beauty. Sure enough, she was distracted from her schoolbooks and her head was turned. The possibility of leading an independent life at university and beyond had glimmered briefly but was now snuffed out forever.

By the time Clementine passed her Higher School Certificate in the summer of 1903, there was no more talk of academia. She left Berkhamsted and Miss Harris behind, albeit with happy and grateful memories. Lady Blanche had been so successful at dispensing with Clementine's academic ambitions that she saw fit to reward her daughter by taking a house for them that winter in Paris, in the rue Oudinot in the seventh arrondissement. She even permitted Clementine to attend a few lectures at the Sorbonne. More to Lady Blanche's taste, however, was the fashionable Voisin, a smart restaurant near the Palais Royal. Clementine loved the glamour but worried that such lavish spending was unwise. Lady Blanche explained that it was merely part of a civilized education, and in truth the grammar school pupil was feeling ever more at home in high society. In the spring of 1904, she was sent to stay for three months with the von Siemens family, the founders of the German electrical engineering company of the same name, in a beautiful house on the lake in Wannsee, a fashionable suburb of Berlin. Here she perfected her schoolgirl German, learned to ride and absorbed all that upper-class Berlin life could offer. A certain Continental polish merely inflated her reputation. On her return to London there were plenty of invitations and soon lots of suitors too, with Nellie jokingly keeping a "file" of proposals under "Discussed," "Answered" and "Pending."

Chief among the pending was the eligible Sidney Cornwallis Peel. The younger son of a viscount (and grandson of former prime minister Sir Robert Peel), he was constant, fifteen years her senior and rich. He took her to the theater and sent her white violets every day. Lady St. Helier thought her job was done. But Clementine was a romantic, and she knew she was not in love. Despite all the pressure from her relatives to accept his hand, poor Sidney was simply not exciting; his letters veered from pleading to peevish and were generally, as he conceded himself, rather dull. He appears to have sensed that she was underwhelmed, writing in one of the few that have survived: "It was stupid of me to allow myself to be goaded into a black rage."[16] She broke off one engagement but was later secretly betrothed to him for a second time.

Then, in April 1906, she found her nerve again—at her cousin Sylvia Stanley's wedding. Sylvia was in pain from a broken arm but insisted that the ceremony go ahead. Her passionate determination to marry the man she loved contrasted sharply with Clementine's own tepid feelings and she parted from Sidney for the last time.

Afterward she seems to have panicked; after all, she needed to escape from her mercurial mother and what she would later confess to have been a "very difficult childhood."[17] Within weeks she was engaged again, this time to Lionel Earle, a wealthy civil servant with intellectual tastes. He was twice her age, and she had known him for barely a month. When he joined her for a fortnight's holiday in the Netherlands, she saw him for the pompous bore he really was. Distraught, she broke off yet another engagement and had to return early wedding presents. The resulting emotional stress led to two months in bed.

Now that Nellie had also finished school, Lady Blanche gave up the lease on the house in Berkhamsted and moved to London to take a firmer hand in her daughters' social careers. It is not clear how she financed the rent, but Lady Blanche first opted for 20 Upper Phillimore Place, in Kensington, where Clementine had no choice but to earn her keep, supplementing her small allowance by giving French lessons at a half crown an hour. A year later Lady Blanche moved again, this time more permanently, to a cream-painted stucco house nearby at 51 Abingdon Villas (not then a modish address). Here Clementine also began working for her cousin Lena Whyte's dressmaking business. Needlework bored her, but she learned to make clothes and even hats—for herself as well as for clients. Later she compared these years to the struggles of Scarlett O'Hara, the heroine of *Gone with the Wind*, who keeps up appearances by making her gowns from old curtains.[18]

It was a very different existence from the idle luxury in grand houses enjoyed by her Stanley cousins Sylvia and Venetia, or the aristocratic circles in which her mother wanted her to move. Her clothes, for all Lady St. Helier's generosity and her own needle and thread, made her feel like an outsider. So too did her inability to return hospitality. She was all too aware of the sniggers about her lack of fortune and knew that the less charitable found a snobbish glee in calling her "the Hozier." She was also considered cold; but while certainly reserved, she was in the main trying to protect herself in a world that was both cliquey and savage. "Nobody knew who I was, so I felt terribly out of place," she recalled to one of her assistants later in life. "I hated it."[19]

Dressing in this era of upper-class Edwardian leisure was time-consuming and expensive, a process that involved high-maintenance coiffures, hats and numerous outfits. Just one "Saturday to Monday" country house weekend required several large trunks of different clothes, as outfits were changed four times a day. For her peers, there were servants who washed, starched, ironed, stitched, fetched and brushed and pinned up hair, whereas Clementine performed most of these chores herself. It is little surprise that as soon as she could afford one in later life she insisted on hiring a lady's maid, and kept one long after the role had largely gone out of fashion.

Lack of an adequate wardrobe meant that some invitations had to be refused, but Clementine had inherited her mother's genius for making the simplest outfits elegant. She was usually able to hold her own for an evening at least. Several contemporary accounts pour praise on her beauty. The diarist Lady Cynthia Asquith wrote that she should have been a queen, describing her as "classical, statuesque, yet full of animation . . . her superbly sculpted features would have looked so splendid on a coin."[20] The society magazine the *Bystander* described Clementine in a 1908 issue as having "most delicately aquiline features, fine grey eyes, and a delightful poise of the head" with "the grace and distinction and soft strength of early Grecian art: she is divinely tall." Sir Alan Lascelles, the future royal secretary and most pernickety of aesthetes, told Clementine's daughter Mary that he would never forget his first glimpse of her mother in the Christmas holidays of 1903, when he was a sixteen-year-old schoolboy and she just two years older. Upon her announcement by the butler, the doors were thrown open to a large gathering, and in walked "a vision so radiant that even now, after sixty-one years, my always moving, always fastidious, eye has never seen another vision to beat it."

The "beautiful Miss Hozier" was gratifyingly admired but Lady Blanche remained Clementine's harshest critic. For all her own wanton pleasure-seeking, she insisted her daughter return from balls by the impossibly early hour of midnight. When Clementine inevitably arrived home late, her mother would reprimand her in full view on her doorstep. On one occasion, Lady Blanche even boxed her ears, an assault so traumatic that Clementine ran without hat or coat the three miles to Mary Paget's house in Harley Street. The sympathetic Mrs. Paget went to reason with Lady Blanche before Clementine would agree to return home.

A year after finishing school, during the summer season of 1904, Clementine attended a ball given by Lord and Lady Crewe at their home in Curzon Street. Among the guests in this Liberal household was Winston Churchill, now a rising young politician. Already a controversial figure, he was barred from most Conservative homes because earlier in the year he had defected from the party to join the Liberals over his opposition to tariff reform. (Winston was committed to the principle of free trade on the basis that it would keep food prices low, while the Conservative government was seeking to protect British industry with import duties.) Considered a renegade and class traitor by the Tories, he was viewed as pushy and puffed up even by admirers. His notorious adventures during the Second Boer War (the conflict doughtily defended by Clementine against her French classmates in Dieppe) and the insalubrious way in which his famous father, Lord Randolph, had died (reputedly from syphilis) lent him an air of raffish danger. A prolific author as well as a soldier and MP, he was already a celebrity.

Upon arriving at the ball, accompanied by his American mother, the voluptuous Jennie, Winston was arrested by the sight of a fawn-like girl alone in a doorway. He stood motionless, staring at her. He asked who she was and it transpired there were many connections between them: Jennie's brother-in-law, Sir Jack Leslie, was the girl's godfather and some years earlier Jennie herself had been a great friend of her mother. So Lady Randolph—whose supposed collection of two hundred lovers over her lifetime outnumbered even Lady Blanche's—introduced Winston to Clementine. The great wordsmith was struck dumb, not even managing the customary invitation to dance. Clementine assumed she had been introduced out of pity, and in any case did not care for what she had heard about this notorious publicity-seeker. He was, to boot, shorter than her and with his pale round face was not exactly handsome. Clementine signaled to a male friend, Charles Hoare, for rescue. He swept her away onto the dance floor, where he asked what she had been doing talking to "that frightful fellow Churchill."

It was an encounter that left no lasting impression on either of them. Winston had a habit of clamming up when first meeting beautiful women, as he had no capacity for small talk. He was also chauvinistically judgmental: he and his private secretary Eddie Marsh would habitually rank a woman on whether her face could launch "a thousand ships," merely two hundred, or perhaps just "a covered sampan, or small gunboat at most."[21] Of course only an armada would do for him, so he had spent years chasing the "thousand ships" Pamela Plowden, daughter of the Resident of Hyderabad, Sir Trevor Chichele-Plowden. "Marry me," he had once declared, "and I will conquer the world and lay it at your feet."[22] At other times, though, he was capable of "forgetting" to see or even write to her for months on end, and she detected something tellingly unphysical in his manner. In any case, his future was uncertain and his finances even more so, and Pamela Plowden was not a woman to gamble with her own comfort. Nor could she remain constant; after rejecting Winston's proposal in 1900 she married the less demanding Earl of Lytton and proceeded to take numerous lovers.

Winston, unlike so many other powerful men then or since, was not tremendously fired up by sex. For him, like the hero in his semi-autobiographical novel *Savrola*, "ambition was the motive force and he was powerless to resist it."[23] Pamela rightly understood that any wife would always take second place to his career and that, although viewing their beauty with semireligious awe, he could be brusquely dismissive of women's conversation. His belittling of Lucile, the heroine in his novel, with the line "Woman-like she asked three questions at once"[24] is indicative of his general attitude.

Winston felt he *ought* to have a wife, however. In the running around 1906 was shipping heiress Muriel Wilson, another willowy beauty with expensive tastes. Once again the sexual spark was missing, and in any case she found politics boring and could not envisage sacrificing her life of pampered luxury to the inconveniences of public duty. Her firm rejection was humiliating.

Before that he had flirted with the American actress Ethel Barrymore, who had caused a sensation in London when, in 1902, she arrived in a low-cut bodice pinned with flowers. Winston took her to the Churchills' family seat, Blenheim Palace, and upon her return to America he bombarded her with political news from Britain. He proposed to her two years later but her lack of interest was made all too clear when she inadvertently praised one of his greatest parliamentary foes.

Earlier still he had visited the West End music halls, once launching a rousing tribute to the dancers at the Empire Promenade, who were then under attack from antivice campaigners. "In these somewhat unvirginal surroundings," he recalled later, "I made my maiden speech." The nature of his interest in the dancers is debatable. On one occasion he went home with a Gaiety girl, who when asked the next morning how it had gone, replied that Winston had done nothing but talk into the small hours "on the subject of himself."[25] So, as he approached his midthirties, he was still to marry or, as the newspapers liked to point out, grow a mustache or hairs on his chest. The press began to label him with that undesirable tag "confirmed bachelor."[26]

One evening in March 1908, Clementine returned home tired after a day of teaching French to find a message from Lady St. Helier asking her to make up the numbers at a dinner the same evening. Clementine was reluctant: she had no suitable gown and was out of the requisite clean white gloves. But, under pressure from Lady Blanche, she eventually picked out a simple white satin princess dress and did her duty for her benefactress.

At 12 Bruton Street, Mayfair, Winston's faithful private secretary Eddie Marsh found him lingering in his bath. He was grumpy about the prospect of a dinner party that he fully expected to be a "bore." Marsh tactfully reminded him of Lady St. Helier's many kindnesses, and after more fuss eventually his boss rose from the bathwater to dress.

Clementine was already starting on the chicken course with the other guests by the time Winston arrived. Ruth Lee, the wealthy American who, with her British husband, Arthur, later donated their country house Chequers to the nation, wrote in her diary that Winston had taken the "vacant place on his hostess's left. He paid no attention to her, however, as he became suddenly and entirely absorbed in Miss Clementine Hozier, who sat on his other side, and paid her such marked and exclusive attention the whole evening that everyone was talking about it."[27]

Winston's fascination was piqued by one of the very necessities that, in Clementine's eyes, made her an outsider: never before had he met a fashionable young woman at a society dinner who earned her own living. Not only was this in itself to his mind worthy of respect but she was also ethereally lovely—another admirer had compared her to a "sweet almond-eyed gazelle." At twenty-two, she knew far more about life than the ladies of cosseting privilege he normally met, and she was well educated, sharing his love of France and its culture.

Through the influence of her aunts and her schooling, here was a woman who was actually interested in politics, if still unversed in its cut and thrust. She was receptive to new ideas, especially, it seemed, from him. For her, his gauche behavior at the ball four years previously had seemingly given way to a maturity and eagerness to please. She found his idealism and brilliance liberating.

After the ladies had left the table, Winston seemed exceptionally keen to finish his cigar and join them. He strode straight over to Clementine and monopolized her so obviously for the rest of the evening that the other women teased her when she finally left to fetch her coat. Years later, when asked whether she had found Winston handsome at that first meeting, she replied tactfully: "I thought he was very interesting."[28] His one false move was an unfulfilled promise to send her a copy of his biography of his father, Lord Randolph Churchill: the omission "made a bad impression on me," noted Clementine later.

Thereafter he wasted little time. Within a couple of weeks he had invited Clementine and Lady Blanche to his mother's house, Salisbury Hall, near St. Albans, in Hertfordshire. There, Clementine had an early taste of political life when his promotion to the cabinet as president of the Board of Trade (at the precocious age of thirty-three) was announced during her stay. No doubt the excitement of being at the center of national events lingered in her thoughts as she embarked, soon after, on a long-standing trip to pick up Nellie from a tuberculosis clinic in the Black Forest and visit her grandmother in Florence.

Winston's first letter to her, on April 16, demonstrates a dramatic change in tone from his gushing notes to women such as Pamela. He wrote about how much he had enjoyed their discussions at Salisbury Hall, paying particular tribute to her cleverness. Here at last was a woman he could talk to rather than worship. "What a comfort & pleasure it was to me to meet a girl with so much intellectual quality & such strong reserves of noble sentiment," he wrote, adding that he hoped they would lay the foundations of a "frank & clear-eyed friendship" with "many serious feelings of respect."[29] Clementine fired off an equally telling letter to Jennie: "You were so kind to me that you make me feel as if I had known you always. I feel no-one can know him . . . without being dominated by his charm and brilliancy."

In those days it was customary for MPs elevated to the cabinet to stand for reelection. So while Clementine was in Germany, Winston began campaigning in his largely working-class seat in northwest

Manchester. In one letter to her, he referred in glowing terms to the help given to him on the stump by the famously good-looking Lady Dorothy Howard. Why he thought it fitting to praise this other woman for fighting on his behalf in every slum, crowd and street "like Joan of Arc before Orleans" can only be imagined. As can Clementine's reaction to his observation that Dorothy was "a wonderful woman—tireless, fearless, convinced, inflexible—yet preserving all her womanliness." On April 23 she replied: "I feel so envious of Dorothy Howard—It must be very exciting to feel one has the power of influencing people . . . I feel as much excited as if I were a candidate."[30]

This expression of political interest—with its hint of jealous concern—must have greatly pleased Winston, who may have been testing Clementine for her reaction. In a quick crossfire of correspondence, on April 27 he added: "How I should have liked you to have been there. You would have enjoyed it I think." He exhibited, moreover, a new mood of measured self-revelation, not least when he wrote: "Write to me again. I am a solitary creature in the midst of crowds. Be kind to me." Here at last the rumbustious adventurer of popular folklore felt safe enough to admit that he was lonely. Indeed, in all the seventeen hundred letters and notes that Winston and Clementine would send to each other over the next fifty-seven years, isolation among people would prove the most persistent theme.

To the woman who had since Kitty's death felt unneeded, this was a clear signal that she might at last have found a new role to play. And despite his praise for Dorothy Howard, there was no reason for Clementine to regard her as a threat. Howard was too didactic on both women's suffrage and teetotalism—neither cause dear to Winston's heart—and he later referred to her as a "tyrant," if also "a dear." But he was at the same time something of a tease and liked to provoke Clementine to jealousy.

Her commitment was also tried when, for all Howard's efforts, on April 23 Winston lost the Manchester election. Now Clementine could see for herself the violent reactions he sometimes aroused. The *Daily Telegraph*, which had never forgiven him for abandoning the Tories for the Liberal Party, reported: "We have all been yearning for this to happen . . . Winston Churchill is out, Out, OUT." She could not help but admire, however, the way he picked himself up from this defeat before winning another election in Dundee the following month. She was now avidly reading the newspapers to monitor his every move.

Unusually self-sufficient, Clementine did not tell even close friends about her feelings, but she was convinced that she was in love. She saw Winston again several times in June and July but never alone. At times she would refuse his invitations, simply to avoid gossip, although she did agree to meet him at Salisbury Hall again in August. In the meantime, she was horrified to discover that a serious fire had broken out at a house where she knew him to be staying. Relieved to read in the *Times* that no one had been injured, she rushed to the post office to wire her joy to him.

Winston took this as a sign and persuaded his cousin Sunny, the Duke of Marlborough, to invite her to Blenheim. She demurred—not least because she was down to her very last clean dress. But Winston was insistent, promising that his mother and Sunny would look after her. "[Sunny] is quite different from me, understanding women thoroughly, getting into touch with them at once," he wrote rather naively. "Whereas I am stupid and clumsy in that relation . . . Yet by such vy different paths we both arrive at loneliness!"[31]

Clementine could refuse no longer. On August 10 she left the Isle of Wight, where she had been staying, and took the train to Blenheim. As she traveled through the English countryside, she wrote in shaky handwriting to Lady Blanche back in London: "I feel dreadfully shy & rather tired . . . I . . . can do nothing more intelligent than count the telegraph posts as they flash by." Soon afterward she was walking up the front steps into the gloom of Blenheim's great hall. There to greet her, below the muscular victory arch, were Winston; Jennie; the Duke; Winston's great friend F. E. Smith and his wife, Margaret; plus a private secretary from the Board of Trade. It was clear this was to be no low-key visit.

Alone in her high-ceilinged bedroom, she found a fire in the grate despite the August heat—an extravagance that no doubt offended her frugal nature. She looked in dismay at the bathtub, the hot and cold water jugs, the towels and sponges, knowing she had no way of dressing to the standards that her hosts would expect. Her spirits were lifted only when there was a knock at the door; noticing her unusual lack of a lady's maid, Jennie had discreetly sent her own. Yet despite this act of kindness, Clementine failed to sparkle at dinner, feeling impossibly shy in that cavernous Blenheim saloon with its forbidding military frescoes. Winston talked so much that perhaps he never noticed. He did, however, promise to show her the famous rose gardens overlooking the lake the following morning.

Punctual as ever, Clementine descended to breakfast at the appointed hour only to be left waiting and waiting. Fearing that she would flounce out at any moment, Sunny hastily invited her for a drive around the estate while he sent word of the emerging crisis up to Winston—who was still slumbering in his bed. The walk was hastily rearranged for the afternoon, when finally Winston escorted Clementine to the gardens. They strolled down the hill, following the twists and turns in the path through the cedars and oaks planted for suspense and drama by the great landscape architect Capability Brown. They toured the rose garden, only some of its flowers drooping from the heat, and admired the glimpses of the great lake through the leaves. Yet by the time they began to make their way back up to the house, still nothing of much import had been said.

Finally, a summer shower drove the couple to take shelter in a little Greek temple folly, but there was by now a certain tension between them. Clementine spotted a spider scuttling across the floor, and with steely determination quietly decided that if Winston had not declared himself before it reached a crack in the flagstones she would leave regardless.[32] Happily, just in time, Winston asked at last if she would marry him. Without any further unnecessary hesitation she agreed, on condition that he promise to keep their betrothal secret until she had asked for her mother's consent. But as they were leaving the temple, a seemingly intensely relieved Winston spotted Sunny and could not help himself, shouting: "We're getting married! We're getting married!" Despite this minor betrayal, she later sent him a note via the footman: "My dearest One, I love you with all my heart and trust you absolutely."[33]

The next day Clementine left Blenheim with a letter from Winston to her mother, asking for Lady Blanche's permission to marry her daughter and promising to give his prospective bride a "station" in life worthy of "her beauty and virtues." He could not bear to wait for the answer, though, and at the last moment jumped on the London-bound train beside her.

Lady Blanche considered Winston just right for her unusual offspring. He did not have the fortune she would have liked, but he was brilliant and ambitious and could earn his own living—and at least he was marrying for romance rather than money. In an approving letter to her sister-in-law, she said: "I do not know which of the two is the more in love."[34] Soon afterward Winston wrote to Clementine, "[There are] no words to convey to you the feelings of love & joy by wh my being is possessed. May God who has given to me so much more than I ever knew how to ask keep you safe & sound."[35] Clementine responded gleefully: "I feel there is no room for anyone but you in my heart—you fill every corner."[36]

News of the engagement drew mixed reactions. In Dieppe, Madame Villain ran through the streets crying out the news in delight. The chattering classes in London took a more negative view of the marriage's prospects, deciding that Clementine would either be crushed or prove insufficiently malleable. Her grandmother predicted that the woman she'd known as such a fearful child would obediently "follow" Winston and "say little."[37] Lord Rosebery, the former prime minister, forecast the pair would last six months, because Winston was "not the marrying kind."[38]

Clementine told people that she was under no illusions that being married to Winston Churchill would be easy but she did think it "would be tremendously stimulating." She was also excited about her ring—"a fat ruby with two diamonds," she boasted to Nellie. But somehow, now that she was engaged she was more reticent with him, writing: "Je t'aime passionément—I feel less shy in French." It appears her reserve worried Winston; he wrote to F. E. Smith: "Is it fair to ask this lovely creature to marry so ambitious a man as myself?"[39]

Even so, he would not brook a long engagement. A date was fixed for the wedding at St. Margaret's, Westminster, for a month's time. Clementine wanted everything to be perfect, but as the days flew by with so much to be done she felt herself sinking. The newspapers were now following her every step. She was young, beautiful and marrying a celebrity; she was news, with all the personal invasion that entails. Photographs of her face were everywhere. The *Daily Mail* took a particular interest in a dress fitting that lasted, by its calculations, six hours. By contrast, Winston—tied up with his politics as ever—was rarely to be seen. There were moments when she began to falter, but her brother, Bill, steadied her. He reminded her that she had already broken off at least two engagements and that she could not humiliate a public figure like Winston Churchill.

There was a reason other than nerves for her wobble. Shortly after their engagement, Winston had embarked on an eleven-hundred-mile round trip to a Scottish castle on a rocky promontory north of Aberdeen, where another beautiful young woman was waiting for him. Over the past year he had become close friends with Violet, the slender-waisted twenty-one-year-old daughter of his relatively new boss, the Liberal prime minister Herbert Henry Asquith. Although spoiled and immersed in a life of almost royal luxury, Violet had a brilliant mind—in her stepmother Margot's view "alas too brilliant"—and found most men her age dull. She held Winston, however, in the "high esteem he held himself." In fact, they were remarkably alike—opinionated, garrulous, idealistic, willful and pugnacious. Both, moreover, loved and lived politics. She met him at balls and dinners, or when he came to visit her father; soon she was clearing her diary to see him all the more. Later Violet would insist they had always been just friends, but all the signs are that she was deeply in love. She declared herself "inebriated" by the way he talked and "enthralled" by his genius. Unfortunately, Winston was not in search of a female version of himself.

Upon learning of the engagement on August 14, Violet had reputedly fainted and then written a venomous letter to Clementine's cousin Venetia Stanley, who was to be a bridesmaid at the wedding. Winston's new fiancée, said Violet, was as "stupid as an *owl*," no more than "ornamental," and incapable of being "the critical reformatory wife" Winston badly needed in his career to "hold him back from blunders." Venetia replied by noting that the *Manchester Guardian* had (generously) included in a list of Clementine's accomplishments six languages, music and brilliant conversation, adding, "I think he must be a good deal in love with her to face such a mother in law."[40] Even so, Violet's stepmother, Margot, remained convinced that Clementine had no brains, character or strength and was in fact "mad," whereas Violet's patronizing view was that she was "sane to the point of dreariness." Asquith himself predicted merely that the match would be a "disaster."

Clementine later admitted to finding such a reception as Winston's new fiancée "petrifying" and had instinctively opposed his decision to go ahead with his long-planned visit to Violet's holiday retreat—where Miss Asquith was caustically remarking that at least the engagement would provide "the Hozier" with a rest "from making her own clothes." Winston fatefully concluded it was still his duty to make his peace with the other woman who loved him, and once there, he and Violet went for romantic cliff-top hikes—but their time together soured when she slipped and cut her face, leaving her miserable and, in her own words, looking "worse than the vampire in *Jane Eyre*."[41] By the time he left a few days later, she was almost hysterical.

Although the Asquiths were invited to the wedding, they did not come. Not that Violet had done with Winston; far from it. But Clementine would soon discover that she had more than one rival on her hands for his attentions.

CHAPTER TWO

More Than Meets the Eye

1908–14

Waking up at dawn on her wedding day in a large, chilly room at Lady St. Helier's mansion did nothing to boost Clementine's spirits. Exiled by her mother from her own home to make room for guests, she was cut off in Portland Place from the bustle of family life. She longed to return, even if only for breakfast, for one last taste of the familiar before taking the leap into the unknown as Mrs. Winston Churchill.

Alas, a maid had taken away her day clothes, leaving her nothing to wear but her wedding dress. Feeling trapped, Clementine crept down the majestic staircase in her dressing gown while the house was still in shuttered darkness and Lady St. Helier asleep. The only soul about was a young under-housemaid blacking the grate in the morning room. Seeing a friendly girl of similar age, if not prospects, Clementine unburdened herself of her troubles. The good-hearted servant quickly abandoned her work to scurry upstairs to her attic.

Minutes later, a figure slipped out of a back door in the classic uniform of an off-duty maid. Wearing a dark, close-fitting cheap coat over a pretty print dress and black-buttoned boots, she hopped on a bus west to Kensington. A conductor, recognizing his famous passenger from the newspapers, suggested Clementine must have made a mistake. London was abuzz with the excitement of an aristocratic beauty marrying a global celebrity. Crowds of the scale normally seen only at a royal wedding were already beginning to take up their positions on the streets. But now here was the bride riding a bus *away* from where the ceremony was due to take place.

Nothing would deter her from returning to Abingdon Villas, however, and she arrived to astonished gasps, not only at her presence but also her unexpected attire. A merry time with Nellie and Bill restored her resolve and she soon headed back (by horse-drawn brougham this time) to prepare for the two p.m. service at St. Margaret's in Parliament Square.

It was September 12, 1908, and many grandees were still away on holiday, including half the cabinet, who had sent their regrets. Among the thirteen hundred guests who did turn up to Parliament's parish church were David Lloyd George, the Liberal chancellor of the Exchequer; F. E. Smith, one of the few Tories who had forgiven Winston's defection to the Liberals; and General Sir Ian Hamilton from his army days.

A number of places on the bride's side—it was anyone's guess exactly how many—were occupied by her mother's former admirers. Some were mischievously placed together, such as the gossipy poet Wilfrid Scawen Blunt and the Scottish peer Hugo Charteris, but significantly it was Bertie Mitford who sat in the front row beside Lady Blanche, who was resplendent in a purple silk gown trimmed with white fur. On the groom's side of course was Winston's mother, Jennie, competitively dolled up in beaver-colored satin and a hat decorated with dahlias. A fading beauty of fifty-four, she was now married to a man a mere fortnight older than Winston by the name of George Cornwallis-West.

The bells of Big Ben struck two o'clock, and four minutes later Clementine entered the fifteenth-century white-stone church on the arm of her handsome brother, Bill, now an officer in the Royal Navy. She walked down the aisle framed by rows of soaring white Gothic arches, bathed in the autumn sun streaming through the windows. Draped in shimmering white satin, a veil of tulle clipped to her hair by a coronet of fresh orange blossom, she wore diamond earrings from Winston and clutched a bouquet of fragrant white tuberoses and a white parchment prayer book. Behind Clementine were five bridesmaids—Nellie, cousins Venetia Stanley and Madeline Whyte, Winston's cousin Clare Frewen and a friend, Horatia Seymour. All wore amber-colored satin gowns and carried bunches of pink roses. More roses and camellias tumbled across their large black satin hats.

The choir sang "Lead us, Heavenly Father" while members of the congregation climbed on their seats for a better look. Many thought Winston fell short as the dashing groom in the presence of such elegance, and flanked by his dapper best man, the mustached Lord Hugh Cecil. He was losing hair and gaining weight, his face "settling into the attitude of pugnacity it was to become famous for."[1] *Tailor and Cutter* magazine branded his morning suit "one of the greatest failures as a wedding garment we have ever seen," claiming that it lent him the appearance of a "glorified coachman." When Clementine reached this unprepossessing figure before the altar, he somewhat bizarrely held out his hand and warmly shook hers.

Dean Welldon, who had been Winston's headmaster at Harrow, proceeded to sum up what was now expected of the bride. A statesman, he declared, should be able to depend "upon the love, the insight, the penetrating sympathy and devotion of his wife." Her role, and the influence she would exercise in her husband's future public life, was so important as to be "sacred." Winston's vows after this portentous address were loud and clear, hers so soft as to be barely audible. The whole ceremony was a rehearsal for her future; when signing the register, Winston deserted her for an animated political discussion with Lloyd George.

When the married couple finally emerged from the church, mounted policemen held back the cheering throngs along the route to the reception back at Portland Place. There, guests were treated to a display of the wedding gifts: twenty-five silver candelabra and a large collection of wine coasters, pepper pots and silver inkstands paraded alongside a gold-topped walking stick sent by King Edward VII, and £500 in cash from the fatherly figure of German-born financier Sir Ernest Cassel. Clementine's aunt Maisie had given her a chain set with "myriads" of sapphires, opals, amethysts and topazes, Winston's aunt Cornelia a diamond necklace. Alongside these treasures were a fresh turbot with a lemon stuffed in its mouth—a gift from Madame Villain of Dieppe—and a manual entitled *House Books on 12/- a Week*.

The crowds had been won over by Clementine's grace and beauty, and so had the press. In one of the next day's papers a cartoon of a grinning Winston holding a stocking appeared over the caption: "Winston's latest Line—Hoziery." "Undoubtedly," proclaimed the *Times*, the event had "captured the public imagination." The *Daily Mirror* hailed it as "the Wedding of the Year."

They spent their first evening as husband and wife at Blenheim—the palace having been tactfully vacated by Sunny, the duke. It can only be guessed who was the more nervous. Both were almost certainly virgins and at nearly thirty-four, Winston's manly pride was at stake. He had been worried enough beforehand to seek advice from an expert—his mother. By the time they left Blenheim a couple of days later for Baveno on Italy's Lake Maggiore, it appears the young couple had got the hang of things. On September 20, Winston was able to report to Jennie that they had "loitered & loved,"[2] and with surprising candor he described sex to his mother-in-law as "a serious and delightful occupation." Perhaps Winston applied the same energy and attention to the details of lovemaking as he did his other "occupations." Within a month of their return from their honeymoon Clementine was pregnant.

While the newlyweds were busy loving in Italy, Clementine's cousin Venetia had traveled to Slains Castle to stay with Violet Asquith. A week after the wedding, Venetia burst into the dining room to announce that she could not find her friend, who had last been seen at dusk, book in hand, on a cliff-top path. Guests, servants and villagers were summoned to search the sharp rocks at the foot of the sixty-foot drop, shouting, "Violet!" into the moonless mist as the sea crashed angrily about them. It was treacherous work lit only by lanterns and toward midnight hopes started to fade. Her father sobbed into his wife Margot's arms. She started to pray.

Shortly thereafter, cheers went up from some fishermen: Violet had finally been found unhurt on soft grass near the house and was already regaling her rescuers with thrilling tales of having slipped on the rocks and knocked herself unconscious. News got out and reporters quickly descended on the castle, demanding photographs and interviews. Sensational headlines such as MISS ASQUITH'S PERIL and HOUSE PARTY'S THRILLING SEARCH followed, but Violet's eagerness to oblige the press led Margot to suspect that the "accident" might not have been altogether accidental. Doctors could find no evidence of a blow to the head and the more Margot tried to avoid publicity, the more thrillingly near-fatal Violet's story became. Some even began to speculate that Violet had attempted suicide, although it seems almost certain that she had merely intended "to cause [Winston] a pang."[3] Either way, Violet was becoming a specter at Clementine's feast.

Margot removed Violet and the family from the eerie atmosphere at Slains, a vast, ancient and reputedly haunted castle perched on the edge of a desolate headland, but for some time after the so-called Rock Affair her stepdaughter continued to show signs of "almost hysterical"[4] behavior. Violet's father, the prime minister, feared more unhelpful attention and had to intervene personally to stop her racing off to meet Winston when he arrived back in Britain. With time, her mood calmed, and she finally returned to London. But Winston was still concerned, and in November he arranged for her to have lunch with him and his new wife. Violet behaved well, but the conversation was no doubt strained and the newly pregnant Clementine would not have been in her best form. Winston's decision to catch a cab alone with his guest afterward appears thoughtless, but according to Violet's account he was eager to impress upon her that Clementine "had more in her than met the eye." With what Violet herself described as "cloying" self-restraint she responded: "But so much meets the eye."[5]

Though mostly sensed rather than heard, the continuing criticism from such quarters was wreaking havoc on Clementine's fragile confidence. Violet and her family were at the center of a snobbish circle of brilliant intellectuals with immense power and privilege. Her bosom pal Venetia, Clementine's super-confident Stanley cousin, could finish the *Times* crossword without needing to write in a single letter. By contrast Violet thought Clementine "very nervous & excited in public" and prone to "beginning her sentences over & over again & constantly interrupting herself." Her eyes, reputedly her best feature, were actually "tired & pink." But Violet also noted that her figure was *"Divine"* and (rather condescendingly) that the content of her conversation was beginning to improve. Clementine, meanwhile, understandably enjoyed it when others turned a critical eye on Violet—although she would wisely refrain from joining in. She knew the esteem in which Winston held her rival and could not help but be jealous. The sentiment was mutual.

Clementine's pregnancy made Winston's bachelor apartment in Bolton Street impracticable. Although fitted with electric lighting, it was tall and narrow with endless flights of stairs. Every surface—even in the bathroom—was covered with model soldiers, polo team photographs, tiny silver cannon or books. This was no place for Clementine to make her first real home, and by the time she returned from her honeymoon, it was even less so. Jennie had given her bedroom a surprise Edwardian makeover, dressing it with sateen bows for the full boudoir effect. A natural minimalist, Clementine could barely conceal her horror; she now considered her mother-in-law a "trial."[6]

For her part, Jennie had welcomed Winston's choice of bride but this marked the beginning of a fraught relationship between the two women. Clementine saw how Winston adored his mother despite her faults. She had seemed a "fairy princess" to him as a child, and later he had harbored somewhat Oedipal feelings for her. Aged twenty he had written in a letter: "How I wish I could secrete myself in the corner of the envelope and embrace you as soon as you tear it open."[7] Even now Winston often chose to walk arm in arm with his mother, leaving Clementine feeling like an intruder.

In recent years Jennie had marshaled her formidable intellect, contacts and womanly charms (although some argued not her critical faculties) to advance Winston's career. Having pioneered the role first of active political wife and then mother, Jennie was a hard act for Clementine to beat. A flashing-eyed voluptuous beauty—once described as "more panther than woman"—and one of the first American heiresses to marry into the British aristocracy, Jennie had many male admirers, including the king, but the bed-hopping that had lately benefited her son offended Clementine's rigid moral code, as did her marriage to the young and impecunious George Cornwallis-West, which she viewed as "vain and frivolous." (Cornwallis-West was in fact pursuing a flamboyant affair with the actress Mrs. Patrick Campbell and the marriage ended as widely expected in 1914. Jennie cited his refusal to grant her conjugal rights as grounds for divorce and became dependent on her sons for support.)

When that marriage broke down, Clementine, according to her daughter Mary, "resented the way [Jennie] leant so heavily on her elder son . . . They never had a classic falling out. It's just that [Clementine] never joined in the chorus of praise for her mother-in-law."[8] She also railed at Jennie's extravagance. Winston's mother, a friend explained, was a woman for whom "life didn't begin on a basis of less than forty pairs of shoes."

Clementine blamed Jennie for Winston's own excesses and was appalled to discover how she and her late first husband, Lord Randolph, had neglected their eldest son throughout his childhood. His mother, she felt, had only "discovered" Winston when he became "famous," after his father's death. While at school he had sent Jennie letter after letter pleading with her in vain to visit him, the crosses for his kisses so numerous they would fall off the page. At fourteen, Winston was still writing, "I long to see you my mummy," but Jennie considered him too "ugly," "slouchy and tiresome"[9] to bother with. Her selfishness and his lack of a settled home life made him feel "destitute."[10] For both Winston and Clementine a steady, loving childhood had been unknown.

Clementine could also empathize with Winston's pain at his father's

obvious preference for his younger, less troublesome brother, Jack.
Lord Randolph barely spoke to Winston unless to deliver a rebuke;
some historians go so far as to suggest his father actively loathed his
son. Winston was a disappointment to him: the poor results he
achieved on his entrance exam consigned him to the bottom class
at Harrow and he was considered not to have the brains for the bar,
let alone Oxford, although the more enlightened teachers recognized that he had unusual gifts. Even by upper-class Victorian standards their parental neglect was unusual. Friends and relations
would urge them to "make more" of Winston; one kindly soul,
Laura, Countess of Wilton, even wrote to him as self-appointed
"deputy mother," sending him money and food. Jennie failed even
to remember her sons' birthdays.

As children both Winston and Clementine had relied on middle-
aged women outside the family for emotional sustenance, in his case
none more so than his nanny Mrs. Everest, whose unconditional love
was the only thing that made him feel safe. It was she who had ensured Winston was extracted from a prep school where the sadistic
headmaster repeatedly flogged him. Mrs. Everest had also tried to
rein in his spending and instructed him to be a "kind" gentleman. He
loved her gratefully, but his upbringing nonetheless left him selfish
and "emotionally insatiable."[11]

A sickly youngster with a lisp and weak chest, Winston had been
bullied at school—at seven he had on one occasion been pelted with
cricket balls. Clementine had also been taunted in her early years by
more rumbustious children and both had eventually developed strategies for self-protection—in his case naughtiness, in hers reserve—to
hide their insecurities from public view. But neither had lost an instinctive sympathy for the underdog.

They both also knew what it was to lose a father and to endure a
mother's "frantic sexual intrigue." Just as there were stories that she
was not Hozier's child, it was rumored that Winston had been conceived before marriage. Witnessing Lord Randolph's public decline
from young political titan to raging invalid had been a further agony
for his son. Only twenty when his father died a grotesque death re-

putedly from syphilis in 1895, Winston never established a connection with him and always felt in his shadow. The penetrating screams of Lord Randolph's last days may have contributed to his own rejection of casual sex.

Thus Winston, like Clementine, craved comfort and protection. Marriage allowed him to recapture that sense of security he had felt in Mrs. Everest's nursery, to be folded at long last within a woman's comforting embrace. Since his Victorian upbringing deterred him from talking about sex in an adult way, he adopted baby talk instead. He began addressing Clementine as "Puss Cat" or "Kat," while he became "My Sweet Amber Dog" or "Pug," and there was much mention of lapping cream and stroking warm, furry coats. Respectable women were in any case at this period presumed to be unburdened by libido, and Winston had a particular dislike for overt sexual predators.

Nor, again like Clementine, did he form close friendships easily. Precocious and bumptious, he had been unpopular with his peers as a child, probably not helped by the fact that his contacts outside the immediate family before he went to school were primarily with servants. When he twice failed to get into the Royal Military College at Sandhurst, the elite training academy for British Army officers, the specialist tutorial college he was sent to observed, "[T]he boy has many good points but what he wants is very firm handling."[12]

These were, then, two insecure people with much in common. One crucial difference was that Winston had spent much of his childhood at Blenheim Palace, while Clementine knew what it was like to live in cheap lodgings. He had always had servants and had never drawn his own bath or traveled on a bus. Just because he was now married and—as the son of a younger son in an aristocracy run on primogeniture—far from rich, he saw no reason for this to change. Clementine, a former habitué of the Dieppe fish markets, was terrified of spending money they did not have in an effort to live up to his exacting requirements.

In early 1909, they bought a lease on 33 Eccleston Square, a cream stucco house in semifashionable Pimlico. This was to be their first family home and Clementine was finally able to decorate in her own simple style, although she let herself go in her bedroom, where she appliquéd an Art Nouveau design of a large fruit tree in "shades of orange, brown and green."[13] She never experimented so flamboyantly again, which is arguably just as well. A later tenant, the foreign secretary Sir Edward Grey, showed the mural to the French ambassador, who was reportedly struck with "horror." (But Grey also wrote to her saying Eccleston Square was the "nicest" house he had ever had in London and that it gave the "impression of belonging to nice people.")[14]

Clementine insisted on having her own bedroom from an early stage. Indeed, after Bolton Street the couple would not share a bed at home again. They kept different hours, she preferring to rise early and he to retire late. And it was not just the Sandhurst college that recognized he needed "very firm handling." Winston was quickly made to observe the "protocol of the bedchamber": Clementine needed refuge from her husband's "dominating brilliance," so he was allowed entry to her room by invitation only, thus placing him in the position of supplicant, always hoping to "kiss her dear lips" and "end up snugly" in her arms. Occasionally, upon turning in, she would leave a note indicating that he might be in luck that evening. But he could never bank on it.[15]

Winston was not the only member of the family who needed "handling." Jennie showed no signs of retreating gracefully, grabbing the chance to decorate her son's new bedroom and insisting on choosing the color for the front door. As Clementine's pregnancy progressed and she went to rest in the country, however, Winston chose to defer more frequently to his wife. He dutifully reported on marble basins, bookcases, paints and progress in chasing up the builders. He commended her on her thrift, which saw old carpets being reused despite the odd stain and shabby edges, while cheap linoleum was put down in the servants' rooms.

Clementine was seven months into her pregnancy before they were finally able to move in. She passed some of the time at Blenheim with Goonie, the wife of Winston's brother, Jack, who was also expecting, and the two struck up a mutually supportive friendship, but she could not shake off her fears about the birth. Goonie—whose real name was Gwendoline—had her baby first and Winston used her "smooth and successful" delivery of a healthy boy to reassure Clementine. He insisted she had suffered little but was himself still nervous about the impending event: "I don't like your having to bear pain & face this ordeal. But . . . out of pain joy will spring."[16]

Not that his concern prevented him from leaving her on her own to pursue politics and steep himself in male society. At the end of May he went to Blenheim for the annual camp of the Queen's Own Oxfordshire Hussars, of which he was an officer. He greatly enjoyed it but Clementine could not face a large house party. In those days expectant mothers were rarely seen and their condition barely alluded to (most thought the word *pregnancy* suitable only for medical books). So on June 1, just shy of a month before she was due to deliver, she went to stay in relative seclusion with Lady St. Helier's daughter in Buckinghamshire. At this point Clementine's old tremulous self returned to the fore. On her way she stopped for lunch at what looked like a "respectable" commercial travelers' hotel in Slough, only to be "terrified" when she found it "infested by several dirty men."[17] On another occasion she locked herself in a train lavatory for fear of cutthroats climbing through a carriage window.

Although anxious about her well-being, Winston was unwilling to change his ways. Their frequent separations—a pattern that would last throughout their marriage—threw them into stark contrast with other political couples of the time. (Stanley Baldwin and his wife, Lucy, spent only one night apart in their entire life together.) These periods apart gave rise to some seventeen hundred letters, telegrams and notes between them that survive today, and a habit of putting their thoughts to paper that persisted even when they were under the same roof.

Diana Churchill was born at home on July 11, and although it was not yet customary for fathers to attend the actual birth, Winston was at least nearby. Even now, however, Violet remained in his thoughts; he wrote to her three days later claiming (unconvincingly) that Clementine had invited her to "come back again to see the baby." "After four almost any afternoon Miss Churchill receives,"[18] he wrote proudly from his desk at the Board of Trade.

Winston was still visiting Violet regularly and she continued to behave possessively toward him. "I was with him heart and soul,"[19] she wrote later, and she certainly took any opportunity to have him to herself rather than spending her time looking around for a husband of her own. One diary entry records a game of golf in "golden autumn sunshine with seagulls circling overhead"; "Winston," she crowed, "is very pleased with my swing."[20] Clementine, meanwhile, was feeling neglected and doubtful of her capacity to fulfill the "sacred" role of being Mrs. Winston Churchill. The minute she was allowed out of bed, she deserted her husband and newborn baby, fleeing to a cottage near Brighton for ten days with Nellie. It appears that in her distress she did not even consider breast-feeding Diana, a task delegated to a wet nurse sixty miles away back in London. Winston was left to supervise care of the baby—now referred to as "Puppy Kitten" or "PK"—and demonstrated an interest so unusual for fathers at the time that he suspected the nanny thought him a "tiresome interloper."[21] Clementine wrote back to Winston, "[K]iss my sweet PK for me," and admitted to being "very jealous" that he was going to give their daughter her bath.

Of course a baby offered Winston all the appeal of a new project, albeit one that he could hand over to a professional at will; whatever excitement he may have derived from becoming a parent, his career remained all-consuming. If Clementine believed she might change this by leaving him and PK behind, she would rapidly discover she was mistaken. Such was evident from his two fleeting visits to his wife in Sussex. He urged her to recover quickly—specifically because he wanted her to be fit enough to "play a great part" in an expected election in the autumn. He conceded that she was competing with politics for his attention but evidently intended to do little about it. "My darling, I do so want your life to be a full & sweet one," he wrote defensively. "I am so centred in my politics, that I often feel I must be a dull companion to anyone who is not in the trade . . . Still the best is to be true to oneself—unless you happen to have a vy tiresome self!"[22]

Clementine decided to prolong her absence and went on to visit her aunt Maisie at Alderley Park, Cheshire, this time with Diana and her nurse. A Stanley gathering—plus effusive praise for her baby—helped Clementine to rally her competitive if not exactly maternal spirits. "None" of the six other children present was "fit to hold a candle to [their] P.K. or even to unloose the latchet of her shoe,"[23] she boasted to Winston. But for all her attempts at defiance she recognized she could never hope to wrest him away from politics by abandoning him. Her sole course of action, if she wanted their marriage to work, was to join him in his "trade" and play her hand more deftly.

She began immersing herself soon after in his social reforms. The newly confident and partisan tone in her comments on September 11 on Lord Rosebery's more conservative alternative to Lloyd George's progressive budget bears testament to her studies. Rosebery's proposals, she wrote, would not help the poor, but then as a peer married to a Rothschild, she declared him to be unfamiliar with "the sordid consideration of how to make both ends meet." Clementine finally rejoined her husband in London later that month, determined to throw herself into his world. Her role was becoming clear.

Although she had performed more impressively at Berkhamsted School than Winston at Harrow, Clementine had still missed out on years of schooling, and of course, she had not gone on to university. His father had not considered the young Winston intellectually capable of taking a degree—and so Winston had not applied for Oxford as he might have wished—but during his service in India as an army subaltern in the late 1890s Winston had immersed himself in history and philosophy so as to compete with those he deemed to be "silver-tongued" graduates on their own terms. Accustomed as he was to conversations with his well-educated American mother, he now set about similarly improving his wife, sending her detailed bulletins on his political strategies and providing her with lengthy compulsory reading lists. She would detect a "note of indulgent criticism"[24] from Winston if she were not completely in command of current affairs or political history, and this spurred her on all the more—although she did complain to Violet (of all people) that Winston was "force-feeding" her books by the dozen. One of his set texts was Maeter-linck's *The Life of the Bee*—an interminable work suggesting that humans could learn from the orderliness and self-sacrifice of the hive. Bees were bores, in her view, as was mathematics.

Politics she found absorbing, however. Her letters from the coun-tryside, where she was hoping to boost her health while Winston was away in his Scottish constituency or consumed by ministerial duties, now dealt only briefly, if at all, with Diana's welfare before moving swiftly on to Winston's career. "I see the Board of Trade Return states that English Industries have improved since last year," she wrote from the Crest Hotel in Crowborough, Sussex, where she stayed for several weeks in October 1909. "I hope you will bring this out strongly in one of the speeches. The rascally *Daily Mail* lies in its throat when it says the contrary." She was finding Winston's world to be infinitely more alluring than being cooped up in a domestic bub-ble with a tiny baby. She particularly disliked any expectation that she would sew (her time as a dressmaker had left her with a loathing for it). "My sweet Pug, I feel imprisoned here. I long to be in the thick of it with you," she wrote to him in the same letter. "I long to put my arms around you and kiss your darling cheeks and curls and lips." That was just how he liked it.

Their first wedding anniversary, in September 1909, had also seen them apart, a sheepish Winston writing to her from Strasbourg that he hoped, after a year together, that she had "no cause—however vague or secret—for regrets." Marriage clearly suited his needs: he felt more confident and able to be himself. Clementine never ridi-culed his obsession with military matters, as others did, and he con-fessed to her: "I feel so safe with you & I do not keep the slightest disguise."[25] Her response was more circumspect: "The year I have lived with you has been far the happiest in my life & even if it had not been it would have been well worth living."

Winston's tender words did not banish all jealous thoughts of Violet—or of other women (known in their pet language as "cats"). "What was my Pug doing with Mrs Rupert Beckett??" she demanded to know in one letter. "My Secret Police keeps me informed of his doings!"[26] An exasperated Winston was reduced to insisting that he had "not spoken to a single cat of any sort except [his] mother!!!!!"[27] His reassurance did nothing to prevent what seems to have been a blistering row the next time they met. Winston found Clementine's raging insecurity embarrassing: "Dearest, it worries me vy much that you should seem to nurse such absolutely wild suspicions wh are so dishonouring to all the love & loyalty I bear you." He urged her to raise her thoughts—"We do not live in a world of small intrigues, but of serious & important affairs"—adding: "You ought to trust me for I do not love & will never love any woman in the world but you . . . Your sweetness & beauty have cast a glory upon my life."[28]

Clementine regretted her jealous outbursts but she was tormented by the idea that Winston would conduct himself like Hozier, or follow the example of his equally unfaithful father. Some women found him insufferable, but others, like the American-born Duchess of Marlborough, Consuelo, were charmed by his "boyish enthusiasm and spontaneity."[29] In the long run, he would prove a far more faithful companion than the previous male figures in Clementine's life, and she would eventually learn to contain her fears of female rivalry. The only whiff of sexual scandal dated to his early twenties, when a disgruntled fellow army officer alleged that he had indulged in acts of "the Oscar Wilde type." The saga was swiftly ended by a hotshot lawyer and a libel suit: Winston won £500 in damages and an apology, and the allegations were withdrawn.[30]

As Winston grew accustomed to matrimony, he learned to live with his wife's explosive temper. The slightest setback, such as cold soup or a late delivery, could send her into a fury. Happily, the storm would soon pass with the help of Winston's understanding and patience; "cast care aside," he would say consolingly. Perhaps witnessing his mother's rages—Jennie was a great thrower of hairbrushes—had inured Winston to female fury. Or perhaps he saw that Clementine was a harsh self-critic; she would, after the event, frequently regret her loss of control. "When I am a withered old woman how miserable I shall be if I have disturbed your life & troubled your spirit by my temper. Do not cease to love me, I could not do without it." But then he too was often impossible to live with—even if he rarely directed his notorious temper at her. He was loving and fun, but also demanding, selfish and rash. Their marriage was never destined to be smooth, but they made a pact that lasted until the end: they would always try to make it up before bed. "Let not the sun go down upon your wrath," he would say, quoting St. Paul's letter to the Ephesians.

In marriage, at least, he was often the first to sue for peace. After a row in January 1913, he wrote: "I was stupid last night—but you know what a prey I am to nerves and prepossessions," before adding in a postscript: "don't be disloyal to me in thought. I have no one but you to break the loneliness of a bustling and bustled existence."[31] In reply, pleading with him to spend more time alone with her, she lamented, "I always say more than I feel & mean instead of less."[32]

Other than Clementine's jealousy, money was the most frequent flashpoint. Upon Winston's appointment as president of the Board of Trade before they had married in 1908 Asquith had promised him "the same level, as regards salary & status as a secretary of state."[33] That should have entailed an income of £5,000 a year, on which the family could have lived comfortably; in the event, he was paid only half that. Other investments and the royalties from his books had already been spent (as had Jennie's American fortune). This left the Churchills living an upper-class life on a middle-class salary. In a confidence shared with Violet—perhaps as a deliberate taunt—Clementine revealed how she had refused to continue buying Winston's expensive pale pink silk underclothes from Army & Navy. In the end he had won that battle by protesting that he could wear nothing else next to his delicate skin. She hated the extravagance; he could not imagine living without it.

When it came to food, drink and comfort, Winston was, as F. E. Smith once put it, "easily satisfied with the best." He frequently announced at short notice that he was bringing home important people to dinner—including on one occasion the king of Portugal. If Clementine asked what she was expected to feed them, his answer might be Irish stew "with lots of onions," but for grander occasions, it was typically lobsters and roast duck. These endless dinner parties involved several courses, champagne, fine wines and then brandy and cigars. Although she tried to economize—for a house of its size, Eccleston Square was run on an unusually small staff of five—the shame of unpaid bills returned to her life. Worse, she discovered with horror that Winston (like her mother, brother and sister) was a gambler. She would wave final notices at him in despair and he would simply ignore her, or suggest pointless schemes such as removing two phone extensions to save a mere £3 a year. Clementine's ideas for balancing the books were more radical. On one occasion she sold Aunt Cornelia's diamond necklace. Appalled and ashamed, Winston rushed to the jeweler's to buy it back but was too late.

Not that Winston was incapable of solicitude toward his wife. Wilfrid Scawen Blunt was struck by the way he took "all possible care of her" when they visited him in the country. Clementine was afraid of wasps; when one settled on her sleeve, Winston "gallantly" took it "by the wings and thrust it into the ashes of the fire."[34] On November 30, 1909, Clementine organized a dinner party, complete with cake and candles, to celebrate Winston's thirty-fifth birthday. A delighted Winston wore a paper hat while sitting on a sofa holding her hand— a rare public display of affection for the time that led one of the guests to note in his diary that he had "never seen two people more in love."[35]

Although devoted to Winston, Clementine began around this time to revel in her power over other men. At a fancy-dress party she dazzled Scawen Blunt, an inveterate womanizer, who now thought her "the most beautiful of women." She was in "a kind of mermaid's dress which looked as if she had no clothes at all underneath her outer sheath of crimped silk. She whispered to me that it was almost so."[36] Winston rarely wrote in such physical terms, his letters seeking more maternal than sexual favors. Clementine very occasionally referred to "wanting" more from her husband than a kiss.

Winston's growing esteem for his wife's intellect did not extend to backing her calls for women to be given the right to vote. To his absolute fury, his prominence made him an obvious target for the suffragettes, who regularly disrupted his speeches. On one occasion in late 1909 a suffragette lunged at him with a dog whip as he descended onto the platform at Bristol station, lashing out at his face and pushing him toward a moving train. A small crowd watched in horror, but Clementine leaped in a flash over the piles of luggage and, just in time, pulled him back with all her might by his coattails. She almost certainly saved her husband's life—while endangering her own. She had shown herself to be braver in real danger than all the male dignitaries cowering nearby. And yet, despite the attack, Clementine's belief in the cause of women's suffrage never faltered and she attended several major court cases against members of the movement. Later she looked back on those years of violence as necessary, concluding that "the day would not have been won" without women "with a passion" that "exceeded constitutional and legal bounds."[37]

The female vote was just the first of many issues on which she would part ways with her husband's more conservative views. He promised that he would never "crush" her convictions and even fretted about her reaction when he "answered the suffragettes sternly."[38] He knew what female suffrage meant to her; before their marriage she had often dressed in the suffragist uniform of collar and tie. Yet he went on to oppose bills in 1910 and 1912 supporting women's right to vote (both of which were unsuccessful), on the grounds that they were not ready for the vote and that the "mass of them did not want it." Although he had some sympathy for the principle of extending the vote, he spoke for a lot of husbands when he said that he refused to be "henpecked on a question of such grave importance."[39] "The truth is," Winston informed a golfing partner, "we already have enough ignorant voters and we don't want any more."[40] Women's suffrage remained a sore point between them until the outbreak of war in 1914 pushed the subject into the political long grass.

Winston believed that a husband must be the dominant partner. He was once outraged at a dinner party when Amy, the wife of his cousin Freddie Guest, took revenge on her husband for flirting with another woman by ordering a valet to remove his clothes and then locking him out of her bedroom. "Clemmie, don't you ever behave like Amy," Winston warned her. "If you do, I'll leave you right away." He counseled Freddie that the honor of the entire family was at stake if he did not claim his conjugal rights. Amy (who was thought to be influenced by suspect American notions of female independence) did not relent, but a crisis was averted when another door was found unlocked and Freddie entered the room by peaceful means.[41]

The macho pronouncement was an insight into Winston's thoughts, if not his deeds. Women were, in his view, lesser beings who were unjustifiably "cocksure"; he particularly disliked the sort of "young unmarried lady teacher" that Clementine might have become if she had been allowed to go to university.[42] Winston did not care for women to venture their own views—with the exception of Clementine (and perhaps Violet)—and preferred them merely to listen to his. As Clementine learned how to manage him and drew closer to him intellectually, however, he softened a little. When the Representation of the People bill of 1918 went through Parliament he voted for women of property aged over thirty to be enfranchised (albeit partly on the grounds that they might shore up his vote). In 1928, though, he abstained from a bill that succeeded in granting women the vote on the same terms as men, thereby earning himself another rebuke from Clementine for being "naughty."

Clementine was learning how to advance her views by subtle, but effective, means. She could not see eye to eye with Winston on the female vote but was thrilled by his work with the chancellor of the Exchequer, Lloyd George, to provide labor exchanges and workers' pensions and generally improve working conditions, including the introduction of the statutory tea break. As she threw herself into politics, she developed an astute judgment of the characters involved, the goals that were achievable and the dangers to be anticipated. Perhaps before Winston himself, she foresaw that Lloyd George's radical "People's Budget" of 1909—which raised taxes on cars, petrol and land to pay for the foundations of the welfare state—would make politics "very bitter." There were many in Winston's own family who refused to speak to him over his support for Lloyd George; acquaintances would cross the road to avoid greeting a couple they viewed as class traitors because the budget sought to redistribute wealth from the rich. One summer's day, a Lady Crichton was shopping for china in South Audley Street when Clementine drove by alone in a "ravishing" black-and-white-striped dress. She waved gaily to Lady Crichton, who greeted her back before informing her nine-year-old daughter, "Poor Clemmie, so few people will speak to her these days."

In truth, Clementine saw it as heroic to be denigrated for helping the poor and she exulted in watching Winston's popularity with the working classes soar as a result. They "love & trust you absolutely," she cooed after attending a political meeting in Bingley. "I felt so proud."[43] It was not so easy for Winston, who took great pride in his aristocratic family and was wounded by their hostility. But if he wavered, Clementine was there to stiffen his spine and act as his radical conscience. "Do not let the glamour or elegance . . . of old associations blind you," she warned. Real Tories "are ignorant, vulgar, prejudiced. They can't bear the idea of the lower classes being independent & free."[44] Later in her life, she was to say that these reformist years were her happiest. This was when Winston's political outlook (even if in part aimed at undermining the rise of the Labour Party) was most in tune with hers—although he did not entirely share her absolutist approach.

Clementine once stormed out of Blenheim, for instance, when Sunny asked her not to use his ducal writing paper to write to "that horrible little man" Lloyd George. Winston was not there to broker a peace, and so when she descended the staircase "like wrath itself" shortly afterward, she ignored Sunny's pleas for forgiveness. Winston was undoubtedly distressed at the family rift this caused and a rare cross tone entered their correspondence at this point. A few days later, Clementine could no longer bear his disapproval. If Winston ceased to love her, she would be raw and unhappy inside and like a prickly porcupine outside. As so often with "Clemmie," Winston surrendered, replying that he only wished he were more worthy of her.

This prickliness was not purely a product of principle; Clementine was not an easy person to get to know and rarely felt it safe to share her private thoughts even with close friends. Her daughter Mary confirmed that "her inner reserve never left her, and throughout her life, she fended off attempts to make intimate relationships."[45] She had two allies from before her marriage—her cousin Sylvia and Horatia Seymour (the Liberal-supporting, unmarried daughter of Gladstone's private secretary)—both liked by Winston. But his life, needs and social circle were displacing her own, and she spent much of her time with people she did not trust. These included the wily Lloyd George, despite her admiration for his achievements, and Winston's best friend, F. E. Smith. She not only disapproved of Smith's Tory influence but feared that her husband would be led astray by his drinking and gambling. But Winston relished their trips away with the Hussars—including nighttime swims in a lake together—declaring: "No cats allowed. Your pug in clover, W."

Others she simply disdained, including some of Winston's relations—notably Ivor, Freddie Guest's brother, who once lost his temper during a bridge match and threw his cards at Clementine's head. Despite his contrite apologies the next day, she swept out, this time with an embarrassed and reluctant Winston in tow.

Winston worked hard on repairing the bridges she burned. When Ivor Guest's mother, Winston's aunt Cornelia, invited them to come visit again he urged Clementine to accept. "We have not too many friends," he pointed out. "If however you don't want to go, I will go alone. Don't come with all your hackles up & your fur brushed the wrong way—you naughty."

"I will be very good I promise you," she replied. For Winston's sake she even tolerated sitting next to Asquith, who was notorious for "peering down Pennsylvania Avenue," as gazing at a woman's cleavage was then known.

Now in her late twenties, Clementine was attracting many a lustful eye. After a day at the seaside with the Churchills, an artist friend, Neville Lytton, wrote, "Clemmie came forth like the reincarnation of Venus . . . I had no idea she had such a splendid body." (Lytton was a convert, having previously been a critic—one of many—of her puritan streak.) Scawen Blunt not only admired her looks but increasingly came to think of her as "one of the nicest" women in society.[46]

Clementine was beginning to appreciate that her allure was not simply a cause for personal pride; it was also raising Winston's stock. That did not mean, however, that she would take the advice given by Alice Keppel, one of Edward VII's mistresses, that if she truly wanted to advance her husband's career she should take a wealthy, influential lover. Clementine turned down her offer to find a suitable candidate, an act Mrs. Keppel viewed as "positively selfish."[47] She was not to be another lion-hunting Jennie.

In January 1910 there was a general election, triggered by the House of Lords' rejection of the People's Budget reforms. It was the first of fifteen campaigns Winston and Clementine would fight together, and she took an active role: after all, Jennie had energetically canvassed for Winston in previous elections. He held his seat in Dundee—perhaps in small part helped by Clementine's Scottish ancestry—but overall the Liberals scraped together just two more seats than the Conservatives. The new government saw Winston promoted to become, at thirty-five, the youngest home secretary since Robert Peel. He was now in charge of prisons, the police and the grisly duty of signing death warrants. The burden of deciding the fate of forty-three men and women who had been condemned to death by hanging was to weigh heavily on him.

Clementine now proved her worth. Winston would later tell his doctor Lord Moran how helpful it had been to talk to his wife during what he claimed were prolonged bouts of depression, a condition that famously became known as "Black Dog." "Alas, I have no good opinion of myself," he would confess to Clementine. "At times I think that I could conquer everything—and then again I know that I am only a weak fool." Certainly, his temperament was not suited to his new position, but his daughter Mary raised questions about whether his mood swings really amounted to depression. His Black Dog moods are viewed by members of the Churchill family today as largely Winstonian hyperbole, and Mary thought in any case that the Dog was "kennelled" by his love for Clementine and the confidence she now brought to him.[48]

Winston's workload was nevertheless onerous, as Asquith would often delegate to him the job of winding up major debates—especially after dinner, when "Old Squiffy," as the prime minister was known, was frequently incapacitated by drink. Clementine would sometimes be sent to the "fighting front" to deliver speeches on her husband's behalf. Pushing the boundaries of what was strictly proper for a gentlewoman, she energetically toured labor exchanges and prisons, and gave away prizes at police sports days. When she was at home with Winston, however, she found he was no longer his ebullient self.

A second election was called in December 1910 specifically to decide the issue of the reform of the House of Lords, and whether it should be prevented from blocking the government's bills to help the poor. The result, which narrowly returned the Liberal administration, paved the way for constitutional legislation (the Parliament Act of 1911) that would assert the supremacy of the Commons over the House of Lords and enable it to force its finance measures through. After the poll, Winston decided on a short trip to Clementine's Stanley relations at Alderley to recuperate. Now pregnant with her second child, she had caught a bad cold and regretted not being able to join him. Perhaps he felt a pang of guilt at this latest absence, for when Clementine woke up from a nap one evening she found her room transformed by his orders "into a Paradise of exquisite flowers." "You are a sweet Darling Lamb Bird!!"[49] she told him.

The new baby (she was convinced this time it was a boy) was due in mid-May 1911 but kept his mother hanging on for another two long weeks. Always anxious during pregnancy, Clementine found the wait unendurable. She was prescribed Veronal—an early form of barbiturate used to treat insomnia "induced by nervous excitability." When Randolph finally put in an appearance, he was immediately granted more attention than his sister. Clementine even breast-fed him. Winston was delighted and although he swiftly left for the Hussars, his regimental camp at Blenheim, he could not help crowing. "Many congratulations are offered me upon the son," he wrote to Clementine.

Now that she had produced the requisite male heir—nicknamed the Chumbolly—there was no pressure on her to recover quickly. "My precious pussy cat," Winston said soothingly. "Just . . . enjoy the richness wh this new event will I know have brought into your life." The paternal pride was in full flow: "The Chumbolly must do his duty and help you with your milk . . . At his age greediness & even swinishness at table are virtues." Clementine was equally enamored, writing of her happiness "contemplating the beautiful Chumbolly who [grew] more darling & handsome every hour," adding, "Just now I was kissing him, when catching sight of my nose he suddenly fastened upon it & began to suck it, no doubt thinking it was another part of my person!"[50]

While she recuperated, Clementine took Randolph and Diana out of London—not to the splendors of Blenheim or Alderley, but to the scene of her impoverished youth in Seaford. Randolph's first holiday was spent in a low-key town of shingle beaches and suburban holidaymakers. Winston joined her briefly in the rooms she rented at Rosehall, an Edwardian semidetached house in Sutton Park Road. She had to remind him to bring his own wine. They were unlikely surroundings for a Churchill, and his first introduction to the concept of "lodgings," but Clementine retained an affection for Seaford and its people—including an old boatman who had taught her to swim—and wanted to share it with her children. She might have been a Churchill too now, but she was not willing to surrender all that she had been before. Three years later she took the children to see her mother in Dieppe, and was annoyed with herself for overpaying for mackerel in the fish market when she should have known better.

Clementine returned to London in late June 1911 for the coronation of George V, whose father Edward VII had died the previous year. For a time, she remained devoted to Randolph, a far cry from Diana's first months, but once he was weaned she embarked on a string of child-free holidays, beginning with a jaunt with Goonie to Garmisch in the Bavarian Alps. Winston was to join them but was detained by the threat of food shortages following a series of strikes. Perhaps in retribution, she reported having been leered at by a "grotesque hugely fat man in only bathing drawers," claiming that she would have liked to "have him put to death."

Clementine was becoming more accustomed to Winston's absences and more tolerant of his work. Now that she had dutifully produced a son and joined forces with her husband in political battle, her self-confidence was growing. This new assurance impressed even Violet, who declared to an astonished Venetia that she had "conceived a sudden & great affection for Clemmie."[51] Clementine's new status, allied to her adequacy at bridge, made her welcome, along with Winston, as a guest of the Asquiths in Downing Street. Margot liked to criticize Winston at these events, even to Clementine—leading to a number of sharp exchanges—but she was nonetheless fond of them both. "I have a great feeling for Clemmy," she wrote to Winston. "She is so rare not to be vain of her marvellous beauty."[52] Clementine never quite relaxed with the Asquiths—she was wary of Violet until the end and she disapproved of the prime minister's intimate relationship, from 1912 onward, with her cousin Venetia Stanley.

Clementine was aware that she was now a woman of consequence and was intent on living up to the part. Her brother, Bill, confessed to Winston that he held her in "an awe which no-one else can rival."[53] Her social cachet grew still further in October 1911, when Winston became first lord of the Admiralty, in those days a position of imperial grandeur. She took up hunting, earning herself a fearless reputation in the saddle. She launched battleships with a regal grace. She also demonstrated extraordinary courage in her official duties. In February 1912, the Liberal-led government, needing to reward the Irish Nationalists for propping them up in the Commons, was intent on advancing the cause of home rule against fierce opposition from Unionists. Clementine became fearful for Winston's safety as he prepared for a trip to Belfast—an act deemed "provocative" by the Unionists—just as Ireland teetered on the brink of civil war. Although pregnant for the third time, she insisted on accompanying her husband, despite warnings that she would be putting herself at "considerable risk"; there were police reports that huge numbers of bolts and rivets had been stolen from railway yards and many revolvers "taken out of pawn."

On the Churchills' arrival, hostile loyalist crowds pressed menacingly up against their car, lifting it from the ground and hurling abuse at its occupants. In the end the couple was whisked to relative safety in a Catholic stronghold and Winston was able to deliver his speech. Nevertheless, it was a terrifying episode and may have contributed to the miscarriage Clementine suffered the following month. Initially she appeared to make a swift recovery and went to "comfortable shabby lodgings" at Oriental Place in Brighton in mid-March to recuperate. But when she returned home, she was still not well. Winston, needless to say, was away and so she had to tell him by letter that it was "so strange to have all the same sensations that one has after a real Baby, but with no result." "I hope," she wrote, "I shall never have another such accident again."[54] As it was, she made sure she did not conceive for well over a year and was from then on even more afraid of pregnancy.

Her natural sense of frustration at the inferior status of women boiled over into outrage at some of the more prejudiced attitudes of the day. In a letter to the *Times*, signing herself as "One of the Doomed," she opened fire on a male correspondent who had opposed giving votes to women on psychological and physiological grounds. Even the Asquiths were impressed when, under the title "Ought not women to be abolished?," Clementine mocked the biologist Sir Almroth Wright's views that women were "unbalanced" if not outright "insane." "Now this being so," she wrote from her sickbed, "how much happier and better would the world not be if only it could be purged of women?" Her put-down was hailed by Asquith himself as "the best thing I have read for a long time" on what he called the "Woman Question."[55]

Fresh from her triumph, she decided to visit Paris for a few days in April, staying at the Hôtel le Bristol with Randolph's godmother,

Lady Ridley. It was immediately clear to her companion (if not to her absent husband) that Clementine was, in fact, very unwell and a top French gynecologist declared she needed a month in bed. Clementine returned to London, but Winston remained absent. There followed months of doctors, relapses and enforced exclusion from his flourishing career, during which Clementine's spirits sank to an all-time low as she began to think she might become a permanent invalid. "I am a poor wrecked ship," she told Winston. "You must take me in hand as if I were one of your battleships." Winston finally acted, finding a new doctor who helped her recover, but she was never to retrieve her full physical strength.

When Clementine was once again on her feet, friends who saw her with Winston thought they still seemed like young lovers, full of affectionate banter. At one sociable lunch, the diarist and newspaper owner George Riddell recalled her laughing saucily about the number of "bastard" children among the aristocracy before turning to Winston and saying, "I've got you. The real question is how to keep you now that I've made my capture." "Well my dear," Winston replied, "you don't have much difficulty in doing that."

With Winston's new job came a splendid eighteenth-century official residence in Whitehall. Admiralty House had two thirty-five-foot drawing rooms, a library and seven bedrooms, but after four years in Eccleston Square Clementine was reluctant to leave her first real home. The Admiralty was only a stone's throw from the garden door to Number 10 (and Violet) and it would require a dozen servants, whereas she could afford no more than nine. She was so concerned about slipping standards and unpayable bills that she delayed moving for more than a year, and even then never took full possession of the staterooms on the first floor. The fireplaces were tiny, the rooms huge, and most of the furniture unspeakably ugly. Naturally, Winston reveled in the grandeur of what he called "our mansion," his one concession a promise to watch his spending. "I am afraid it all means vy hard work for you—Poor lamb," he wrote. "But remember I am going to turn over a new leaf! . . . The only mystery is 'what is writ-ten on the other side!'"

More to her liking was the *Enchantress*, a 4,000-ton yacht with a 196-man crew—all at the first lord's disposal. Leisurely cruises to sunny places could be enjoyed at least partially at the taxpayer's ex-pense, provided they were combined with naval inspections. Free of the maternal and domestic duties that burdened her at home, Clem-entine grew to love life on board, although Violet's frequent presence was a strain. In May 1912 they traveled by train to join the *Enchantress* in Genoa, and while Clementine rested, still recovering from her miscarriage, Violet took the opportunity to monopolize Winston, their laughter drifting back to Clementine's sleeping compartment. After a stopover in Paris, "poor Clemmie was in tears of nerves & exhaustion." On another cruise a year later, Violet was still accusing her of various "lacunae," including being "completely impervious to the 'point' of places and situations."[56] Yet she could hardly fail to no-tice how Winston now relied on his wife. If ever he returned from a jaunt, his first question would be "Where's Clemmy?" and if he could not find her, he would be "quite gloomy."[57]

Clementine began to sense her value to him. Even when he was away she would, if well, attend social events on her own, speaking to the right people (for him) and—usually—saying the right things. She had not won over everyone—the die-hard man of action Admiral Beatty, who saw her on the *Enchantress*, dismissed her as an "amiable fool"[58]—but Clementine was learning fast, and when in form she was an operator on her own terms, albeit always on Winston's behalf. She knew how Winston liked to conduct business over the dinner table—at which he excelled—and thought carefully about whom to invite. When she met Lord Kitchener (then a member of the Committee of Imperial Defense) at Lady Crewe's house, for instance, she knew he could be useful and she ventured his name. "By all means ask K to lunch," Winston replied. "Let us be just à trois. I have some things to talk to him about."[59]

With time it became quite normal for her to sit in on his most important and sensitive discussions; he trusted her fully. She also got into the habit of checking over his speeches before he delivered them, sending him a handwritten reminder in early 1914, for instance, that she was waiting for "a little visit with the Speech. Miaow, but sitting tight."[60] Sometimes she suggested cutting passages she considered elaborate or harsh, advising, "I would not say that Winston."[61] Equally, he was thrilled when she found much to praise, such as when he allowed himself to show emotion and sympathy. She patiently coached him through his speech impediment, which caused him to pronounce *s* as *sh* and made him difficult to understand at times of stress. Often she would sit in the public gallery at the Commons, smiling encouragingly if he struggled—for all his later global fame for oratory Winston had long since found public performance an ordeal. In 1904, before his marriage, he had once dried up mid-speech in front of a packed House of Commons and after an excruciating silence while he fumbled in vain for the right word he had had to sit down. He never spoke again without notes and rehearsed his speeches painstakingly for the rest of his life—and more often than not with Clementine present to criticize or praise as necessary. This was just one reason why Lloyd George observed that she was no ordinary politician's wife. He told Winston that Clementine was his "salvation." He was "full of [her] praises," Winston later informed her, remarking that "[her] beauty was the least thing about [her]."[62]

In the summer of 1912 Clementine decamped to a grand beachside house in Sandwich, Kent, lent by Nancy Astor. She entertained Winston by writing him vivid tales of Randolph's tantrums—he would roar with rage if his meals were too milky—but merely mentioned in passing how Diana was saying her prayers "so sweetly." Parliament was sitting, so Winston could come down from London only every now and then, but his arrival was more often than not swiftly followed by an excursion to the beach to make "a nicely bevelled fortress." Clementine would be entrusted with finding the best sand in advance for these elaborate fortifications, and to have buckets, spades and, of course, cigars at the ready. As Winston happily immersed himself in a reversion to his childhood, she could only look on, watching him play boisterously with his children in a way that seemed beyond her reach.

Perhaps this distance explains why Clementine seemed only too eager to escape her maternal responsibilities. During one lengthy trip to Spain and Paris with friends in early 1914, a wistful tone entered Winston's letters to his wayward wife with reports of "continuous complaints" from Diana (now four) and Randolph (nearly three) about her "non-return." A week later he worked on her again with: "I asked Randolph this morning whether he wanted you to come back & why & he said 'Becos' I lurve her.' So now you must come my sweet pussy."[63] He too was missing her—for one thing, the household did not run as smoothly "when the Cat's away." But there was another reason her return was required: the cost of running Admiralty House, as she had expected, was proving ruinous. "The expense of the 1st quarter . . . is astonishing," he warned her in 1914. "Money seems to flow away."[64] In truth, the overspending was, as usual, largely due to Winston's extravagances; Clementine was doing "all [she could] to help to keep down expenses." (Her longest jaunt had been funded for the most part by the ever-generous Sir Ernest Cassel.)[65]

Nor was money the only sore point. Winston had taken a fancy to flying, then still in its perilous infancy. When many other pilots he knew—including his instructor—died one by one in a string of crashes, Clementine, now pregnant for the fourth time, became almost hysterical with fear. She pleaded with him to stop, but he was enthralled. It was only when, in June 1914, she had a dream that her baby had been born a "gaping idiot" that he finally relented. He did not fly again for three years. Of course, by then he had more serious concerns to occupy his time.

In July Clementine took the children, their nanny and a maid to Overstrand, a then-fashionable Norfolk seaside resort. There she rented the six-bedroom Pear Tree Cottage on the low cliffs overlooking the beach. By now five months into her pregnancy, she was unable to pursue her hobbies of tennis, hunting or even swimming for fear of suffering another miscarriage, so she spent an unusually lengthy time with Diana and Randolph. She reported to Winston that she was "finding out a lot of things about them" and told him, "You will be surprised to hear that they are getting quite fond of me." She was thrilled when Randolph called her "my darling sweetheart mummy."[66]

It was otherwise a deeply worrying time. On June 28, the gunshot in Sarajevo that killed Archduke Franz Ferdinand, heir to the Austro-Hungarian throne, had "rung around the world." Fired by the Bosnian Serb Gavrilo Princip, it triggered a catastrophic series of events that would culminate in the outbreak of the First World War. Clementine was dismayed to be in exile, removed from the feverish buzz of London as it prepared for the unthinkable. Winston came down by train one weekend, and on another occasion he rowed ashore from the *Enchantress*, but mostly he was away, engrossed with buttressing the nation's naval defenses. She envied how he was living a thrilling life "to the tips of [his] fingers" and felt excluded and superfluous. She used a neighbor's phone to try to keep in touch, but his line was usually engaged. Knowing that Violet was only yards from him in London, she longed to be with him but her children were enjoying their seaside holiday, she knew her condition required her to rest and in any case the family car had broken down, making travel more difficult. There is also little indication that Winston was keen to have his family around him at such a challenging time.

To appease her thirst for news, however, Winston occasionally took astonishing risks in sending Clementine classified information by post. It was soon all too clear to her that on the Continent, war was inevitable. The Austrians had threatened the Serbs, Russia had set its sights on Austria, and Germany was making hostile noises to virtually everyone. Ultimatums were issued and ignored. Navies were sent out to sea and armies mobilized. Spoiling for a fight, Germany then launched an attack on Britain's ally France through the neutral territory of Belgium. On August 4, with the great powers of Europe thus ranged against each other, Britain itself had little choice but to declare war.[67]

Overstrand was on open coastline now vulnerable to attack. But while other holidaymakers were packing up, Clementine found her options still further curtailed when the local cinema screen flashed up the message: "Visitors! Why are you leaving? Mrs Winston Churchill and her children are in residence . . . If it's safe enough for her, surely it's safe enough for you!" Whatever her inward fears, she could now only see it as her duty to stay put and appear calm. This defiance won her much credit and a wealthy Tory MP sent her an emerald and diamond ring in tribute. Assiduous as ever, she returned it, earning praise from Winston for her "high and inflexible principles." But in truth she felt both exposed and rejected. Since the beginning of her marriage she had had to compete with politics—and Violet—for her husband's attentions. Now not only was she pregnant again and on her own, but she would have to contend with the all-consuming preoccupation of war.

CHAPTER THREE

The Pain and the Pride

1914—15

No one could have foretold Clementine's crisis but with hindsight it is astonishing that Winston failed to bring his family back to London as soon as war broke out—not least because he had written cabinet briefings on the vulnerability of the North Sea coast to the enemy. Indeed, it was only a matter of months before the eastern seaboard of Britain—although farther north at Scarborough, Hartlepool and Whitby—began to suffer German naval bombardment, and with it considerable loss of life. For the first time women and children as young as six months were slaughtered on a barbaric new home front. War no longer merely scythed through uniformed young men on foreign battlefields, it was crashing through homes, gardens and shops on British soil.

Winston may have told himself that Clementine was coping remarkably well; outwardly, she appeared as calm and determined as ever. Or maybe he thought it better that she was out of London, which was beset by fears of zeppelin bombing raids—although the first such attack did not come until May 1915. He professed to being a "little anxious" about her, but in truth he was finding the challenge of war, for all its death and destruction, exhilarating. He was engrossed by the job of running the greatest fighting force of the world's greatest empire; Clementine and the children were out of sight and mostly out of mind. It took the actions of her sister, Nellie, finally to reveal just how near to hysteria Clementine was.

Both sisters had considered it too dangerous for their mother to remain in Dieppe and so Nellie was dispatched to bring her back to Pear Tree Cottage. Lady Blanche arrived safely but exhausted just as "spy-mania" began to afflict Overstrand, with several unproven sightings of enemy "agents" on the cliffs. Already haunted by fears that these supposed Germans might be planning to kidnap her, Clementine was furious that Nellie had failed to accompany their mother. Once back in England, her sister had peeled off and gone to Buckinghamshire to help the Astors convert their mansion into a nursing home, before traveling with a medical unit to the front line in Belgium as an interpreter. Clementine had counted on Nellie to look after their mother so that she could finally slip away to see Winston. She was instead trapped with two little children and a "taxing" mother fearful of a German attack, her hopes of rejoining her husband dashed. Unable to sleep and heavily pregnant, she became overwrought.

"I feel disgusted with Nellie," Clementine raged in a scrappy note to Winston on August 14. "I feel quite ill this morning, as I have had a very bad night & this on top of it has really upset me. I long to see you . . . You are always so sane and sensible my darling one, & you would calm my hurt and angry feelings . . . [I]n the midst of your work it is wrong of me to bubble over like this, but my heart is full & I can't help it." Shortly after writing this, Clementine appears to have lost control and even to have attempted self-harm. "It is absurd to savage myself and to knock my head against the wall," she scribbled later in another heart-wrenching note. "I feel bruised all over and as if I had walked 20 miles and nobody loved me. I am just going to lie down for a little as I have now reached the stage of idiocy when all I can do is to cry feebly."

Later still, she poured out her terrors of capture. "If I *am* kidnapped I beg of you not to sacrifice the smallest or cheapest submarine . . . I could not face the subsequent unpopularity whereas I should be quite a heroine . . . if I died bravely and unransomed . . . If you do get a letter from me praying to be saved it will have been extracted by torture!" And then finally she pleaded with him to let her come home. "I long to be comforted," she cried.[1]

Winston's response to what appears to have been some sort of breakdown is not recorded. What seems clear is that Clementine needed to expel her demons—and grab his attention—before she could return to her cool and rational self. A little later she wrote to Winston: "I feel better since writing to you my Darling. Do not misjudge me for being so garrulous, Your loving very tired Clemmie."

Her obvious distress must have finally prompted Winston to summon her back, as somehow Clementine returned with the children to London shortly afterward for the last few weeks of her pregnancy. As soon as she was by his side, she happily devoted herself to his welfare and career. She sent notes downstairs to his study from her bedroom urging him to go to bed early. "You look weary from want of sleep," she wrote in one, reminding him, "[T]omorrow you will need all your cool brain and judgment." It was as if she were an entirely different woman from the desperate semimarooned wife in Overstrand.

With the declaration of war came the need for a rapid and effective mobilization of the navy he had been frantically building up for the past thirty months. Amid a frenzy of patriotic flag-waving, men of all classes volunteered to join up—and those not in uniform were soon looked upon as rather suspect. The poet laureate Robert Bridges, swept up by the excitement, promised young men that they would be "cleansed" through "suffering" and would find "beauty through blood." For Clementine, like so many others, the reality was less poetic. At the end of August, Nellie had been captured by the Germans in Belgium; her brother, Bill, was commanding the destroyer HMS *Thorn* and Winston's brother, Jack, was in France with the army. There was precious little "beauty" in the news coming in daily of so many young men already dead for the thousands of families grieving their loss. Confident predictions that it would "be all over by Christmas" were giving way to gloomy fears of a long, hard slog. And yet Clementine no longer nursed feelings of self-pity or isolation. She was back in partnership with her husband at what she called "the pulse of things," where she belonged. How much more rewarding it was to contribute to the war effort than to shepherd small children to the beach or tend her mother! Later she would look back at what she called those "wonderful" opening weeks of the war when they "were so happy." She thrilled at the initial success of Winston's naval preparations and "the excitement of swiftly moving events," and later felt "guilty & ashamed" that even the appalling casualties of those early battles had had so little effect on her. Instead, she said later, "I wondered how long we should continue to tread on air."[2]

When the navy won a major battle in late August 1914, it was Clementine who sent word to the war secretary, Lord Kitchener, while her husband dressed for dinner. "Winston," she wrote, "thinks this is rather a Coup."[3] She also set a precedent by accompanying him to such male conventions as the inspection of battleships, where she would personally congratulate admirals on their victories, rewarding them with invitations to lunch. Winston briefed her so thoroughly on naval operations that she was better informed than most cabinet ministers. Now that she was so bound up with his work, he wanted to be with her more. Asquith noted one evening that Winston "wouldn't leave Clemmie"[4] even to dine with him at Downing Street.

Clementine quickly identified an area in which she could provide Winston with particular support—assessing the weaknesses and insecurities of his colleagues and their capacity to make trouble. Perhaps her own anxieties sharpened her understanding of other people's, but in any case her perspicacity contrasted with his own rash emotionalism. He had a tendency to trample over others' feelings, viewing them as immaterial to the overwhelming necessity of winning the war. He quickly moved, for instance, to replace an aging commander in chief of the Home Fleet, Admiral Sir George Callaghan, with a younger man, ignoring entirely the warnings from his senior advisers about the "disastrous" consequences for morale. It was only when Clementine intervened that he finally listened. Saying that she hoped he would not be "vexed" at her views, she warned him that Callaghan needed to be handled carefully or his bitterness would "fester." A mere medal would be insulting, but a seat on an Admiralty board would soothe his feelings and ensure that he was not seen across the navy to have been "humiliated." She also advised Winston not to underrate the ability of wives to cause mischief if they deemed their husbands to have been maltreated. Surely he did not want a "league of Retired Officers' Cats" blackening his name and making his task still more difficult? Winston saw sense and gave Callaghan a job as an adviser just as Clementine suggested.

Her success in her first major intervention encouraged her to offer further opinions. Although Winston took exception when others attempted to disagree with him, often frightening people into submission as a result, Clementine was never afraid of him. She became highly skilled at arguing her case, often opening with "If I were doing it . . ."

As first lord of the Admiralty, Winston was charged with winning the war at sea, but as a trained soldier with battle experience, he could not help involving himself in affairs on land as well. He began to make a habit of crossing the channel to meet Sir John French, the commander in chief of the British Expeditionary Force, to discuss the wider military picture. Although Winston seemed oblivious to the mockery and resentment provoked by such interference, Clementine sensed the danger. She knew her husband always wanted to be at the center of any major military decision but that others found his "relish for warmaking"⁵ repellent. When he determined to meet Field Marshal French again at the end of September, she tactfully stepped in: "Now please don't think *me* tiresome, but I want you to tell the PM of your projected visit. It would be very bad manners if you do not & he will be displeased and hurt." She also made sure her husband consulted the popular but solitary Lord Kitchener, so that he would view Winston's trip as a legitimate fact-finding "mission" rather than a disruptive "weekend escapade." She observed that in the reverse situation Winston would be disgruntled if Kitchener visited naval commanders without paying him a similar courtesy.

In any case, she argued, why could he not content himself with running the Admiralty? It made her grieve to see him so gloomy and dissatisfied with the high position he had reached, when at thirty-nine he was the only young and vital member of the cabinet, and someone on whom the prime minister leaned more and more. The army accounted for only "1/8 of the allied forces—Whereas you rule this gigantic Navy," she concluded masterfully, "which will in the end decide the outcome of the war."[6]

She had argued her case well. "She has got him tighter than a cleverer woman would have got him," Margot Asquith observed in her diary. She still underestimated Clementine but confessed to being fascinated as to what Winston's wife "could do with him."[7] Winston did indeed write to Kitchener, asking whether he had any objection to his having a talk with French. A (temporarily) placated Kitchener replied that he did not. "How right you were,"[8] an impressed Winston wrote to Clementine on September 26, 1914, from HMS *Adventure*, "at full speed" on the crossing to France.

This respect did not, however, prevent him from embarking on other reckless escapades before she had the chance to stop him. One notable example was his spur-of-the-moment decision to leave for Antwerp, a strategically important port and, as the stronghold of the king and queen of the Belgians and their government, the center of resistance to the Germans. On October 2, the day the baby was due, news had come in that the battle to hold Antwerp was all but lost, and the royal couple was now planning to flee the besieged city with their ministers. Winston could not resist the call of romantic heroism and quickly volunteered to dart over to shore up their resolve. Within hours he was on his way with his entourage, dressed bizarrely in cloak and yachting cap, and in possession of a fleet of armored Rolls-Royces.

Clementine was aghast at the danger in which her husband was placing himself (in her view wholly unnecessarily) and concerned that the thrill of conducting his own miniwar had gone to his head. After a couple of days in Antwerp, Winston telegraphed Asquith for permission to resign his cabinet position as first lord of the Admiralty to take formal charge of British forces in the port. His lust for action met with a "Homeric laugh"[9] from his colleagues—Asquith called the request a "real bit of tragi-comedy"—and he was permitted to stay only until a professional army general could relieve him on October 7. Antwerp in any case fell a few days later, tarring the entire escapade (and therefore Winston) with embarrassing failure.

Clementine was sufficiently astute to see that while his courage was commendable, his conduct in Antwerp had made him vulnerable to accusations of adventuring. She remained troubled by these thoughts as she went into labor late on the night of October 6. In the early hours of the following morning she gave birth not to another boy, as she had fervently hoped, but to a red-haired daughter, who was named Sarah Millicent Hermione. Nellie, who had fairly swiftly been released by her German captors to resume her work with the British wounded, wrote from Mons to congratulate her but also felt the need to warn her not to "neglect Randolph and Diana for the newcomer."[10] Clementine's first concern, however, appears to have been Winston's safe return from Antwerp later in the day.

She was worried about his likely reception, and in this she was not alone. Violet, still taking the closest interest in Winston's fortunes, believed that the escapade had done him "great," if "undeserved," harm. Clementine's cool analysis—colored by a natural desire to have her husband close by when she was about to give birth—compared tellingly with his dangerous impulsiveness. Just seven weeks after her breakdown in Overstrand, she was now thinking more rationally than Winston. War had helped her to rediscover her sense of purpose—and it was not as a mother. As she later told her future daughter-in-law, Pamela Digby, she had "decided to give her life totally" to Winston. She would "live for him"[11] and could only really be happy when it was clear that he needed her. With her husband—and her country—under attack she had a role, and despite the rival needs of her newborn baby and two young children, she was not going to let maternal duties hold her back.

As the conflict dragged on, Winston continued to confide in Clementine his hopes, fears and frustrations. She became well versed in the machinations of the War Council as it struggled to come up with ways of breaking the trench-bound stalemate on the Western Front. By the end of 1914, there had been ninety thousand British casualties, all for no significant gain. Morale at home had also been hit by the naval shelling of coastal towns and the grim realization that there was no end in sight. Often the only "doe" (Asquith's pejorative word for women) at high-level dinners when the most grisly news was discussed, Clementine observed just how many of Winston's colleagues were lacking in energy or ideas. So when he decided to support a seemingly more hopeful plan to the east, she readily familiarized herself with the details.

It entailed capturing Constantinople (now Istanbul) by taking control of the Dardanelles straits, between the Turkish mainland and the Gallipoli peninsula. The idea, approved by the entire War Council in January 1915, was to weaken Germany's firepower by eliminating its new ally, Turkey, and creating a direct link to Britain's struggling ally Russia.

Clementine took great interest in the personalities involved, spotting the danger in the appointment as Winston's first sea lord in late October of the volatile Admiral Lord Fisher. An infatuated Winston saw in his "dear" Jacky Fisher—who at seventy-three was being brought out of retirement—technical brilliance and devotion to the navy. Clementine registered truculence, a volcanic temper and a genius that was on the borderline of madness.

Fisher, a notorious womanizer, sensed her distrust of him and deeply resented her influence over his "beloved" Winston. Two years previously, when he had taken exception to Winston's filling three naval positions with officers close to the king, he had savagely rounded on Clementine, accusing her of persuading her husband to behave like "a Royal pimp." "I fear," he had continued in a letter to Winston, in April 1912, "this must be my last communication with you in any matter at all . . . I consider you have betrayed the Navy."[12] Incredibly, such was Churchill's curious attraction to Fisher— described by Violet Asquith as "something like love"—that he had ignored this unfounded slur on his wife and had brought him back into the fold.

No doubt the incident had taught Clementine to tread carefully, however, and to avoid prompting public suggestions that she was shaping any aspect of her husband's work. For his part, Fisher remained in post as first sea lord despite no fewer than seven threats to resign and a series of deranged rants in writing bestrewn with capital letters. No matter that Fisher vowed that anyone who disagreed with him would find their wives "widows, their children fatherless, their homes a dunghill." Winston still kept him on—a purblind decision that led to speculation that he was as irrational as the old admiral himself.

Winston even asked Clementine to look after the "old boy" for him when he had to travel overseas. Early in May 1915 he went to Paris to take part in negotiations to bring Italy into the war. Clementine had previously noticed how Fisher seemed to become agitated whenever he was left in charge in Winston's absence, and so on this occasion she invited him to lunch with her at Admiralty House. The meal passed uneventfully, and Fisher appeared to depart in good spirits. Only when she emerged from the sitting room herself a while later did she realize that he was still lurking in the corridor. He then bluntly informed her that, far from negotiating with the Italians, Winston was actually in the arms of his Parisian mistress.

It says much about her new understanding of her husband that Clementine treated this intelligence with derision. "Be quiet, you silly old man," she retorted. "Get out!" He went at last, but when Clementine informed Winston of this disturbing episode, he once again brushed away her fears about Fisher's mental stability.

Fisher's erratic changes of opinion about the viability of the Dardanelles plan (these might occur as often as four times in one day) served only to confirm Clementine's doubts. His wavering also did nothing to improve the quality of the preparations for such an ambitious strategy, or to secure the appropriate number of men and ships. From the start, the forces were ill equipped; on the eve of departure one key battalion lacked doctors and drugs. Here Clementine's skill at organization made an impact for the first time. Even her longtime critic Asquith noted that she had "showed a good deal of resource" in arranging for the necessary "details" to be picked up en route at Malta.[13] So caught up was Clementine with every detail of the plan that five-year-old Diana sensed the general air of anxiety, and concluded her prayers every night with "God bless the Dardanelles" without being entirely sure what the Dardanelles were.[14]

Naval bombardment started on February 19, 1915, and initial progress was good, but Winston quickly became convinced that the commanders on the spot were failing to press home their early advantage. Unaccountably, after the loss of a handful of Allied ships, the admirals ordered the fleet to withdraw, thereby providing the hard-pressed Turks with the chance to replenish their depleted stocks of ammunition. Thus, when the army was sent in to launch amphibious landings in April it encountered ferocious fire, resulting in huge loss of life. Winston's old friend and wedding guest General Sir Ian Hamilton was appointed overall commander of the land operation—another choice Clementine regretted. Winston was seduced by Hamilton's dash and chivalry, but she detected a worrying lack of staying power or initiative. Her fears were now borne out by a shocking strategic failure by the army command eventually leading to General Hamilton's being recalled to London.

The whole exercise was fast descending into yet another bloody trench-bound "slogging match." Even so, Fisher blocked Winston's attempts to send further naval reinforcements. Then Kitchener, one of the initial advocates of the whole plan, effectively killed it by also refusing to send more troops. In April grave news came in from the Western Front: the Germans had launched their first poison gas attack and British forces had been left inexcusably exposed by a dire shortage of effective shells to fire back.

As war secretary, Kitchener bore the brunt of the "shell scandal," but the whole government was tainted. Then on May 15, at the peak of the crisis, Lord Fisher again decided to quit. His private secretary handed over the letter of resignation with the words "I think he means it this time." Winston remained unconvinced, believing for some time that it was yet another false alarm[15] and bizarrely continuing to insist that his relationship with Fisher was "deep and fiercely intimate."[16]

Fisher's resignation was real, however, and served to highlight the appalling mess of death and ineptitude evident throughout the Dardanelles campaign. In fairness, the tragedy was the work of many, but a single scapegoat would suffice. Winston was still seen as a traitor by the Tories, an insufferable ego by the Liberals, untrustworthy by the king and a blood-smeared hothead by voters: he was the obvious choice.

Some military analysts believe that with a combination of determination, boldness and more men the Dardanelles exercise would have succeeded, as Winston constantly argued. Although controversy still rages, he had his supporters in this view. In 1954 Clement Attlee (the Labour MP who beat Winston in the 1945 election to become postwar prime minister) was to describe the campaign, in which he had served, as "the only imaginative strategic idea of the war."[17] The concept of the assault—rather than its execution—would later be defended by historians as eminent as Alan Moorehead. But Winston's natural belligerence meant that he had failed to carry his colleagues with him at the time and no one else, including Asquith, was willing or able to take on overall strategic control. Asquith knew it was his own skin or Winston's, and for him that left no choice. In the event, Winston was held liable for one of the bloodiest British military failures in history. The exact number of Allied fatalities is a matter of contention, but it is believed that Britain lost around 29,000 men, Australia 8,500, New Zealand 2,800, India 1,800 and France 9,800 (including deaths from sickness). Clementine would have to endure hearing "Gallipoli" shouted at her husband as a term of abuse for decades to come. Her instincts about Kitchener, Fisher and Hamilton had proved right, but she had still been unable to save her husband from his own misjudgments.

Yet her loyalty never faltered, nor did her sense of outrage. Hearing that Asquith was about to remove Winston from the Admiralty, on May 20 she wrote in high dudgeon to the prime minister himself:

"If you throw Winston overboard you will be committing an act of weakness." Conceding that Winston might have faults in the eyes of some, she nevertheless blasted, "[He has] the supreme quality which I venture to say very few of your present Cabinet possess; the power, the imagination, the deadliness to fight Germany." She concluded: "If you send him to another place he will no longer be fighting. If you waste this valuable war material you will be doing an injury to this country."[18] Whether Clementine's eruption did Winston any good is unclear—he lost the job that he had so loved. Asquith was amazed that one of his ministers' wives should dare to address him in such a manner. He could only assume that she had broken down under the strain, for hers was to his mind the letter of a "maniac."[19] His wife, Margot, forgetting her growing admiration for Clementine, now declared that she had the "soul of a servant," that she and Winston were a "shallow couple" and were together guilty of "blackmail and insolence," as well as "black ingratitude."[20] But what had Clementine to be grateful for?

Her blood was up. She declared to her cousin and friend Sylvia Henley that after writing to Asquith, her one remaining ambition was to dance on his grave. She thought the prime minister effete and complacent and above all out to save himself, leading him to block the release of documents that might have vindicated Winston and revealed his own failings. Kitchener's responsibility for the fiasco, meanwhile, was simply overlooked. On June 3 he was even rewarded with the Order of the Garter.

Clementine's sense of betrayal was profound, not least because the Churchills had regularly socialized with the Asquiths. Indeed, a fortnight after Winston was sacked from the Admiralty they were somewhat eccentrically invited to dine with them at Downing Street again. Margot, hearing that Clementine had been "behaving like a lunatic & crying daily over Winston being turned out of the Admiralty," asked her to visit in her private sitting room for afternoon tea beforehand. Clementine "answered pleasantly on the telephone" and duly arrived "looking cool & handsome in a muslin dress." Margot, with her beaked nose, gray corkscrew curls and hard, inquiring eyes, could not resist finding something to criticize. Noting in her diary that Clementine had "lost her looks since her last baby and she is fatter," she also thought her weight gain had "taken away her refinements & given prominence to her Xpressionless protruding eyes."

The prime minister's wife assumed a friendly front, however, and put her arms around the younger woman, giving her "a little squeeze" and saying (perhaps not with complete sincerity), "Darling I've been thinking & feeling a lot for you." Clementine, whose mood was far from conciliatory, firmly pushed her away. "I saw I was in for it," Margot wrote, deciding now that Clementine was "a very hard insolent young woman with little or no sense of humour . . . frivolous, bad-tempered, *ungrateful* & common *au fond*."

The meeting became no more harmonious when the talk turned to the government and Asquith himself. Clementine got up to go but Margot implored her to "sit down" and "calm" herself. She claimed to have forgiven Clementine for sending that letter but urged her to give some thought to the damage done to "poor Henry," as she called her husband. This was too much for Clementine, who in Margot's words proceeded to "harangue" her hostess on the prime minister's "defects" "in fish-wife style." She "screamed on" until Margot "stopped her & said: '[G]o Clemmie—leave the room—you are off your head.'" Clementine declared she had no desire to be "forgiven" and stormed toward the door. Margot roared a retort as she was leaving that cut Clementine to the quick: "You are *very very* foolish as you will do Winston harm in his career."[21] Nothing Margot might have said could have been more wounding.

Despite this teatime confrontation, the planned dinner went ahead. Afterward, the prime minister led Clementine alone into the Cabinet Room and "spoke very faithfully to her." He later claimed to have "parted on good & even affectionate terms," having quelled her "rather hysterical mutiny."[22]

Although he held Winston in some esteem and enjoyed his company more than that of other cabinet ministers, Asquith, in truth, never rated Clementine's qualities. He sought unquestioning adoration, not criticism, from beautiful women, and went out of his way to repay her defiance with considerable spite, complaining that she was not "quite in [her] best looks" and that her unbending moral code (and insistence on driving everywhere at a "snail's pace") made her a "thundering bore."[23] When, in March 1915, Clementine refused a generous gift of a beautiful couture dress from Edward VII's mistress Mrs. Keppel (the same woman who had offered to procure her a rich lover), the lascivious Asquith sneered about her stuffiness and pride. He was particularly crushing as to her intelligence, describing it as "by no means a deep well,"[24] and made a point of showing his preference for the gregarious Goonie—"worth (I think) 100 Clemmies"[25]—and the more freewheeling Nellie, declaring the younger Hozier "much cleverer and more original."[26]

There was some truth in his view of Clementine: she was shy, critical and reserved, and could certainly be prudish about more exotic lifestyles. So it was perhaps not surprising that people who deemed themselves brilliant sophisticates found her uncomfortable. Conversely, Clementine had long been genuinely shocked that Old Squiffy was a premier who, even in wartime, appeared unwilling to put fun (or the sizing up of attractive females) on hold. His busy social round of golf, bridge, car rides and luncheon parties carried on, even as a generation of young men was being slaughtered in the Flanders mud or on the Gallipoli shores.

Nor was Clementine alone in her disapproval. Asquith had been warned by a senior colleague, Lord Chancellor Haldane, to curtail his champagne habit, and Margot too had come under fire for wearing osprey plumes to a society wedding: since Germans had "the monopoly of the osprey plume trade," her thoughtless choice suggested, albeit wrongly, that she might be "at heart pro-German."[27] To families receiving the dreaded War Office telegram, the whole impression was of lack of discipline, energy or even compassion.

A great peacetime social reformer, Asquith no longer seemed concerned for the poor, but nor did he ever really change gear to deal headlong with the catastrophe befalling his country. Torpid and out of touch, he continued to regard "energy under the guise of lethargy" as one of his greatest qualities.[28] And all the while he indulged his obsession with Venetia Stanley, writing her billets-doux during cabinet meetings, arranging assignations and generally making a fool of himself over a woman thirty-five years his junior. Such was his obsession that he disclosed state secrets to her, leading some historians, including Winston himself, to argue that she became, over time, Britain's biggest-ever security risk. When he fired Winston from the Admiralty, Asquith's judgment may have been affected by his distress at the news that Venetia was to marry a junior minister, Edwin Montagu. Interestingly, she had made up her mind to inform him that their affair was over while staying with Clementine, who may well have encouraged her. Venetia's decision to marry was, for Asquith, the "most bitter memory" of his life.

No wonder Clementine railed at such a man throwing the focused—and warlike—Winston to the wolves. As he was to write later, nothing in his life caused him so much pain as his disgrace over the Dardanelles and his removal from the Admiralty. He maintained an admirable dignity in public; in private he was in agonies about his fall from grace. For all of Clementine's ministrations—cozy fire, favorite food, traditional comforts—he would sit in an armchair and scowl at the futility of having "nothing to do." "None of us," he would say, "can do anything without power."[29] It was "odious," he said, to watch from the sidelines Asquith's "sloth and folly."

On June 30, despite the ignominy being heaped on Churchill, Clementine fulfilled a promise to her kindly old headmistress, Beatrice Harris, to return to Berkhamsted School to open a new wing. Upright and dignified, she planted a tree and, in a speech to the schoolgirls, paid tribute to the "stoic fortitude with which women bear the most agonising sorrows."

Upon his removal from the Admiralty at the end of May, Winston had been made chancellor of the Duchy of Lancaster in the new coalition government, a nonjob often given to politicians to keep them quiet on their way out. Gone was the bustle of executive power and the elixir of being at the center of events. For the devoted Eddie

Marsh, who followed Winston from the Admiralty, the summer of 1915 was a melancholy time. To see Winston torn from his naval work, he said, was like watching Beethoven go deaf. When he left his Admiralty office, Eddie picked up a photograph of Lord Fisher inscribed "Yours till Hell freezes," tore it into pieces and dropped them into a wastepaper basket.[30]

Now that the Conservatives under Andrew Bonar Law had joined the government—in what Asquith hoped would be a post-Dardanelles display of national unity—Winston found himself ever more an outsider. Unable to see himself as anything other than indispensable, he had fatally misread others' feelings, particularly those of members of his old party still bitter at his defection eleven years before. His removal from the Admiralty had, in fact, been part of Bonar Law's price for shoring up the Asquith regime, although Clementine largely blamed the "Welsh Judas" David Lloyd George, one of the architects of the cross-party arrangement, for what she saw as horse-trading Winston's future for his own advantage.

Both Churchills now felt that Winston was being conveniently blamed for everything by everyone; indeed sometimes it seemed more firepower was being directed at him than at the real enemy in Berlin. His isolation—political and social—was complete. Many former so-called friends cut him off, and even Violet now deserted him in favor of defending her father. Those few still close to him at the time—and thereafter—believed it was only his marriage that saved him from self-destruction; the darkness of his moods frightened them. For her part, Clementine feared her husband would "die of grief," and yet even then she never lost her faith in his greatness.

General Hastings "Pug" Ismay, who became a great Churchill favorite when he served as Winston's chief of staff during the Second World War, was convinced that only Clementine's unbreakable loyalty preserved Winston's "sanity" in the First. The Dardanelles "experience had the most tremendous impact on him, an impact that people never realised" and one that lasted in the back of his mind even after he became prime minister in 1940. Clementine, who had shared all his ups and downs, was "his rock during that terrible time," Ismay believed, "because [Ismay could not] imagine what other comfort he could have had."[31]

In fact there was to be another comfort. The Churchills had been renting a country retreat, Hoe Farm near Godalming in Surrey, a rambling fifteenth-century house altered in the 1890s by the architect Edwin Lutyens. With ten bedrooms and the numerous bathrooms Clementine insisted on, there was room for Goonie and her brood too (fortuitously, they shared the rent). One Sunday, desperate to lift his spirits, Goonie handed Winston one of the children's paint boxes and asked: "Are these toys any good to you? They amuse some people." It was a revelation. The very next morning, Clementine rushed out to buy him his own paints, easel and canvas. For short intervals at least, Winston discovered he could escape his sorrow by throwing his energies and thoughts into what he liked to call his "daubs." He became transfixed by "a wonderful new world of thought and craft" and applied himself with childlike enthusiasm. Clementine ensured much praise was poured on his early rudimentary efforts, which pleased him no end, of course. Remarkably, he had never been to an art exhibition, so she took him to the National Gallery, where he spent half an hour studying the brushstrokes in a single van Dyck. "Grandmama had an appreciation of art,"[32] says her granddaughter Edwina Sandys, one that she now tried to pass on to her husband. Later Winston would say that if it had not been for painting he could not have withstood the strain.

Not only had Winston been kicked out of power, the Churchill household had also been shorn of its trappings—including a London base, a full cabinet salary (due to the first lord's senior ranking) and the beloved yacht *Enchantress*. Asquith offered to let them stay on in Admiralty House, but Clementine's pride would not allow her to accept charity from the man who had, in her view, sacrificed her husband to shore up his own waning popularity. Eccleston Square was still let, so the couple were without a roof over their heads in London. In early June they moved, albeit temporarily, into a large house belonging to Winston's aunt Cornelia and her son Ivor Guest next to the Ritz hotel.

Domestic life had comforted Winston immediately after his downfall, but denied his normal refuge in work he now found the all-day commotion of rumbustious children overwhelming. His son, Randolph, a beautiful child with golden locks and flashes of charm, was a particular handful, once pushing a nursery maid into a full bath in her clothes, and on a later occasion phoning the Foreign Office claiming to be "Mr. Churchill." Having endured parental coldness in his own childhood, Winston did not have the heart to punish him. Diana, too, exhibited a naughty streak, although she was generally shy and nervous. Clementine seemed to lack both the inclination to coax her out of her shell and the strength to keep her children in order. Neither was there a Mrs. Everest to provide firm but loving discipline, only a series of undertrained and underpaid nursery maids who left as soon as they could.

This may account for why Winston spent many nights half a mile away with his mother at 72 Brook Street, Mayfair, a graceful Georgian house with arched windows and a much-admired interior designed more for photogenic dash than practicality. Jennie, whose homemaking talents were now widely admired, wove a particular magic with fine rugs, furniture and paintings, a silver bedroom, flowers everywhere and the luxury of a seven-course dinner elegantly served. Tablecloths were banned from her marble dining table (a style swiftly copied by many a London hostess) and a maid would burn incense to complete the theatrical mood. Here Winston was the undisputed center of attention and could escape the demands of family life. She had a "heart of gold," Winston would say of his mother, hardly endearing her to his half-deserted wife.

In mid-June, Clementine and the children went to live with Jack and Goonie at 41 Cromwell Road, their redbrick terraced house opposite the Natural History Museum in South Kensington. Winston's restless soul could never be content with such hugger-mugger family life. He had been considering the possibility of returning to soldiering and now resolved that if he was to be prevented from waging the war at his desk in London, he would fight it on the front line. As his mother instinctively understood, he deliberately sought danger to ease his pain. He would take up his commission as a major in the Oxfordshire Hussars and rejoin his regiment in France.

On November 11, 1915, after being excluded from the newly formed War Council, Winston wrote to Asquith resigning from his government post to place himself at the "disposal of the military authorities." The announcement prompted his old sweetheart Muriel Wilson to write: "I just wanted to tell you how much I admired you for your courage." (It was one of several affectionate letters from his former amours over the years that highlighted the degree to which the women who had rejected Winston nonetheless continued to cherish him.)[33]

The following Tuesday, there was a small farewell lunch at Cromwell Road, whose hall and landings were piled up with bags and military equipment. It was a family occasion, apart from Eddie Marsh and, more surprisingly, Violet and Margot Asquith. Taking action at last, Winston was in good form, trying on his uniform and enjoying the rumpus. Eddie and Jennie were blinking back the tears, the latter distraught that her brilliant son was being "relegated to the trenches." As at any such gathering, the prospect of death was, of course, the "uninvited guest."

Unbeknownst to Clementine, Winston had already written a letter to be given to her in the event of his demise. Much of it concerned their finances—notably what to do about overdrafts and other debts. But he also wrote: "Do not grieve for me too much . . . On the whole, especially since I met you my darling one I have been happy & you have taught me how noble a woman's heart can be . . . Meanwhile look forward, feel free, rejoice in Life, cherish the children, guard my memory. God bless you. Good bye W."

Despite the terrible likelihood that he would be killed or maimed, Clementine remained admirably calm, organized, even cheerful throughout. She seemed fortified by an unshakable conviction that Winston was preordained for greatness, and this was merely another stage in his journey. Although thousands were being slaughtered by the day across the channel, she appeared incapable of believing that her husband could become yet another casualty statistic. Perhaps her brave front was born more of necessity than delusion: she knew that when Winston was this low, she had no choice but to be "up." Certainly, just a year on from her breakdown in Pear Tree Cottage, and despite all the trials she had endured since, her self-control and courage at such a moment were exemplary. She was now a woman with conviction, one who knew her worth in a true partnership. Violet's star was finally waning. She herself observed that it was Clementine who now commanded center stage, while she was unable to have any "interchange with Winston" that day. "Only the implicit passed between us," Violet wrote in sadness about the man she had loved and lost.

CHAPTER FOUR

I Believe in Your Star

1915–16

Major Winston Churchill arrived in Boulogne, in northern France, on November 18, 1915, to be met on the quayside by a staff car. He was swept off to the champagne and hot-bath comforts of general headquarters at St. Omer, where he dined with his old friend and commander in chief, Field Marshal French. Such a reception befitted Winston's former VIP status as a cabinet member and his own sense of importance. But it sat uncomfortably with the new reality of his position as a middle-ranking officer bound for the trenches.

He could have remained in the well-appointed Château de Blendecques, but both Clementine and Winston knew there would be little benefit for him in a staff post at GHQ, other than the obvious one of increased personal safety. Winston would never be happy doing things halfheartedly and in any case he had a point to prove. So within a few days he was at the front, with its stinking mud, bloated rats and rotting corpses. It was the first—and only—time in his life when he lived in discomfort, or cheek by jowl with the lower classes.

The ducal grandson, former first lord of the Admiralty and ex-nabob of the *Enchantress* was now widely reviled at home and ankle-deep in the squalor of war. No major British offensives were launched during his time on the Franco-Belgian border at Ploegsteert (or Plug Street, as it was dubbed by the Tommies), but it was a wretched existence all the same. During the unforgiving winter of 1915–16, when there were only eighteen rainless days in five months, it was impossible to get dry or warm. No wonder he took pleasure in escorting visiting staff officers—often from his own exalted social circles—on tours of the trenches, where they would be splattered with mud, tear their pristine uniforms on barbed wire, and on occasion endure gut-twisting fear.

Although they resented him at first as a privileged impostor, Winston's men came to love him for his stoicism and good humor. His bedroom in a semiruined farmhouse was pierced three times by shells and his dugout obliterated. Snipers were a constant danger and there were terrifying nighttime sorties into enemy territory. Yet he displayed to his men a fatalistic, almost romantic, attitude to the prospect of his own death. He also talked down the dangers to Clementine, at first absurdly insisting that it was all "a vy harmless thing"[1] and there was "certainly nothing to complain about . . . except cold feet."[2]

This did not mean he intended to tolerate unnecessary hardships. He kept Clementine frantically busy with lists of urgently required (but often scarce) items, such as periscopes, sheepskin sleeping bags, small face towels, trench wading boots, leather waistcoats, big beef-steak pies and chocolate. Later came demands for brandy, cigars, fancy headed notepaper and a tin bath complete with copper boiler. Regularly thereafter she would send him hampers of carefully cho-sen delicacies, which he shared around his fellow officers, prompting raucous cheers for Clementine in her absence. Winston was, more-over, favored by the personal support of French, who had written to Clementine to reassure her that he was going to do all he could to "take care" of him.[3] There is little doubt that he was one of the most cosseted officers on the Western Front.

In fact, Winston reported on November 19, "I am very happy here . . . I did not know what release from care meant." For Clemen-tine, however, left at home to march alone, there was no correspond-ing sense of escape. Earlier that same day she had written: "Altho' it's only a few miles you seem to me as far away as the stars, lost among a million khaki figures . . . Write to me, Winston. I want a letter from you badly."[4] His reply was deliberately defiant; he claimed to have "lost all interest in the outer world" and "its stupid newspapers."[5] As if needing to talk himself up, he added: "Do you realise what a very important person a major is? 99 people out of 100 in this great army have to touch their hats to me." Within a couple of days, the brave face slipped altogether and he was struggling to conceal his private rages and longing for political power. Nor could he keep from her the true savagery of conditions in the trenches, with "filth and rubbish everywhere, graves built into the defences . . . feet and clothing breaking through the soil, water & muck on all sides" and "enormous rats" creeping and gliding "to the unceasing accompaniment of rifle & machine gun fire."[6]

Recognizing Clementine was his most loyal—perhaps his only—follower at home, he pressed on her the need to "show complete confidence in [their] fortunes" and told her, "Hold your head very high."[7] Fortunately, she drew intense pride from Winston's courage in willingly suffering such horrors; she also soon recognized that it was working wonders for his reputation. "Wherever I go I find people awestruck at your sacrifice," she told him.[8] The *Observer*, for instance, was running articles about Major Churchill's "blaze of glory."

His new "military halo," as she called it, and the fact that he never gave up his parliamentary seat, provided her with a glimmer of hope for his future rehabilitation as a national figure and so, when not scouring London's shops for his creature comforts, she set about what amounted to a "Bring Back Winston" campaign. She dealt with his constituency affairs to the best of her ability and long before the term came into use, she was tirelessly schmoozing newspaper proprietors such as Lord Rothermere, editors including C. P. Scott of the *Manchester Guardian*, cabinet ministers, MPs and military chiefs, even including General Hamilton. She sang Winston's praises, pointed out his courage in leading by example and duly reported back to him any positive reaction. She also kept a constant lookout for openings and tried to act on them. When she got wind of plans to create a minister for air, she immediately engineered a lunch with Lord Curzon (who was to become president of the Air Board) to suggest that her husband would be ideal for the job. "Oh my darling I long so for it to happen, & feel that it would except for the competition for the post inside the Cabinet,"⁹ she wrote somewhat optimistically.

She courted the more amenable journalists, dealt with daily press inquiries and sent Winston all his cuttings—most of which were still unflattering, although she reassured him that press hostility was not a major concern "becos' the public [was] very fond of [him] personally." She understood the potency of *his* celebrity—a quality so lacking in many of his powerful enemies. But she avoided giving much of herself away to journalists, even when they were agreeable. It was a policy she would retain for the rest of her life, granting few interviews and no in-depth ones. Around this time she wrote that she had "determined with great courtesy to hold all newspaper men at arms' length," a safe distance from which they might regard her with "curiosity, interest & respect." She believed that if she allowed them to "come closer" they would "observe the flaws in [her] armour!"¹⁰ Understanding the dangers to a woman who projected herself in public, she still lacked confidence in her own abilities.

Despite her exhaustive efforts, the restless Winston would issue her with such peremptory instructions as "[K]eep the threads in your fingers" and "[L]et me know what you see," and told her to send "*verbatim*" reports of relevant conversations with key players. On January 19, 1916, he wrote: "I should like you to make the seeing of my friends a regular business." Such commands were unnecessary, and he later apologized for one particularly "miauling" letter. She was already sending him regular bulletins on political events, discussions and plans; she attended the relevant functions and her diary was full of meetings and "reconnoitre" sessions. She was, in effect, an early twentieth-century amalgam of special adviser, lobbyist and spin doctor, and she became widely admired on the political circuit. The Labour man Ramsay MacDonald thought her "the queen of wives" and Lloyd George considered her "charming and delightful," as well as expert at "managing" Winston.¹¹

Of course she did not enjoy Winston's previous status or access to secret information. Women were yet to be given the vote, there were no female MPs, and when they visited the Commons to watch debates they had to do so in the Ladies' Gallery, like cloistered nuns behind a grille. What Clementine could do was confined by her sex, but studying politics—and politicians—at Winston's side had imbued her with a sense of the people who mattered and what to say to them. After seven years at the center of power she missed the hubbub almost as much as he did. Indeed, there were times in her life when she hinted at regret that she could not enter politics on her own account, that her sex unreasonably contained her. "I don't believe that it is so difficult to be a statesman or a strategist," she told her husband a few years later. "All one needs is core common sense but to be born with trousers instead of petticoats!"[12] Another time she mused about being "reincarnated" so that she could "go into public life."

Jennie also wrote frequently to Winston, urging him not to stay in the trenches too long. She still invested much of her energy in her famous elder son, but at the front he became unresponsive to her (and to Violet). His daily missives were to Clementine. During his rational moments he recognized that she was the one indispensable figure in his life; later he referred to her as his "vy wise & sagacious military pussy cat."

As well as managing her husband, Clementine was once again running a household on too little money. Winston urged her not to deny herself reasonable comforts—and sent her £100 for urgent bills and later £300 for emergencies—but Clementine was otherwise making do on £140 a month, a great deal less than she had enjoyed at the Admiralty. Fortunately, Jennie came to live with them, contributing £40 a month to the household kitty, but money was tight and the family car was sold for the cash. Even so, Clementine made a point of showing generosity to others. She spent the princely sum of £25 on "a really beautiful Louis XV" gold box as a thank-you gift for Winston's ex–private secretary, Eddie Marsh, because nothing cheaper was good enough.

There is at this time surprisingly little in Clementine's letters about Diana, Randolph or Sarah—and only passing mention that Diana had been suffering from neuralgia, often screaming in agony for twenty minutes at a time. In any case, as ever, the children were largely entrusted to the care of one short-term nanny after another. As her daughter Mary later noted, many women at such a time would have found "real consolation" in the "company of their children." Clementine loved them and was "devoted to their welfare" but the whole focus of her life and her emotions was out there in France. Very occasionally, she would mention how Diana's new haircut made her look like Peter Pan, that Sarah was "on the verge of voluble speech," or how Randolph was showing a precocious interest in the war, and she once crowed with maternal pride after a birthday party when they looked "quite beautiful and quite different from the other children." She wrote more frequently, however, about her concerns over Winston's health, fretting that he was not inoculated against typhoid and waking in the night from nightmares of his shivering in the cold, a thought that made her utterly "miserable."

Perhaps Clementine's greatest concern of all in this testing time was how to prevent her impetuous husband from damaging his prospects further. She could not have been more opposed, for instance, to Winston's knee-jerk desire for immediate and unsuitable preferment from Field Marshal French—a divergence of views that would generate a great deal of heat between them. Clementine now saw clearly that Winston's best interests lay in staying at the front and being seen to rise up the ranks by merit. She was forthright in her assertion that only in this way could he begin to repair the damage done to his reputation back home. Yet still she occasionally expressed fears that she had gone too far: "I do hope that when you think of me, it is not a picture of a harsh arguing scold, but your loving & sad Clemmie,"[13] she told him. "I love you very much more even than I thought I did . . . & now I feel more than half my life has vanished across the channel." No doubt she remained mindful of Jennie's favorite piece of advice: never scold a husband, otherwise "he will only go where he is not scolded."

Clementine's courage in standing up to Winston is remarkable. All his adult life, he dominated those around him, with many a tough general or hard-nosed minister holding back from contradicting him. As one admiral, David Beatty, would complain: "It takes a good deal out of me when dealing with a man of his calibre with a very quick brain."[14] Winston was forceful, impatient and very quick-witted. Phenomenally knowledgeable on a range of subjects, he had a fierce temper and a cutting tongue. Disagreement with his point of view was "obnoxious" to him, and when combined with personal affection, Violet Asquith observed, "it became a kind of treachery."[15] In short, it was difficult for almost anyone, however powerful or self-assured, to withstand the full force of his invective. Whenever Clementine herself lost face-to-face against this invincible opponent (sometimes because she became "over-emphatic"[16]) she would remarshal her arguments in writing. But she would only rarely give up, however exhausting the fight became.

This refusal to cede ground on important matters persisted throughout their marriage and was one of her most conspicuous traits. Often it was *only* Clementine who would point to Winston's faults; his lack of real empathy with others and tendency to bully meant that he often mistook silent acquiescence for positive support. As Clementine told him, he had to learn how to take people with him by inspiring their trust rather than cowing them into submission. It was a lesson she would have to teach him time and time again.

Her campaign in late 1915 to prevent him from taking command of a brigade—an indefensible promotion straight from major to brigadier general—was particularly hard fought. Winston was only too eager to be elevated to a higher authority, and wealth and social distinction generally still counted for much in the British Army, but the old order was fading fast and Clementine rightly feared that he would be seen once again as a character of vainglorious ambition. "I hope so much my Darling that you may still decide to take a battalion first," she opened one letter; "I prefer you to win your way than to be thought a favorite [of Field Marshal French]. I *feel* confidence in your star."[17] The field marshal was in any case a spent force. A weak-willed womanizer, on the battlefield he was slow and complacent. Whatever his failings, Winston remained devoted to him, but Clementine took a more objective view. "Do not my Dear be shocked & angry with me for saying this," she pleaded. "I know he is your friend," but with victory seemingly further away than ever he needed to be re-placed by a "fresh un-tortured mind."[18]

In the same letter, an increasingly desperate Clementine tried several different approaches: "I long for you to be not so much in the trenches . . . but everyone who *really* loves you & has your interest at heart wants you to go step by step . . . Do get a battalion now and a brigade later."

Clementine's instincts were sound, but she detected in Winston's letters a coolness toward her—as well as a stubborn determination to have his way. "During this last week I feel as if I had missed your thoughts—or is it fancy?" she asked three days later, on December 9. He answered tersely the next day with news that he was to be given the command of the Fifty-Sixth Brigade, no matter what "criticism & carping" came his way, and that she was secretly to order a new khaki tunic for him with the insignia of a brigadier general. Clementine realized the battle was up; there was this time no point in trying to dissuade him further. She now affected to share his enthusiasm, however wrongheaded she still believed it to be, telling him she was "thrilled" while steeling herself to defend Winston's actions from his detractors once again. "Just come back to me alive that's all,"[19] were her closing words.

In the event, fearing questions in the House of Commons, Asquith blocked French's offer of a brigade, leaving Winston bitter and Clementine saddened but ultimately relieved. She quickly canceled the tunic and tried to boost Winston's battered spirits: "My own Darling I feel such absolute confidence in your future—it is your present which causes me agony."[20] In return, he sent her two letters raging about Asquith's treachery, which he later wisely advised her to burn. He vowed to sever every last link with the prime minister, but despite her own enmity toward Asquith, she pleaded caution: "Do not burn any boats!"

Knowing that Asquith was deep down fond of Winston, she now saw that there was a greater benefit to be had from winning him back to the Churchill cause than from permanently setting such a powerful operator against them. She still believed in her husband's "star" but warned him that his constant demands for information and persistent rejection of her considered advice were becoming intolerable: "You must not beat your poor Kat so hard; it is very cruel & not the right treatment for mousers. I am absolutely worn out tonight."[21]

Winston was in open despair at his exile from power, complaining: "I see so much to be done that will never be done . . . My Darling, what should I do if I had not you to write to when I am despondent?" He now regretted not following her "counsels" in the past, even though they were on occasion "too negative." But crucially he conceded, "[T]he beauty & strength of your character & the sagacity of your judgment are more realised by me every day."[22] In one of his sweetest letters, Winston told her, "[My] greatest good fortune in a life of brilliant experience has been to find you, & to lead my life with you . . . I feel that the nearer I get to honour, the nearer I am to you."[23]

Winston returned home on leave for Christmas 1915, a welcome family get-together and reprieve from the strains of the past few weeks. He stayed for just a long weekend, and, making use of the opportunity to see his political contacts, he had very little time alone with Clementine. It seems she found him attractive in uniform: there was something virile and valiant about a man in khaki. They cut it rather close and had to run for his train back to the front. She recalled being out of breath and unable to speak, but wrote later: "I could not tell you how much I wanted you at the station."[24] It is probably the most explicit note between them that survives. It also raises the question of just how much time and energy there was left for their marriage when they were investing so heavily in the remnants of his career. He relied on her completely, and she was giving her all to his cause, but there was little sign that he thought much about her needs or desires.

Although exhausted by the frantic activity of Winston's visit, Clementine immediately got back to work the next day, inviting Asquith's great rival, Lloyd George, to lunch at Cromwell Road. Winston fancied that the Welshman was intent on toppling Asquith as prime minister and that herein lay his opportunity to sweep triumphantly back to office. Sure enough, Clementine was able to report back on Asquith's weakening grip on power, but although Lloyd George had previously declared to Winston that he planned to overthrow Asquith at the earliest opportunity, he was now busily backtracking.

While Winston continued to have faith in his former colleague, the meeting had placed a great strain on Clementine. Lloyd George had uttered all the right things, saying repeatedly, "We must get Winston back," but she found herself incapable of believing him. In her view he was at even greater fault than Asquith in Winston's downfall, as he had failed to stand by his ally in his hour of need. "I don't trust him one bit," she reported, characterizing Lloyd George as "fair of speech, shifty of eye, treacherous of heart."[25] So for now, Winston had to make do with promotion to lieutenant colonel in command of a battalion of the Royal Scots Fusiliers. The men had recently come out of battle, having sustained horrific casualties at Loos, and Winston tried to raise their spirits by lavish praise of Scotland. "A wife, a constituency, & now a regiment attest the sincerity of my choice!" he declared to them, presenting himself as an honorary Scotsman.[26]

Feeling reenergized after a few days' rest at Alderley with her Stanley cousins, Clementine decided to swallow her pride and "reconnoitre Downing Street." She thought herself "not good at pretending" but she would deploy all her charms to woo the Asquiths. Sure enough, on January 7, 1916, Margot invited her to tea again at Downing Street and this time the prime minister's wife was in a "very good mood." Clementine bumped into Asquith himself in the hall, and although reticent at first and looking as though he had suffered a "good deal," he stopped for a chat, asking after Winston with "compunction in his voice."[27]

She spoke to him at greater length when she was invited to lunch with the Asquiths the following Sunday. It was the first time they had had a proper conversation since Winston's departure in November, and Asquith asked her a great many questions about her husband. "I was perfectly natural (except perhaps that I was a little too buoyant)," she reported back, "but it was an effort."[28] Clementine's intention was to reestablish "civil relations" with the seat of power, and believing she was getting the measure of the prime minister, she begged Winston not to do anything that might jeopardize her progress, or without first permitting her to interject her "valuable (!) opinion."[29]

Winston was not satisfied with this account and demanded a "verbatim report of the Kat's conversation with the old ruffian." Asquith had not talked much about politics, she wrote, but rather "trivialities and femininities which you know he adores." She had sensed that Asquith wanted her answers to his inquiries about Winston's life in the trenches to be "reassuring, & my good manners as a guest forbade me making him uncomfortable which I could easily have done." She knew she had to behave impeccably as she would otherwise not be "bidden again."[30]

Clementine was playing the long game, but Winston was tiring of the wait. Although absorbed in his new regiment, military service was not enough. His second in command was the likable Sir Archibald Sinclair and once he would have drawn comfort from this male comradeship, but now he felt obliged to maintain a "smiling face" while keeping to himself his agony at being sidelined as the country continued to bleed to death. He felt "remote, forgotten, ineffectual."[31] "It is such a relief to write one's heart out to you," he told Clementine. "Bear with me."

As well as looking after Winston's interests, since the first German gas attack back in April Clementine had been spearheading a successful appeal to housewives to help make emergency gas masks for the front (the first time a woman had ever undertaken such a role). In June she had also gone back to work organizing canteens for munitions workers. The factories were working day and night to avoid another "shell scandal" but management rarely provided proper catering for the staff. Clementine was invited to join the Munition

Workers' Auxiliary Committee, formed by the Young Men's Christian Association (YMCA), and was put in charge of refectories across North London. Over the next few months, she took on responsibility for opening, staffing and running nine canteens, each feeding up to five hundred workers at a time. Although she had no previous experience in managing anything beyond the household, she turned out to be surprisingly effective. It was tiring and time-consuming work—not least because she was reliant on a combination of trams, tubes and trains to make her tours of inspection. Arriving home late at night, she was sometimes too exhausted to answer Winston's letters straightaway. Many replies were written at five or six in the morning, suggesting a very long day indeed.

Her new position of authority gave her the chance to advance her feminist beliefs. It was a small but significant step toward sexual equality when she introduced a rule that women workers could smoke in exactly the same canteens and rest areas as their male colleagues. The thousands of women now employed in heavy industry for the first time fascinated her. She took a great interest in their lifestyles, noticing that these often young and pretty women became "terribly skilful very quickly." They expected "good money" too, she noted, but even Clementine could not countenance equal pay with men. A woman earning thirty-five shillings a week felt like a millionaire, she declared, although a man earned more for the same work.

Although socially Clementine still mixed exclusively with her own class, she gradually endeared herself to the workers. Her obvious concern for the less fortunate and unusual dedication to the job of providing them with good meals distinguished her from other upper-class women drafted in to help with the war effort. Having watched her husband work at close quarters for the previous seven years, she adopted his professional approach—typically working from nine in the morning to half past seven at night. Her colleagues were "surprised" at her speed and efficiency as well as her high expectations of her team; she wrote to Winston, "I get very tired [but] I find the others get tired first . . . It is no use scolding me becos' it's all your fault—You have taught me to work outside office hours."[32] Clementine was honing impressive leadership skills.

Despite her aristocratic origins, her relatively impoverished childhood and brief experience of work while unmarried had also fostered in Clementine an instinctive sympathy for the worker's point of view. Her natural reserve belied a populist touch, including the odd harmless flirtation. In mid-December she had visited a free canteen for traveling soldiers at London Bridge station, where four hundred men were about to embark for France. "One very tough man talked to me a little & I asked him about his experiences," she told Winston. "Just as he was going he turned back & said 'If you will wait for me till I come home I'll marry you!' "[33] She was touchingly proud of the compliment.

Around the same time, she began to take an interest in how Winston dealt with his rank and file, urging him to treat them kindly and with respect—a refrain she was to maintain throughout their marriage. Winston did strive to improve conditions for his soldiers; he instituted a delousing operation as soon as he arrived, and arranged for sports days and concerts to entertain men about to return to the line. He was keen for her to know that he was a fair and compassionate commander. "My dear don't be at all anxious about my being hard on the men," he wrote in one letter. "Am I ever hard on anybody? No. I have reduced punishment both in quantity & method."[34] Nevertheless, she was right to worry, as his sense of natural superiority over the lower classes sometimes induced him to issue the most absurd orders. His idea that batmen—military servants assigned to commissioned officers—should also act as bodyguards and willingly sacrifice their lives for their superiors was reportedly drowned out by laughter from his men.[35]

More than seven million British women worked during the First World War, many of them for the first time. Upper-class women had previously lived lives free of household chores or virtually any sort of toil, leaving them with plenty of time to read, dress up and socialize. Many, like Clementine, found the new work hard but also liberating and confidence-boosting. New horizons were opening up beyond husbands, parties and homes.

Until it became necessary to replace men away fighting at the front, it was widely presumed that women were simply not capable of carrying out demanding jobs. Just before the war, there had been a debate in the press about the role of women, in which some seriously argued that if they were required to make decisions their brains would melt down under the strain. Although he had admired Clementine's teaching of French when he first met her, Winston was certainly against her being out of the home too much now that she was his wife. He had reservations about her canteen work, fearing that it would distract her when she should be focused entirely on him. On one occasion, when she was absorbed in setting up a huge new refectory for a big factory at Hackney Marshes in East London, while also nursing her mother, who had hurt her leg, Winston instructed her not to "neglect" to "represent" his interests, telling her, "[D]on't let them drift or think I have left the game." He wanted her to spend as much time lobbying on his behalf as she did on the canteens—a request that would have excluded any time for sleep. He nevertheless pleaded: "I have no-one but you to act for me."

Clementine continued to do her best to charm the men of influence, but she discovered, as an outsider, that "everyone 'in office' seem[ed] to be unbelievably smug" and wondered, "Were we like that when we were in power?" Reporting back in detail on January 29 on her supper with Winston's friend F. E. Smith, now attorney general, she attributed his apparently slavish (and unhelpful) support of the government to the "sedative effect" of a "dignified position" and "heaps of money." She equally waspishly reported having put on "3 layers of armour" for lunch with Reginald McKenna, the chancellor of the Exchequer, who turned out to be a "noxious creature" of "tepid counter-jumping calculation."[36] Winston's successor at the Admiralty, A. J. Balfour, resembled, under her close examination, a "shabby maiden aunt's tabby cat" and was, in common with all the others, "smug, purblind, indifferent, ignorant, casual." With such uninspiring, complacent leadership, she feared that the war would "go on forever."[37]

She wanted recognition for her efforts and was not afraid to seek it. "Now don't scold your Kat too much for being a hermit. Here in two days I have hobnobbed with [Edwin] Montagu, [Augustine] Birrell [a cabinet minister], Lloyd George & a South African potentate! Tomorrow night I am dining with [Sir Ernest] Cassel. Please send me home the Distinguished Conduct Medal at once & much praise."[38] Suitably impressed, Winston replied: "You have indeed been active . . . Persevere, the D.C.M. is yours."[39]

For the first time, Clementine's own work won public acknowledgment. At Ponders End on February 4, 1916, Lloyd George (then munitions minister) promised to open her biggest canteen yet—and Violet and Jennie turned out to watch. Alas, the workers had taken exception to some of Lloyd George's more draconian labor policies and threatened a walkout during his visit. When the manager informed them that they would upset Clementine if they did so, they immediately desisted—a courtesy that made her feel "very superior." To express their gratitude, the workers presented her with a bouquet of flowers and a shell-shaped brooch enclosed in a gold box studded with turquoises, pearls and even diamonds. "I nearly fainted with emotion," she wrote to Winston. "Don't tell anyone about this as it sounds vain, but I want you to know about my small success. I really have worked hard but now I shall have to redouble my efforts to deserve all this. I feel I must give the men fat chickens every day to eat!"[40]

Back in October 1914, Winston had rebuked Violet Asquith for her plans to train as a nurse, instructing her that "the duties of women" specifically include tending men "at the 'apex' of responsibility." "No, my dear," he had written sternly, "you must remain at your father's side and mine . . . We who are directing these immense and complicated operations . . . need every comfort, care and cosseting . . . We are your duty. This is your war-station. I command you to remain here."[41]

In the event, Violet did not go into nursing. For many years she remained as instructed at Winston's side, much to Clementine's displeasure, but she finally conceded defeat with his expulsion from the Admiralty and move to France. She decided, at the age of twenty-eight, that the time had come to marry someone else. Maurice Bonham Carter, her father's principal private secretary, had pursued her for years and eventually won her by promising to guarantee her freedom in marriage. Unfortunately for him, she took him literally; for years she was to conduct an affair with prominent economist Oswald Toynbee Falk, a close friend of John Maynard Keynes, proving just what an unsuitable match she would have made for Winston, who demanded undiluted attention.

Violet's wedding, on November 30, 1915 (Winston's forty-first birthday), was a lavish occasion. Clementine reported to Winston that the prime minister looked "happy, sleek & complacent," although the photographs carried by the newspapers captured a decidedly unsmiling bride. The event had briefly turned London "topsy-turvy in excitement" and even Clementine had not been entirely impervious to all the pomp, bursting with pride at Randolph's triumph as a page. "He looked *quite* beautiful in a little Russian velvet suit with fur . . . & at Downing Street afterwards he was surrounded & kissed & admired by dozens of lovely women."[42] Nevertheless, she was unable to resist a little jibe at Violet, noting that she and Maurice had looked "dreary & blue-stockingy"[43] on return from their honeymoon.

The wedding took place against the backdrop of the apocalyptic stalemate on the Western Front. By the end of 1915, 285,000 British lives had been lost in the trenches in France and Flanders to no obvious strategic advantage. In December, the evacuation of the Dardanelles began, where countless more had been killed. The disastrous failures of these two campaigns had prompted a massive fall in public support for the way in which the war was being conducted. Fewer were now prepared to volunteer for service and yet the need for men was greater than ever, leading to the introduction of conscription as a last resort in January 1916.

Clementine had felt Winston's absence deeply at Violet's wedding, but she had been fortified by her pride that her husband was away serving at the front by his own volition. "Since you have rebecome a soldier I look upon civilians of high or low degree with pity & indulgence," she had written defiantly. "The wives of men over military age may be lucky but I am sorry for them being married to feeble & incompetent old men."[44] Yet she had also warned him against deliberately "over-exposing" himself to danger: "[T]he world might think that you had sought death out of grief for your share in the Dardanelles. It is your duty to the country to try to live."

In December, Winston had toured different sectors of the front, talking to friends and commanding officers, and he had returned even more despondent and desperate at the thousands of lives being squandered through ineptitude and complacency. He poured out his frustration to Clementine in a series of letters. She advised him to "try not to brood too much," saying, "If you are not killed, as sure as day follows night you will come into your own again." She warned him that a premature return would harm his political prospects, perhaps fatally. When the war ended, they would be proud that he had spent much of it as a fighting soldier rather than a desk-bound politician, she told him presciently in January 1916. Soldiers and their wives were now, in her view, the only "real people."

Clementine feared Winston's rash streak. For her part, she was intent on showing a "detached & smiling face to the world"—as she wrote pointedly—sharing her troubles only with the trustworthy Goonie, whom she described as her "safety-valve." She urged him to follow suit and to confide in Archibald Sinclair—"a safe & loyal" friend—but no one else. She warned him specifically not to share his views on the "PM's character or policy" with "curious acquaintances."

Winston replied that her letter had been "splendid," but his restlessness soon overrode its counsel. After only two months at war he had decided to return. On January 16, 1916, he instructed her to start

spreading the word among his closest political associates and to contact "the Fiend himself"—their pet name for Lord Fisher—to discuss
his return. She refused to do so but she was, in truth, torn. Advising
him to stay in the trenches would improve his chances of a future
political comeback; biding his time on the front would show selfless
courage and would win praise and respect—but he also might be
killed.

Beneath the outer appearance of cheerful calm, privately she was
struggling. This was one of the few times she mentioned religion in
her letters, telling Winston that she could "see only miles & miles of
uphill road" and asking whether his men had faith. "Tell me if being
near danger makes you think of Christ. Being unhappy brings Him
to my thoughts but only, I fear, becos' I want to be comforted not
becos' I want Him for Himself."[45] She started to talk of Winston coming back "D.V.," standing for "Deo volente," or "God willing." It appears she had begun to doubt that he definitely would. The crushing
sadness of early 1916 was captured by Winston's friend the artist John
Lavery, in a portrait of Clementine with her daughter Sarah, which
still hangs in the study at Chartwell, the country house that was later
to become the Churchills' long-standing country home (which is
now open to the public).

Clementine's charm offensive with the Asquiths was going well,
however, and in mid-February she was invited to spend a "useful"
weekend with them at their country residence, the Wharf. Those
childhood games in Seaford now stood her in good stead, as she gave
Asquith an enjoyably challenging game of golf—although, no doubt
fortuitously, the prime minister narrowly won. Clementine had as-
tutely surmised that a little well-planned sport would serve to entertain and relax the prime minister and provide uninterrupted time
alone with him to press Winston's case. Despite her tactful inquiries,
Asquith resolutely refused to discuss the war, even as they heard the
boom of shell fire from across the channel. She gauged from their
conversations, however, that he was still fond of Winston and would
actually like him back in the government—"if it could be done without a row." So she suggested that Winston write a friendly private

letter to him, as otherwise with the PM "it [was] so much out of sight out of mind." She informed Wintston that it would be extremely unwise to let "him see that you consider he has behaved badly: he only waddles off as quickly as possible & avoids you in future."[46]

On February 25, she raised the stakes by issuing a reciprocal invitation to dinner at her house. She knew success depended on securing eight acceptable, amusing bridge players for the prime minister's "comfort & happiness." After working "like a beaver" on this and every other aspect of the evening, she was able to proclaim the event a triumph. The "old sybarite thoroughly enjoyed himself" and the Churchill family "presented a solid & prosperous appearance." She made sure to sit next to Asquith himself and he duly went home some time later in "high good humour."[47]

As Clementine continued to battle for her husband night and day, she ventured to ask for just a little family life in return. For once, she mentioned what "sweet companions" the children had become and talked about looking "forward with longing to the time when" Winston would come back to her and how they would once again have a "country basket" (their name for a rural retreat). "Only you must not become too famous or you won't have time for these pastoral joys!" She asked him to promise that in future he would keep an hour of every day, a day of every week, and six weeks in every year for the "small things of Life . . . and Leisure with a big L."[48]

When Winston was granted leave in early March he suggested she meet him at the Lord Warden Hotel in Dover. He would have just ten days back in England, and he gave her precise instructions on how to arrange them, asking her to organize one dinner at his mother's, at least three at home, two plays alone with her and one "man's dinner out somewhere." She was also expected to "work in all [his] friends" at lunches, arrange a day's painting and find a servant to look after him. "I put it all in your hands my dearest soul." His orders were carried out to the letter. When he arrived in Dover on a destroyer, there she was, waiting patiently for him as instructed.

Despite Clementine's efforts, the leave did not go as planned. The diary was changed or abandoned as Winston was swept up by events in the Commons and decided to take part in a major debate. He was now being urged by several associates—most of whom she thought "wrong-headed"—to give up soldiering and return to politics forthwith. They included F. E. Smith; the editor of the *Observer*, J. L. Garvin; and a newer confidant, the newspaper tycoon Sir Max Aitken (later Lord Beaverbrook). Incredibly, and to Clementine's great dismay, Winston also made time, on more than one occasion, to see the "malevolent" Lord Fisher. Although Fisher had in effect caused Winston's ejection from the Admiralty, he was now forcefully urging Winston to come back and lead an attack on the government over its patent mismanagement of the war.

Fisher's advice—and that of Winston's other counselors—could not have been more opposed to Clementine's, or to the step-by-step rehabilitation campaign she had waged so tirelessly over the preceding months. When Winston invited Fisher to lunch at Cromwell Road, Clementine rounded on the old rogue with: "Keep your hands off my husband. You have all but ruined him once. Leave him alone now!"[49]

It was to no avail. The suggestion that he alone could take the government to task appealed to both Winston's vanity and his sense of frustration. He decided to make a dramatic intervention in a Commons debate on naval spending—a move that jeopardized all Clementine's painstaking work to ease his eventual return. She had managed to arrange another supper with the Asquiths on March 6— by coincidence, the evening before the debate—but now the reunion was to be a far more combative affair. There was unseasonably heavy snow, and Clementine made sure the fires were banked up regardless of the expense. She went to great trouble over the food and, thinking of the lustful Asquith, her own appearance. Conversation over dinner was tense, however, and took a sharp turn for the worse when Clementine and Margot left the men to their brandy and cigars. Winston informed Asquith that the next day he intended to denounce his successor at the Admiralty, Arthur Balfour, as inept. Knocking back another large drink, Asquith expressed his strong disapproval, thinking such a theatrical move premature and unwise.

The following afternoon, Winston spoke in the Commons at some length. At first, it went quite well, as he made a powerful and valid case against the navy's inactivity. But then, to Clementine's despair, disregarding all her counsel and apparently any sense of reason, he called for Fisher, the chief architect of his downfall, to be returned to the Admiralty as first sea lord. To this day, it remains unclear how Fisher exercised such fatal power over Winston. The result of this unfathomable move was the loss of any residual parliamentary support and despondency among his small circle of friends; Eddie Marsh sat watching Winston from the Strangers' Gallery in tears.

There was now a suspicion that the horror of the trenches was beginning to affect the balance of his mind. Even Violet asked herself if Winston was "deranged." Indeed, many thought his career had been destroyed—like his father's—by some strain of insanity. What is perhaps stranger still is that he appeared astonished at the hostility of the reaction. It was as if he had not heard a word Clementine had said. Admiral of the fleet Sir Hedworth Meux, also an MP, summed up the feelings of many on the floor of the House of Commons when he roared: "We all wish him a great deal of success in France, and we hope that he will stay there!"[50]

In the ensuing furor, Clementine had hardly any time alone with Winston. He chose this moment to avoid her and seek comfort instead from Violet, specifically asking for a meeting away from home to ask whether she was "against" him "like the rest of them." Violet told him she could "never" be against him, but neither could she support Fisher's return. What was beyond her was to urge him to go back to the front. Only Clementine had the steel for that.

On his departure a week later from the pier in Dover, Winston handed his wife a letter for Asquith requesting to be released from his military duties so that he might return to politics full-time. Clementine stayed at the Lord Warden Hotel again that night, writing a covering note for the prime minister and pondering her next move. Exhausted after days of what she described as an "inferno," she finally crept into bed and "prayed for happier days & calmer waters."

She considered Winston's letter extremely ill advised and felt that a delayed return from France was more essential than ever if he was to repair his freshly damaged reputation. Her spirits did not improve when her car broke down several times in the pouring rain on the way back to London. Perhaps the sea air drove some sense into Winston, however, for he telegraphed Asquith to ignore the letter Clementine was to send him. This came as a relief, although she feared that when he was alone again in France, his resolve would weaken.

She longed for him to come back, she wrote to him on March 13, when he returned to the front, but only when he would be "welcomed & acclaimed by all, as you *ought* to be and as I know you will be very soon." She closed with a very Clementine touch: "Whatever you finally decide *I loyally agree to*."[51] "You have seen me vy weak & foolish & mentally infirm this week," he confessed in a letter written at the same time in France. Although his words bore traces of resentment, even self-pity, he acknowledged "how sweet & steadfast" Clementine had been "through all [his] hesitation & perplexity."[52] Suffering from bronchitis, she now became more blunt than usual. She told him that his speech on Fisher had done him "harm" and that without it the demand for his return would perhaps have "come sooner," before finally reassuring him: "But come it will—It must."

Clementine knew what she was advocating—that he should stay in the trenches—could well end badly, with "a wicked bullet" finding him that "[he] might but for [her] escape." She felt "lacerated" by his dilemma and dreaded one day returning home from "canteening" to a telegram with "terrible news." But she also knew that without a political career he could never be happy. It was therefore in his interest to come home by way of others' demands rather than his own sense of impatience. She cited in support a conversation with the former attorney general Sir Edward Carson, who had echoed her views about the folly of a precipitate return. The words *come back* must be spoken by others, she said, and if he returned merely to criticize the government his own star would suffer all the more. "The Government may not wage war very vigorously," she observed, "but when on the defensive they are very strong."[53]

His tone now became notably sterner. He replied acerbically that she seemed to want him to stay in the trenches until the "Day of Judgment." (He had, in fact, been there for less than five months.) She should, he commanded, "be careful not to use arguments or take up an attitude in conflict with my general intention, & do nothing to discourage friends who wish for my return. On the contrary labour as opportunity serves to create favourable circumstances."[54]

In a letter dated April 6, she made one last attempt to persuade him to stay, an effort that confirms the acuity of her political sense. "To be great one's actions must be able to be understood by simple people. Your motive for going to the Front was easy to understand— Your motive for coming back requires explanation." The reason his Fisher speech had failed was that "people could not understand it." Now beginning to take stock of her own worth, she added: "I have no originality or brilliancy but I feel within me the power to help you now if you will let me. Just becos' I am ordinary & love you I know what is right for you . . . & some day . . . perhaps not for five years, you will have a great & commanding position."[55] She was right, of course, in her extraordinary conviction. Only it took a lot longer than five years.

Winston's self-absorption was such that it threatened to break their marriage. She had given him her love and wisdom but he was a man possessed, unwilling to listen. His letters were full of instructions— even orders—soured by his sense of grievance. "These grave public anxieties are very wearing," she had written on March 25, making her point with a new and chilly distance. "When I next see you I hope there will be a little time for us both alone. We are still young, but Time flies, stealing love away, and leaving only friendship which is . . . not very stimulating or warming."[56]

Evidently this frightened him. It appears to have been unexpected. "Oh my darling, do not write of friendship to me," he pleaded. "I love you more each month that passes & feel the need of you & all your beauty." He even admitted that he was "devoured" by "egotism." "I reproach myself so much with having got so involved in politics when I was home that all the comfort & joy of our meeting was spoiled." He promised that next time would be different, "with no wild & anxious hurry," and vowed, "I am going to live calmly." Sometimes, he claimed, he thought he would "not mind stopping living vy much" but wished to meet her "in another setting, & pay you all the love & honour of the gt romances."[57]

This last letter arrived in time for Clementine's thirty-first birthday. A few weeks later he was back in London for good. Despite his promise, Winston never would learn how to "live calmly."

CHAPTER FIVE

Married Love

1916—18

It was a typical Randolph prank. With a faint suggestion of menace, he had dared his younger cousin Johnny to pour the contents of a chamber pot out of a bedroom window. A harmless downpour on the hydrangeas it was not, however. Randolph had omitted to share with Johnny the fact that the target was no less a figure than the new prime minister.

It was the summer of 1917 and Lloyd George was admiring the views over the Surrey hills from the terrace of the Churchills' new "country basket," a run-down Tudor manor called Lullenden, near the town of Lingfield. The ever-dapper Welshman appears not to have commented on being drenched in this way, although he can scarcely have failed to notice. Perhaps his pride was at stake. Or perhaps Winston's was. A regular visitor, Lloyd George must surely have known that Randolph's cherubic looks belied his character and that he was doubtless to blame. Unrestrained by either his adoring father or his concerned but distant mother—and cared for by untrained local girls when both parents were busy in London during the week—the six-year-old was becoming distinctly unruly.

Randolph took pleasure in terrorizing the other children—his sisters Diana and Sarah, and cousins Johnny and Peregrine. On one occasion he pushed three-year-old Sarah and four-year-old Peregrine inside a model trailer and sent it careering down a steep hill. Fortunately although the trailer, a present from newspaper proprietor Lord Riddell, was smashed to pieces, the pair emerged almost unscathed. Johnny would try to laugh off Randolph's tyrannical behavior, but eight-year-old Diana found her younger brother difficult to bear. Doll-like in looks and timid in character, she was becoming more and more withdrawn. Her eyes were forever cast downward under astonishingly white eyelashes—her family nickname was the "gold-cream kitten."

The children had been sent down to Surrey that summer to escape the increasingly ferocious air raids on London; thereafter they had been left largely to their own devices. Winston's brother, Jack, was away at war; Goonie was socializing in the capital; and Winston and Clementine themselves were preoccupied. Even when the adults came down on weekends, they spent little time with their offspring, sticking to the rambling main house with its seventeenth-century galleried hall while the youngsters camped out in a converted barn, leading, some have suggested, an almost *Lord of the Flies* existence. Allowed to roam across the farmlands all but unchecked, they drank water from the pond and untreated milk straight from the cows.

It was probably here that Sarah picked up the glandular tuberculosis that would dog her childhood and eventually necessitate, around the age of six, a traumatic operation. Clementine never forgot her daughter panicking as the doctors put the chloroform mask over her face. She managed to fight her way off the operating table and run for it, and her mother could only watch with horror as her little girl was caught and held down with force. Young Sarah was left with a scar on her neck and an equally permanent terror of physical restraint.

The elder children went by pony and trap to the village school at Dormansland. Randolph was taunted about the Dardanelles, but he appears to have shrugged it off; the teasing confirmed that his father was a boss and he exulted in the reflected superiority. At home flustered nursery maids tried a variety of punishments to chasten him—a hard slap seems to have been the favorite. Yet Randolph neither respected nor feared such underlings. He even claimed to be guilty of additional misdemeanors for the satisfaction of proving he could withstand any sanctions they devised. One maid, maddened by his impudence, filled his mouth with mustard. He screamed but swallowed it. So much for Clementine's delightful Chumbolly, now known by the equally unsuitable nickname of "the Rabbit." And so much for her bucolic idyll.

Winston had come back uninjured from the trenches in May 1916, whereupon he immediately set about his rehabilitation as a palatable public figure. It had proven painfully slow. As she had predicted, in returning home on his own rather than by popular demand he had provoked a fresh torrent of abuse in the press. The *Daily Mail*, invoking the toxic legacy of the Dardanelles, had accused him of being a "megalomaniac politician" who had "sacrificed thousands of lives to no purpose"; in November 1916 the popular weekly journal the *World* ranked the expedition as "one of the greatest military disasters of all time."

Both Lloyd George and Asquith continued to take great pains to distance themselves from Winston. For well over a year, he had been given neither a government job nor much hope of one, despite growing admiration for his frequent and knowledgeable interventions on the floor of the House of Commons. Coming up to his forty-second birthday, he could only look back at the promise of his youth and wonder where it had all gone wrong. So despairing had he become at his ongoing isolation, at a time when the war was taking yet another turn for the worse, that he wrote to his brother, Jack: "I am learning to hate." Even Violet had deserted Winston, effectively choosing her father over her onetime hero. His criticism of the Asquith administration's direction of the war had made him "an enemy of the Government from which he was an exile," she explained. "My father was the leader of that Government and my loyalty to him must range me in the enemy camp."[1] Here was yet another casualty of Winston's egotistical insistence that his allies must be fully "on his side" or be considered wholly against him.

Lloyd George had finally maneuvered the flailing Asquith out of power in December 1916, following the disastrous Somme offensive (in which twenty thousand British soldiers had died on the first day alone) and the consequent collapse of Tory support for his coalition government. But even after the fall of his nemesis, Winston remained untouchable. Validating Clementine's long-nursed suspicions, Lloyd George fought shy of bringing him into the new government in even the most junior role, let alone the War Cabinet. As he had observed, some of his partners in the new coalition disliked Winston more violently than they did the kaiser, and his own desire as the son of a teacher to rise to power easily outweighed any feelings of loyalty.

Winston had found this prolonged exclusion impossible to comprehend. In his view, he had done his penance on the front and knew a great deal about the higher direction of the war, as well as what the men actually fighting it most needed. He also clung to the conceits that he enjoyed a huge following in the country, that his enemies were without reason and that his rightful place was in Downing Street itself. As Violet later put it, while Winston certainly had "vision" he lacked "antennae."[2]

Throughout this time only one person had been in a position to disillusion him. Clementine alone could repeatedly tell him why he was deemed untrustworthy and why he had made so many enemies. But while she saw beyond the brusqueness, the scorn for lesser beings, the refusal to listen to rival points of view, others could—or would—not. Genuinely fretting about his despondent state of mind, she had devoted every minute of her time and every drop of energy left over from her canteen work to his welfare. Sometimes, in her devotion to the cause of returning Winston to office, she had gone for weeks without seeing the children. No wonder they were acting up.

Deliverance finally came soon after the publication in March 1917 of the preliminary findings of the Dardanelles Commission—which partly exonerated Winston. Three weeks after the commission's report appeared, the US entered the war; Lloyd George now badly needed a minister of munitions with energy, efficiency and imagination, capable both of working with the Americans on supplies and, crucially, of avoiding another catastrophic shell scandal now that the conflict was entering a new phase. In July, he decided to hand the appointment to Winston—allowing him, in his own words, to become the "escaped scapegoat." It was just as Clementine had hoped. She had long surmised that if only the facts about the Dardanelles were made public at the right time, her husband would no longer have to shoulder the entire blame for the tragedy and could work his way back into favor on merit. Even so, she never forgave Lloyd George for taking seven long months after becoming prime minister to give Winston a chance to rehabilitate himself. More than 340,000 British soldiers had been killed in action in the twenty months since Winston had left office, and it seemed as if virtually every family in the country (although not the Churchills) had in the interim been bereaved.

Ensuring adequate supplies of bombs, grenades, ammunition, guns, planes, trucks and ambulances to the military was a more important job than ever now that the Americans were on board. It was a gigantic operation. Winston presided over twelve thousand civil servants in the ministry and two and a half million munitions workers in the factories, some of whom benefited from Clementine's canteens. The return of a ministerial salary allowed them to move back into Eccleston Square when their tenant, Sir Edward Grey, moved out (although not before destroying the Art Nouveau experiment in Clementine's bedroom). But, according to custom, the appointment also triggered a by-election in his Dundee constituency. While he ecstatically plunged into his war work, Clementine took over much of the campaigning. The Churchill name inevitably attracted a lot of jeering, but Clementine gamely dealt with the hecklers while lending a compassionate ear to their complaints. In large part thanks to her, Winston was returned with a sizable majority of over five thousand, although the attacks on his name continued.

He remained surprised and hurt by the hostility wherever he encountered it. His aunt Cornelia—one of the more sensible of his relations—counseled him to be cautious: "You are just the man for the job [but] my advice is stick to munitions & don't try & run the Govt.'[3] Yet Winston was perhaps even more restless than when he had been at the Admiralty, and still wrapped up in inflated ideas of his own importance. At a banquet in July 1918 held to welcome the thirty-six-year-old assistant secretary of the US Navy Department, one Franklin D. Roosevelt, Winston was so self-absorbed that he virtually ignored the guest of honor. Roosevelt had been a little overawed by the venerable setting of the great hall of Gray's Inn, and he came away thinking forty-three-year-old Winston was a "stinker." While Winston could not even remember having met him, Roosevelt was never to forget the slight.

The Churchills' home in Eccleston Square quickly became an alternative nerve center for the war, with ministers and messengers coming and going and secretaries pounding away on typewriters. Winston delighted in conducting life at breakneck speed, not excluding his frequent journeys between London and their country home. A reckless and impatient driver, known to mount sidewalks in order to bypass traffic, he drove far too fast, sometimes losing control and colliding with other vehicles. On one occasion, his car overturned just outside Dormansland with Clementine at his side—they were fortunate to escape with mere bruises.

These jaunts to Lullenden, although increasingly brief and rare, were a highlight for the children. Clementine could only look on as Winston, happy to be at the center of world events once more, played with the youngsters as if one of them himself. He was glamorous— arriving with guards, secretaries, important guests and a great deal of fanfare. And he was fun—playing "gorilla," when he would drop out of a tree on unsuspecting children, or "bear," in which he would chase them through the woods growling gloriously. As soon as he had had his fill, however, he would instantly retreat into an unreachable adult world, leaving the overwrought youngsters for someone else to deal with. Randolph, in particular, could not contain his pride at having such an exalted and exotic creature as his father. In turn, Winston sucked up his son's adoration and returned it without qualification. The unfortunate consequence was that Randolph felt immune from Clementine's reproving glances, and from any real sanction.

Now that he was back in the saddle, Winston's state of mind was positively joyful. But a buoyant Winston was also a selfish and dictatorial one. He expected to live exactly as he pleased. "Churchill on top of the wave," Beaverbrook later commented, "has in him the stuff of which tyrants are made."[4] Clementine had shared his humiliation, and helped him to absolution, but now her wishes were largely ignored. Once again, particularly after she became pregnant for the fifth time in early 1918, she was distressed by his frequent trips to the front. She thought more of his work could be conducted safely from his desk in Whitehall, and that when he did have to go to France he should cross the channel by sea. Instead, though he knew of her desperate fear of planes, he flew whenever he could, sometimes twice or more a day. A field near the house at Lullenden was specially redesignated a "flying station" so that Winston could land and take off whenever he pleased on the weekend as well. She should not worry, he told her in his egocentric way, as flying gave him a "feeling of tremendous conquest over space" and, he told her, "I know you'd love it yourself."[5]

His courting of death in this fashion caused her to writhe in her bed, haunted by nightmares of crashes and flames. She was so consumed by dread and foreboding that she could not stop herself from pouring out her fears in front of her bewildered children. Whenever Winston was in the air, Lullenden was suffused with gloom and tension—and with some justification, for he was involved in a number of potentially fatal accidents. One of his planes caught fire over the channel, another somersaulted after takeoff and yet another crash-landed. These tiny, fragile aircraft were also, as Clementine knew, at the mercy of storms or passing squalls. Winston remained obstinately undaunted. Despite numerous warnings, he refused to give up his reckless habit of boarding planes with a lit cigar.

He was not, however, entirely inconsiderate. Indeed, he fretted as to whether he and Clementine were more or less happy than "the average married couple." When away in France on their tenth wedding anniversary in September 1918, he wrote to her: "I reproach myself vy much for not having been more to you. But at any rate in these ten years the sun has never yet gone down on our wrath . . . My dearest sweet I hope & pray that future years may bring you serene & smiling days . . . your ever devoted if only partially satisfactory, W."[6]

His fine words did not mean he was prepared to change his ways, of course, and he seemed genuinely surprised when she took umbrage. Although normally an exemplary correspondent, on one occasion, after he had been away a whole month, she stopped writing to him completely to demonstrate her distress. He was outraged. "When I reflect on the many and various forms which yr naughtiness takes, I am astonished at its completeness & its versatility. So there!" Winston told her on September 15, 1918, signing himself as her "vilely neglected Pig."[7]

He also continued to ignore her fears about money, stubbornly refusing to bow to reality and live within their means. Lullenden, now bought for £4,000 in Clementine's name with a hefty mortgage, was proving highly costly to run. It satisfied Winston's craving for a substantial country residence, with seven bedrooms in the main house alone, and the date 1694 carved into the stone fireplace in the hall (although its history was actually even older), but it failed to meet several of Clementine's romantic dreams. The soil was too poor to establish the rose garden she longed for and there was no money for a tennis court. The house did not even have electricity at first, and remained bitterly cold and damp in winter, while the sixty-seven acres of farmland were hugely expensive to manage, especially with wartime labor shortages.

Once Winston was back at work, the management of Lullenden fell to Clementine. Now that she saw it at close quarters she was horrified at what she considered the brutality of farming. She disliked the life of constant pregnancy and milking that the cows had to endure, and the slaughter they faced when no longer productive. Meanwhile, in a desperate bid to cut costs she brought in three German prisoners of war to work the fields. Their presence alarmed the neighbors, and with good reason: one even attempted to poison the water supply. She had to send them away, and so the hay crop rotted on the ground, the brambles and thornbushes rioted and the ditches became clogged with undergrowth and dank water.

Just caring for the house and gardens cost £450 a year. The farm, which Winston had foreseen as a generator of income, was actually costing even more. Yet he was still swept up by a romantic vision of playing the country gentleman—even if he was never around to see it through. He spent an enormous £1,000 on expanding the vegetable garden, improving the cowshed and pigsty and increasing their live-stock. He even bought a horse and cart for local trips and to pick up coal from Lingfield station.

One day, when Clementine was five months' pregnant and alone at the reins, the horse bolted at the sight of a steamroller. The cart overturned, throwing her out and shaking her badly. Thoughts of her miscarriage never far from her mind, she was terrified that she would go into premature labor, but happily it was only her knee and the cart itself that were damaged. The incident did nothing to endear the country to her, though. She felt ever more a townie.

Her cousin Madeline Whyte rented a cottage nearby for a month to help out, but Clementine—whatever her public demeanor—was in reality succumbing to anxiety and exhaustion. With Winston away so often, she became even more agitated when *he* neglected to write, failing to disguise her true feelings with vague attempts at humor. "I *would* have enjoyed a letter from you these last days, but I am not fretting or pining for you, but just think you are a little pig. 'What can you expect from a pig but a grunt?' . . . But I haven't even had a grunt from mine."[8] Feeling abandoned, she decided to make contact with an old school friend from Berkhamsted, only to make the haunting discovery that she had just died giving birth to twins.

Clementine had been frightened to be with child again in the spring of 1918. As her daughter Mary noted, it was hardly "her mo-ment of choice."[9] Pregnancy exhausted her, made her feel neurotic and threatened to strand her in the country because she had no fixed abode in London. It also prevented her from participating (albeit in a supporting role) in Winston's high-powered and enthralling world. One of a growing number of young women who wanted to take control of their bodies so that they might be able to do more in life than simply produce babies, she urged Winston to read a controver-sial new booklet entitled *Married Love*, lent to her by the sympathetic Goonie. Written by the pioneering birth-control campaigner Marie

Stopes, and dedicated specifically to husbands, it aimed to ensure that men took their fair share of responsibility for contraception by spelling out the practicalities and benefits. It was a message that Clementine was keen for Winston to take on board. "I can't think why this pamphlet was not written years ago,"[10] she told him emphatically. It appears Winston was sufficiently taken with the notion that he discussed it at a dinner of the Other Club, a male-only political talking shop.

Contraception at the time was still surprisingly primitive, almost taboo. The main options were withdrawal, the hugely expensive and little-known Dutch cap, or abstinence; none was exactly satisfactory and only one was reliable. It seems, however, that Clementine's efforts with Winston may have paid off. This was to be her last pregnancy until a point in her life when she was actually ready for another child.

In the meantime, she despaired at the thought of another baby when she already found her existing children so challenging—Randolph in particular. Since her early excitement at having produced a son, her feelings toward him had cooled, making her doubt her abilities as a mother. Although the children all had loving nicknames, this concealed the fact that she found it difficult to bond with any of them. Margot Asquith liked to observe that she had "little or no maternal feeling." Now she feared that she might (like her dead friend) be carrying twins—with all the expense and worry that would entail. She also knew that after ten years, Winston's father had tired of his mother, Jennie, and divorce had been under serious discussion. It lingered in the back of her mind that, a decade on from their wedding, she also would be found wanting; she knew too well how often men exploited their wives' pregnancies as "excuses" for conducting affairs. Perhaps worst of all was the idea that Winston's political resurgence and the restrictions imposed by her condition might make her redundant as his counselor in chief.

It is a little surprising that she did not abandon her canteen work at this stage. She continued to drive herself extremely hard. One society hostess was amazed that, although obviously worn out, she insisted on leaving a dinner party at eleven p.m. to make her night visits to the factories. But then the canteens were the only part of Clementine's life that was her own. She knew she was good at her job and thrilled in the praise she received. At the end of 1918, in recognition of her efforts, she was made a Commander of the Order of the British Empire (CBE). It was a great honor and gave notice to all those doubters and critics that, given the chance, she could be much more than a powerful man's ornament.

While laborious and challenging, the work was of course unpaid, and so it did nothing to solve the Churchills' growing financial crisis. Around the time she found out she was pregnant, they had been forced to relet Eccleston Square—to the Labour Party—as they needed the income to meet the bills for Lullenden and Winston's way of life. Winston was back in the cabinet but he was not earning as much as before. They could not afford to buy another London home and Cromwell Road was no longer available as it too was let out. Winston sometimes spent the night at the Munitions Ministry in the old Metropole Hotel just off Trafalgar Square (now the luxury Corinthia Hotel) but mostly he stayed with friends. For a while, when both were in town the Churchills were reduced to camping out in friends' spare rooms. The choice was limited—the Dardanelles had seen to that.

The Hamiltons were one of the few couples to offer them a roof, at 1 Hyde Park Gardens. The two couples had shared the experience of daily abuse over the Dardanelles, but their relationship was hardly warm. Clementine had of course not rated Hamilton as a commander of the operation and held him partly to blame for the disaster. In return Lady Jean Hamilton was among those who found Clementine rather aloof. She did, however, feel some feminine sympathy for her, as she considered Winston to be an "awful, utterly unthinkable" husband.[11]

Clementine normally avoided casual female intimacy, and particularly those maternal exchanges on baby recipes and sleeping patterns—and especially husbands—that some other women find supportive. But when the Churchills came to stay in June 1918, it was quickly clear to Jean Hamilton that Clementine, then four months' pregnant, was on the verge of breaking down and in desperate need of sisterly support. Perhaps Lady Jean's kindness—and her own anguish—persuaded Clementine to open up. In any case, she waited until the two women were alone one evening after dinner before seizing her chance. Knowing that Lady Jean had long tried for children without success (and was on the verge of adopting), she begged her hostess for help. Greatly distressed, she explained how she had neither the money to pay her medical bills nor anywhere safe to give birth (considering Lullenden, which still had no piped water, too rustic and remote). "She asked if I'd like to have her baby," an astonished Lady Jean recorded in her diary. "I said I would." Lady Jean even offered to let her give birth at her house, and in return Clementine "said if she had twins [Lady Jean] would have one."[12]

It was an extraordinary idea and one that begs many questions: Even with the expenses of Lullenden, could they really not afford the £25-a-week fee for a nursing home? Was Clementine's pessimism getting the better of her or was she simply being realistic about their finances? Was it the prospect of twins that she found so overwhelming?

Whatever Clementine's motives, the incident appears to have finally prompted Winston to take action to help his wife. Soon afterward his aunt Cornelia agreed to lend her house, 3 Tenterden Street, just off Hanover Square, for Clementine's confinement. The immediate crisis passed and Lady Jean went ahead with her original adoption as planned. Aunt Cornelia's generosity gave Clementine some peace of mind as well as a comfortable home. Moreover, she was able to stay in London and follow the progress of the war, thus making herself useful. Her astute comments on strategy and the need not "to waste [their] men" as the war finally drew to a close undoubtedly impressed Winston. He was full of details of weaponry and destruction and felt, now that the Americans had entered the war, that victory was in sight, but it was she who had the foresight to look to the future and the need for him to reinvent himself as a man of peace, as well as of war.

She often worried that his actions and publicly expressed views gave an impression that he was a lesser man than he really was. So she urged him to spend more time in Britain. "Darling do come home and look after what is to be done with the Munition Workers when the fighting really does stop . . . I should like you to be praised as a reconstructive genius as well as a Mustard Gas Fiend, a Tank Juggernaut & a flying Terror." She advised him to redeploy the workers into pulling down slums "in places like Bethnal Green, Newcastle, Glasgow [and] Leeds" and replacing them with "lovely garden cities."[13] She was particularly keen to make sure that the women who had contributed so much toward the war effort would not now be abandoned but perhaps trained to make the furniture for these dwellings. With his public image at the forefront of her mind as ever, she perceived the need for Winston to rebrand himself a social reformer and thus further diminish the stain of the Dardanelles.

Winston was also looking forward. Certainly, he had been struck by the role played by women during the war, recognizing that it had changed Clementine and would likewise transform other women's lives. "I think you will find real scope in the new world opening out to women, & find interests wh will enrich yr life,"[14] he wrote to her in September 1918. He was prepared to go only so far on female emancipation, however. There were certain male fortresses that should not be breached. In 1919, when Nancy Astor became the first woman to sit as an MP, she was ignored by men she had known for years, including Winston.[15] When she asked him why he had been so rude, he retorted: "Because I find a woman's intrusion into the House of Commons as embarrassing as if she burst into my bathroom, when I had nothing with which to defend myself, not even a sponge."

The world outside, though, had changed forever. Women had called off their suffrage protests during the war, depriving many former opponents of their chief objection to the female vote. True, many who had taken on tough, demanding and relatively well-paid jobs were to lose them when the troops returned from the front. But total war had brought about a social revolution. British society was never to be quite so unequal again and women, including Clementine, were no longer seen as hysterical weaklings. They led more of their lives outside the home than ever before; they were more visible and more demanding of respect.

Earlier in the war, the speaker of the House of Commons, James William Lowther, had chaired a conference on electoral reform that had recommended limited women's suffrage. The result, in early 1918, was the Representation of the People Act, which granted the vote to property-owning women over thirty such as Clementine. Like Winston, the majority of MPs—385 to 55—supported the legislation as recognition of women's contribution to the war effort.

This limited measure was not, however, the sole area of female advance. Women's fashion was also becoming more liberating. The elaborate corseted outfits of the Edwardian era—perfected by the likes of Jennie—were out. Bras were becoming commonplace, and easier, looser and often cheaper and more practical outfits could be worn on top of them. A certain androgyny was in vogue, and Clementine's slender, athletic figure and taste for the unadorned was right on trend.

By the autumn of 1918, when Clementine was enduring the final months of her pregnancy, it was clear that victory was in sight. Under the "Hundred Days Offensive" the Allies were gradually pushing the Germans out of France and retaking parts of Belgium. With the rapidly improving military news, Clementine began to think more of family and future and there are hints of her urging Winston himself to plan for a happier, more peaceful life.

War had dominated the Churchills' lives for more than four years. It had tested their marriage and their sanity. It had made them social and political pariahs. And it had driven them to virtual bankruptcy. But by its end Winston had proven himself a resourceful, innovative and driven minister, and had won the respect of many of his critics, not least by his courage in volunteering to fight on the front. His reputation had undergone a remarkable recovery and his life and career were once again full of promise. Clementine had also done much to prove her worth. Even though the birth of their fourth child was just days away, she wanted badly to be with him when the glorious moment of the Armistice finally came. So, minutes before eleven o'clock on Monday, November 11, she ran excitedly into his office off Trafalgar Square.

Outside there was a strange but expectant silence. Then, just as they heard the strokes of Big Ben, they saw through the windows a solitary office girl come down into the street. Soon there were hundreds pouring out of doors or leaning out of windows, cheering and waving. Within minutes the roads were full of smiling faces. Elated by the scene, Winston ordered a car, and as he and Clementine climbed inside they were surrounded by well-wishers, some standing on the running boards as the vehicle inched its way through the crowd.

Slowly the car crept along Whitehall to Downing Street, where they intended to offer their congratulations to Lloyd George. It had been so long since Winston and Clementine had been cheered rather than booed—now at last they were experiencing together the joy of being hailed as heroes.

CHAPTER SIX

Loss Unimaginable

1918—22

Four days later Clementine gave birth to a single red-haired girl, named Marigold but quickly known within the family as Duck-adilly. The arrivals of Sarah and Marigold thus respectively marked the beginning and end of the Great War. Randolph's dominant position as the only son remained unchallenged. Despite the plush surroundings of Tenterden Street, and even without the feared complications of twins, it was a difficult delivery, and mother and baby both suffered.

Marigold was just ten days old when Parliament was dissolved and a new election announced. Fortunately, for once, Clementine was not dragooned into electioneering. She was not really needed; the result was all but a foregone conclusion. Triumphant in war, Lloyd George's coalition secured a massive victory at the polls. For all his bellicose reputation, Winston actually swam against the tide in speaking out against calls for harsh treatment of Germany, making Clementine very proud of what she considered a true manifestation of his Liberal beliefs. But his stance against "Hang the Kaiser" sentiments and vengeful demands for enormous reparations was hardly designed to please a victorious but war-shattered nation. He won back his seat in Dundee, but the Churchills once again felt the chill of disapproval.

Now in his midforties, Winston was soon busy plotting the next step in his career. He fancied a return to the Admiralty—a backward step but one that would solve the family's perennial housing problems and, perhaps, help lay to rest the ghost of the Dardanelles. It is safe to presume that Clementine had had more than her fill of the navy, however, and saw the folly in such a move. After a lavish Christmas at Blenheim—their first with Sunny for many years, and one that heralded a rapprochement between the cousins—Winston started work in January 1919 at the War Office. Lloyd George, now mostly away at the peace negotiations in Paris, had made him both secretary of state for war and secretary of state for air. His job ostensibly involved, in the first instance, demobilizing millions of troops and preventing a collapse of morale, even mutiny, during the long wait to go home.

In the meantime, Winston allowed himself to relax and enjoy the splendors of Blenheim at Yuletide. Clementine endured the overwhelmingly Churchillian celebrations for Winston's sake, but she never enjoyed them as he did. Blenheim still offended her Liberal sensibility. The staff were numerous but invisible, and behind the forbidding splendor there was an overwhelming air of sadness. During another such Christmas a housemaid had gone mad, running through the staterooms screaming. Eventually she was cornered by four burly footmen and that night dispatched to a lunatic asylum. On an even earlier occasion, the butler had drowned himself in an ornamental pond.

Winston was oblivious to Clementine's discomfort. He was particularly delighted that F. E. Smith was also a guest; his old friend was the ideal sparring partner for the late-night political discussions that Winston so adored. With F.E. and his brother, Jack, Winston could play at soldiering again, just as he had done as a child. He would line up the children in opposing "armies" of French and English soldiers for a series of mock battles in the great hall. The rules were obscure except to Winston and Jack, and no one enjoyed them as passionately as the brothers themselves. Perhaps only Randolph joined them in the rougher elements of the game.

Clementine rather disapproved of such boisterous antics—as well as the louche atmosphere at Blenheim since Sunny's marriage to Consuelo had collapsed. She was also nervous about the future. Although his new hybrid job came with a handy £5,000 a year (cabinet pay had been restored to its prewar levels), her antennae had already detected discontent about Winston's bagging of two senior positions. The *Daily Mail*, that continuous critic, had dubbed the arrangement "grotesque." It would be better to give up the "Air" and focus on the War Office, she suggested, as such an act would be interpreted as a "sign of real strength . . . After all you want to be a statesman not a juggler."[1] He ignored her advice—on this occasion to his credit. Although he failed to drive it through at the time, Winston rightly saw the sense in establishing a single ministry of defense to encompass all the armed forces and his double appointment was a step toward its creation. Clementine's unfailing eye for Winston's own best interests could sometimes blind her to the bigger picture.

As before, his many duties frequently took him away to France and elsewhere, leaving Clementine behind. On one of these trips he bumped into the fiancée of his cousin Reggie Fellowes—the man-eating twenty-nine-year-old divorcée Daisy Decazes de Glücksberg, the beautiful daughter of a duke and heiress to the Singer sewing machine fortune. She invited Winston to her room for afternoon tea to meet her "little child"—and in the paternal glow following Marigold's arrival he agreed. But upon turning up, he discovered the "child" was Daisy, lying naked on a tiger skin spread over a chaise longue. When later relating the incident to Clementine, Winston insisted he had left immediately. She appears to have been surprisingly relaxed about the encounter—perhaps because she believed such lack of subtlety was unlikely to succeed with her husband. In later life she even enjoyed repeating the tale to others.[2]

She was, however, extremely put out by his frequent absences. Perhaps that was why she "forgot" their eleventh wedding anniversary in September 1919. Given her fastidiousness in other matters, there must be a suspicion that she chose to overlook the day as a protest. It is likely that her conscience was pricked—or her anger abated—by a loving letter from Winston that arrived on her breakfast tray that morning. Its contents made her "very happy." "I woke up and remembered suddenly the importance of the day," she wrote to him afterward. "I love to feel that I am a comfort in your rather tumultuous life." The most revealing passage in her note offers an insight into what it was that kept her in such a challenging marriage: "My Darling, you have been the great event in [my life]. You took me from the straitened little by-path I was treading and took me with you into the life & colour & jostle of the high-way."³ But in what was also surely another plea for him to invest more in their relationship, now that the war was over, she went on: "How sad it is that Time slips along so fast. Eleven years more & we shall be quite middle-aged."

Winston was in France in March 1919 when their latest nanny, a young Scottish girl by the name of Isabelle, was struck by the influenza epidemic that killed 150,000 people in England alone over the course of the devastating winter of 1918–19. Delirious with fever, Isabelle grabbed Marigold, wanting to take her with her to bed, and Clementine struggled to retrieve her child from the dying girl's arms. No doctor would come, as all were too busy with other cases. Sick with the flu herself, Clementine tried to nurse Isabelle through the night, but in the small hours the poor girl succumbed. Clementine was terrified that the tiny Marigold might have caught the disease too, and spent several anxious days watching to see whether the tell-tale symptoms would emerge. Happily, none did, but even during the height of the crisis, with her husband's interests always to the fore, Clementine had instructed Winston not to return home until she and the entire household were free of infection.

Winston was in any case immersed in his work and needed little persuasion to avoid family dramas. He had been appointed war secretary *after* the great conflict had ended, of course, and some of his critics suspected he was spoiling to prove himself elsewhere. Looking east Winston had been deeply troubled by the 1917 Russian Revolution and was implacably opposed to the Communist Bolsheviks. His romantic attachment to kings led him to view Czar Nicholas II, who had been executed by the Bolsheviks, as a tragic hero, and the revolutionaries' leader, Vladimir Lenin, as a barbarian.

The rest of Europe, sick of bloodshed and devastated by war, lacked both the will and the resources to intervene and simply hoped the Russians might settle their differences themselves. But now that the Germans were defeated, the Bolsheviks' proclamation of world-wide revolution aroused Winston's natural aggression. "Kiss the Hun and Kill the Bolshie"—avoid excessive punishment of Germany but use force against the Russian Reds—was how he described his view-point to Violet. It was not a sentiment shared by the majority of his compatriots, who, after such a long war of attrition, were repelled by the idea of more slaughter and wanted the "Hun" to be taught a sharp lesson. At the Paris peace conference, Lloyd George signed up to pu-nitive measures against Germany under the terms of the Treaty of Versailles, including the imposition of massive reparations and the surrender of a tenth of the country's prewar territory and all its over-seas possessions.

With the prime minister preoccupied elsewhere, Winston was given a largely free hand at home. He set about launching a dogged campaign in Parliament, the cabinet and the press in favor of inter-vention on behalf of the White Russians, who were fighting the Communist revolutionaries. He was convinced the British public would support him as soon as they were made aware of the "foul baboonery" of Bolshevik atrocities. As one historian has noted, this was just one of many subjects on which Winston sounded "like a stuck record, more likely to turn listeners off than on."[4] He began providing the White Russian General Denikin with "surplus" British war matériel and repeatedly lobbied Lloyd George and the Ameri-cans to support large-scale military support for the antirevolution-aries. Incredibly, by mid-1919 Britain was on the brink of another war.

Tensions continued to mount over the next few months, but chaos among the White Russians and fading support for Winston at home prevented a full escalation of hostilities. Indeed, while newspa-pers were decrying MR. CHURCHILL'S PRIVATE WAR, some on the left were calling for him to be tried for treason for intervening against the Reds without public support or political approval. Clementine soon found herself facing the sound of angry mobs chanting, "Arrest Churchill!"

To avoid any further military imbroglios, in 1921 Winston was extracted from the War Office (although not before he had been embarrassed by the discovery that his beautiful cousin, the sculptor Clare Sheridan, had been conducting an affair in Moscow with another Bolshevik leader, Leon Trotsky). An exasperated Lloyd George moved him to the Colonial Office, a reverse step back to the department that he had dominated at the beginning of his ministerial career. Winston, who had hoped to become chancellor of the Exchequer, was bitterly disappointed by this turn of events, and by Lloyd George's decision to entrust the Treasury instead to the less glamorous Sir Robert Horne (yet more evidence, in Clementine's eyes, of the prime minister's untrustworthiness). For all of his wife's efforts to persuade Winston to recast himself as an advocate for peace, he had willfully chosen a course that had led him to be painted as a warmonger. It was a perception that would prove almost impossible to change and was, for a long time, disastrous.

In early 1919 the Churchills were still without a permanent London home or the means to procure one. House prices had soared since the war, and unlike the Admiralty, neither the War Office nor Winston's later appointment as colonial secretary brought with it an official residence. With a newborn baby and three other small children, Clementine endured a merry-go-round of temporary and often unsuitable abodes mostly rented from friends or extended family for just two or three months at a time. In desperation, she even offered her impoverished younger sister four guineas a week to move out of her redbrick house at 15 Pimlico Road, although Nellie seems to have rejected the idea. Clementine soon realized that the only way to restore the family finances was to let go of Lullenden, now little used anyway, particularly in winter.

In March, the Churchills invited Sir Ian and Lady Jean Hamilton to the country for Sunday lunch, having already hinted to them that they were thinking of selling. Perhaps they were lucky with the weather—Lullenden was rather seductive in the spring sunshine—or maybe Winston and Clementine were simply at their most beguiling as hosts. In any event, the Hamiltons decided to rent the house, even though Winston quoted an outrageous £500 a year, and were subsequently induced to buy it. Falling victim once again to a certain sharp persuasiveness, they handed over £9,800 for the property and a small number of wildly overpriced livestock. (Sir Ian himself later admitted that its actual worth was closer to £3,000.)[5]

The Hamiltons' largesse, or perhaps gullibility, was the Churchills' gain. With a great deal of luck, they would emerge from the Lullenden experiment having more or less broken even. But it had brought home to Clementine the folly of trying to live like a country squire without the matching income. By contrast, Winston seems not to have given their narrow escape from ruin much thought. Meanwhile, the sale, due to complete on September 30, 1919, would leave them without a roof over their heads. The search for a home in London appropriately grand for Winston and affordable for Clementine became ever more frantic.

Finally, in July they found a huge early Victorian property at 2 Hyde Park Street. It offered a respectable address and wonderful views across the park at an astonishingly low price that included a useful mews house at the back. The Churchills made an offer of £2,300 for the lease and were so delighted with what seemed to be a bargain that they did not at first bother with a structural survey. Only in August, when the building's state of health was thoroughly inspected, did the truth emerge. The whole building needed a huge amount of expensive and time-consuming work, well beyond what they could ever afford. In its current state, it was simply uninhabitable.

They tried hastily to backtrack but, alas, too late. The vendor, Lord Wellesley, the future seventh Duke of Wellington, threatened to sue if they did not proceed with the deal. Thanks to a mixture of naïveté and Winston's distaste for anything less than the best, the couple and their four children were now facing both homelessness and financial ruin. They could not afford to make the house safe, nor could they pull out. Clementine's natural hopes of finding somewhere secure to raise her family seemed to have been permanently dashed and all the insecurities of her childhood revisited her. Knowing that the family was now perilously close to having nowhere to go, she tried desperately to delay the sale of Lullenden, while writing begging letters to London friends such as Sir Ernest Cassel, asking to be put up in the capital for a few days at a time.

The Churchills' lawyers were meanwhile still battling with Lord Wellesley over the frighteningly high cost of the repairs.[6] It only exacerbated their parlous financial position when, at the end of the year, they agreed to buy another smaller home (now demolished) at 2 Sussex Square for around £7,000. As if oblivious to Clementine's mounting distress, incredibly Winston was also instructing agents (fortunately without success) to find him yet another "country basket" in his favored county of Kent. The crisis highlighted the difference between them: Clementine struggled to see a way out; Winston simply assumed there would be one. At the eleventh hour, in January 1920, salvation duly arrived, in the form of their faithful benefactor Sir Ernest Cassel (who appears to have acted out of little more than generosity of spirit, loneliness and a certain political sympathy). He agreed to buy the Hyde Park Street lease from them for the original asking price while he looked for a long-term buyer. For the first time—but by no means the last—the Churchills had been bailed out in the nick of time by a generous friend.[7]

In the spring of 1920, Winston took off with a group of other men for the south of France—the first in a pattern of separate vacations that would persist for the rest of their marriage. No expense was spared; as one historian put it, Winston liked to "travel in comfort and arrive in luxury."[8] He left Clementine behind to supervise the children's school holidays and prepare Randolph for Sandroyd, a preparatory boarding school near Cobham in Surrey. Remembering how much she had enjoyed her own schooldays at Berkhamsted, she took the relatively unusual step for her class at the time of enrolling her elder daughters, Diana and Sarah, at Notting Hill High.

Not until January 1921—shortly after Clementine's grandmother Lady Airlie died at ninety—would she and Winston finally take their first holiday together since before the outbreak of the war. Clementine had never really loved her stern grandmother, and the old countess's death revived painful memories of her youth. Her escape with Winston a few days later to a hotel in Nice therefore came as a welcome tonic. By this point, although only thirty-six, she was neither physically nor emotionally robust and she increasingly questioned whether she had enough energy or strength to sustain her highly stressful lifestyle.

Yet even this was not to be an intimate break alone. They were joining Cassel and his granddaughter Edwina, the future Lady Mountbatten, and had barely unpacked their suitcases before Winston was called back to London. Perhaps these separations helped to keep their relationship fresh; Clementine certainly tried to adopt a philosophical approach when they occurred. But they sometimes left her feeling isolated, even abandoned, and there are hints that she began to harbor doubts about the viability of her marriage at this point. Winston was so often engrossed in his work, and without a war there no longer seemed a need for her to help him. This was not what she had had in mind for their life together in peacetime.

Time, as she had written to him, was slipping by so fast; she was still struggling to reconcile herself to the fact that she was now approaching middle age. When Winston went back to London, Clementine stayed on to visit Lady Essex at St. Jean Cap Ferrat. Freed of domestic or maternal duties—even of advising Winston—she played a great deal of tennis, having over the years become a notable amateur player. Winston became worried that her innate competitiveness would lead her to play too much and reverse any improvements in her health. He was particularly concerned, he admitted candidly, because he wanted her to help in the forthcoming election. "You will want to be fit for the political fights that are drawing near," he informed her.[9] And in a later letter: "Do stay until you are really reequipped to fight. I shall need you very much . . . you can render me enormous help."[10] She was so enjoying herself, however, that she ignored his pleas to take it easy and entered several prestigious amateur tournaments. It was exhilarating to feel free and young again, and she extended her stay still further. She even, uncharacteristically, unwound enough to allow herself a little flutter at the casinos, which were still illegal back in Britain.

Meanwhile, Winston was left in charge of the children. He visited Randolph a couple of times at Sandroyd (where the headmaster described the boy as "combative") and sent Diana and Sarah to the seaside at Broadstairs with a maid to recover from a series of coughs and colds. Marigold, now nearly two and a half, was at home with Winston in London as he liked to have at least one "kitten" in residence to brighten up the house. A merry little heartbreaker, she loved to run around the dining room, her face bright with laughter. Marigold's other party trick was to sing the popular song "I'm Forever Blowing Bubbles." She had a "sweet, true little voice," as a member of the family described it, but was unusually prone to sore throats, which in the days before antibiotics were taken far more seriously. Infections were difficult to treat once they had taken hold. On at least one occasion during Clementine's absence, Winston was sufficiently worried to call in the doctor.[11]

Winston also had news of another sort for his absent wife. At the end of January, a distant cousin was killed in a railway accident and as he was childless his Irish estate, known as Garron Tower, and a large pile of cash were passed on to Winston. This unexpected windfall had the potential to net him some £4,000 a year, almost as much as the salary he received as a minister. Winston had been a part-time journalist since the army days of his youth and following his marriage he had, when possible, been supplementing the family budget with prolific newspaper and magazine articles—part of every holiday would be devoted to writing thousands of words in the face of impending deadlines. Now, however, he could afford to be more choosy, turning down what Clementine considered to be unsuitably "trivial" or "pot-boiler" commissions that she feared might undermine his public standing, and his chances of high office. Even she, constitutionally insecure about their finances, now looked forward to a "care-free" future. While Winston promptly celebrated by rushing out to buy a Rolls-Royce cabriolet, Clementine exulted in the security of knowing that bills could be paid, a delicious feeling she compared to "floating in a bath of cream."

Characteristically, the Churchills shared their good fortune with the impoverished Nellie. She had married the handsome Bertram Romilly, who had been badly injured during the war, and now found herself running a household and raising two small children on a modest disability pension. They lent her £500 to open a hat shop, while also giving sixty-eight-year-old Lady Blanche, a distant grandmother who had escaped social disdain after the war by returning to her previous bohemian lifestyle in Dieppe, an additional income of £100 a year.

Winston's appointment as colonial secretary on February 13, 1921, brought the prospect of much exciting travel. One of the first trips was to Cairo for a conference on Middle Eastern affairs the following month and (perhaps aware of his wife's restlessness) he suggested to Clementine that she join him on board ship straight from her extended holiday in the south of France. She was thrilled at her first chance to accompany Winston on official business abroad and was "living in blissful contemplation," she wrote, of their "smooth and care-free future."[12] Before departing on their adventure, Winston summoned Diana and Sarah back from the seaside to say good-bye and visited Randolph again at school. He disliked leaving them all for long stretches, but Clementine seemed undeterred by the fact that she had now not seen her children for going on two months. At least Jennie was on hand to keep an eye on them (and the latest inexperienced young girl hired to oversee them), reporting back that they were all "great darlings."

At Winston's side, and unburdened by domestic responsibilities or financial worries, Clementine glowed with a fresh vitality. The glamorous T. E. Lawrence—Lawrence of Arabia—joined them and became a close friend. She played lots of tennis and met politicians, ambassadors and leading archaeologists, and they both lived and traveled in great luxury. There was even time for magical visits on camelback to the Pyramids of Giza with Lawrence. In such exalted company Clementine established herself as something of a cool customer. While others sweated and swooned in the heat, she remained unflustered, apparently unaffected.

The conference delivered many of Winston's aims to bolster British interests in the region, helping to bring about postwar political settlements in Transjordan and Iraq and a pledge to establish a Jewish national home in Palestine under a British mandate. But he had arrived to a wave of hostility and several credible death threats. Even from the safety of the armored car provided to transport them around, the sight of angry crowds of Egyptian nationalists pelting stones at them was no doubt unnerving. Perhaps her experience in Ireland in 1912 had inured Clementine to the threat of mob violence; certainly Winston's bodyguard Walter Thompson was astonished by her courage, noting that "nothing seemed ever to disturb or to dishearten her."[13] When their train was stoned and the first windows smashed, Clementine put down the book she had been reading but, according to Thompson, "seemed more annoyed than interested."[14] She tolerated the constant intrusion of bodyguards without complaint, but she was no pushover. She had "an icy way she could look at a man when things went to the snapping point of endurance," he recorded.[15] It was not just her composure that was remarkable. Clementine's slender, neat and elegant appearance (in contrast to poor Winston, whose pale skin would turn an ever deeper pink in the heat) was also widely noticed. Thompson was not alone in hailing her around this time as "the best-dressed woman of her day."

Clementine did not hurry home at the end of the conference—she spent two leisurely weeks wandering back via Alexandria, Sicily and Naples. By the time she finally returned on April 10 she had been away for a good three months. Rested, fulfilled and happy, she was pleased to be reunited with the children. Randolph, now nearly ten, was grumpy and demanding, and Marigold was suffering from yet another cold, but Clementine was hugely moved that they had all made a "Welcome Home" banner, which they hoisted as she drew up in the Rolls-Royce outside their home in Sussex Square. At such moments, her reserve melted away and she joyfully scooped them up in her arms. If only she could always be so spontaneous. But perhaps this was a new beginning: Winston's career was back on track, she was by his side, and she had at last a secure home. There was even money in the bank.

Her contentment was not to last. Four days later her brother, Bill Hozier, was found shot dead in a Paris hotel room. Just thirty-three, he was handsome and charming and had gone into business after retiring from the navy at the end of the war. But like his mother and his twin sister Nellie, he had a weakness for gambling. Winston, who had once or twice helped him to cover his losses, had recently made him promise to stop betting on cards. When he died, he had not long ago deposited ten thousand francs into a bank account. Even so, it was soon confirmed that he had killed himself.

Life for little brother Bill had never run smoothly. As a child he had been uprooted from his upmarket prep school Summer Fields after barely a term without ever being properly registered, because Lady Blanche could not pay the fees. Although the grandson of an earl, instead of following his peers to board at one of the great public schools, as Eton, Harrow and Rugby are known in Britain (because they were once theoretically open to any member of the public irrespective of occupation or religion), he was sent to the grammar school at Berkhamsted. It was a relegation (in his eyes) that he bitterly resented for the rest of his life. Unlike Clementine and Nellie, who had adapted so well to school life in Berkhamsted, Bill could not—or would not—relate to the local boys. The effect on both his studies and his morale was recorded in school reports as "disastrous."

In search of his rightful place, Bill had left school early and in 1903 joined the navy. Here too he failed to shine. Indeed, Lieutenant William Ogilvy Hozier's naval career might have been destroyed at the tender age of twenty-two if Winston had not used the power and influence of his office as home secretary to rescue him. His commanding officer, Captain Ryan, had excoriated Bill in a report on August 8, 1910, as "inexperienced and highly inefficient." Instead of rising to the challenge, Bill convinced himself that he had been harshly treated and sought a transfer to another ship. Knowing that Clementine was fond of her brother, Winston had repeatedly intervened on the young officer's behalf by trying to discredit Captain Ryan with the then–first lord of the Admiralty Reginald McKenna. It was an extraordinary episode, even in an era when it was not uncommon for cabinet ministers to ask one another for favors for their families,[16] and though well intentioned, it gave Bill the unfortunate impression that any complaints he might have would command Churchillian endorsement.

At the news of his death Clementine rushed over to her distraught mother in Dieppe and took charge. Suicide was not a crime in France at the time, but it was a sin in Catholic doctrine, and at first it seemed that the family might not be allowed to bury Bill in consecrated ground. Winston pulled strings for his brother-in-law one last time, however, and the British vice consul was dispatched to put pressure on the local clergyman to accommodate Lady Blanche's desperate wish for a "decent" funeral. Yet nothing would quite expunge the terrible feeling of shame, or the abiding grief. Clementine was frantic to avoid any impression that her only brother was "a mere scapegrace disowned by his family." She was also aware of muttering—even among certain Churchills—about "bad blood." So, in order to lend the occasion an appropriate grandeur, she delayed the time of the service until late in the afternoon to make it easier for her husband to attend. "Oh Winston my Dear do come tomorrow," she pleaded, "& dignify by your presence Bill's poor Suicide Funeral."

Winston did not fail his wife or her family. He dropped everything and dashed across the channel, arriving just in time for the service. In his will, Bill left him his elegant gold-topped malacca cane; Winston would use it for the rest of his life.

Two months after Bill's suicide, death visited the Churchills again, when Jennie died, equally unexpectedly. She was sixty-seven, vibrant, still sexy and particularly proud of her shapely ankles. For years after her second marriage had collapsed she had been mostly lonely and alone, resorting to taking her maid with her on trips to the theater. She still had admirers, but she had been forced to reconcile herself to no longer being the most beautiful woman in the room.

In truth, she had long been a little jealous of the much-fêted Clementine and Goonie for displacing her as the centerpiece in the lives of her sons. Jennie's feelings were particularly apparent when, on her shopping trips to Paris, she would buy expensive designer hats from Worth for herself and bring back cheap little things from Le Bon Marché for her daughters-in-law. Clementine could not help noticing the potential heartache inherent in relying on one's adult children for company. To her great annoyance, Jennie would command Winston to visit her frequently and to help with her interminable financial crises. Grandchildren were similarly summoned at whim.[17]

In June 1918, Jennie's life had changed when she entered her third marriage, to the kind and debonair Montagu Porch. Another youngster—twenty years her junior—he was genuinely devoted to her. Although she continued to style herself as Lady Randolph rather than Mrs. Monty Porch, she had never known such happiness. Her spirits revived, she reveled in dressing up (she had in recent times been spending a staggering £5,000 a year on clothes) and socializing with a zest not seen since her prime. It was in May 1921, during a convivial stay with her friends the Horners at their country house at Mells, that—while descending the stairs in a pair of vertiginous heels—she tripped and fell. The local doctor diagnosed a broken ankle and Jennie returned home to her London house at 8 Westbourne Street, Bayswater, to recover. All seemed well. But then gangrene set in and the foot had to be amputated.

Jennie bore her misfortune and pain with extraordinary fortitude and humor. Clementine, whose Sussex Square house was only minutes away, could not fail to be impressed by her mother-in-law's courage. The two women, who had never been close, finally became more intimate. Clementine found herself less judgmental of Jennie's extravagances and, as she grew older, more understanding of her libido. They had more in common than either had originally thought. If, after the death of Lord Randolph, Winston had become Jennie's lifework, there was now a clear understanding between them that he had in recent years become Clementine's alone.

Secure in her own place, Clementine realized that Jennie's example had taught her much in terms of resilience and resourcefulness. It is likely that Clementine's war work, arranging medical supplies for the Dardanelles expedition or canteens for the munitions factories, was at least in part inspired by the hospital ship Jennie had chartered during the Boer War. Jennie was also brave in isolation—Monty was away in Africa when she was injured and had stayed on after receiving assurances from Winston that she was out of danger.

Then, early on the morning of June 29, 1921, Jennie suffered a sudden and violent hemorrhage. Winston ran crying through the streets in his dressing gown when he heard the news to be with her, but by the time he reached her bedside it was too late. "I do not feel a sense of tragedy," he wrote to Jennie's friend Lord Curzon the same day, "but only of loss." He was later to tell Clementine that losing his mother had been like an "amputation" and had made his life "seem lonely & its duration fleeting."[18] He kept a bronze cast of Jennie's hand near his desk for the rest of his life.

It had been such a grisly spring. Clementine was determined to enjoy her summer. At the beginning of August all four children were packed off to seaside lodgings in Broadstairs under the care of yet another new nanny, a young French nursery governess called Mademoiselle Rose. The plan was that after a couple of weeks Diana, Randolph and Sarah would leave Marigold behind with Mademoiselle Rose and join their parents for a holiday with the Duke and Duchess of Westminster on their estate in Sutherland, a beautiful bolt-hole in the Scottish Highlands. In the meantime, Clementine visited the Westminsters alone at their Cheshire stately home, Eaton Hall, an enormous high-Victorian palace (since demolished). Without Winston—who was working—or the children, she would be blissfully free to relax, socialize and take part in one of her beloved tennis tournaments without distraction.

The children dutifully wrote to their mother about shrimp fishing, rowing boats and sunburn. But from the beginning both Randolph and Sarah also alluded to Marigold—or Baba as the other children sometimes called her—being unwell. She seemed to be rallying, however, and in any case she had coughs and sore throats so often no one suspected anything unusual. Then, with terrifying speed, the infection began to spread around her body, her temperature soared uncontrollably and she started finding it difficult to breathe. Eventually a local doctor was called but his remedies were limited. Even now the inexperienced and probably overstretched Mademoiselle Rose hesitated for two more days before taking further action. Only when the terrified landlady of the lodgings absolutely insisted did she finally call Clementine with the dreaded news that Marigold had developed septicemia, a severe form of blood poisoning that can lead to organ failure. The little girl had by now been ill for a fortnight.

Clementine left Eaton Hall at once and dashed down to Broadstairs as quickly as she could, while the three elder children were sent up to Scotland as originally planned with a maid. By the time she arrived, Marigold was in a critical condition. Winston shot down from London soon afterward and a specialist doctor was summoned. It was too late. On the evening of August 22, a few days after Clementine's arrival, Marigold said to her mother, "[S]ing me Bubbles." Summoning every ounce of control, Clementine began the song that Marigold loved so much:

> *I'm forever blowing bubbles*
> *Pretty bubbles in the air*
> *They fly so high, nearly reach the sky*
> *Then like my dreams they fade and die.*

The little girl put out her hand and whispered: "Not tonight . . . finish it tomorrow." Both parents were with her when Marigold died the next day, three months short of her third birthday. Winston shed many a tear and was unable to speak. Clementine, according to Winston's secretary, "screamed like an animal undergoing torture."

They buried Marigold in Kensal Green Cemetery on August 26 and erected a simple, unassuming headstone engraved with the words *Here lies Marigold, dear child of Winston and Clementine Churchill.* After they had dismissed Mademoiselle Rose, it was as if a book had been slammed shut. Clementine and Winston boarded a night train for Scotland to rejoin the other children, but to the end of her life, Clementine would barely speak of Marigold again. Mary, born after her sister's death, grew up puzzled by the identity of the little girl whose framed picture stood on her mother's dressing table.

Religious in her youth, it is possible that Clementine now turned to her faith to carry her through. The Churchill household was far from pious—Winston had once told his mother: "I do not accept the Christian or any other form of religious belief"[19]—but now she took to slipping off to church alone.

For nearly two weeks, they all stayed at Lochmore, a rambling fifteen-bedroom Victorian pile owned by Bendor and Violet Westminster, with views over the water to mountains beyond. It was a rare occasion when all the family was on holiday together. The weather was kind, and the Westminsters organized picnics in the hills, riding and boating. There was comfort in each other's company. Alas, it came to an end all too quickly when Winston left to join the Duke and Duchess of Sunderland's house party at their Dunrobin estate, where the guest of honor was the Prince of Wales. Clementine wearily made her way back south to London without him to prepare the children for the new school term. Somehow she kept going with all the rituals and errands of her life, her daughter Mary later writing that she did not "indulge her grief" but "battened it down."

That Winston should part from his family at this point in favor of the social anesthetic of a large crowd might be regarded either as heartless, the behavior of a man afraid of contemplating his loss, or both. His letters to Clementine during this time are surprisingly distant, writing of his "many tender thoughts" of "[her] sweet kittens" as if they were not also his. He even seemed surprised that he could not shed his grief in quick order. Little more than a fortnight after Marigold's death, he wrote about tennis, painting, politics and grouse shooting, adding only toward the end of the letter: "Alas I keep on feeling the hurt of the Duckadilly." Obviously, removing himself from his family had not had the desired palliative effect. Meanwhile, on September 18, Clementine had taken Diana, Randolph and Sarah to the grave, where they had watched a white butterfly settle on the flowers. "The children were very silent all the way home," she told him.

Inside, she would never get over her grief, or quite dispel a gnawing sense of guilt. Outwardly, however, she gathered her strength, snapped herself out of her misery and a few days later decided to jolly the children up by hiring a smart car and setting off on a splendid picnic. Not long after, as if fate could be any more spiteful, Ernest Cassel died suddenly from a heart attack at his London home. Clementine could not believe she had any feeling left, but she may have wept more tears at the loss of one of their only true and loyal friends than for her daughter. For Cassel she could allow herself to cry whereas for Marigold her sorrow felt limitless and frightening.

By the end of 1921, Clementine was an emotional and physical wreck. Her deep depression—marked by severe listlessness alternating with near-hysterical outbursts—appears to have been far more serious than Winston's brooding periods of Black Dog. The doctors were flummoxed as to what to do and merely prescribed another vacation. Only the thought of a break on the French Riviera after Christmas kept her going through December.

On Boxing Day, Winston chose to go on ahead to Cannes without her in the company of Prime Minister Lloyd George, and happily indulged himself in his normal round of politics, painting, writing and hunting. Clementine was to join them as soon as the school term started. Once again, luck turned cruelly against her. Within hours of Winston's departure, Diana, Randolph and several servants were one by one struck by another outbreak of a deadly strain of influenza. By the evening of what Clementine came to call "Black Monday," Sussex Square resembled a hospital ward with two nurses tending five ailing patients (a cousin, Maryott Whyte, who had come to help, had also contracted pneumonia). A few days later, Clementine herself collapsed from nervous exhaustion and the doctor ordered her to bed for a week. Too tired to read let alone receive visitors, there was nothing to stop her reliving Marigold's death a hundred times.

She sent Winston a note of such anger and distress about his silent absence that she later panicked and sent a telegram asking him to destroy it unopened. She followed this up with another long letter explaining her "deep misery & depression," and how she wished that she were "basking" with him in the Riviera sun. She had endured, she said, "one of the most dreary & haunted weeks" of her life.[20]

Winston's response was not wholly sympathetic. "My darling, I cd not bear not opening yr letter . . . I am so sorry you had such a churlish message." He had, he explained, sent her a lengthy handwritten letter, but it had been delayed in the post. It did not contain an offer to return to be at her side, however, but yet more bad news. "I must confess to you that I have lost some money here, though nothing like as much as last year. It excites me so much to play—foolish moth."[21]

By the time Clementine was finally free from sickroom duties and fit to travel, Winston had returned to London. She soon replaced him in Cannes and it was now that Clementine's suspicions were confirmed: she was pregnant again. Seeking consolation following the loss of Marigold, it seems she had decided to try for another child. But she did not let her condition stop her from pushing herself hard on the tennis court. She even won the mixed doubles handicap in the Cannes lawn tennis tournament. She returned to London in the spring revivified, but her extended holiday had done nothing to strengthen her maternal ties with her children, or to remedy their problems. Randolph was becoming increasingly obstreperous, Diana nervy and insecure, and Sarah still suffered from glandular tuberculosis.

Nor had Winston's work at the Colonial Office been free of trouble. The devolution of powers to an Irish assembly had for decades been arguably the British government's most pressing colonial issue. A home rule bill had finally been passed by Parliament in 1914 but had never come into force due to the war. In response, radical Irish republicans had formed a volunteer paramilitary force and staged the failed Easter Uprising in 1916. The fiercely nationalist political party Sinn Fein had gone on to win a majority of the Irish seats in the 1918 general election; within a matter of weeks they had proclaimed an Irish republic and a bloody war of independence ensued.

The savage treatment of the nationalists by British forces—most notably the hated Black and Tans—had done nothing to quell the sporadic violence in Ireland, a problem in which Clementine took a great interest. The solution was by no means simple—the massive support for Sinn Fein in the south was balanced by that for the Unionists in the north. Nevertheless, Clementine felt sympathy for the nationalists since they had helped the Churchills escape loyalist mobs during their trip to Belfast in 1912. She consequently pleaded with Winston to ensure "some sort of justice" in Ireland and to draw back from "iron-fisted" or "Hunnish" treatment of the Irish rebels, urging him to recognize that in their place he would not be cowed by harsh or vindictive British retaliation. It appears that her pleas for moderation may well have softened his approach and perhaps even altered events. Winston duly invited Michael Collins, a key Sinn Fein negotiator, to his home in Sussex Square and devoted much of the second half of 1921 to Irish affairs. The resultant truce was followed by a treaty that, approved by the Dáil (the lower house of the Irish parliament) in January 1922, would eventually lead to independence for southern Ireland.

Yet this forward step did not halt the Irish Republican Army's murder spree. When Sir Henry Wilson, MP, security adviser to the Northern Ireland government, was assassinated on his front doorstep in London in June 1922, a hit list was found of other targets. Winston's name led it. He was instantly assigned a security detail. When Randolph and Diana returned from roller-skating in Holland Park shortly afterward they found the house surrounded by police, with several more conducting a thorough search inside. Winston announced he would sleep in the attic and erected a metal shield in front of the door. He stayed there until dawn clutching a revolver and slept there every night for months, while the heavily pregnant Clementine remained as usual in her bed without protection of any sort.

In mid-August 1922, Winston decamped to the Duke of Westminster's chateau near Biarritz. So it was that Clementine found herself without her husband for most of the last weeks of her final pregnancy. For all his sentimentality about the "kittens," Winston was not one to endure the waiting and hard slog of labor and birth.

Clementine sought respite at Frinton-on-Sea on the Essex coast. This small town, with a grassy seafront and firm golden sand, had become fashionable with Londoners and was one of her favorite destinations for a bucket-and-spade holiday with the children. She chose to rent a large modern house called Maryland for the considerable sum of forty-five guineas a week (some £2,300 or $3,500 today). It was near a smart tennis club, and although her condition stopped her from playing, she entered Randolph and Diana to represent her. Alas, they had not inherited their mother's application or talent and they won the booby prize and came in last. Ignoring their growing hatred of the sport, Clementine insisted they continue to play regularly. Giving up was not an option. There were to be no excuses, no complaints, just the determination to carry on with life—however challenging it became.

"I'm getting very stationary & crawl even to the beach with difficulty. I long for it to be over," she told Winston that summer. "It has seemed a very long nine months." Exactly a year had passed since Marigold had started to fade, and Clementine wrote to Winston to remind him of the anniversary of her death. He replied: "I think a gt deal of the coming kitten & about you my sweet pet. I feel it will enrich yr life and brighten our home to have the nursery started again.

I pray God to watch over us all."²² Only a few days later he wrote again to reassure Clementine that "yes," he had been thinking of the loss of Marigold, but that most of all he had been thinking of her.

In September Winston and Clementine were reunited in London for the birth. Duckadilly could never be replaced, let alone forgotten, but the new baby, "Mary the mouse," would help Clementine to ease the pain. She arrived safely early on the morning of September 15, to much celebration. Winston took advantage of the occasion. It was the one and only time in their marriage that he would betray her trust.

CHAPTER SEVEN

A Country Basket

1922—29

As he hurtled down the country lanes of Kent in the family Rolls, Winston chatted about a property he was thinking of buying. His three elder children were in the back enjoying a "mystery" car ride, while Clementine remained at home recovering from her delivery. For Randolph, Sarah and Diana, it was a rare few hours alone with their father and they were all patently excited.

Presently, twenty-five miles outside London, he pulled up outside a large empty house, which seven-year-old Sarah at first thought "wildly overgrown" and "untidy." True, the house was smothered with ivy, but at the rear it commanded views over the Weald of Kent toward the South Downs. Grassy slopes gave way to a secret valley with a lake fed by a busy little stream, and trees and shrubs offered tantalizing opportunities for hide-and-seek. Sarah soon felt quite "delirious," and when Winston asked his children, "Do you like it?" all three exclaimed, "Oh do buy it!" Their father offered merely, "Well, I'm not sure . . ."[1]

In truth, Chartwell was already his. He told them so just as they were pulling into Parliament Square that evening. They were, of course, eager to share the news with their mother, but if Winston hoped the children's enthusiasm would bring Clementine around he was mistaken. She was appalled and deeply hurt. Later she was to say that this was the only time in their marriage that he had been less than candid with her.

Since the windfall of their sudden inheritance, they had both been longing for another "country basket," but Lullenden had taught Clementine a few bitter lessons about the fortune-crunching qualities of large unmodernized properties. She had stated plainly that she feared their Irish inheritance would be wiped out by a foolish indulgence and had set her heart on something more manageable. Winston, true to form, harbored more grandiose aspirations. He had spotted Chartwell—a former foundling house near Westerham dating back to the reign of Henry VIII—the previous year. The building itself was ugly, but Winston had been seduced by its seclusion and its quintessentially English views.

Clementine, who had been playing tennis nearby, came over to see the house and was similarly entranced by its elevated position at 650 feet above sea level, which she compared to flying in a plane. Doubts soon set in, though. To the south lay that lovely vista, but the other sides were dominated by a steep wooded bank and hordes of light-sucking rhododendrons and laurels. Even worse, the rhododendrons were purple, a color she detested. The house itself had suffered the most ponderous of Victorian makeovers. Downstairs the rooms were small, dark and mostly faced away from the view, and the upstairs was infested with earwigs. It was ravaged by dampness, and she knew it would be ruinously expensive to heat. So that, she had thought, was the end of it.

Winston had allowed her to continue in this belief, while behind her back he negotiated a price (ultimately settling on £5,000, equivalent to about £210,000 today) for both the house and the surrounding eighty acres. He was accustomed, as Clementine wryly observed, to living his life exactly as he pleased, and here was another occasion when his unbounded ego blinded him to reality. Chartwell would become the Churchills' principal residence for forty years—and their only long-term home—just as Winston had intended. But in that time it would drain their finances and sap her energy. From the very beginning she would escape whenever she could.

Clementine accepted her role as its new chatelaine with grace, if not enthusiasm, and quickly set about transforming it into a haven. She would at least be granted her rose garden, and he would have fun damming the spring to create three lakes (thus topping the two at Lloyd George's Surrey estate near the village of Churt). Clementine too competed with the prime minister, in her case over apples: each sent their rival "samples" of the "goodness" of their orchard, daring the other to concede the superiority of its fruit. Meanwhile, a new east wing was to be built, with a top-floor bedroom for her that (perhaps tactically on Winston's part) was double the size of his. Directly below would be an elegant drawing room, and the floor beneath that would feature a large dining room with a line of arched French windows looking onto the gardens, as well as sisal matting and bleached oak furniture that still look modern today. Visitors considered that this prominent new wing lent the house the appearance of a large brown galleon. Imposing, yes, but hardly stylish in the manner of, say, a Georgian rectory.

In September 1922, all of this was still to come. To realize their dream the Churchills first needed an architect. Unfortunately, the obvious contender, Edwin Lutyens, was unavailable. Instead they hired Lloyd George's favorite, Philip Tilden, who not only shared Clementine's concerns but quickly discovered dry rot. As a result, the works would ultimately cost twice the original estimate and take eighteen months to complete.

The bills started to mount—along with Clementine's concern—at the same time as the coalition government of which Winston was a member was falling apart. Conservative backbenchers were in rebellion against Lloyd George, whom they deemed to be incapable of curbing the mounting electoral threat from the Labour Party (boosted by the recent economic downturn) or of resolving the intractable unrest in Ireland. Then on October 19, 1922, just days before a general election was called, Winston was rushed into surgery to have his appendix removed. In those days this was no minor operation and under doctors' orders he was put out of action and sent to a nursing home to recover until mid-November.

Back then, well-heeled new mothers were also expected to rest. But now, a mere five weeks after giving birth, Clementine found herself assuming Winston's place on the stump once again. Taking

Mary—"an unbaptised infant," as the *Dundee Courier* acidly recorded—she made the five-hundred-mile trip to his Scottish constituency for what was to be a bitter campaign. Her pluck drew little sympathy from his constituents, many of whom were angered by Winston's warmongering, the government's failure to help the unemployed and its brutal repression of the Irish. At the hustings she was met by jeering crowds waving red socialist flags and green IRA banners, while on one occasion someone caused a near riot in a hall where she was speaking by throwing sneezing powder into the audience.

Newly enfranchised women, as Clementine had privately predicted, were particularly hostile. Some even spat at her, although one onlooker described her "bearing" under fire as "magnificent—like an aristocrat going to the guillotine in a tumbril."[2] On reflection, it may have been wiser if the ever-elegant Clementine had dressed down a little and not worn pearls, but no one could fault her courage.

She represented Winston faithfully, despite her private belief that his virulent anti-Labour line was ill judged. A more heartfelt Liberal than her husband, she was genuinely moved by the deprivation she witnessed on Tayside and could see the appeal the Labour Party held for those who had so little. Winston's "Smash the Socialists" sentiments, as she referred to them, captured few votes while positioning him as the left's natural bogeyman. Yet for all her considered arguments he continued to ignore her pleas to take "a less hostile and negative" attitude. As always in public she defended him, trying in vain to present him as a "Cherub Peace Maker" with "little fluffy wings round [his] chubby face."[3] When she stood defiantly beside him at the count—he had risen from his sickbed to be present—her judgment was confirmed: he came in an inglorious fourth, behind a Scottish Prohibitionist, the Labour candidate and even another Liberal candidate.

The 1922 election was, in fact, a pivotal point in the history of the country, as well as in Winston's career: for the first time Labour won more votes and seats than the two wings of the now-split Liberal Party put together, although it was still the Tories who formed the new government. Winston now lost patience with the Liberals' over-all leftward drift (and growing electoral impotence against Labour) and consequently soon found himself "without an office, without a seat, without a Party, and without an appendix," as he drily observed. Being out of Parliament, where he had sat almost continuously since 1900, was to prove an ordeal that would tax his spirits and test his marriage for the next two years. Henceforth the Churchills' politics were to pull ever further apart.

With builders at work on Chartwell and nothing to detain them in London, Winston and Clementine set off to the south of France. For the next six months, they rented a villa called Rêve d'Or in the wooded district of La Croix des Gardes, above Cannes. All the children joined them for Christmas and New Year, but Winston returned to Britain three times during this period to escort the elder ones to and from boarding school. Most of the time he remained in France, however. Before the days of easy flights to the Caribbean, well-heeled Brits would congregate on the Riviera to escape the worst of the winter, transplanting the London social whirl to the Continent. Consuelo, Sunny's former wife (now married to the Frenchman Jacques Balsan), wintered not far away at Lou Sueil, in what Clementine wistfully described as a "scented nest," a light-filled, elegant and comfortable house surrounded by umbrella pines and mimosas. These months away from everyday politics were in many ways idyllic: Clementine was able to practice her tennis, Winston could paint, they celebrated her thirty-eighth birthday in style and he gave her a diamond brooch. Under the Riviera sun, that extraordinary Churchillian energy quickly returned, as did his appetite for work. Winston wrote the first volume of *The World Crisis* (which was serialized by the *Times*, netting him £20,000). The house was always bustling; not only did servants accompany them everywhere, but Winston's secretary and researcher were present too. This may have been one of the longest periods they spent together in their marriage, but they were still rarely alone.

Meanwhile, Chartwell was proving to be the money pit Clementine had feared. Sitting on the boulevard du Soleil in Cannes, she tried to impose control on the works from afar by sending detailed written instructions. The contrast between Winston's ambitious whims and her efforts to pare back brought numerous flashpoints. Tilden also annoyed her with what she saw as unnecessarily fancy interior doors, firebacks and a weathervane. He even ordered, without consultation, a costly kitchen range (although admittedly the monogrammed copper saucepans were her indulgence).[4] Just as she had at Admiralty House, she was constantly fighting to keep staff and other costs to a minimum. However grand a lifestyle her husband desired, they would have to get by, she decreed, with two housemaids at most.

When they returned at last from France, in mid-May 1923, Chartwell was still a mud-splattered building site. For a year they were obliged to rent a place nearby, putting further strain on their creaking finances. Winston begged his wife "not to worry about money or to feel insecure," but he also had a confession to make. From the safe distance of Bayonne harbor in southwest France, where he was luxuriating on the Duke of Westminster's four-masted yacht, he wrote to her back in England with bad news. On top of the £5,000 purchase price, he had already sunk three times that sum into the renovations, with no end in sight. Even complete the house was unlikely to be worth more than £15,000 (later, after the rebuilding bill had ballooned to £19,000, it was valued at less than £12,000), yet Winston seemed unconcerned. Chartwell was no Blenheim, of course, but he nonetheless viewed it as a dynastic seat, one that should never be sold and would eventually pass to Randolph. Clementine much preferred the culture and people of London, but they could no longer afford, even with the Irish inheritance, to keep two large residences. Her beloved Sussex Square would have to go. She had not wanted Chartwell, or the crushing cost of it, but she was now effectively trapped.

When the Churchills finally moved into the house, on Maundy Thursday in 1924, Clementine was absent, having chosen to visit her mother in Dieppe. Normally she took solo charge of domestic ar-

rangements; on the occasion of their move into Sussex Square, for
instance, Winston had excused himself in favor of a luxurious boar-
hunting excursion to France. This time she was the one who was
running away. Removing herself was always her most powerful
weapon. Realizing he had won the war but lost the final battle, Winston crafted a letter designed to bring her back and win her over. First
he enthused about how the children had worked "like blacks"—as he
put it in the language of the day—to help him. Next he claimed to be
overindulging—"I drink champagne at meals & buckets of claret and
soda in between." He then related how her bedroom was now a
"magnificent aerial bower" and that "genial weather" was bringing
the garden into glorious bud. He rounded off with:

> *Only one thing lack these banks of green—*
> *The Pussy Cat who is their Queen.*

By this stage in their marriage, Winston rarely reproached his
wife—he knew it to be counterproductive—and he was genuinely
anxious when she was displeased. Her antipathy to Chartwell disappointed him and her absence wounded him (although less so when
the holiday was his). His physical comfort was provided by a host of
staff, but only Clementine's presence could bring those deeper feelings of security; he depended on her constant attention and advice.
Sometimes when she was away he would climb into her unmade bed
just to feel close to her,[5] and he would even claim to be "frightened"[6]
without her. During one of her escapes, this time to Lou Sueil, Winston forgot his pride altogether and simply pleaded: "Do not abridge
yr holiday if it is doing you good—But of course I feel far safer from
worry and depression when you are with me & when I confide in yr
sweet soul . . . You are a rock & I depend on you & rest on you. Come
back to me therefore as soon as you can."[7]

The sad truth was that Clementine found his dependency draining; like a child, he was petulant, moody and demanding. This was
to be a torturous time in their marriage and they spent long stretches
apart. As everyone in the household discovered, being out of office

made Winston exceedingly grumpy and "a kicker of wastepaper baskets, with an unbelievably ungoverned bundle of bad temper. It is better to stay away from him at such times and this his family seeks to do."[8] Staying away was something Clementine would resort to more and more. In response, Winston would not change himself but he would try to make Chartwell more agreeable to her—including installing a tennis court and later a croquet lawn. Her imminent return after a lengthy absence would prompt a frenzy of smartening-up—on one occasion dozens of seedling sycamores and elders had to be frantically dug out when he spotted them from his bedroom window and judged them likely to displease her.

He did, however, take advantage of her periodic flits. During one such—to compete in a tennis tournament in Cromer—he built a tree house in an old lime tree by the front drive. In common with his sandcastles, this elaborate structure unleashed his inner child. It stood two stories high and twenty feet aboveground; the children adored it and Clementine's much-mocked fears for their safety—not entirely unfounded—merely made her feel excluded from the rest of the family's fun.

The more childlike he was, the more she felt duty-bound to play the responsible adult. In the summer of 1924, while she was away with the children on Anglesey, he seized the opportunity to build another lake. It proved more difficult—and messier—than he had anticipated. Two years later, when she went to stay with Consuelo at Lou Sueil, work was still going on. Inspired by Capability Brown's creations at Blenheim, Winston was consumed by ostentatious waterworks. He tried to compensate for the mud and expense by also building a swimming pool, as Clementine and the children loved to bathe. Some giant *Gunnera* plants—donated by her once whip-happy aunt Mary Hozier—disguised the filtration works and an oak tree concealed the boiler, which was said to be big enough to heat the Ritz.

When Clementine took to the water she did so in an elaborate skirted bathing costume (one guest mistook it for a dress), with her hair coiled under a stylish sun hat. Swimming was a regular feature

of her disciplined exercise and dietary regimen; she would also sometimes resort to a strict "tomato diet" to lose weight. She made the
most of her slender form (and limited budget) with a fashionable
pared-down wardrobe of muted grays and blues that was to become
much admired. Her beauty—particularly her "natural-looking" eye-
brows, "wonderful" bone structure and china-white teeth—was
deemed intrinsic and unaffected (although she had regular manicures at Harvey Nichols in London). Because she distrusted hairdressers, she fastidiously arranged her hair herself—in neat curls
around her face—and washed it, to her family's alarm, with undiluted benzene to give it shine. Without fail immaculately presented,
whether in town or country, she appeared, to her admirers, to be
growing more beautiful with age. Perhaps Winston was the only one
not to notice.

He was, as usual, engrossed in his career—but Chartwell, if not
a rival, at least provided a sufficiently all-consuming distraction. He
wanted the kitchen garden to produce a huge range of fruit and veg-
etables, whereas Clementine yearned for flowers. She expected a constant supply of scented hyacinths, freesias and sweet peas to put in
vases; one year alone she ordered a thousand tulip bulbs. Such activity made Chartwell a major employer, with twenty full-time staff.
The male employees included three gardeners, a chauffeur, a butler,
a farmhand, an "odd man," a groom and a carpenter, in addition to
estate workers, researchers, two secretaries and a valet for Winston.
Clementine's domestic staff included a lady's maid, two housemaids,
a cook, a nanny, a nursery maid and a parlor maid. Such an army of
retainers sounds excessive, but the house had five reception rooms,
nineteen bed- and dressing rooms, and what was then a daringly
numerous eight bathrooms.

Furthermore, both Churchills were exceedingly demanding.
Winston in particular insisted on a rigid if eccentric regimen, and
Clementine ensured the staff complied with it fully. It was no easy
task. Her nephew Peregrine remembers that "for everyone except
[Winston] life at Chartwell was continual chaos."[9] Winston was
treated like a pasha—his clothes were laid out (two shirts a day,

cream in the morning, white in the evening) and his newspapers were folded and piled with the *Times* always on top. Order (three yellow and three green toothbrushes laid out in a row and used strictly by rotation)[10] and cleanliness were obsessions for each of them. Even Winston was forbidden to enter the house if wet or muddy, and would stand dripping outside until maids were able to place newspapers across the polished floors. Fortunately Randolph was often away at boarding school in the early years—firstly Sandroyd, then Eton at the age of thirteen—for it is unlikely he would have been as compliant as his father.

Winston took a bath twice a day, poured exactly at midday and again at seven p.m. by his valet. The bath had to be two-thirds full and heated to precisely 98 degrees Fahrenheit, rising to 104 degrees Fahrenheit once he had plunged in. He ordered the overflow to be blocked up as he did not like to lose water but was fond of somersaulting in the tub—an alarming maneuver that caused gallons of displaced water to seep down onto the coats of visitors in the cloakroom below. Rather than attempting to persuade Winston to change his habits, Clementine took the pragmatic approach of fitting a special drain in the floor of what amounted to a 1920s forerunner of a wet room. His valet would then towel him dry, after which he refused to put on a dressing gown; if he wished to go to another room he would do so undressed. New members of staff would be shocked to see a very pink, 224-pound naked man with stooping shoulders scurrying toward them exclaiming, "Coming through, don't look!"[11]

Nudity was not uncommon in the Churchill household. Clementine would also summon a secretary while in the bath. "Please order the car for eleven," she would say, while unself-consciously sponging herself, or "Book me a doctor's appointment for next week." If the instructions were numerous and complex, the heat and steam in her little bathroom could become overwhelming and on at least one occasion a secretary succumbed by fainting to the floor. Her lack of prudishness meant that it was not unknown for her to issue orders to workmen with her hair in curlers, face smothered in skin cream, wearing only a bathrobe.

Clementine devoted herself to running the large house for Winston's pleasure. The wood gleamed and smelled of beeswax, the glassware sparkled, cushions were puffed, the silverware polished, the paintings perfectly aligned in vertical rows. "She was a perfectionist, and at times, she sacrificed too much on the altar of that stern goddess," her daughter Mary later remarked.[12] She never quite shook loose the tearful girl with a spot on her pinafore, but maintaining such standards, even with a large staff, took its toll on her nerves. Her maids learned fast—or left faster. The slightest imperfection could prompt a terrifying put-down: "You stupid goose!" was one of Clementine's milder outbursts. Yet she disliked having "people around her who were frightened of her" and could deploy tact and gratitude to equal effect.[13] One of her youthful smiles would reward a job well done.

Despite all the expense and effort, however, Chartwell remained problematic.[14] The windows and roof let in the rain. The wiring was faulty and the drawing room ceiling once collapsed, bringing a chandelier down with it. An embattled Philip Tilden wrote to a firm of surveyors, "Mrs Churchill who has very great influence over Mr Churchill has given it as her opinion that the house is falling down."[15] Another battleground was the subject of trees. Winston wanted to keep them all; Clementine was uncompromising about cutting undesirable ones down. Former members of staff talk in hushed tones to this day about the great "copper beech incident." It was Winston's habit to make mischief in her absence, but once when *he* was away she gave orders for a large copper beech to be felled. She had argued in vain that it darkened her sitting room and she disliked the purple-black of its leaves. On his return, he was incensed. But Clementine had won.

Inside, her style was in evidence almost everywhere, whether in the porcelain blue of her sitting room or the primrose yellows of the drawing room. The carefully positioned mirrors to lighten the rather gloomy interiors were her inspiration, as were the colorful curtains at the windows. The principal chambers were graced by a sprinkling of good (but never quite top-quality) antiques and there were fine

French glass (not crystal) chandeliers. She regarded the services of an interior designer a gross extravagance and liked nothing better than to find an attractive piece of furniture going "for a song." "She was very frugal," remembers Shelagh Montague Browne. Nothing was thrown out "until it was completely falling to bits."[16]

Flowers from the gardens were placed in every room and arranged in her signature style. "Grab them by the necks and just drop them in the vase, dear," she would instruct staff. She could be furious if she found fussy arrangements, and on formal occasions would only countenance white. "Once someone put colored ones in too," recalls a former member of staff. "You would have thought there had been a major international incident." (Clementine was aware of, if powerless to alter, her habit of overreacting, telling Winston, "[I]t is a great fault in me that small things should have the power to harass & agonise me.")[17]

By such means she made the best of a challenging house. The results of her perfectionism were admired, even copied. Yet some visitors thought her considerable flair unable to conceal Chartwell's many drawbacks—the place reminded Harold Macmillan of a government department and others of a male Oxbridge college.

Winston had certain set ideas about interior design, even if he left the work of implementing them to others. He penned a lengthy "dissertation," for instance, on the necessary characteristics of dining room chairs: there should be no fewer than twenty, they should have arms and be both fairly narrow and comfortable. Those shown in William Nicholson's painting of the Churchills at breakfast, which now hangs in the Chartwell dining room, were specially commissioned to meet these exact specifications.

A gift for their silver wedding anniversary in September 1933, Nicholson's painting was meant as a conversation piece, and guests liked to exchange observations about its inaccuracies. Winston and Clementine did not breakfast together (he believed that "one of the secrets of a happy marriage is never to . . . see the loved one before noon")[18] and it is most unlikely that a cat would have been allowed on the table in her presence. Never as sentimental as Winston, Clementine was a stickler for hygiene—although when they were without important company she would allow diners to eat cutlets with their hands to extract more of the meat. At a relatively early age for the era, the children were permitted to dine with their parents and even with their guests and were consequently precociously aware of national and international events. They grew up unusually at ease in adult company—but perhaps less so with those of the same age as themselves.

Winston was indulgent of his cats and over the years there were several, including Mickey, a tabby; Nelson, a gray; and the marmalade-colored Tango, all of whom he would address as "darling." (During the Second World War Clementine ordered Tango's death to be kept from him until news on the fighting had improved.) In his wife's absence he encouraged them to sit on chairs at table, poured cream from a jug straight onto the tabletop for them to lap up, and insisted that his poodle Rufus was served—albeit in a bowl on the floor—before his guests. Winston also had a penchant for describing Chartwell's various varieties of fowl as his friends and addressing them by name. When he could not bring himself to carve one of his flock at table, Clementine would take over.

Winston preferred to dine on hearty English cooking. Heaven forfend the cook should he or she fail to provide a regular supply of such favorite dishes as clear soup (never creamy), oysters, pheasant, lobster, dressed crab, Dover sole, chocolate éclairs and roast beef and Yorkshire pudding. Clementine indulged her own lighter preferences only when she took her meals on a tray in her room—which she did more frequently as the years passed by. Although she never now cooked herself—she described herself as a "theoretical rather than practical cook"[19]—she attended high-class cookery courses with such famous chefs as Marcel Boulestin (a celebrated West End restaurateur whose books popularized French cuisine) simply to ensure her kitchen stayed abreast of the best techniques. She had particularly exacting standards for a béchamel sauce and would quiz staff in detail on how they planned to prepare one. In truth, it was cheaper to pass on her knowledge and train a maid than to employ an experienced cook. Similarly, she took pains to devise menus that mini-mized unnecessary expense. This took time as even lunch involved three courses. Every morning at half past eight she would spend a full half hour in her bedroom discussing the day's meals with the cook (dressed in a spotless white apron) to ensure that all was to Winston's taste.

Such culinary exactitude masked an ulterior motive. Feeding Winston well was her way, she once confessed, of "managing" him. "You must give him a good dinner," she explained to a riveted Lloyd George.[20] Sometimes her food was so good, Winston would refuse to enter the conversation at table and she would have to take over. No wonder then that Winston, who unlike his wife rarely found time to exercise in middle age, was straining the buttons on his waistcoat. (She made her concerns about this clear by prominently placing scales in his bathroom.)

Her efforts to manage his wardrobe proved less than successful. At the time of their marriage, he had been widely regarded as the worst-dressed member of the Asquith administration, a Conservative MP once apparently mistaking his curious garb in the chamber for a pair of pajamas. Even now his bow tie was often willfully askew. At Chartwell he favored a ragged coat or paint-splattered jacket and bat-tered hat; his work attire still consisted of an old-fashioned winged collar and black frock coat. A barber came to visit once a month but in truth there was little to work with. What he lacked in hair, he more than made up for with a large and theatrical collection of hats. He was perhaps one of the few men in Britain whose wardrobe was more playful than his wife's.

At least twice a day Clementine's lady's maid laid out an entirely fresh outfit (including underwear) on her bed while she bathed. Her children remembered her smelling "delicious" and being dressed in the softest fabrics—attributes that in their eyes added to her already goddesslike status. She was an early riser—waking around five or six—and would put her hair in curlers while she dealt with her cor-respondence, before breakfasting on her own in her room at eight. As she grew older she frequently took an afternoon nap. However brief this was, she expected her pillowcases to be changed for fresh ones immediately afterward.

Winston was no less particular, but many of the servants preferred working for him as they found he forgave more easily. Ultimately, these exalted expectations—and the fact the Churchills were notoriously ungenerous payers—meant the turnover of staff at Chartwell was rapid. Only the most dedicated (for instance, the cook Georgina Landemare) or eccentric (such as the tipsy valet David Inches) lasted the course. Clementine constantly fretted about finding and training new staff—a preoccupation that Winston, unburdened by such concerns, airily dismissed with the observation that "servants exist to save one trouble and shd never be allowed to disturb one's inner peace."[21] "Do not worry about household matters. Let them crash if they will," he once advised. It can be said for certain that Winston would have been the first to complain if they had.

The only corner of the house immune to Clementine's signature style was her husband's bedroom. A swashbuckling shrine to military memorabilia with a single bed, it was, like all his other bedrooms—even those at Admiralty House and Number 10—relatively humble, a bolt-hole adjoining his vaulted study, where the windows were sealed with putty because of his terror of drafts and noise, particularly anyone whistling. Some distance away was Clementine's far more splendid sky-blue, barrel-domed boudoir, with its imposing four-poster bed dressed in red moiré silk. In summer white roses from the garden graced her desk, and *her* windows would be thrown open to capture the fresh air. "There was never any question of them being in the same bed, or same room or even in the same part of the house," recalls their niece Clarissa Churchill, who spent her holidays at Chartwell. "They were nowhere near each other."[22]

It was a grand life. Even Winston occasionally became alarmed at the cost of it all—at one point in 1926 expenditure rose to £477 a month (equivalent to £25,000 or $38,000 today).[23] He would then send Clementine unintentionally ironic memoranda on economy. Savings to be made, he decreed, included fewer holidays (his tended to be infinitely more expensive than hers), selling livestock (on which he himself had lavished money) and inviting fewer guests outside family (although they had invariably been selected for his pleasure). Purchases of cigars, champagne and wines, dress shirts and even boot-polish should be cut, he pronounced, although there is little evidence that the chief culprit in these areas observed his own edicts.

Once or twice he suggested letting Chartwell, although he quickly dropped the idea when Clementine jumped at it. Far more worrying was his suggestion of "going into milk"—just one of a stream of money-losing ventures. As she often did when hell-bent on winning an argument, she set down her case in writing. All previous such schemes, she pointed out—across no fewer than seven pages— had been disastrous. Winston had invested in English Shorthorn cattle, Swedish Landrace pigs, sheep, chickens, geese, turkeys and ornamental Australian black swans, but Chartwell had not thrived as a working farm. For Winston could not bear to have an animal slaughtered once he had said good morning to it. Dairy cows were likely to be no more remunerative.

She was right to urge caution on his agricultural adventures but her natural tendency to worry made her too negative about some of his other pursuits. Winston's devotion to painting was literally paying off. When he had begun writing about his hobby in 1921— receiving the enormous sum of £1,000 for two articles in the *Strand* magazine—she had warned that the professionals would be "vexed & say you do not yet know enough about Art." In fact, his articles, entitled "Painting as a Pastime," were an enormous success and eventually became a book.

Nevertheless, the prospect of financial ruin continually shadowed their lives. Clementine knew their future depended on his ability to churn out books and articles at a ferocious rate—and he constantly sent her drafts for her "deeply interesting" suggestions. Many assumed that the Churchills had a cushion of family money like other upper-class British politicians; they certainly appeared to live extremely well. But by the late 1920s the Irish inheritance had been exhausted by the cost of rebuilding and maintaining Chartwell. True, Churchill made some money out of libel damages—he was frequently excoriated in print and as an experienced litigant he always won. From time to time the elder children would also be told, "Papa and Mummie are economising," a notice that would be followed by lectures about the need to turn off lights and reprimands for long telephone calls. But overall their life of luxury continued largely intact. All the while they "lived from book to book, and from one article to the next."

However fervent the promises of economy, the largesse would swiftly creep back. Hospitality was a great source of joy for Winston and sometimes the Churchills would host a grand garden party, ordering a marquee of olive green and yellow for the grounds, and laying on music (usually of the Gilbert & Sullivan variety favored by Winston). Clementine would fret about the cost but would partly assuage her worries by taking out insurance against rain, with the payouts related to the scale of the deluge. Winston liked not only to offer guests the best food, Pol Roger champagne (or "panya" as he called it) and Romeo y Julieta Cuban cigars, but to show off his latest Chartwell project. With such immoderation came bills, and visits from angry local tradesmen in search of payment. The Churchills acquired a humiliating reputation for tardiness in settling accounts, reminding Clementine of her childhood. Sometimes she would lose her temper with Winston over his extravagance, which would inevitably lead him to become doggedly defensive. As one of his political colleagues once aptly put it, reasoning with Winston was like arguing with a brass band.[24] On one such occasion she got so frustrated that she threw a plate of spinach at him. She missed, but it left a mark on the wall.

Within the household, their quarrels were the stuff of legend. As she grew older Clementine became increasingly forceful. "When her nerves were stretched, she sometimes turned on Winston with vitriol in her voice and the flashing eyes of a Fury,"[25] remarked one senior staffer. Her raised voice could be heard from behind a closed door, only for Winston to emerge afterward head down and muttering miserably, "She called me a bloody old fool!"

Only rarely would lack of money prevent them from going on holiday, as both considered time away one of life's essentials. But their disagreement as to the joys of the British seaside—Clementine relishing the very simplicity and ruggedness that so horrified Winston—meant they seldom traveled together. His celebrity made him a trophy guest for the likes of Maxine Elliott, an aging American actress who owned the modernist Château de l'Horizon at Golfe-Juan on France's Côte d'Azur. She competed for his presence with Lord Rothermere at Cap Martin, or Lord Beaverbrook at La Capponcina near Nice. On the odd occasion that Clementine accompanied him to these resorts she was horrified at their vulgar displays of self-indulgence. "God," she wrote to her daughter Sarah, "the Riviera is a ghastly place." She scarcely ever stayed long, which one fellow guest attributed to the fact that the "Churchills simply hadn't a bean." Winston cared little, but being relatively poor among the super-rich brought back painful memories for her. "Clementine worried dreadfully," the guest surmised, "and used to feel that the others were laughing at her behind her back because of her clothes."[26] As well as disliking the company, she did not paint, write or gamble, and so she felt excluded. She also worried about Winston's losing money in the casino—which he did—although once when she was with him his luck on the tables improved; she woke up to find her bed layered with banknotes from his winnings.

The exception to Clementine's horror was Lou Sueil: she took solace in Consuelo's understanding of the peculiar pressures of being married to a Churchill. She also felt in tune politically there. Now that Winston was drifting back to the Tories, his loathing of Bolshevism seemed to have hardened his heart against the poor. Many of his Riviera cronies were even less sympathetic and so Clementine treasured Consuelo's social conscience all the more.

By the mid-1920s Winston was convinced that only the Conservatives were capable of countering the Labour Party. Clementine felt duty bound to follow his reconversion—at least publicly—taking the spitting, brick-throwing and booing alongside him, but as Mary related, she never made a "good Tory," and occasionally her "natural radicalism would burst through the layers of reasonable compliance like a volcanic eruption, often to people's astonished bewilderment."[27] Even Violet recognized Clementine as a true "natural Liberal"[28] who never ceased to promote to Winston what she saw as Liberal values. Clementine's feelings about Tories, whom she described as variously stupid, inefficient and reveling in "slaughter & the Army," were doused with suspicion.[29] "Do not . . . let the Tories get you too cheap," she warned Winston as he pondered a return to his old party. "They have treated you so badly in the past & they ought to be made to feel it."[30]

Winston nevertheless decisively split with the Liberals over the reunited party's decision to support Labour after the 1923 election, a move that shut the Conservatives out of power even though they had won the most seats. He tried to justify his "re-ratting" to her by arguing that certain senior Conservatives now harbored more agreeably moderate and progressive views. She conceded that the Tory leader, Stanley Baldwin, was showing a "genuine feeling" for working people, but all this hardly compensated for Winston's readiness to compare the Liberal Party's association with Labour to missionaries assisting cannibals.

Winston's political inconsistency over the years had left the couple with few real friends, particularly mutual ones. They did not move in fashionable or intellectual circles, and neither did they meet new people on the country house circuit, as Winston disliked spending weekends away. Most Chartwell guests in the early days were therefore relations or Winston's political colleagues and hangers-on. In the first year, they entertained Nellie's husband, Bertram Romilly, then Goonie and later Nellie herself. But there were sometimes tensions between the two Hozier sisters. Clementine's sole surviving sibling spent much of her time caring for Bertram, an invalid from his Great War injuries, but was by nature a garrulous and easygoing character, known for wearing long strings of pearls over her some-

what threadbare clothes. Clementine could be critical of her for getting "up to mischief" when she had the chance. But what was
considered "feckless" by some was seen as fun by others. "If you
couldn't like Nellie," recalls one former member of Clementine's
staff, "you couldn't like anyone."

Winston too was very fond of "Nellinita," whom he helped financially, and had taken an interest in her increasingly wayward sons.
Esmond, her youngest, shared a passing resemblance to his uncle (as
Esmond's future wife, Decca Mitford, was to point out) and that,
together with Winston's kindness, prompted speculation that the boy
might be his natural child. He was, however, a born rebel, a leftie
who would run away from his public school, Wellington College, in
January 1934 to launch a popular Communist teenage magazine, *Out
of Bounds*, and live as a squatter. In the absence of much help from her
disabled husband, Nellie washed her hands of Esmond, and he was
subsequently sent to a remand home for juvenile offenders before
making off for Spain to join the International Brigades and fight in
the civil war. Headstrong and idealistic, he had charisma and charm,
so while he infuriated his uncle, he was too likable for Winston to
give up on him entirely. Clementine, by contrast, was harsher on
both Esmond for misbehaving and Nellie for not controlling him.

Goonie's son Johnny was another Chartwell regular who attracted rumors about his paternity. Indeed, Johnny encouraged the
talk that he might be Winston's son, which thoroughly annoyed
Clementine. A successful artist in adult life, he once sent his aunt a
painting as a birthday present; she secretly tried to dispose of it but
promptly gave it away instead when she was caught by a member of
staff. If he asked after it, she said it was hanging on her bedroom
wall.[31] Few, if any, who knew Winston and the family well give cre-
dence to the idea that any of Winston's nephews was actually his illegitimate son. The rumors were most likely the product of prevailing
assumptions about the sex lives of powerful men, as Clementine in
her heart of hearts no doubt knew. What hurt was that while Johnny
and others gleefully spread the gossip, Winston declined to quash it.

She desperately wanted the Churchill family to remain united and untainted by the sexual intrigue that had dogged her own youth.

On October 29, 1924, another general election, precipitated by the collapse of the Labour government Winston had so despised, saw the Tories restored to power and secured Winston's return as a Conservative MP for Epping, a seat he was to represent for the following forty years. His immediate but unexpected appointment, just before his fiftieth birthday, as chancellor of the Exchequer—Clementine initially thought he was teasing when he told her—mercifully furnished them with a grand London residence again, and effectively completed his homecoming to his old party. Clementine grew fond of 11 Downing Street—then a spacious family home—and would work tirelessly in Epping so that Winston could focus on his demanding task at the Treasury. But the fact remained that her husband was now the second-most prominent member of a government whose politics were anathema to her.

"The Tories don't want to be made to think!" was one of her private complaints. Certainly they could never provide her with the thrilling pride she had taken during Winston's reforming partnership with Lloyd George. Local constituency Tories may have regarded her "as a fashionable beauty" with a "model-like carriage," but most of all they noticed an unnerving "direct gaze."[32] She had so obviously disliked accompanying Winston to Conservative rallies preceding the 1924 election that he had felt compelled to offer an explanation: "She's a Liberal, and always has been. It's all very strange for her. But to me, of course, it's just like coming home."[33] Clementine later told her closest staff that she did not vote Liberal again—out of loyalty to Winston—but she was never to overcome her "latent, almost subconscious, hostility"[34] to the Tory party.

His defection had left her politically high and dry. No longer sharing the same vision, she felt unable to pursue a role of her own on the national stage with any conviction. In 1920 she had told him that the one time she had plowed her own furrow—her admirable work in the munitions canteens of the First World War—already seemed like a "dream"; even then she had believed that *if* she had genuinely possessed "real organizing ability . . . it died with the War."[35] Now, by contrast, Winston had secured his highest position yet. As Clementine wrote in September 1926, he was having "an anxious but thrilling . . . time with power & scope which is what the Pig likes."[36] "Pig" liked it so much, in fact, that he desired an upgrade in his pet name, informing Clementine that he now wished to become a "Lion."

An economic brief did not play to his strengths, however. Despite Clementine's efforts to encourage him to help the poor and widows (which he did through small raises in state pensions), his first budget in 1925 was widely attacked. Many pundits deemed it ill judged— John Maynard Keynes deplored Winston's decision to rejoin the gold standard, which tied the pound to gold at unsustainably high prewar levels (and led to soaring unemployment). Others thought it a wealthy man's charter by way of its tax cuts for high earners. As the son of Queen Victoria's ex–private secretary put it, Winston's "sympathy for the poor was eloquent; his sympathy for the rich was practical."[37]

During his time at the Treasury Winston had to contend with a period of intense social and industrial strife, much of it arguably of his own making. Clementine may have felt estranged from her husband's politics, but her skill at creating an elegant home with exceptional food nonetheless made her an asset in his attempts to defuse the various crises that arose. Winston was never a man who spent a lot of time at the club, as he loved his home comforts too much; thus Chartwell was to provide the setting (as, to a lesser extent, did 11 Downing Street) for some of the most difficult meetings of his chancellorship. Both sides in the 1925 prebudget debate on whether to return to the gold standard were bidden to discuss the issue over the Churchills' dinner table, while during the miners' strike of 1926, the Labour opposition leader Ramsay MacDonald was seated beside the owners of the coal mines—a gathering pretty much unthinkable anywhere else. Flawless hospitality became part of Winston's surprisingly inclusive political style, based on the principle that good food, wine and Clementine's charm (when she was around) made almost anything possible. "It is well to remember that the stomach governs the world," he once wrote.[38] It was an approach he would readopt at a time of even greater crisis.

Day visitors were not normally recorded in the book kept on the chest in the hall, but "dine & sleep" guests were. The latter were to increase dramatically in number after Winston's return to government, lending Chartwell the air of a frantically busy small hotel. Arrivals would crunch up the semicircular gravel drive to the great front door, whereupon they would be shown into the drawing room with its dominating portrait of Winston and sofas ranged companionably either side of the fire. The real Winston, who himself never liked to hurry from the bath, would rarely be ready to greet even the most distinguished visitors. That role would fall to Clementine. She would smile and receive them gracefully in the hall, while surreptitiously sending up a string of messengers (including certain trusted guests) to bang on his bathroom door.

Lunch was timed to start at 1:15 on the dot, but Winston would still be splashing in the water at 1:20. Dinner was scheduled for 8:30 but it was unusual for him to descend to the drawing room, where Clementine would have long since finished her predinner sherry, before 8:45. Perhaps in reaction to his poor timekeeping, she herself was obsessively punctual. Certainly she found his casual rudeness—and the inconvenience it caused to others—intolerable; she frequently made her anger clear to Winston, who would respond to her eye-flashing fury with: "Oh I'm so sorry, yes, yes, so sorry." Later he would say conspiratorially to the staff, "I'm afraid, Mrs. C is very angry with me,"[39] thereby recruiting their undying sympathy.

Clementine welcomed numerous British politicians to Chartwell over the years, among them prime-ministers-to-be Anthony Eden, Harold Macmillan and Edward Heath. But she was also to play hostess to some of the world's powerful and famous, including US president Harry Truman, Queen Elizabeth the Queen Mother, Charlie Chaplin and Albert Einstein, Laurence Olivier and Lawrence of Arabia (who would arrive by motorbike but dined in the robes of an Arab prince). Members of many of the grandest dynasties came only once. Clementine, although proud of her aristocratic lineage, made a point of showing indifference to the very elevated and—albeit not averse to her own comforts and retinue—was scornful of conspicuous wealth. Her daughter Mary would even sometimes later accuse her of "inverted snobbishness."

An invitation to Chartwell was flattering, and was usually extended for Winston's sake rather than Clementine's. Some guests were summoned to cheer him up when out of sorts, others to inform, advise, help or stimulate him. Almost all found Mrs. Churchill an alluring hostess. One first-time visitor recalled an "almost physical shock" that Winston had such "a life-force of a wife, someone so clever, opinionated and interesting in her own right."[40] Visitors were equally surprised when Clementine, seated opposite her husband at dinner, occasionally admonished him with "Winston, I wouldn't say that!" or challenged him with "Winston, you have suddenly changed your mind about that!" Her voice was young sounding, crisp, quite high but confident without being particularly plummy for the time. She was charismatic—and, while there was an air of mystery to her, she had a knack for making guests enjoy the (usually false) impression that they were being taken into her confidence. Few who were treated to her wide smile and big-eyed gaze did not succumb. Sarah compared her mother to a "chandelier," an idea that also appealed to Mary as "she did give forth great life and sparkle."[41]

A memory that lingered long after a stay at Chartwell was her full-throated laugh—"a sound of real joy" was how one guest put it. "She would cackle like a hen," recalls an ex-member of staff. "It was very contagious."[42] Like Winston, she found a play on words funnier than people's foibles, including her own. She enjoyed it when they hired a chauffeur called Bullock, for instance, and Winston referred to the car as "the Bullock cart," but the casual comedy of life's ups and downs largely passed her by. Shelagh Montague Browne remembers that Clementine had more wit than humor: "She couldn't really laugh at herself, as she took things very seriously . . . She had a razor-sharp wit . . . she just would not get the amusingly absurd."

There were times when she would not even attempt to conceal her disapproval of a guest. She took a principled if sectarian stance on many subjects and could "erupt" at someone spouting the opposing view, particularly if the culprit were a brash and wealthy Tory. She was savage in her put-downs, and the fact that her target was a visitor to her house made scant difference. Only the shy were spared. As a finale, she might storm out of the dining room, leaving her family, including Winston, helpless with embarrassment at what they collectively referred to as one of "Mama's sweeps." And yet Winston harbored a secret pride at his wife's feistiness—relating afterward in awestruck tones how she had given so-and-so "a most fearful mauling." On one occasion he told his guests with particular glee that "Clemmie dropped on him like a jaguar out of a tree." At other times—if she had already taken exception to someone—she would shut herself in her room before she lost her temper. The company would be informed that she was unwell.

Absorbed in his own interests—politics, painting or landscaping—Winston left her alone for long periods, even when they were in the same house. He needed to know she was nearby and in constant attendance, but very often, when he was busy, he did not want her at his side. She learned over time when not to interrupt him; her life at home, however, orbited his all the same. His welfare and ambitions consumed her every moment. Much of her own time was spent reading history and biography to bolster her understanding of his world—in 1932 she remarked to Winston that her book on the American Civil War was "full of abuse of politicians who try to interfere with Generals in the field—(Ahem!)"[43]—but she had few outside pursuits other than tennis and visits to art galleries.

Nor did she have many friends of her own, especially at Chartwell. Her cousin Sylvia Henley, her old friend Horatia Seymour and Goonie would come to stay for occasional weekends, but even with these trusted women she rarely opened up completely. She found it difficult to make new friends, or get really close to old ones. Unlike other politicians' wives, such as Diana Cooper, she had no independent court of supporters—let alone lovers—of her own. The various spells of unpopularity that Winston had brought upon them during his career had cut her off from the circuit.

She sought companionship instead from some of the female staff—and more than one found her need for intimacy overwhelming and left. "It was a bit like working with the royals," recalls one former assistant. "If they liked you they wanted you there all the time." Secretaries were chosen for their compatibility with Churchill family life and lack of competing outside interests (such as boyfriends) more than for their proven office skills. One newly widowed recruit did not last long as she was trying to rebuild her own life outside work and had a habit of answering back. After an argument with Clementine over the color of a pair of shoes, in which the secretary refused to back down, she was "let go."

The younger ones—some only seventeen or eighteen and generally drawn from a similar social stratum to Clementine herself—were more pliable. They worked long and unpredictable hours and were fairly isolated so many ended up practically living with the family. "You will see warts and all," new employees were informed by a long-term staffer, "but you're not to talk about it."[44] With a couple of them Clementine struck up enduring friendships—and frequently gave them affectionate hugs. Many more were to disappoint her by leaving and not bothering to stay in touch. Margery Street, her secretary for many years, became very close, but alas she too left, returning to her native Australia in 1933.

The exception to this procession of well-bred "gels" addressed as "Miss" was Grace Hamblin—or "Hambone," as the Churchills called her. A gardener's daughter who started work at Chartwell in 1932 and took over from Miss Street the following year, she faithfully remained with the couple until Winston died and was the linchpin of Clementine's life. She ran Chartwell, employing the staff and dealing with the household bills. Beautiful, funny and astonishingly efficient, she had a knack for knowing what Clementine wanted even before

Clementine herself. In the absence of other friends, Clementine depended heavily on Grace, who would over time become perhaps her greatest confidante and a favored holiday companion. Sarah, Diana and Mary also came to rely on this selfless woman, whose dedication was such that she gave up all prospects of a family of her own. She was far more than a servant, yet always willing to serve. For her first few years at Chartwell Grace was expected to enter the house by the back door, something she did not appreciate.[45] It would take another world war for the Churchills to reconsider their outdated views on class.

By the late 1920s, it had become clear that regular escapes from Winston were essential to Clementine's health. As she later told Mary, "[I]t took me all my time and strength just to keep up with [him]. I never had anything left over."[46] When she was asked after the war how her husband had managed to pack so much into his life, she said that he "never did anything he didn't want to do, and left someone else to clear up the mess."[47] When she ran out of fuel, she would flee. A favorite excuse was taking the "cure" for fatigue (exacerbated by low blood pressure) at any number of Continental spas. As life at Chartwell grew ever more exhausting so her absences grew longer and more frequent. Even when she was in Britain, she spent little time with her children. Winston demanded more of her attention than they did—and got it. As Mary recalled, "Father always came First, Second and Third."[48] One of Winston's more astute biographers explained that as Clementine "was primarily interested in Winston and so was Winston, their relationship to each other was always closer than with their five children."[49]

When she was at home, Clementine was in Mary's words a "mixture of tenderness and severity."[50] Sarah more bluntly called her "an authoritarian figure with whom you could not argue."[51] It certainly took courage to speak to their mother. The children, who when young were most of the time confined to a nursery wing away from the rest of the house, felt a constant need to be witty and clever in her presence, so as not to be boring. Winston would occasionally raise concerns about whether they should be wearing undershirts; Clementine appears to have left such details to others. She was also plainly incapable of the unself-conscious play that her husband occasionally delighted in. As Mary noted, although they "loved and revered her," Clementine's children did not find in her a "fun maker or a companion." There was, however, one occasion when Clementine created a magic for her family all of her own.

Every year she spent months planning Christmas so as to create a golden spectacle that would live on in her children's and grandchildren's fondest memories. Randolph came back from Eton; Jack and Goonie would arrive with their three children (known as the "Jagoons") and Nellie and Bertram Romilly with theirs (Esmond and his brother, Giles). The children would put on a play in the dining room; log fires danced in the fireplaces; holly, ivy, laurel and yew decorated the rooms; and if the weather obliged, Clementine would help the servants to make a snowman beforehand. In 1927, there was enough snow for the elder children to build an igloo and it was cold enough to skate on the lakes. Upstairs, under lock and key, was the "Genie's Cupboard" containing neatly wrapped presents ready for the big day. With the house packed to the rafters, glorious food on the table, a hundred real candles twinkling on the tree, glorious scents of pine and wax, and champagne in silver ice buckets, Clementine made Winston's fairy-tale vision of Chartwell come alive. "My grandmother," recalled Celia Sandys, "organized the best Christmases I have ever known."[52]

Christmas was the one time of the year when Clementine could bring all her family together with little risk of outside distraction. It was a rare private moment in the family life of a public man and so it *had* to be perfect. Her unstinting pains were also in part compensation for her prolonged absences and what she knew were her shortcomings as a mother over the year as a whole. Sarah and Mary drew closer to Clementine as they grew older, but Diana's prickly relationship with her mother lasted for the rest of her life.

Clementine took her eldest daughter with her to France in 1926 when she was seventeen, and they lunched together at Voisin in Paris as she had done at the same age with her own mother. It was one of the first times they had spent alone together, and Diana enjoyed the more relaxed atmosphere without her father around. But, suffering from puppy fat and painfully shy behind a talkative exterior, she could never quite live up to her mother's expectations. Clementine thought Diana plainer than her sisters and Diana developed a protective habit of walking apart from the others, head down and singing tunelessly. Following her birth in 1909, Winston had written to Clementine that their first child "ought to have some rare qualities both of mind & body," before presciently adding that "these do not always mean happiness or peace."[53] As it was, Diana was very naughty when young and certainly not outstanding at her London day school in Notting Hill or the boarding school she attended afterward. She grew up plagued by self-doubt, acutely emotional and always in search of an escape route from boisterous Churchill life. At one point she invested her hopes in a career on the stage—an idea that received little if any encouragement at home. Maybe Clementine saw too many of her own vulnerabilities in her daughter to warm to her or appreciate her compassionate qualities.

Diana also wanted for her father's affections. Although his first-born, she could never compete with Randolph. "Tender love to you my sweet one & to both those little kittens & especially that radiant Randolph," Winston had written to Clementine when Diana was just four. "I repent to have expressed a preference. But somehow he seems a more genial generous nature: while [Diana] is mysterious and self-conscious."[54]

The more independent Sarah had inherited some of her father's toughness and seemed better able to cope with being a Churchill. Funny, beautiful and at ease with the rich and famous around her, she was a "daddy's girl" and, some say, half in love with her father. She, like him, enjoyed holding an audience—in her case as an actress—but being a Churchill set her apart from other girls her age and she realized early on that she was a "loner."[55] Her problem would be how to find a man who could measure up to the titan who was her father.

The most problematic of all the young Churchills, though, was Randolph. Winston took the traditional view that children (and their discipline) were the responsibility of their mother. Worse, though undeniably loving, he was a dilettante parent. All the children adored helping him build brick walls and caring for his menagerie of animals. With Randolph alone, much to Clementine's consternation, Winston would use the front door of Chartwell for shooting practice, as can still be seen today. These brief spurts of paternal preferment were golden treats for his son, his approval godlike. But what Randolph needed was a constant father figure who would upbraid him when necessary. In place of boundaries, Winston proffered indulgence.

Randolph was unpopular at school and uncontrollable at home. Later on he would tell his first wife that his mother's dislike for him had been evident even in childhood, recalling an incident while boarding at Sandroyd when he was only nine years old. "My mother came down on a Saturday to take me out and slapped my face in front of the other boys," he said. "That was the moment I knew she hated me."[56] One theory is that Randolph, deprived of maternal love, spent the rest of his life seeking out an alternative mother figure. His cousin Anita Leslie attributed his varying behavior—he was capable of acts of great kindness as well as beastliness—to his "craving for affection."

Clementine's already difficult position as sole disciplinarian of a bumptious and insolent child was aggravated by his habit of running to Winston for an instant reprieve. The most draconian sanction imposed by his father was banishment from his presence. Even this was rarely enforced. Hence Clementine imposed what little sense of order she could through exhortation, sometimes patrolling the area outside Winston's study in person to ensure that all was quiet. It was a dispiriting task in a house overrun with high-spirited children—or as Winston put it, "all bunged up with brats."[57]

When Randolph started at Eton in 1924 Winston specifically asked for him to be spared corporal punishment, remembering his own sadistic treatment at school. It made no difference; the boy was regularly beaten for being "bloody awful all round." Winston continued to disregard criticism of his precocious son from his teachers, and, worse still, he encouraged Randolph to ignore their frequent castigations. Randolph, as a teenager, refused to get out of bed in the mornings and stayed up unreasonably late at night. Winston compounded his indolence by treating his heir as an adult long before he had learned to behave like one. Having been put down and shut out by his own father all his early life, he actively encouraged his adolescent son to participate in dinner-table conversations with such eminent figures as Lloyd George and Lord Beaverbrook, as if he were their equals. To Clementine's horror, by the time Randolph was in his midteens Winston would raise his cigar to signal silence even from cabinet ministers so that his son could speak. She saw the damage being done and thought Randolph increasingly without self-restraint. For his part, Randolph observed the apparently contrasting views of his parents and decided to ignore his mother's killjoy preaching.

This is not to suggest that Winston was entirely blind as to how his son was developing. In April 1928 he expressed concern to Clementine about how forcefully sixteen-year-old Randolph had argued in favor of a "rabid" brand of agnosticism with a senior MP and more generally about his "brutal & sometimes repulsive" remarks.[58] Clementine tried to remain positive, but she could not dispel the idea that their son would remain "an anxiety" and that his conduct might later come between them.

Over time, as Randolph's antics extended well beyond the school playground, anxiety gave way to anger, even on Winston's part. When Bernard Baruch, an important American contact, came to Chartwell in the mid-1920s while Randolph was still a teenager, Winston recognized that his son's behavior was damaging the entire family. As Winston and his bespectacled guest were about to enter the dining room, Randolph started to play on the gramophone "Barney Google (with the Goo-Goo-Googly Eyes)," a hit tune inspired by an

American comic strip character. A livid Winston snatched the record from the turntable and smashed it to pieces on the floor.[59] But the occasional bout of rage combined with otherwise unqualified adoration was not effective parenting. Evelyn Waugh, who later became one of Randolph's drinking cronies, was damning in his assessment of Winston's inaction, dubbing him a "most unsuccessful father."[60]

With Clementine variously absent or devoted to Winston, the Churchill offspring saw little of either parent, even by the standards of British upper-class families of the period. Mary remembers becoming "aware that [their] parents' main interest and time were consumed by immensely important tasks" and that by comparison their children's needs were "trivial." Winston and Clementine were simply not the sort of parents who could be expected to show up at school events, and if on rare occasions their mother did attend, the children were "ecstatically grateful." Sarah remembered one school prize day when Clementine had, unusually, agreed to officiate, although sadly the school was unable to think of a single suitable prize that could be given to her daughter. "When my mother came . . . she looked so beautiful I was almost ashamed of her. She was not 'mum-shaped,' and she made what was referred to as a rather racy speech."[61] The event underlined the pressure the children felt to match up to Clementine's expectations, whether intellectually or physically— something Sarah was not alone in believing she failed to do: "I felt clumsy and awkward and wanted very much to be pretty," she later confessed.[62] Perhaps as a consequence Sarah was nearly expelled from school after developing what she herself called "certain rebellious instincts."[63]

Marigold's death had, at least, persuaded Clementine that she could no longer rely on cheap, inexperienced nannies to care for her children, and especially the young Mary. In 1927, she hired twenty-seven-year-old Maryott Whyte, an impoverished cousin known within the family as Moppet. Trained at the prestigious Norland Institute, which was known to train the very best nannies, she provided the steady and loving environment for Mary that her elder siblings had lacked. She took much of the load off Clementine and insulated

Mary from the pressures of being a celebrity's daughter. Clementine's critics claim she relinquished her parental duties at this point and that Moppet became a virtual foster mother, but the appointment most likely represented a well-meaning attempt not to repeat the failings of the past. "Moppet was a big, bundling woman who was terribly sweet," remembers Clarissa Churchill. "She was an ideal person to be brought up by."[64]

Clementine herself had enjoyed no such loving stability as a child. Lady Blanche had not always been kind to her, and when her mother started drinking in later life there were times when she was outright "malicious." She had scarcely provided Clementine with a mothering role model. True, the life of a woman on her own was far from easy in those days, and Lady Blanche had been disappointed by so much. Yet she had never made much effort to conceal the fact that Clementine remained too fastidious for her tastes. Then, in March 1925, came news that seventy-seven-year-old Lady Blanche was dying and that she needed her daughter in Dieppe by her side. Clementine loathed the town—not only did she blame its casino for luring her family into penury and confining her brother, Bill, to an early grave in the cemetery up on the hill, she also felt haunted by Kitty's death from typhoid fever all those years ago. But of course she had to go.

As Clementine nursed her mother through the struggles of her last days, Winston's reaction was to send his wife an eloquent, if perhaps overindulgent, tribute (as well as a rare acknowledgment that his children were not pure Churchill): "When I think of all the courage & tenacity & self denial that she showed," he wrote from 11 Downing Street, "I feel what a true mother . . . she proved herself, & I am more glad & proud to think her blood flows in the veins of our children."[65] By contrast, on paper at least, Clementine was matter-of-fact, outlining holiday plans one day, describing Lady Blanche's "agonising struggle" a couple of days later. Death in the end came quickly, she wrote to Winston in a brief note, enclosing instructions for Moppet to send her some black clothes.

She did not mention grief in her letters, nor indeed her feelings as to whether Lady Blanche really had been a model of self-denial or a "true mother." But, shopping in the Brompton Road in London a few days after the funeral, an evidently distracted Clementine was hit by a bus. She took a taxi home without assistance, but her doctor prescribed her six weeks' rest in Venice to recover. Her physical wounds were the least of it; emotions were running high and she desperately wanted Winston to make the effort to be with her. Although a year later he was to permit himself a ten-week stretch away from the office (to finish a book and take a long Mediterranean holiday), now he pleaded expense and things to do as justification for staying behind. He also claimed, "Every day away from Chartwell is a day wasted."

That was a sentiment she simply could not share. Indeed, theirs was now a marriage in which they disagreed on a great deal, including politics, holidays, gambling and even their own son.

CHAPTER EIGHT

Temptation and Redemption

1929–39

As the results flowed into 10 Downing Street on the evening of May 30, 1929, Winston was in a terrifying rage. He swore profusely as he sipped his whisky. His head lowered, like a bull's before a charge, his face flushed to crimson, he felt his chance had come and he had blown it. Once a hope for the future, he was now a disappointment from the past.

This was the so-called flapper election—for the first time, women were allowed to vote on the same basis as men. Clementine, Diana and Randolph had helped Winston to fight and hold his Epping seat—albeit with a severely reduced majority. But his record as chancellor was in no small part to blame for the drubbing being delivered to Stanley Baldwin's Conservative government in the country as a whole. Within days, the Labour Party under Ramsay MacDonald would form its second administration. When the Labour cabinet then split in 1931 over its response to the Great Depression, Baldwin would lead the Tories into a national government with the embattled MacDonald. By 1935, he would even be restored to Downing Street as prime minister. But unlike after the Dardanelles disaster, or the loss of his seat in Dundee, any remaining hopes of a way back for Winston gradually faded. He was to be out of office completely, and miserable about it, for a decade—the period frequently referred to as his "wilderness years." During this lengthy "Siberian exile" he relied on Clementine to comfort him and stand by him no matter what; the effort would test their marriage to the breaking point.

Winston had lost favor with the people as well as with his party. His gold standard decision in 1925 had been blamed for the economic slump of the late 1920s (he himself came to regard it as the greatest mistake of his career) and his confrontational handling of the Great Strike of 1926 had made him look coldhearted and trigger-happy. Ministerial colleagues, tired of his egotistical interference in their own departments, had been only too keen to join the general criticism. Neville Chamberlain protested that working with Winston, "[y]ou never get a moment's rest!"[1] Overall, it was clear that his post at the Exchequer had not played to his strengths and the consequences had reinforced his reputation for poor judgment. The backbiting, meanwhile, did nothing to help reconcile Clementine to his return to the Conservative fold.

The election result also deprived the Churchills of their London home. At a time when others in their circle were settling into opulent middle age, Winston and Clementine were reduced once again to living out of suitcases in short-term lets, staying with friends or stints in hotels. Three years would elapse before their finances were sufficiently robust to allow them to buy another place in the capital. Even then, 11 Morpeth Mansions, occupying the upper two floors of a red-brick mansion block close to Westminster Cathedral, was certainly not the grand London villa they might once have expected. The study and kitchen were tiny, the spiral staircase narrow, and at the time flats were generally seen as rather lower-class. But the views over the Palace of Westminster offered some compensation, and Clementine transformed the place with her usual magic.

Even while at the Treasury, Winston had continued to write books at a prodigious rate to bring in extra money, sometimes churning out two thousand words a day during the parliamentary recess. Now his output increased still further in an attempt to plug the £5,000-a-year hole left by the loss of the chancellor's salary. His advances and serialization payments, plus the proceeds from the sale of American publishing rights, amounted to a handsome sum, giving him the unusual and welcome feeling of a cushion of wealth—at least until the Wall Street crash in October 1929. Winston was on a three-month American lecture tour at the time and in New York he witnessed a ruined investor throw himself to his death from the fifteenth floor. Without Clementine's knowledge, Winston had been using his own funds (and borrowing more) to speculate heavily in American stocks and lost £10,000 (over half a million pounds in today's money). Although he tried to keep the bad news from her as long as he could, when he arrived back at Waterloo station on November 5 he buckled, confessing all before they had even left the platform.

By the end of that year, they were on the edge of bankruptcy. Only Winston's monumental day-and-night productivity as a writer kept the creditors at bay. With no money to pay for heating or servants, Chartwell had to be mothballed for the winter, while Mary (the only child still living at home as Diana was attending finishing school in Paris before going on to the Royal Academy of Dramatic Art in London, Sarah was at boarding school and Randolph was studying at Christ Church, Oxford) was moved into a butler's cottage with Moppet. Even holidays were canceled. When Winston attempted to boost the family coffers with another US speaking tour toward the end of 1931, Clementine made sure to accompany him. The money should have made good his Wall Street losses—£10,000 had been promised for forty bookings—but after delivering just one lecture in New York, he was knocked down late one evening by a taxi on Fifth Avenue and rushed to Lenox Hill Hospital with frightening head, chest and thigh injuries. Clementine was summoned so quickly from her room at the Waldorf Astoria Towers that she forgot to put on her shoes. She stayed at his bedside overnight until he was out of danger, but the tour had to be postponed.

Their parlous financial state allowed little time for convalescence, however. Winston had to write an article about his injuries for the *Daily Mail* to cover his medical costs, and within a few weeks he had pushed himself back to work to deliver at least some of the lectures. News of their latest misfortune traveled home, and as would happen so often in their lives, wealthy admirers clubbed together to help them. When Winston arrived back at Paddington station in March 1932 (Clementine had traveled on ahead), there was a gleaming new

Daimler waiting for him by the platform, a gift from 140 disparate benefactors including Charlie Chaplin, the Prince of Wales and his former arch-critic John Maynard Keynes. It was a magnificent gesture, but not one that would pay the bills.

These years marked the beginning of a long period of brittle health for Clementine. In the immediate aftermath of the 1929 defeat a tonsil infection led to a serious case of blood poisoning and she was sent to Preston Deanery Hall nursing home at Northampton, where a near-starvation "curative" regimen caused her to lose six pounds in five days and drop to 120 pounds. Unsurprisingly she felt "giddy & prickly" and one day, after a visitor left, she panicked, thinking she was about to have a "fainting fit" or even a heart attack. Although she pleaded with Winston to come and "hold her paw," she conceded he was probably "too busy." In the absence of her husband, a medicinal brandy would have to suffice.

This illness was followed by bouts of mastoid disease, a potentially fatal infection of the air cells behind the ear. So severe was the pain at one point that her doctors were forced to operate twice in a day. Clementine rose to the challenge and "astonished" them with her courage. The drama drew the best out of Winston as well: he took the trouble to sit by her bedside, patiently reading her psalms. Clementine was so touched that he had spent time alone with her that she actually welcomed her illness, telling him, "[I]t has brought you so close to me . . . you are always deep in my heart and now your tenderness has unlocked it."[2]

He was notably less attentive during her increasingly frequent bouts of nonspecific nervous exhaustion. Despite his much-hyped Black Dog, in truth he had no understanding of real depression, whereas at times Clementine's was acute—a condition someone would later describe as her "high metal fatigue." Few on the outside would guess but she would spend the rest of her life trying increasingly invasive and unorthodox methods of overcoming it. Even as a child, her niece Clarissa had thought her "neurotic." "Aunt Clementine was always going to bed instead of coming to lunch," she recalls. "Obviously living with Winston was quite a business; overall she must have been a tough cookie to take it . . . [But] she was always conscious of her health. It was accepted within the family that she was a hypochondriac and she was definitely hysterical, no question . . . Maybe she felt in some way inadequate, although Winston just doggedly went on when this happened and didn't pay much attention. True, I never saw her not completely self-controlled. But when people are trying to control themselves all the time in public, they find it too much and need to go to bed."[3] So frequently did Clementine absent herself from her guests that the painter William Nicholson (another Chartwell regular) took to sending her illustrated notes addressed to "Mrs Churchill in bed." The challenge of being married to Winston did not always command the respect it deserved.

Clementine devoted her whole life to her husband, yet as her future daughter-in-law, who would later live with them and come to know them both intimately, once calculated, she may have spent up to 80 percent of their marriage without him.[4] In part this was because Winston was often away working or pursuing his other interests. But as Pamela Digby Churchill later noted, the Churchills "expect their women to understand them totally. And they don't spend much time trying to understand their women . . ." Pamela would also observe a lack of "tenderness" on Winston's part, despite the pet names and their idiosyncratic "wow wow" greeting. "I think in his heart, he adored her, or I assumed it, but I don't think it ever occurred to him that she might need perhaps a little more."[5]

Winston does appear to have sensed that the demands of being married to him were in large part to blame for Clementine's nervous condition, but as his own doctor noted, he scrupulously avoided "anything depressing"—including visiting hospitals[6] or discussing his wife's seemingly intractable problems. Nor, as Clementine knew all too well, did he enjoy the company of any but the most optimistic people; he tolerated her frequent absences in search of a cure because there was a chance she might return in a better state of mind. There was no question of a change in him, however. Even out of power, Winston continued to thrive on ceaseless rush and bustle; he was miserable without it. His staff could stand the commotion for only so many years (three or four seems to have been the general limit) before they left, completely spent. But the option of resigning for a calmer life was not open to Clementine. Following his ejection from office he continued to take for granted her undivided attention and support, apparently oblivious to the extent of her growing detachment. She took to reciting out loud a couple of lines from a popular elegy reputedly written for an overworked governess:

> *Here lies a woman who always was tired,*
> *For she lived in a world where too much was required.*[7]

As well as politics, painting and writing, Winston devoted much time during these years to his "cronies." Clementine disapproved of many of these ever-present hangers-on, whom she likened to "dogs round a lamp-post."[8] Rather than scions of ancient noble families like himself, Winston was drawn to a collection of self-made buccaneers, of whom the most favored by him (and disliked by her) were known as the "Three Bs." Clementine had long since proved herself a better judge of character than her husband and she waged a constant battle to prevent these adventurers from taking advantage of him—or from excluding her. As her erstwhile rival Violet put it: "His cause was her cause, his enemies were her enemies, though (to her credit) his friends were not invariably her friends."[9]

One of the Bs, Brendan Bracken, was an unmarried loner who had cast off his own family back in Ireland. He would let himself into the Churchills' home and overnight on their sofas without warning, cut articles about Winston out of her scrapbook without permission and once promised to take an excited twelve-year-old Randolph to the zoo and then nonchalantly failed to turn up. She was furious when Bracken had the cheek to call her "Clemmie"[10]—a privilege she jealously reserved for the very few. She made her feelings clear in withering put-downs or icy stares that prompted another guest to brand her "the coldest woman [she] ever met."

Most of all Clementine took exception to the rumors that the mysterious Bracken was Winston's illegitimate son. Bracken fanned the flames by mischievously addressing Winston as "Father," and Winston in turn enjoyed the resulting sexual frisson otherwise so absent from his life. Her husband's delight in the ruse—and the fact that even her own children began to believe it—only deepened Clementine's dislike for Bracken. When she finally confronted her husband to come clean as to whether the red-haired "reprobate" really was his son, he teasingly replied: "I've looked the matter up and the dates don't coincide."

She was rarely wrong about people and seldom changed her mind, yet with Bracken she did. He was not, as she had feared, another charlatan, using his connection with Winston for his own gain. Beneath his brash exterior he had a warm and generous nature. During Winston's period as chancellor, Clementine had tried to exclude him from their lives because she thought him bad for Winston's image, but such was his undying fealty to her husband, and persistence, that by the early 1930s, her anti-Bracken "vendetta" had thawed.[11]

But she was never to change her view of F. E. Smith, who in 1919 had become Lord Birkenhead. Here was a man for whom excessive alcohol consumption amounted to a virility test and she dreaded the idea of his leading her husband—and later Randolph—astray. Winston, contrary to legend, was not a hard drinker by the standards of his day; in truth, he disliked any loss of control. The Johnnie Walker Red Label whisky placed by his side as soon as breakfast was over was heavily diluted and sipped so slowly it lasted until lunchtime. But as a man unusually prone to tears he relished reports of his drunkenness, which lent him an air of machismo. While Winston was indeed able, as he put it, to take "more out of alcohol" than it took out of him, Clementine was right to fret about the arrogant Birkenhead's influence over her son. Both Randolph and Birkenhead lacked Winston's self-restraint and would suffer equally for it. Yet Birkenhead—who spoke of an "intimacy" with Winston that had "a quality" almost "feminine in its caressing charm"[12]—was perhaps his greatest friend. When he died, from drink, in 1930, Winston broke down and spoke of feeling "so lonely."[13]

Clementine disliked Birkenhead but she was horrified most of all by the hold over Winston of the third B, the Canadian Lord Beaverbrook—born William Maxwell Aitken—a rapacious wheeler-dealer of uncertain loyalties and a shady past once described as 25 percent thug, 15 percent crook and the remainder genius and goodness of heart.[14] Winston accounted for his fixation with this latter-day Machiavelli by quipping, "Some take drugs, I take Max," but Clementine was appalled at the newspaper magnate's manipulative power games, and she almost always (and often correctly) vehemently disagreed with his political advice. She also abhorred his neglectful treatment of his long-suffering wife, Gladys, who died in 1927 aged just thirty-nine, and worried that the presence of his "close friend" Mrs. Norton would corrupt Diana's and Randolph's teenage minds. She set out to counter his sway wherever she could, in what became a prolonged contest for Winston's ear. If her husband was to be dining with Beaverbrook without her, it was not unknown for Clementine to escort Winston to the door pleading with him not to be taken in by that "microbe."[15] For his part, Beaverbrook appears to have regarded her dislike as a challenge, sometimes sending her fruit and flowers when she was ill, but at other times deliberately trying to outsmart her.

In 1932, Winston took a trip to Bavaria, where he toured the old battlefields trodden by his ancestor the first Duke of Marlborough (about whom he was writing a book). While there he was struck by displays of what he considered to be a distinctly unhealthy militarism. Although widely mocked on his return to Britain, even by his few remaining friends, he sounded warnings about "bands of sturdy Teutonic youths, marching through the streets and roads of Germany, with the light of desire in their eyes to suffer for the Fatherland."[16] From then on "Germany's card was marked in Churchill's mind" and he was soon viewed in Berlin as an "enemy of its 'rightful' progress as a major power."[17] When Adolf Hitler became German chancellor in January 1933, Winston was swift to denounce both the man and his "pitiless" ill treatment of minorities, who obviously included Jews, decrying the terrible dangers of the führer's grievances over Germany's treatment by the Treaty of Versailles. A year later he was predicting in the Commons that air power—which he called a "hellish invention"—would irrevocably alter the course of future wars and that therefore Britain needed to expand the RAF as a matter of the greatest urgency. He also informed the House of Commons of "terrible" news: "Germany is arming—she is rapidly arming—and no one will stop her."[18] His words fell largely on deaf ears. "I was disgusted by the D.M. [*Daily Mail*]'s boosting of Hitler,"[19] Winston wrote to Clementine in dismay in August 1934.

Such was his isolation, indeed, that MPs on both sides of the House would pointedly leave the chamber whenever Winston stood up to speak, considering his stream of warnings about Hitler tedious and absurd. The *Times* declared that his alarmist prophecies made even "Jeremiah appear an optimist." Supported by five MPs at most, he was lampooned by cartoonists, shouted down by students, and looked ill and beaten. Although determined to "bugger on regardless," he felt battered by the abuse from the evangelical voices of appeasement and found public appearances an ordeal. As part of the wall of mockery, there were even sniggering doubts about his virility, not helped by admissions such as: "The reason I can write so much is that I don't waste my essence in bed." Now coming up to sixty, he clearly appreciated the young, pretty secretaries who worked devotedly for him late into the night, but there was never a whisper of anything untoward. Certainly the once green-eyed Clementine no longer appeared perturbed by potential rivals; on one occasion, she invited his old love the actress Ethel Barrymore down to Chartwell to cheer him up.

Just how much Clementine shared Winston's concern about the Nazi peril in those early days is not clear. She made sure to keep abreast of the news, and cut out articles on events in Germany for Winston that she thought might be of use. When she was away, he wrote to her frequently about his concerns, and detailed new evidence in support of his case, but in the early thirties she rarely addressed the subject directly in her replies. In fact, in 1931 she suggested it would be folly ever to engage the Germans in war again, as the last time they had not really been defeated but merely "stifled by numbers."

Whatever her private thoughts on the German issue, in most other areas their marriage was turbulent. They were profoundly at odds over how to deal with what was now widely viewed as Randolph's "pathological" self-importance. Even Winston had finally recognized that his indulgence was spoiling his son, writing to him in 1929: "You appear to be leading a perfectly useless existence." Calling Randolph insolent and self-indulgent, he continued: "I have tried—perhaps prematurely—to add to our natural ties those of companionship & comradeship. But you . . . give nothing in return for the many privileges & favours you have hitherto received. I must therefore adopt a different attitude towards you for yr own good."[20]

Unfortunately, Winston's tougher "attitude" was short-lived and Randolph quickly reverted to his old sense of freewheeling entitlement. This became further inflated when, in June 1932, Winston threw a roast-duck-and-champagne twenty-first-birthday party for him at Claridge's. More than sixty titled and powerful men and their sons sat down to a dinner at which Lord Rothermere hailed Randolph as "Britain's Young Man of Destiny" and Winston spoke of handing on the "sacred lamp" of power. Randolph repaid his father's devotion by bedding other men's wives, appearing in the newspapers in drunken brawls and on one occasion throwing the half-blind Bracken's glasses into the sea out of jealousy.

Clementine rarely put pen to paper regarding her son at this time, but Mary recalled bitter rows and recriminations between her parents on the subject and a distinct chilliness in their relations. For the first time there were hints that their ever more regular separations might become permanent. Indeed, Pamela believed that the only subject that ever really came between Clementine and Winston was Randolph.

Nevertheless, the boy continued to worship his father. If Papa failed to indulge him quite as before, it was his distant mother he blamed. Randolph became notoriously misogynist, most pointedly in his attitude to women in politics. On one trip with Winston to the US, a female reporter from the *Toronto Star* quoted him as saying that he thought women "simply did not fit in" with British political life and that their presence caused a lamentable "lack of dignity."[21] No doubt Clementine felt even greater dismay when Winston began to seek Randolph's advice on his speeches—he was thrilled with his son's suggestion that he should be more "garrulous."[22]

Although Winston would now rebuke Randolph when he was rude to his mother, and send him from the room when he refused to apologize, his inclination was still to relent. He clung to the idea that he could salvage the relationship, whereas Clementine felt she had no option but to break any remnants of a bond between mother and son. "He was so badly behaved—Randolph would get possessed by the devil in drink—that Clemmie couldn't handle it anymore," recalls John Julius Norwich, a Churchill family friend. He believes to this day that she really did "hate" her son, and that he in turn held her in equally low regard. "I remember [Randolph's] passionate admiration for his father . . . He never mentioned his mother at all."[23]

The tragedy was that on the odd occasion they did spend time together away from Winston and Chartwell, Clementine and Randolph enjoyed each other's company. In October 1930, when he was just nineteen, Randolph dropped his studies at Oxford—against her advice—to take up an exciting invitation to give a lecture tour in the US. Word soon came back that he had met a young woman named Kay Halle, from Cleveland, Ohio, and was planning to marry her. Clementine hurriedly set out for New York in February 1931 to try to persuade him that he was too young to settle down. Given their history of antagonism, it was a risky strategy. She was to travel solo by luxury liner—which she exploited to the full by ordering manicures, pedicures, massages and dinner in bed. "Papa is amused & rather outraged at the idea of me going to America without him," she wrote to Randolph. "But I think I should prefer to go alone & not as the appendage of a distinguished man!"[24]

Upon reaching her son, Clementine was surprised by his warm

reception. They sat talking long into the night. "His joy at seeing me was really sweet & I felt much moved," she said. Away from the pressures of being Winston Churchill's heir, she saw her son in a new light: "[Randolph] is a darling. He has quite captivated me . . . & he seems to enjoy my company . . . It is quite like a honeymoon."[25] Not only did she successfully scotch his wedding plans, but she also spent six enthralling weeks with him touring the country. Randolph escorted his mother through the louche delights of Prohibition-era speakeasies as well as to the more formal charms of lunches with senators, ambassadors and members of the great political dynasties. They also swam in warm waters, played golf and took a look at the White House, if only from the outside. The US fashion for heavy makeup and obsession with face and figure was her sole disappointment: American women were in her view "clothes pegs & painted masks" who were lovely to look at but "inane & dull."[26]

Clementine and Winston had been known to be "hostile" to America as a result of President Coolidge's crushing announcement in 1928—when Winston had been in charge of the national purse strings as chancellor—that he would not forgive Britain's crippling debts from the Great War. Clementine had been hawkish, too, in her attitude to American ambitions to supplant Britain as a world power, advising Winston that it was "no use grovelling or even being civil" to the US.[27] She had railed about Coolidge's "coldness, smugness, self-sufficiency, boastfulness, Pharisaicalness & cant" and had even described Americans as "Swine"[28] who intended to "do [them] in." (It was a common belief among upper-class Britons of the time that Americans were somehow less civilized and less educated than themselves.) Now that Clementine had mingled so enjoyably in American society, her whole conception of the Land of the Free was dramatically altered. She found she loved the sights of Washington and the shopping in New York, and realized that many Americans were "extremely nice!"[29] She particularly relished attending a "wonderful club for women" called the American Women's Association, which introduced her to the novel concepts of networking and female leadership.

Sadly, when she and Randolph returned to life in England after this harmonious interlude, their relationship plummeted to new depths of distrust. Randolph successfully took up journalism, but his earnings failed to sustain his wanton lifestyle. He swanned around in a chauffeur-driven Bentley, lived in the best suite in the May Fair Hotel, acted obnoxiously in nightclubs and when he could not pay his bills ran back to his parents for money. To Clementine's horror, in 1934 Winston was, on one occasion alone, obliged to settle pressing gambling debts of £1,500, wiping out a tenth of his entire earnings for the year. He later confessed to feeling "overwhelmed with work"[30] trying to pay for it all, once drawing himself as a pig loaded down by a ten-ton weight.

Randolph's visits, usually marked by a request for yet another sizable check, would inevitably herald horrific rows. His cousin Peregrine Churchill recounted how family dinners at the time were not for the fainthearted: "All those overpowering egos!"[31] Sometimes Winston refused to see Randolph; more than once Clementine banned him from the house completely. Relations deteriorated to the point where Clementine began to fear her son. After a time, she instructed her staff *never* to leave her alone with him.

The early 1930s also highlighted the Churchills' parental shortcomings in preparing their elder daughters for adulthood. Diana had made her society debut in 1927, during the same season as her second cousin Diana Mitford. It was, of course, the latter who had taken London by storm and been pursued by dozens of bewitched young men. Both Diana Churchill and her parents had found the contrast with her namesake humiliating. It did not help that the Mitford girl hero-worshipped Clementine, whom she later confessed to having tried to emulate: "When people say Clementine was so cold, well, she was extremely kind to us as children and, to me particularly, wonderful."[32] Still worse was that even Randolph adored Diana Mitford; according to another cousin, Anita Leslie, her resemblance to his mother only added to his yearning. "She had the same beautiful features, and huge blue eyes that looked as if they had been carved out of sapphires."[33]

Perhaps Clementine had forgotten her own pain at being eclipsed by her vivacious sister Kitty, for she took little care to hide her disappointment from her daughter. Sarah recalled a painful visit to the dressmaker with her "beautiful and elegant" mother, during which Clementine had delivered "a near mortal blow" to the slightly plump Diana by remarking that Sarah was "so easy to dress."[34] The unspoken comparison was clear. On another occasion, Anita found Diana in tears, crying, "Mummy is horrid to me and I haven't been a success. I have sandy-coloured eyelashes."[35] Nor did her dreams of a career on the stage come to fruition. She found she had little real talent, and as there was already an actress called Diana Churchill she could not even trade on her name. By the time Sarah, with her ivory skin, green eyes and auburn tresses, was preparing for her society debut, Diana was neither working nor married; such a failure in an elder sister was considered "a terrible tragedy."[36]

Salvation appeared to arrive in the autumn of 1932, in the form of a proposal from handsome John Bailey, the thirty-two-year-old son of a South African mine owner. Winston ensured that the wedding, held on December 12 at St. Margaret's, Westminster, was suitably grand—so as to demonstrate that although he himself was down, the Churchill dynasty was by no means out. The king sent a blue enamel dressing-table set; Sunny, the Duke of Marlborough, lent the ballroom at his house in Carlton Terrace for the reception; the wedding night was spent at the Ritz. The trouble was that Bailey was in love with the romantic novelist and society beauty Barbara Cartland, but on discovering his "impossible" drinking, she had sensibly run a mile. At twenty-three, Diana had been in such a desperate rush to "escape" from home that she discovered her mistake much too late. The marriage broke down after just a year, another embarrassing failure. Diana's poor choice hardly helped to raise her in her mother's esteem.

Sarah's future was also uncertain. Upon coming out in 1933, she found the round of society balls excruciating—often escaping into the ladies' to play cards with her cousin Unity Mitford. Clementine disliked staying out late and comparing notes with gaggles of super-competitive mothers, but she thought it necessary. Sarah wanted to follow her sister Diana into acting. She was considered more suited to the craft but neither Clementine nor Winston was any happier at the thought. Despite her own thwarted ambition to go to university, Clementine could summon no empathy for either daughter's theatrical dreams, dismissing both girls as without "talent or even aptitude."[37] Yet Sarah had the inner steel Diana lacked. Her doggedness had long since earned her the family nickname of "Mule" and her hopes would not be so easily crushed.

In truth, having received so little parenting themselves, Clementine and Winston were struggling to find their way. Only Mary, still safely ensconced in the country in the capable care of Moppet, seemed to be growing up largely trouble free. Moppet sent her upstairs to do her homework every evening like clockwork and consequently Mary did better than expected at school. The very success of this arrangement, however, would itself become a source of anxiety for Clementine.

In December 1934, the wealthy Guinness heir Lord Moyne, one of Winston's former junior ministers at the Treasury, invited the Churchills on a four-month cruise to the East Indies. The aim was to try to capture a specimen of the giant lizard known as the Komodo dragon for the London Zoo. Too busy with politics and book writing, Winston decided not to take up the offer, but Clementine was determined to go. Her various "cures" had provided only temporary relief from the physical and emotional strains of her life, so an invitation to the palm-fringed southern oceans was opportune.

It was while sailing across these glittering seas on board Moyne's sumptuous motor yacht, *Rosaura*, that Clementine was thrown into the company of Terence Philip. He was tall, rich, suave, an authority on art and unburdened by driving ambition—unlike Winston, in fact, in almost every respect. He was also an entertaining gossip, seven years her junior, and he complimented her lavishly on her beauty and brains while seeking little in return. Clementine met him as she approached her fiftieth birthday and, excited by the attentions of such a man, fell in love.

Apart from the crew, for the first three weeks there was only one other couple aboard—Moyne's agreeable cousin Lee Guinness and his wife, Posy. Clementine and Philip were then alone for a few days before Moyne himself, an amusing *bon viveur*, and his married long-term mistress Vera Broughton, joined them in Singapore. Clementine was known to frown on adulterers and even to refuse to socialize with unmarried couples at all. On board the *Rosaura*, however, romance, sunshine and champagne soon swept her up onto a thrilling high, which made her forget such straitlaced strictures. The ever-growing gloom of European politics, Winston's obsession with his faltering career, and her children's troubles all rapidly retreated over the horizon. Her letters home became shorter and less frequent—hurried notes with only the odd tinge of regret. After years of isolation and anxiety, she had at last found companionship and a release from tension.

Two days after Christmas 1934 the family had waved her off from Victoria station. On her way by train to Messina, where she was to join the *Rosaura*, she had written to say how much she loved her "sweet and darling Winston," telling him not to be vexed with his vagabond Kat. "She has gone off to the jungle with her tail in the air, but she will return presently to her basket and curl down comfortably." Sunbathing on the scrubbed wooden decks of the *Rosaura* as it headed south in the early days of 1935, she was able to take stock of her life. After little more than a week, she wrote a letter that suggests she was now in pursuit of rather more than a Komodo dragon. "Oh my Darling, I'm thinking of you & how you have enriched my life," she began, before continuing in the past tense with "I have loved you very much but I wish I had been a more amusing wife to you."[38] She concluded wistfully, "[H]ow nice it would be if we were both young again." Winston replied that he would "always feel so overwhelmingly in [her] debt," before plucking her heartstrings with: "I hope &

pray I shall be able to make you happy & secure during my remaining years . . . & leave you in comfort when my race is run."³⁹

On a stopover in Madras in January Clementine was photographed dressed in a diaphanous white dress. She appears lean, glowing, relaxed and perhaps at her most beautiful, and stands almost
touching Philip's side despite the expanse of deck all around her.
They look for all the world like two young lovers. She had already
described to Winston, in rather breathless tones, her enjoyment at
frolicking with this other man in the swimming pool that Moyne
had had rigged up on deck. "We hang onto the sides & get beaten
about by the waves," she had written, "& when there is a respite we
turn the hose on to our faces & tummies."⁴⁰

Later, away from the other passengers, she went deep-sea fishing
with Philip in the turquoise waters of the subtropical Bay of Islands
off New Zealand. On board she noticed that the captain of their
launch had only one leg. " 'Bitten off by a shark?' I asked Terence in a
frightened whisper. 'Perhaps only the war' he whispered back—'Can
I ask him?' 'No, certainly not yet!' " When relating how they landed
a "lovely blue tunny" that slithered out of their hands, her tone became yet more familiar: "[W]e nearly fell over the edge with it. I
nearly cried and [the captain] clearly thought we were the most awful
muffs. I said I felt faint & wanted food. So we left the fishing grounds
for an hour & got into a little bay & had luncheon—But I felt so sick
I could only drink claret & suck some very strong peppermints."⁴¹

On other solo jaunts they boated up a river in Sumatra and mo-
tored to a deserted coral island for a picnic. "When we got back I
discovered that I had lost an ear-ring . . . I am lost without a fat pearl
in each ear & they are my only pair," she recounted. "So we went back
& Terence found it."⁴² She fell under the spell of Philip's admiration
over these blissful weeks, conceding, years later, even to her own
family, "[H]e made me like him."

Perhaps Moyne thought nothing of it. Philip, the London director
of Knoedler, the New York art dealers, had a reputation for passing
flirtations and was in any case thought not to be that interested in

women sexually. Or maybe their host merely enjoyed seeing Clementine so happy. There is no proof that anything physical took place between them during the cruise, but there was certainly no lack of opportunity, and Moyne had set a decadent tone by bringing along his mistress rather than his wife. Whether her relationship with Philip was adulterous or not, it seems that he was almost certainly not in love with her. Nevertheless, his open and ardent admiration shook Clementine to her core.

At first, seemingly oblivious to the threat, Winston churned out lengthy typed bulletins about events at Chartwell or Randolph's latest antics. He confessed to feeling "unprotected" without his Kat and wrote that he had been "sometimes a little depressed about politics" and that he would have liked to have been "comforted" by her. But then she began to mention "Mr Philip"—soon he was just "Terence"—rather too often and too enthusiastically. She also wrote more explicitly than before. Early on in the cruise, she had railed against the "indecency" of a Jean Harlow film, but within weeks she was enthusing about the Balinese dedication to sex. Perhaps goaded by her account of their trip to the desert island, Winston sent to her next port of call, Batavia, the capital of Java, an expensive pair of new earrings for her birthday, some "really lovely 'twinklers'" she had long coveted. Gratifyingly, the gift elicited the response: "wow—I love it." The earring retrieved by Philip had been a cheap fake.

The children began to wonder about the drift in their mother's affections. Back in January Sarah had written: "DARLING DARLING Mummy. I imagine you . . . gaily chasing after butterflies and dragons with Mr Terence Phillips [sic]."[43] A month later she pleaded: "Don't forget to come home some time. Papa is miserable and frightfully naughty without you! Your children however are model in every way."[44] Finally Winston wrote that although he had not grudged her this "long excursion," as he called it, before declaring: "Now I do want you back." He was not displaying jealousy as such—he never did—but he was becoming a little impatient.

When she finally returned to him—and real life—on April 30, 1935, Clementine was a revitalized woman with a model's physique that she showed off at George V's Silver Jubilee celebrations a few days later. Of course she soon came crashing back down to earth. She discovered that Randolph, Mary and Sarah had all been ill; that Randolph's antics had become so acutely embarrassing they had elicited the sympathy of the prime minister (Baldwin had remarked to Winston on how "one's children are like a lot of live bombs. One never knows when they will go off, or in what direction"); and that Winston had spent more money on Chartwell, redecorating the drawing room, returfing the orchard and installing new bookshelves.

In short, nothing had changed—certainly not Winston nor his obsession with the Nazis. Hitler had recently announced that his air force was already as strong as Britain's—completely contradicting Baldwin's previous assertions to the contrary. Yet this vindication of Winston's position had done little to shake the general atmosphere of apathy and denial that clouded British foreign policy. In truth, the Luftwaffe was actually superior in strength and still rapidly growing. "How discreditable for the Government . . . to have misled Parliament upon a matter involving the safety of the country," Winston informed Clementine bitterly.[45]

Little wonder she was reluctant to let go of her life on the *Rosaura* altogether. Over the next two years Philip came to Chartwell to visit Clementine a number of times, and they may well have met elsewhere. But in the late thirties he seems abruptly to have moved away to work at the Wildenstein Gallery in New York, where he would die a few years later. Whatever the nature of their relationship, like many another sunlit holiday fling, it fizzled out under the gray skies of England. A coral-pink dove that she had brought back from Bali in a wicker cage also survived only a couple of years. She had it buried under the sundial in the kitchen garden at Chartwell with lines around the base from a poem by W. P. Ker:

> *It does not do to wander*
> *Too far from sober men,*
> *But there's an island yonder,*
> *I think of it again.*

• • •

It was "very nice" to be back, Clementine wrote to her former secretary Miss Street in August 1935, but she added, "Oh Dear I want to start out again very badly! Mr Pug is very sweet but now he says 'NO.'"[46] Her only real option was to throw herself back into family life. Tortured by what she saw as her failures with her elder offspring, she resolved to do better with her youngest child. Until her adolescence, Mary was much closer to Moppet—or Nana as she called her—than to Clementine and quite open about it. If Clementine suggested doing something, Mary's instinct was to consult beloved Nana first. Mama was beautiful and clever—but she was, in Mary's own words, more of a "deity" than a parent. In Clementine's absence, Moppet had performed the maternal role brilliantly, creating a stable home for Mary in which she had thrived. Now that Mary was fast growing up, time was running out for Clementine, and with painful regret, she knew it.

In 1935 Winston spent Christmas away from his family, on a luxurious stint in Morocco with Lord Rothermere and Lloyd George. Clementine seized the opportunity to spend more time alone with her youngest. Their skiing trip to Zürs, in Austria, which Mary remembered as a "great thrill," was their first proper holiday together. Indeed, it was the first occasion Mary, now thirteen, had spent "any period of time" with her mother without Nana.[47] Clementine's decision to take up skiing for the first time at the age of fifty was her way of reaching out to her daughter—and perhaps also a device to separate the girl from Moppet. "Clementine was jealous of Moppet," recalls her niece Clarissa, "because of her good relationship with Mary. But that was Clementine's fault. She wasn't much of a mother as you can imagine." There are reports of painful rows between the two women, with Clarissa confirming that Clementine's jealousy "made it an awful job for Moppet."[48]

She became a stylish if not especially speedy skier, but at least she now shared a hobby with Mary, and she made plenty of time for them to chat and read together in the evening. Only now did Mary come to know and understand her hitherto distant mother as a "person." The experiment was such a success that it was repeated the following winter, and the next. (Winston, disliking both snow and exercise, never joined them.) The more intimate relationship was not without its stresses, though. "I dreaded her displeasure, and the emotional, electric storms that could brew," wrote Mary later.

But the trips established a companionship between them that never really faltered. Thus Clementine's belated efforts with her last child were amply repaid—further highlighting her disappointments and differences with Diana, Randolph and Sarah. "She didn't mean to neglect the others—they were beautifully provided for," Mary once claimed, insisting their mother was not a bad parent. "But she didn't give to the others as she gave to me."[49]

While Clementine was away with Mary, Sarah informed her father that she was in love with an older Austrian-born comedian by the name of Vic Oliver. The pair had met in October 1935, when they had both been appearing in impresario C. B. Cochran's theatrical revue *Follow the Sun*. Before leaving for Zürs, Clementine had gone up to Manchester to see Sarah's first night and she was impressed by her twenty-year-old daughter's dancing, even if it was performed scantily clothed and was not exactly "respectable." Oliver was the show's principal star, although at the time he made little impression on Clementine. Despite the fact that he was eighteen years older, divorced and with a devoted mistress in New York, Sarah had set her heart on becoming his wife.

From the slopes, Clementine professed "horror" at the news, but she decided to leave the matter to Winston and even to extend her skiing trip for a couple of months after Mary returned home for school. In her absence, Winston ignored her appeals to him not to be "severe." All guns blazing, in February he summoned Oliver and Sarah to Morpeth Mansions, deliberately omitting to shake hands with a man he dismissed as "common as dirt," with a "horrible mouth and foul Austro-Yankee drawl." Winston told the comedian that, should he dare to persist with the engagement, he would issue "an immediate public statement" that would be "painful to them both."[50]

Oliver gave way, agreeing to Winston's terms of a year's separation before marrying. But her father's aggression—including addressing her "like a public meeting"—made the Mule all the more determined. "I think I have put her off," Winston claimed triumphantly to Diana. "On the contrary," replied the more perceptive Diana. "I think you have chased her away."

Sensing imminent disaster, Clementine finally returned from her holiday and tried a less confrontational, woman-to-woman approach. Over breakfast at Chartwell, at a time when she knew Winston would not be around, she promised Sarah her own flat in London to use with "total freedom," on the condition that she should give up Oliver. It was an offer that would have been unthinkable just a few months earlier and showed how Clementine's attitudes had relaxed since her adventures aboard the *Rosaura*. It also revealed how desperate she was not to lose her daughter. "Sarah was the closest to Mummy," Mary believed. "She understood her . . . there was a chemistry."[51]

The Churchills were not a family among whom sex had previously been discussed, so Sarah was shocked at what she saw as her mother's "immoral" suggestion—and at the way Clementine now speculated as to whether a man was "executive" (her new term for "good in bed").[52] Sarah was not in any case tempted by the parade of eligible young bachelors her mother hastily invited to Chartwell, executive or not. She was starstruck and was all the while secretly in constant contact with Oliver, even though he had left for the US. She appreciated her mother's conciliatory efforts, but her mind was made up.

In September 1936, with Winston safely out of the country in the south of France, Sarah bolted. Oliver had finally succumbed to her pleas for a lifeline by sending her a ticket to New York on the German liner SS *Bremen*. After withdrawing her savings, amounting to just £4, Sarah told the unsuspecting Clementine that she was going up to Morpeth Mansions for the night to visit her hairdresser. And she did go to the flat. But from there she took a cab to the boat train at Waterloo. Guilty at betraying her mother's trust, she handed a friend a letter to pass to Clementine in person after her departure. Alas, the so-called friend merely posted it and rushed to tip off the *Daily Ex-*

press. By the time Sarah reached the port in Southampton a newspaper photographer was waiting for her. The first Clementine knew of her daughter's whereabouts was when she saw the next morning's headline: MISS SARAH CHURCHILL ELOPES TO NEW YORK.

Sarah's letter, when it arrived, implored Clementine to "please make Papa understand" and asked her not to worry. Clementine was distraught and also certain that Winston would not be mollified. His efforts to stop the marriage reached new heights of paternal belligerence. Randolph was dispatched on the next steamer across the Atlantic, lawyers were instructed to erect legal barriers and private detectives were hired to dig up dirt on Oliver. An increasingly panicked Sarah phoned Clementine to appeal for her help, but Winston was unstoppable. In the melee, Oliver appeared ever more a refuge from the intensity of Churchill life. "I had needed to get away from my happy home for it wasn't a question of having one strong parent but," Sarah later recalled, "two great and strong parents."[53] She quickly and quietly married Oliver on Christmas Eve 1936 with only a lawyer and a cleaning lady as witnesses. Winston had waged an unsuccessful war against his daughter and the whole world had watched him fail.

It was far from the only humiliation of the mid-1930s. Take India and his opposition to the most gradual moves toward self-government. Since the late twenties Winston had devoted energy—and much of his remaining political capital—to an imperial position that even his natural sympathizers recognized was futile, and that served to exclude him from the MacDonald-Baldwin national government of 1931. Curiously, Clementine's instincts for Winston's best political interests failed her on this issue, as she appears largely to have agreed with him that it was essential to retain the British Raj, and even made one of her now-all-too-rare public speeches in support. The Churchills' stance cut them off not only from the Conservative front bench, but also from natural anti-appeasement allies such as the rising MPs Anthony Eden, Harold Macmillan and Alfred Duff Cooper. Duff Cooper later wrote that Winston's attempted blocking of dominion status for India was "the most unfortunate event that occurred between the two wars."[54] Certainly it was a position that would cost him dearly. For all his efforts, the Government of India Act, which introduced limited self-rule, passed into law in August 1935.

Clementine's judgment during the abdication crisis of 1936 put her back on the side of history. She and Winston fought like Kat and Pug over whether the new king, Edward VIII (George V having died in January), should be forced to renounce the throne if he were to marry his twice-divorced American mistress Wallis Simpson. Prime Minister Stanley Baldwin had bluntly informed the king that Mrs. Simpson would be unacceptable as queen, and that he would have to choose between her and his crown. Winston, though, displayed unwavering loyalty to Edward, who had personally turned to him for support. He rose to speak in the king's defense in a debate in the House of Commons in December 1936, begging the government not to take an "irrevocable step." Before he could utter more than a few words, however, he was "howled down" in shame.

It was—as Clementine had warned him—a near-career-ending misjudgment of the mood of the House of Commons. The normally supportive MP Robert Boothby compared it to a dog being sick on the carpet, and many thought Winston's die-hard championing of an unpopular monarch—even if rooted in the romantic ideals of the divine right of kings and the supremacy of love—had undermined his credibility forever. He had woefully misread the majority view (at least among the political classes) that the king should put duty first. Worse, just when there were signs that others were beginning to heed his warnings about the rise of Germany and the need to rearm, he had laid himself open to the damaging charge that he had exploited the whole saga to undermine Baldwin. Only after the constitutional crisis was resolved by the king's abdication a few days later did he finally see the error of his ways. At the coronation of King George VI in May of the following year, Winston turned to Clementine with tears in his eyes and said, "You were right: I now see the other one wouldn't have done."[55]

The saga had shaken even Clementine's faith that Winston would one day reach Number 10. Some thought his reason so flawed that there were once again suggestions that he might be suffering from a form of insanity—or late-stage syphilis, like his father. Clementine had endured so much, but this series of humiliations took her close to the breaking point. Exhausted, depressed, without hope for the future, she started planning her way out. She went to see her sister-in-law Goonie at her house in Regent's Park to say that she wanted a divorce from Winston.[56] "There might have been many times, I'm sure," recounted Pamela, "in the twenties and thirties when she could have left him and nobody would have blamed her." Goonie, however, wisely advised her to go abroad to reflect before she finally made up her mind.

It was only when Clementine left for Austria that Winston appears to have realized that he was in danger of losing his wife as well as his daughter. When Sarah returned to Britain, he invited her to a reconciliation lunch at Chartwell. "I suppose we must call him Vic," he wrote to Clementine, who had decided to stay away. Now civil but still unconvinced, Winston pronounced: "She has done what she liked, and now has to like what she has done." Few were surprised when the relationship with the unreliable Oliver quickly began to unravel. Its demise left Sarah deeply unhappy, though, and by the end of the decade she, Randolph and Diana (who had embarked on another unsatisfactory marriage in 1935) were all drinking heavily. But at least Winston's efforts to broker a peace with his daughter won him favor with his wife; she returned from Austria some time afterward a little pacified.

In October 1935 Mussolini had launched a brutal invasion of Abyssinia, but in Britain the Conservatives under Baldwin's leadership had won the following month's election on the pledge that there would be "no great armaments." It was thus unsurprising—to everyone but Winston—that as the most "belligerent" exponent of rapid rearmament he had again been excluded from the new government. Clementine now saw that his exile might prove propitious. It would, she argued, leave him untainted by the government's continuing blunders. "I really would not like you to serve under Baldwin," she told him from Zürs in January 1936, "unless he really gave you a great deal of power and you were able to inspire and vivify the Government."[57]

From this point on, Winston changed his tactics, seeking to broaden his appeal and win support from a wider spectrum of public opinion (and indeed his own wife). Instead of directing his fire at Labour and the Liberals and the die-hard appeasers in the Tory party, he sought to woo his onetime opponents, together with progressive Conservatives, by integrating their beloved League of Nations and its doctrine of "collective security" into his call for rearmament. This attempt to build an anti-Nazi coalition led Clementine to take a closer interest in Winston's campaign, so that from early 1936 onward whenever she went away for one of her cures she would make sure to have copies of Hansard (the official report of the proceedings of both houses of Parliament) sent out to her so she could keep close track of his speeches.

Events in Europe were in any case gathering pace. In March 1936, while Clementine was still in Zürs, Hitler again flagrantly defied the Treaty of Versailles by reoccupying the demilitarized zone of the Rhineland. Then, in July, nationalist elements of the Spanish army revolted against the left-wing Republican government and a bloody civil war broke out. Despite the fig-leaf policy of nonintervention championed by the British and French, the Soviets moved to prop up the republic while Hitler and Mussolini began supplying military aid to General Franco's rebels—a contravention that if anything Winston actually supported, as, in 1936 at least, he believed that it would be "better for the safety of all if the Communists" were "crushed."[58] By 1938, however, as the civil war dragged on, Winston radically changed his mind. He began to fear that a nationalist victory in Madrid would result in Spain's falling under the influence of Nazi Germany and that therefore Franco's fascists represented a real and growing threat to Britain. He even argued it was in the national interest to seek a once unthinkable alliance with Moscow (a stance that did much to raise his standing with Labour MPs).

LEFT: The young, timorous Clementine had few friends and was devoted to her dog, Carlo. She never got over his death under the wheels of a train. © *National Trust*

BELOW: Clementine with her adored elder sister Kitty (*seated*). Lady Blanche was brazen in her preference for the flamboyant and puckish Kitty; the more reserved Clementine was too timid for their mother's freewheeling tastes.

© *Churchill Archives Centre*

ABOVE: Before her marriage, Clementine was often seen in the tie-and-shirt-collar combination favored by suffragists. Once she married Winston, she spent many years trying to recruit him to the cause, with varying levels of success.

© *From the Collection of Lord Stanley of Alderley*

LEFT: Clementine arriving at St. Margaret's Church in Westminster for the "wedding of the year" on September 12, 1908. © *Mary Evans Picture Library*

LEFT: Clementine was considered to have the profile of a queen. She was hotly pursued by eligible young (and older) men, and broke off at least two engagements. © *Mary Evans Picture Library*

BELOW RIGHT: Winston and Clementine emerge from the church to huge crowds. Her dress was hailed as elegant and beautiful; his attire was deemed to lend him the air of a "glorified coachman." © *Mary Evans Picture Library*

BELOW: Nellie and Blanche Hozier wave the newlyweds off on their honeymoon. © *Mary Evans Picture Library*

ABOVE: Clementine and Winston endured cheers and jeers together. He was widely admired as First Lord of the Admiralty at the beginning of the First World War, but such popularity was not to last.

© *Mary Evans Picture Library*

LEFT: Clementine broke the mold for political wives by accompanying Winston to all-male rituals including watching army maneuvers, such as here at Aldershot in 1910. Her sense of style was noteworthy, and she would become widely admired for her dress sense.

© *Press Association Images*

RIGHT: Clementine was more athletic than her husband and an impressive tennis player. Here she is playing in Surbiton in May 1920.

© *Press Association Images*

LEFT: At the height of the Dardanelles debacle in 1915, Clementine was welcomed back to her old school by the headmistress, Beatrice Harris, who had imbued her with ideas of female independence. Clementine never forgot her encouragement and example.
© Berkhamsted School

ABOVE: Sir John Lavery painted this portrait of Clementine and her daughter Sarah in the spring of 1916, when Winston was away in the trenches. Many believe it captures her profound sadness at the time. © National Portrait Gallery, London

LEFT: Clementine with Marigold, her third daughter, who died in tragic circumstances in 1921 when only two years old.

© Mary Evans Picture Library

ABOVE: Winston, Clementine and Sarah watching the troops of the Brigade of Guards, January 22, 1919. Winston, although often an absent father, was natually warm and spontaneous with his children when they were young.

© Press Association Images

BELOW: Clementine (*far left in white*) visited the Pyramids on camel-back in 1921 with a party that included Winston (*on her left*), Gertrude Bell (*third from left*) and T. E. Lawrence (*fourth from left*). © *Churchill family*

ABOVE: Clementine with the suave art dealer Terence Philip on board the *Rosaura* in 1935. She was thrown into his company on her cruise to the South Seas with dramatic results. © *Churchill Archives Centre*

BELOW: "Fast" but not "wild," Pamela Digby (*third from left*) married Randolph (*center*) in October 1939. The ill-fated marriage launched her career as the twentieth century's most influential courtesan. © *Central Press/Getty Images*

LEFT: Clementine was very proud of her "soldiering" daughter Mary, who became her most trusted confidante. Here she was visiting a gun site with Mary and Winston on June 30, 1944.

© *Press Association Images*

RIGHT: Clementine's Aid to Russia Fund was perhaps her greatest work apart from Winston, of course. It set a new bar for charity fund-raising, raising astonishing sums of money from a cash-strapped nation. © *British Red Cross Museum and Archive*

LEFT: Tablecloth embroidered with names including the Duke of Gloucester, Lady Edwina Mountbatten, the Princess Royal and Clementine Churchill. The tablecloth was embroidered from signatures obtained at the Bring and Buy shop at Streatham Hill Congregational Church.

© *British Red Cross Museum and Archive*

ABOVE: Dressed in her Red Cross uniform, Clementine became a huge success on her 1945 tour of Russia. Stalin was said to resent the popular appeal of Churchill's wife. © *British Red Cross Museum and Archive*

ABOVE: Winston buying a flag for Clementine's Aid to Russia Fund. Such pictures were sometimes released to disguise the fact that he was actually on a secret mission overseas. © *IWM*

RIGHT: Winston described Clementine and her Aid to Russia Fund as the one bright spot in Anglo-Russian relations during the war. © *British Red Cross Museum and Archive*

ARE **YOU** HELPING RUSSIA?

SEND A DONATION TO
Mrs. Churchill's RED CROSS
"AID TO RUSSIA" ✠ FUND ✠

ABOVE: Clementine in 1943. She thought dressing up and a touch of glamour especially important in wartime and rarely failed to deliver.

© William Hustler and Georgina Hustler/National Portrait Gallery, London

RIGHT: Clementine understood that entertainment and a "lack of class feeling" were essential to raise morale during both world wars. Here she takes to the floor with a worker at an arms factory in the North of England in January 1942. © *Press Association Images*

BELOW: Clementine was known for her full-throated laugh, which was more raucous than Winston's quiet chuckle. Many thought her "cackle" rather contagious. Here she is laughing heartily on a visit to Chigwell, in Essex, during the election campaign shortly after VE Day. © *Press Association Images*

ABOVE: Two First Ladies of war: Eleanor Roosevelt was keen to drag Clementine into the limelight with her and here they are broadcasting together in Quebec in September 1944. Clementine admired Eleanor's easy, chatty style and public works, but Winston was not such a fan. © *Press Association Images*

ABOVE: Animals of all sorts played a major part in Churchill family life—not always to Clementine's liking. Here, however, she cuddles the first of two successive poodles named Rufus while taking an elegant afternoon tea with Winston at Chartwell. In an unusually intimate picture taken after he was ejected as prime minister in 1945—and before he returned to office in 1951—Winston looks rather cross and it seems Clementine was, as she often did at his low points, trying to cheer him up. © *William Sumits/The LIFE Picture Collection/Getty Images*

ABOVE: Clementine received the insignia of the Dame Grand Cross of the Order of the British Empire from the king at Buckingham Palace in July 1946. She is flanked by her daughters Mary on the left and Sarah on the right. © *Press Association Images*

BELOW: Relaxing in Hendaye, France, in 1945, shortly after VE Day. Holidays together were rare—they disagreed profoundly on companions and destination. On the left Clementine reads the papers with Mary. © *Mary Evans Picture Library*

LEFT: Clementine addresses the audience after receiving the Nobel Prize for Literature on behalf of her husband in December 1953. She learned to handle big events with aplomb.
© S&G Barratts/EMPICS Archive

BELOW: Clementine attends the premiere in Leicester Square, London, of Sarah's 1951 film *Wedding Bells*. Mary looks the picture of health on the right, but Diana's struggles are clearly taking their toll. © AP/Press Association Images

ABOVE: Clementine was a devoted if not exactly cozy grandmother. Here she is in November 1954 at the christening of Charlotte Clementine Soames, her granddaughter. Also pictured are Mary and Christopher Soames with their children, Nicholas, Emma and Jeremy, as well as Diana (*second from left*)—as godmother—and her husband, Duncan Sandys.

© S&G Barratts/EMPICS Archive

RIGHT: Eleanor was assiduous in maintaining her friendship with Clementine after the war. Here they chat during a reception in London in April 1959 to mark the publication of Eleanor's autobiography.

© Press Association Images

By the late 1930s the Spanish war was to prove a turning point more widely for public opinion in Britain. For many it demonstrated that bloodshed was almost certainly the only way to halt the spread of fascism beyond the German Reich, Italy and now the Iberian Peninsula. Groups of unlikely allies increasingly haunted by the idea that Britain could eventually suffer the same fate began converging on Chartwell, rallying to the only man seen as capable of stopping the madness of appeasement.

One of Winston's recruits—the defiantly odd Professor Frederick Lindemann (later Lord Cherwell)—started to provide much-needed scientific data for his speeches. Soon this professor of physics at Oxford University became one of the Churchills' most frequent visitors. Unlike that of the Three Bs his presence was welcomed by Clementine and she willingly accommodated his many idiosyncrasies—including a dietary regimen that consisted almost entirely of egg whites. In a house where she was so often ignored, he took the trouble to converse with her as well as her husband, despite his hostile attitude to most other women (including his own sister, with whom he was not on speaking terms). He also played tennis with Clementine—albeit insisting on wearing long shirtsleeves, even in hot weather, apparently with the aim of discouraging women from regarding him as a "sex object."

The "Prof" was just one member of what from the mid-1930s was fast becoming an alternative intelligence network devoted to gathering information on Hitler's plans. The emerging nerve center for British and European opposition to Nazism, Chartwell provided the venue for covert meetings between military officers, civil servants, journalists and industrialists, as well as refugee Germans and later Czechs and Austrians. Over time Clementine's "country basket" took on the bustle and tempo of a government department, as messengers arrived at all hours and the telephones continually rang. Once again, Winston had become a magnet for powerful and influential visitors and Clementine found herself welcoming and hosting them all—often in great secrecy. Gradually drawn into the frantic activity, she was universally trusted for her tact and discretion, although some of those who put themselves in danger to pass on information were concerned that Winston's volubility would lead *him* unwittingly to betray them. Part of her role was to ensure he remain appropriately discreet.

She also helped develop a network of informants on Germany's massive rearmament—recruiting a cousin, Shiela Grant Duff, a journalist who fed vital details back from Prague. It was serendipitous that another mole, Desmond Morton—head of the government's Industrial Intelligence Centre and reputedly the model for James Bond's "M"—lived just across the fields and could come and go easily without detection. Others—such as Ralph Wigram, who risked his Foreign Office career and even his liberty by passing secret files to Winston that revealed the shortfalls in Britain's defenses—were unable to take the strain of deception. After telling his wife in December 1936 that he felt a "failure" for not being able to goad the government into action, he mysteriously died at the age of forty-six, some believe by his own hand. Winston's reaction was that the unduly "sensitive" Wigram had taken his government's ineptitude "too much to heart."[59] It fell to Clementine to insist he pause a moment to comfort a brave man's grieving widow.

In May 1937, Baldwin retired as prime minister and was replaced by Neville Chamberlain, who quickly dashed Winston's hopes of office once again. Under Chamberlain's leadership, the division between supporters of appeasement, such as himself, and critics, such as Winston, became if anything even more personal and bitter. Most of the leading figures on either side had known each other for years and some were related. Many had attended the same schools (over a third of Tory MPs had been to Eton or Harrow) and universities. The rebels were socially shunned and scorned, and branded traitors to their government, class, party and even country. Wigram was not the only one to suffer; others also broke down under the strain of finding a room go silent every time they walked in.

Winston's pressing sense of mission turned many of his remaining followers and staff into devoted accomplices, their working hours often stretching to two or three in the morning. So unceasing were his demands that in the summer of 1936 his long-standing secretary Violet Pearman suffered a stroke brought on by overwork. Every moment of the day, including mealtimes, was now feverishly devoted to proving to a disbelieving nation the horrifying scale of the Nazi threat. Talk of fighter planes, bombers, troop movements, tank production, weapons development and the full-scale ruthlessness of the Third Reich dominated almost every waking minute. (The little time left over was spent churning out books and articles to pay the bills.) His endless gloomy prophecies of global cataclysm drove some of the less politically inclined guests to distraction. The painter William Nicholson, for instance, complained that it made him feel "quite sick." Clementine too sometimes felt overwhelmed, once exclaiming to her nephew Johnny in the car on her way up to London, "I can't stand it any longer."[60]

Other upper-class British families were still happily sending their daughters to Berlin to be "finished" in what they considered a more polished and disciplined culture than that of Paris. Society ladies even wore bracelets with swastika charms in tribute to the führer. Many admired how Hitler was putting a muscular pride back into a defeated country, creating a power that, in acting as a bulwark against the Communist hordes to the east, deserved to be hailed as Europe's savior. The stories of atrocities emerging from this civilized nation of art and music lovers were scarcely to be believed. Nancy Astor hosted frightfully smart pro-appeasement gatherings at her mansion, Cliveden, overlooking the Thames, and members of Clementine's own family—including her beloved niece Diana Mitford—were ardent admirers of the Nazis. Diana's marriage in October 1936 to her second husband, Sir Oswald Mosley, the leader of the British Union of Fascists, took place in Joseph Goebbels's drawing room in Berlin, with Hitler as guest of honor. Although Winston remained obstinately outspoken, as the decade wore on and life in Britain remained much the same, most people were, as the British historian Geoffrey Best has put it, "keener on hearing what Hitler said about peace than what Churchill said about war."[61] Part of the problem was the messenger himself: Winston had been wrong about so much else.

At this point his mood turned fatalistic. In February 1937 he told Clementine that money was so short that "no good offer" for Chartwell "should be refused" as, he pointed out, "our children are almost all flown, and my life is probably in its closing decade."[62] No such offer was forthcoming and their finances continued to worsen over the months that followed. When Clementine returned from another excursion to Zürs in the spring of 1938, she discovered that her sworn enemy Lord Beaverbrook had brought them still closer to the edge of financial ruin. In late March, the pro-appeasement press baron had canceled Winston's lucrative fortnightly column in the *London Evening Standard* (worth some £100,000 in today's money) when he called for Britain to rise "in its ancient vigour" against Germany's annexation of Austria, known as the *Anschluss*. Winston thus lost a crucial platform to warn his fellow countrymen about the Nazis (although he was soon taken on on similar terms by the *Daily Telegraph*). This blow may have been only temporary but it was compounded by news that another £12,000 had been wiped off the value of his US investments. He had no choice but to put Chartwell formally on the market. Still worse, its value had sunk to £20,000 in the 1938 recession, down from £30,000 the previous year, but even at this low price there were no takers.

In his frustration Winston was genuinely considering giving up on politics to dedicate himself to books and other moneymaking ventures. Then, at the eleventh hour, the Churchills—and Winston's political career—were saved by the striking generosity of an outsider. Sir Henry Strakosch, who had been briefed on the crisis by Brendan Bracken, stepped in to cover Winston's losses in the American markets. Strakosch, a committed anti-Nazi who was born in Austria and had become a naturalized Briton, had been providing Winston with detailed and authoritative information on German rearmament. Now he saved the Churchills' all-important base at Chartwell, which was withdrawn from the market, and made it possible for Winston to continue his vital work. (On his death in 1943, Strakosch left them a further £20,000.)

After the *Anschluss*, with the once-mighty Austria now part of the greater German Reich, Winston warned that Czechoslovakia would be next. And this time he was proved right: Hitler did not take long to demand control over those parts of the country with large German populations, stoking fears that war was now inevitable. The British fleet was mobilized and air-raid trenches were dug in London's parks. But on September 29, 1938, Neville Chamberlain packed his beloved umbrella and went to meet Hitler and Mussolini in Munich, in search of peace. He was comprehensively duped, effectively sacrificing Czechoslovakia to Hitler's demands in a naïve belief that by doing so he could avert war. When Chamberlain returned to Britain claiming that he had secured "peace with honor," public opinion was radically divided. The Munichois—as they became known— hailed him as a world hero, while the Churchills and their growing band of supporters saw his capitulation as a final act of foolish betrayal.

People the Churchills had entertained in their home now cut them in the street. Some say their isolation at this point was more personally challenging than when Britain was fighting alone in 1940; it was social suicide to be seen with a man widely branded a warmonger and party traitor. "The gloom after Munich was absolutely terrific," recalled Winston's nephew Johnny Churchill. "At Chartwell there were occasions just alone with him when the despondency was overwhelming."[63] Older and wearier than she had been when she faced the opprobrium heaped upon him during and after the Great War, Clementine felt the slights more deeply now. But since Munich she was becoming even more vehement than Winston in her views, haranguing even the mildest Chamberlain supporters for what she called "pussy foot" or pacifist views. She once rounded on the redoubtable Eva, the wife of Admiral Sir Roger Keyes, for expressing pro-government views over lunch at Chartwell, reducing her to tears.

In early October Winston rose to his feet in the Commons and delivered a spectacular denunciation of Chamberlain's efforts to maintain a "friendship" with Hitler despite all his "pitiless brutality." The speech nearly cost him his seat. Elements of his local party, with thoughts of a more malleable MP, began to plot against him. Some within the constituency—and many outside it—branded him unstable, or worse, an "agitator" who deserved to be shot or hanged. As Winston paced back and forth late into the night at Chartwell, desperately writing any number of articles and books to pay the bills, he watched helplessly as his country staggered blindly toward apocalypse while the Men of Munich went on ignoring or distorting the facts in the vain hope that Hitler could be placated with smiling inaction.

Exhausted by all this tension and emotion, Clementine, now fifty-three, was also nursing a painful broken toe. An invitation from Lord Moyne to cruise to the Caribbean, leaving England on November 25, seemed too good to refuse—even without Terence Philip, and despite the mounting international crisis. It might strike us as incredible, or even reckless, that she left at this point, but she was evidently deeply distracted—to the point that she forgot Winston's birthday, blaming the "lonely vast Atlantic" for causing her to lose track of the date.

Her state of mind clearly troubled him, and a couple of weeks later he wrote, "I send you telegrams frequently, but in yr answers you do not tell me what I want to know—How are you? . . . Have the rest & repose given you the means of recharging your batteries?" His letter is that of a man who has lost so much but hopes he can reel his one remaining treasure back to him. "Do you love me? I feel so interwoven with you that I follow your movement in my mind at every hour & in all circumstances . . . Darling do always cable every two or three days. Otherwise I get depressed—& anxious about you & yr health."[64]

The *Rosaura* was the same beautiful boat, but little else resembled Clementine's previous voyage. Lord Moyne was chairing a royal commission into social conditions prevailing in the West Indies and the purpose of the trip was investigation, not adventure or relaxation. As a result, Clementine witnessed the terrible deprivation of the British Empire's Caribbean holdings. Not only did it horrify her, it provoked her to give vent to her anger at what she saw as Tory complacency, and she admitted finding much in common with the Labour members of the royal commission who traveled with her. (The resulting report was so critical that Chamberlain deemed it impossible to publish.)

It was thus her sense of injustice rather than her longing for romance that was reawakened on this trip. But when she learned of the premature death of her hapless old fiancé Sidney Peel, she nevertheless found herself, to her own surprise, sobbing uncontrollably. She remembered his having "made [her] difficult arid life interesting"[65] but she also knew that a privileged existence of comparative indolence with him never would have been enough. Peel's death perversely brought home what life with Winston had given her.

In Jamaica, she told Winston that she was "thrilled" when raucously cheered as the "wife of the future prime minister of England."[66] The crowd hailed Winston as an antifascist scourge and even a savior. Such an unexpectedly enthusiastic reception after years of ridicule and scorn emboldened her. She repeatedly cast her thoughts back home to the dangers that lay ahead, asking Winston at one point whether war was really inevitable. Now she was the one pleading for *him* to write more often with all the news.

He missed her profoundly, writing at the time to his friend Lord Craigavon about "this time of trouble and misunderstanding in which [he felt] much alone."[67] He sent her detailed typed political bulletins marked "secret" on the growing fears for France and the Chamberlain government's woeful unpreparedness for war. She, in turn, became increasingly uneasy about just how isolated Winston must have been feeling in her absence. Even on board the *Rosaura* there were those who opposed his views and still clung to appeasement. When, after listening to a radio broadcast from England on January 24, 1939, Moyne's mistress Vera Broughton led attacks on Churchill for endangering Chamberlain's so-called peace, a revivified Clementine flounced out majestically, booking her passage on the first steamer home the very next day.

Just six weeks later, on March 15, Hitler's troops invaded the rump of Czechoslovakia, followed soon after on Good Friday by Mussolini's annexation of Albania. Now, at last, much of the press—even his old enemies at the *Daily Mail*—began to row in behind Winston, boisterously calling for him to be brought into the government. Around the same time he started to suspect that the Germans were genuinely out to assassinate him, so once again his security had to be stepped up and he reemployed his former bodyguard Walter Thompson. Her doubts and anxieties put to one side, however, Clementine was soon giving rousing speeches in his constituency—denouncing Hitler, calling for national unity and fearlessly blaming Chamberlain's government for the crisis engulfing Europe because of its failure to act in time. "At any rate," she informed a sizable crowd in Chigwell in July, "we have made up our minds to do our duty, whatever may befall!"[68]

CHAPTER NINE

A World of Accident and Storm

1939–40

Clementine sat bolt upright in the Strangers' Gallery, eyes fixed on her husband in the Commons Chamber below. For years the house had mocked Winston and his bellicose warnings about the Nazi threat. Now that his predictions had come true she saw how the house was finally uniting with him in a "temper for war." At dawn that fateful morning—September 1, 1939—Germany had attacked Poland with brutal force. As the news grew worse by the hour, Neville Chamberlain had finally made a somber and weary admission to Parliament: "The time has come when action rather than speech is required." MPs waited feverishly for Winston to intervene, but he left without saying a word.

The following day—a Saturday—Clementine was there again. Britain had at long last mobilized its forces; children were being evacuated from London, and anxious crowds were gathering in the streets. Some seven hundred miles to the east, the Wehrmacht was smashing the valiant but ill-equipped Polish army and laying waste to towns and villages. Britain was honor-bound by treaty to defend Poland. Yet still the glacial Chamberlain failed to make a move. He finally rose to his feet at 7:44 p.m., nearly forty hours after the start of the Polish invasion. His brief, almost nonchalant statement about the government's "somewhat difficult position" prompted such bedlam in the House of Commons that two distraught MPs actually vomited. Once again Winston walked out of the chamber without speaking.

At 10:30 that evening at Morpeth Mansions he and Clementine played host to a stream of grave-faced members of Parliament including Anthony Eden, Bob Boothby, Diana's second husband, Duncan Sandys, Alfred Duff Cooper and Brendan Bracken. Duff Cooper noticed how all those present were in a state of "bewildered rage" but also that Clementine was "more violent in her denunciation of the Prime Minister even than Winston."[1] Chamberlain had led them all to believe he *was* finally going to take a stand against Hitler, but still no word had come and it was now clear that he was once more backtracking on his pledge. As rain pummeled the sixth-floor windows and thunder crashed angrily around the Westminster rooftops, the assembled men begged Winston to take a lead. At last he sat down to write, bluntly warning Chamberlain of the "injury" done to the "spirit of national unity by the apparent weakening of [Britain's] resolve." Then a number of the MPs walked through the storm to Downing Street to deliver the letter in person.

By daybreak the skies had cleared and the air had cooled. Now finally the prime minister issued an ultimatum to Germany to halt its hostilities against Poland within two hours. As he famously broadcast soon afterward, "no such undertaking" was received. At eleven a.m. on September 3, 1939, Britain declared war on Germany and that same day France, Australia, India and New Zealand followed suit.

After listening to Chamberlain on the radio Clementine joined Winston on their roof terrace at Morpeth Mansions. As they watched the first blimps rising slowly over the roofs and spires of London, they thought of the horrors to come. Yet they were far from downcast. Yesterday's finished man today stood at the threshold of a new beginning, and as Winston told a Commons sitting that afternoon the prospect of the "call of honour" thrilled his "being."[2] He noted privately that Clementine was equally "braced" for whatever the future held.

Within minutes of Chamberlain's announcement, the wailing of the first air-raid siren began outside their flat. Joking about German "promptitude and precision," Clementine grabbed a bottle of brandy and "other appropriate medical comforts"[3] before heading down the street with Winston to the makeshift shelter. A German refugee, sensing he would not be welcomed by the jocular crowd, hovered anxiously on the pavement outside. Clementine insisted he should come in[4]—although it soon transpired it was a false alarm.

Winston's newfound status as visionary man of action was such that Chamberlain could not possibly exclude him from the newly formed War Cabinet. Later that day the prime minister summoned him to Downing Street and, while Clementine waited in the car outside, appointed him first lord of the Admiralty—a politically pragmatic decision (not one of the great offices of state but important nonetheless) that seems to have surprised Winston as much as his colleagues. He reported to his old desk at six that evening, and orders instantly came thick and fast—radar was to be fitted to naval ships, merchant ships were to be armed, the Prof was to run a new statistical department. Winston himself set about a quick-fire tour of naval bases, accompanied by Clementine as in the previous war. It was an early indication of how they would work during the years ahead.

Back in London Clementine immediately set about bringing together Winston's supporters—around a dining table, of course. The day after he took office, she arranged a lunch for twenty-four. Alas, Winston had to rush off to deal with a crisis and the meal was abandoned after ten minutes. So began a life with "less schedule than a forest fire and less peace than a hurricane," in the words of their bodyguard Walter Thompson. He confessed to wondering "a thousand times" how Clementine could "endure the almost unvarying smash-up" of all her plans. Never would there be "one meal without a phone call; even one good-morning kiss not witnessed by waiting courtiers. The mere matter of menus [was] the most awful madness! But Mrs Churchill never showed that she was troubled."[5]

And so, for the second time, Winston Churchill was galvanizing the Admiralty for war with his wife at his side. He worked up to sixteen hours a day, seven days a week, and was soon immersed in every detail of naval operations. He also expected his department to function around the clock—a shock for many senior Whitehall staff, who were unaccustomed to starting at their desks before eleven a.m. Unfortunately, only a fraction of Winston's fizzing energy would be put to good use. Although war had been declared, Downing Street vetoed most of his more audacious plans lest they antagonize the Germans. Some within the government were still intent on finding a peaceful solution. Winston was adamant that the navy under his command should ruthlessly hunt down German submarines and battleships, but when he ordered their sinking—"not without relish"— many in the government felt ill at ease. The torpor of appeasement still hung over Whitehall.

It was a virus from which Winston's Admiralty was free, but his stock suffered when Britain's early naval engagements failed to go his way. The sinking on October 14, 1939, of the old battleship HMS *Royal Oak*, while anchored at the navy's chief base, Scapa Flow, in the Orkney Islands, cost 833 lives. It also handed the Nazis a public relations coup by demonstrating that even supposedly "impregnable" harbors were vulnerable to U-boats. Over the course of the next month, 60,000 tons of British shipping were sunk by magnetic mines alone. Billboards may have proclaimed, "Talk Victory," but Clementine wrote to Nellie on September 20, 1939, that the news was "grim beyond words," saying "One must fortify oneself by remembering that whereas the Germans are (we hope) at their peak, we have only just begun."[16] Fortunately the evening of December 17 brought better tidings, with the scuttling of the German pocket battleship *Admiral Graf Spee* off the River Plate estuary in South America following a ferocious sea battle with three British cruisers.

Yet despite this mixed record, many now believed that Winston's fanatical drive made him the only politician capable of leading Britain through the darkness of another war to victory. Crucially, word of his prescience in peacetime and exuberant determination in war had reached the White House and on September 11, the US president Franklin D. Roosevelt had cabled him at Morpeth Mansions asking to be kept "in touch personally" about events. In doing so, he broke all the normal protocols, bypassing the prime minister, the Foreign Office and even his own ambassador.

In public President Roosevelt was denying that he had any intention of sending Americans to fight foreign wars, but in private he had now established a direct connection to the one man in Europe he thought capable of resisting Hitler. The beginnings of this relationship were not auspicious. Winston had snubbed Roosevelt at that London dinner in 1918 and was known across the Atlantic both as "hostile" to America (from his time as chancellor in the 1920s) and as a "drunken sot." On the Churchills' side, Randolph had declared himself "anti FDR" after meeting the president in 1936 during Roosevelt's campaign for a second term. Randolph had been invited to tea at Hyde Park, the Roosevelts' estate in upstate New York, when he went over to try to save Sarah from Vic Oliver. He had reported back that the American could not match Lloyd George for magnetism or charm. Now, of course, such equivocation would need to be put firmly in the past.

Clementine masterminded the move from Morpeth Mansions into Winston's beloved Admiralty House. In this new age of wartime austerity, the Office of Works had converted the attics into a modest flat for the first lord's use, so she no longer needed to worry about the cost of running the staterooms. Clementine decided to keep the curtains with red and blue seahorses hung by Lady Diana Cooper when Duff had been at the Admiralty, but few other remnants of naval foppery survived. When Diana visited, she mourned the disappearance of her bed that "rose sixteen feet from a shoal of gold dolphins and tridents," its blue satin curtains held up by ropes. In its place Clementine had installed a monastic single bunk for Winston and she had covered the walls with battle charts in pastel shades (bright colors gave him headaches).[7]

Under her orders, the first lord's office was transformed into a no-nonsense modern command center. She arranged his desk at an angle so that he would not be distracted by views of the park, and made sure his chair was practical and uncushioned. But she also had two armchairs, upholstered in comforting red leather, positioned beside the coal-burning fire and placed a constantly replenished cookie tin and soda siphon for his whiskies on a nearby table. She did everything she could to ease her husband's burden—he was not to be bothered by domestic cares.

Winston's war had begun "from the first hour" with the sinking of the passenger liner SS *Athenia* by a German U-boat on the evening of September 3. It had become immediately obvious that the navy faced a monumental challenge in protecting British merchant shipping from marauding enemy submarines. Winston's days were long and arduous, but he made a point of joining Clementine—and their guests—for both lunch and dinner. He also kept her constantly informed. If news—good or bad—came in of a battle he would often rush over to tell her. She joined him on the quayside at Plymouth when victorious ships sailed in and she would accompany him to speak to the relatives of those who had lost their lives. It was her idea, when battle survivors were being honored, to set up a special enclosure on Horse Guards Parade for the families of the bereaved in order to show them respect and consideration. More than twenty years since she had last launched a ship, she was invited back to do the honors for the aircraft carrier *Indomitable*. A photograph of Clementine joyfully waving the vessel away became a favorite of Winston's and the inspiration for a portrait.

Winston's appointment as first lord paid £5,000 a year and even more important provided a defense against creditors, who were suddenly reluctant to be seen pursuing a figure so vital to the war. Moving into Admiralty House allowed the Churchills to sell Morpeth Mansions for much-needed cash. They were thus—for now at least—financially secure. The outbreak of hostilities had not only energized Clementine, it had liberated her from one of the constant strains of Winston's wilderness years.

Not that she was solely occupied with the ceremonial and the domestic: she threw herself into all aspects of the war effort and it visibly thrilled her. Clementine was "more beautiful now than in early life" and was as "fearless and indefatigable" as her husband, noted Lady Diana Cooper in March 1940. "She makes us all knit jerseys as thick as sheep's fleeces for which the minesweepers must bless her."[8] Clementine also raised money for those minesweepers (mainly civilian trawler crews whose boats had been commandeered and converted). The way she helped run Fulmer Chase maternity hospital for officers' wives in Buckinghamshire (where she made a point of visiting almost every expectant mother herself) was deemed "beyond praise" by a midwifery magazine.[9] Sadly her attempts to press Chartwell into service proved less successful. Initially she offered the house up for the use of evacuees, whereupon two mothers with seven children duly traveled down from London to take residence—only to leave after three weeks, having found the countryside boring. She then suggested it should be used as another maternity home or hospital, but the medics considered the house unappealing and impractical and turned her down. Eventually the main building was shut up completely; only Orchard Cottage was kept open for family use. Out of sight did not mean out of mind; her diary records as many as fifty visits to inspect for dampness during the war.

Conscious of the need to set an example to the nation, Clementine expected *all* members of the family to do their duty. Mary, just out of school, worked in a canteen and for the Red Cross, and so as to avoid creating an unserious impression she was, temporarily at least, forbidden to attend dances. Sarah continued acting for a while but was keen to distance herself from Oliver (he charged her with desertion in 1941 and they divorced at the end of the war). She joined the Women's Auxiliary Air Force (WAAF) and was assigned to the Photographic Interpretation Unit, where she became a "quick and versatile" analyst of aerial surveys at RAF Medmenham in Buckinghamshire, to the northwest of London. Only Diana, now the mother of two children (and, from 1943, a third) by her second husband, Duncan Sandys, struggled to find a significant role: she became an officer with the Women's Royal Navy Service (WRNS) but resigned her commission for "family reasons" (although later she became an air-raid warden). Diana never accompanied her father on his foreign travels, as Sarah and Mary later did. Both of his younger daughters carried out their duties as aides-de-camp with efficiency and aplomb—and in doing so influenced for the better Winston's views of women's capabilities.

Diana's meek domesticity held no interest for her father and was anathema to her mother, who could not abide the way Diana spoke more about her children, and even the idea of sending them to the safety of America, than about the war effort itself. Clementine believed the war came first; when she discovered one of Winston's great-nieces—Sally Churchill—was about to be evacuated to Canada, she personally ordered the girl's passport to be withheld and had an official stop her from boarding the boat train to Southampton. Her action provoked tears and reports in the national press, but like any modern spin doctor Clementine understood the need for all Churchills, no matter how young, to stay in the country and remain outwardly resolute. Diana had no option but to follow suit.

Meanwhile, Randolph had been spraying around marriage proposals to well-bred "gels" across London in his quest to father an heir in case he was killed in combat. Most recently he had been trying his luck with a Lady Mary Dunn, but upon receipt of a better offer she had fobbed him off on a friend from the country. "I've got a redheaded tart up my sleeve," she told another chum. "She will do for Randolph."[10] And indeed she did. Randolph invited the pony-loving Pamela, the eldest daughter of Lord and Lady Digby, to dinner at Quaglino's in St. James's and three days later asked for her hand in marriage. She was the ninth woman to whom he had proposed in the space of a fortnight, and the first to accept.

Nineteen-year-old Pamela found the prospect of marrying a Churchill irresistibly exciting. She had grown up in a manorial hall at Minterne in Dorset, where her childhood had been one of dull routine interrupted only by occasional visits from Americans whose different worldview fascinated her. Known as the "dairy maid," she was voluptuous, sexy, and wore high heels and tight skirts. Considered "fast" but not "wild," Pamela's "erogenous" manner and "eloquent listening" conquered men by the dozen.[11]

Winston immediately welcomed his prospective daughter-in-law, relishing her flirtatiousness. In turn, Pamela was intensely solicitous of him, soon calling him Papa, lighting his cigar, laughing at his jokes and playing his beloved bezique. He grew as fond of her as if she were his own daughter, one perhaps less complicated than Diana or Sarah, neither of whom warmed to this rival for their father's affections. Clementine would eventually draw Pamela into the bosom of the family but was at first "correct and reserved." In truth, she was fretting about the marriage, mindful of her son's capacity for destructiveness and his lack of money. Winston brushed her concerns aside, exclaiming to her: "Nonsense. All you need to be married are champagne, a box of cigars and a double bed."[12] As Randolph's regiment, the Fourth Hussars, might be posted abroad at any moment, the wedding was hastily arranged for October 4 at St. John's church, in Smith Square. Pamela wore a deep-blue coat trimmed with dyed fox fur and she placed a jaunty velvet beret with a quill over her auburn curls. The groom wore his uniform and as her biographer Christopher Ogden neatly put it: "Both looked plump. Pamela would become more attractive; Randolph less."[13]

As Clementine had feared, it was not a happy union. Pamela did her conjugal duty by quickly becoming pregnant; he failed miserably in his. He lost money they did not have by gambling with rich friends, drank more than ever and was frequently abusive. Pamela's disillusionment with her husband created a natural source of intimacy with his mother. The two women exchanged surprisingly personal details, leading Pamela to understand that lovemaking did not enter the Churchills' lives "a great deal." Her own sex life with Randolph also left much to be desired. "He was a womaniser, but in the sense of wanting to dominate women," Pamela later told her biographer. "When it came to sex, Randolph, like other Churchill men, did not seem all that interested."[14] He also snored and farted with gusto.

Drawing on her own handling of Winston whenever he had been "objectionable," Clementine counseled Pamela on how to deal with Randolph: "Darling, go away. Don't say where you're going. Just disappear. I . . . would go off to a hotel for three days and he wouldn't hear from me." She also seems to have sided with Pamela against her son—once telling Winston in front of her daughter-in-law, "Randolph is treating our Pamela very badly." Clementine "would have liked to have been closer to" Randolph, recalled Pamela, "but she was always scared, and with good reason, that he would embarrass his father."[15]

The first eight months of the war were eerily quiet. Church bells, ambulance sirens and car horns were banned in case they alarmed people. Initially the mood was buoyant, as collective fear, in the words of the British author Harold Nicholson, "changed into determination, the gloom of anticipation mettled into the gaiety of courage."[16] But then the expected "rain of bombs" failed to pour: Hitler was still busy farther east dividing up Poland's spoils with Stalin (under the terms of their recent nonaggression pact), and beyond a couple of botched attempts to bomb German warships, Britain had done little to deter him. In fact, during the early months of hostilities, British attempts to defend the Poles amounted to little more than dropping propaganda leaflets warning Germans that they did "not have the means to sustain protracted warfare."

By the end of 1939 early British grit had given way to a bewildered resentment. The enemy had yet to kill more than three soldiers, but the blackout imposed in Britain to protect from thus far hypothetical raids had already taken four thousand lives in accidents.[17] Moreover, millions had been uprooted from the cities to a countryside they often loathed, while the pets they were forced to leave behind had been put down and left to rot in the streets. Essentials from soap to sugar soared in price. Only the rich appeared conspicuously free of hardship and lived much as before. When they ran out of supplies at home, they moved into luxury hotels, which seemed able to procure almost anything for those able to pay. Even the weather was unjust. Persistent autumn rain turned into the coldest winter of the century; eight miles of the Thames froze solid at a time when only the wealthy had enough coal to keep warm.

Chamberlain's wartime Downing Street merely exacerbated

these feelings of division and inertia. It still ran, or rather dawdled at the leisurely pace of an upper-class London home, just as it had in peacetime. Even now, the seventy-one-year-old prime minister disliked being phoned after dinner or on weekends.[18] Although his staff were, for the first time, expected to be at their desks at what they considered to be the "disgustingly early hour" of nine thirty a.m., many days were still comparatively idle.[19] Senior officials remained convinced that real fighting could be avoided and shuddered at anything resembling a "war mentality."

Clementine was merciless in her criticism of Chamberlain's complacency. Shored up by a large Conservative majority in the Commons, the administration reminded her of the lassitude of the Asquith administration during the first years of the previous war. Winston, by contrast, was magnanimous; now that he had agreed to serve in Chamberlain's government he would brook no disparagement of his "chief." In this ability to leave rancor in the past he was remarkable; later in his life he would claim that the secret of his longevity was "carrying no hatreds."[20] In October 1939 he even invited Chamberlain and his "utterly vague"[21] wife, Anne (as the prime minister's then private secretary Jock Colville once described her), to an intimate dinner for four in the Admiralty House flat. Clementine's reaction is not recorded, but it is unlikely she responded well to the prime minister's habit of remarking on the weather in order to avoid discussing the situation in Europe.

The so-called phony war was overall a misnomer. The navy had already been heavily engaged, with huge losses of merchant ships; several army divisions had been sent to France; and the Royal Air Force was conducting reconnaissance flights over enemy territory. In any event the "phony" phase came to an abrupt end in the spring of 1940, when the Germans invaded Norway, who appealed to Britain for help. The ensuing naval and military expedition was, however, badly bungled. Yet Winston seemed bizarrely willing to shoulder more than his fair share of the blame on behalf of a leader who had for years tried to write him off as mad. At the time, Clementine worried that the Norwegian fiasco would bring Winston down just as the

Dardanelles had done. He himself considered his escape from censure a "marvel," later attributing his good fortune to the fact he had been proved right about so much else.[22]

On May 7, 1940, attention once again turned to the Commons, and a dramatic debate on whether, in the aftermath of its failure in Norway, the government was still fit to conduct the war. This time it was Anne Chamberlain who sat in the gallery. Dressed in a funereal black coat and hat, with a nosegay of violets, she looked "infinitely sad" as her husband was interrupted, ridiculed and bitterly criticized from all sides of the Commons. Perhaps she expected to witness Winston mount a coup there and then. But it was Leo Amery, a Conservative backbencher, who stood up and, echoing the words of Oliver Cromwell to the Long Parliament, roared at Chamberlain: "You have sat here too long for any good you have been doing. Depart, I say, and let us have done with you! In the name of God, GO!"

Although the government won the subsequent vote, it was clear from the thunderous cheers greeting Amery's speech that Chamberlain's Tory administration was fatally damaged. An emergency cross-party coalition would have to replace it, but the Labour leadership refused to serve under Chamberlain. He would indeed have to go—providing Winston with his chance at last. The foreign secretary, Lord Halifax, appeared, however, to be the leading contender and was the favorite of the king. So Winston played a waiting game and continued with what he called his "heavy business" at the Admiralty.

At this critical time Clementine received news that Nellie was in desperate need of her at her home in Herefordshire. Nellie's husband, Bertram, had died on May 6 and her son Giles, a *Daily Express* reporter, had been captured in Norway and taken prisoner by the Germans. Clementine felt painfully torn. It is all too clear that she would have preferred to stay in the thick of things with Winston and some historians have been critical of her for going to Nellie's aid. But she felt she had a duty to comfort her younger sister, and Winston himself was understanding. On May 8, she decided she must go.

Two days later the German army launched a brilliant and

"lightning-fast" offensive through Western Europe toward the channel, invading Holland, Belgium and then France. The invasion of Britain by what Winston called an "avalanche of steel and fire" could now be only a matter of weeks or even days away. Beaverbrook, once one of the staunchest appeasers, acknowledged many years later that "[Britain's] peril" at this point was "beyond comprehension." Such was the febrile atmosphere in Downing Street that to this day there is some dispute as to the exact sequence of events within Britain's seat of power. By Winston's own account, at least, as late as ten on the momentous morning of the tenth of May, Chamberlain was still determined to cling to office. Within the hour, however, even this most stubborn of men had finally conceded that he could not command the support necessary in such a crisis to carry on as head of a national government. At eleven, Winston later recalled that Chamberlain, still looking "cool and unruffled," summoned him and Halifax into Downing Street to announce his reluctant decision finally to stand down.

It was now a question of whom Chamberlain should advise the king to appoint as his rightful successor. A long, tense silence ensued, with Winston remaining uncharacteristically tight-lipped. At last, Halifax spoke only to rule himself out of the running, conceding that a war leader needed to be a member of the Commons. As Winston later wrote, it was now clear that the "duty" of saving his country had "fallen" to him.

Immediately afterward, he hurried to phone Clementine to tell her the news and she boarded the first train back to London. After a frantic afternoon dispatching battleships to positions off the Dutch coast from where they could open fire on the German invaders, Winston duly received his summons to attend the king at the palace. At the same time he heard that Clementine was "safely home," and he insisted on first dashing back to their quarters in the adjoining Admiralty House before making his way up the Mall. There, she was waiting excitedly for him in the drawing room, still wearing her hat. Her prediction had finally come true: at the age of sixty-five, Winston had been called on to serve the nation as its leader. Their true life's work together could now begin—and she would barely leave his side again until it was done.

In Washington, President Roosevelt told his cabinet that he "supposed Churchill was the best man England had, even if he was drunk half the time." For his part, Winston soon made clear to the British people, to Germany and to the US that appeasement was over. Britain was going to fight. "You ask what is our aim?" he declared to the Commons on May 13 as German forces plunged deeper into France. "I can answer in one word—victory. Victory at all costs."

This bulldog oratory was, of course, to become his greatest weapon. Even when he was still at the Admiralty, secretaries had bustled down the corridors, ferrying drafts of his speeches to Clementine—who would duly make suggestions, remedy omissions and point out political necessities. Significantly, together they agreed that, in order to rally people's spirits most effectively, he should stick to simple vocabulary. Now more than ever, the power of his speeches would be weakened if most listeners needed dictionaries to understand them.[23] Ordinary words—beaches, streets, finest hours, beginnings and ends—were to work extraordinary magic on Britain's morale during those early months. Later on, he made similar broadcasts to occupied Europe in French. Many of those who listened were inspired by these stirring messages from the free world, but few knew that Clementine coached Winston before he spoke. After he had delivered a speech, he would often turn to her and ask, "Was that all right?"

From day one Winston knew that American support was critical if Britain were to survive. A week after his father became prime minister, Randolph came into his bathroom one morning while Winston was shaving, just in time to hear him say, "I think I see my way through." Astonished at this display of optimism, Randolph asked him whether he thought that Britain really had a chance. "Of course we can beat them," Winston replied as he threw his Valet razor into the basin and swung around to emphasize his point. "I will drag America in."[24] But US public opinion remained largely isolationist—considering yet another European conflict across thousands of miles of ocean to be someone else's problem. Why should Americans spill their own blood to save a decadent Britain interested only in maintaining its empire? America's ambassador in London until October 1940, the pro-appeasement Joseph Kennedy, whipped up further anti-British sentiment by declaring to an audience in Boston, "[T]his is not our fight," and adding that in any case Britain was finished as a great democracy.

Clementine was worried that Winston remained surrounded by defeatists and appeasers at home, men who had done so much to belittle him in the past. Although he had immediately invited key Labour figures to join his government—including the party's leader Clement Attlee, who later became his deputy prime minister—his first ministerial lineup retained virtually every "guilty man," including Chamberlain himself. Churchill even kept the Tories' chief whip, David Margesson, who had earlier led a campaign to spy on him and other rebels with the aim of breaking them politically and emotionally. Once again Clementine struggled to comprehend her husband's gift for clemency—or perhaps she underestimated the precariousness of his position in those early days of his premiership. Her blood up, she targeted Margesson for one of her notorious dressings-down, and when Winston invited him for lunch, she pointedly refused to attend and went out for a walk instead.[25]

Soon, though, there was little doubt as to who was now in charge. Never before or since has a prime minister accrued such wide powers or exerted similar control over the operation of a conflict. Winston was not only the king's first minister but minister of defense as well—an accumulation of power made possible by the vagaries of Britain's lack of a written constitution plus the sheer force of his personality. "Thus . . . he became virtually a dictator," as one close observer put it.[26] And, like all dictators, Winston invoked fear. He terrified ministers, military commanders and officials by his sheer force of will; even by his family's account, his leadership style was "tyrannical." The same qualities of single-mindedness that made him the right man to take on Hitler were in danger of working against him. The Canadian prime minister Mackenzie King noted with alarm that "he cowed his colleagues . . . He had a way of stifling discussion when it was critical."[27]

Having observed Winston's mistakes during the Great War, Clementine understood the hazards of his tendency to browbeat opposition. She had warned him since before the Dardanelles disaster that a culture of passive acquiescence was potentially dangerous, and now she took it on herself to act as a corrective. One by one key staff were invited to take tea with her, alone—first at the Admiralty flat, where the Churchills continued to live for a month, and later in the White Drawing Room at Downing Street (which she used for her private retreat). Here she made them feel appreciated, giving them her undivided attention while sounding them out for signs of trouble. She "wanted honour and glory for Winston . . . and she was always, always fending off things that might be difficult for [him]," explained Pamela, who was now observing events from close quarters as she had moved in with them in Downing Street.[28]

One private session with a member of his "entourage" in mid-June 1940 took place against the backdrop of a critical moment of the war. France, Britain's only major ally, was on the point of capitulation, and German troops were already marching down the Champs-Élysées in Paris. The outnumbered British Expeditionary Force had retreated to Dunkirk, from where some 338,000 troops had been evacuated by the British and French navies between May 27 and June 4. Despite the miraculous rescue of many men against the odds, army commanders had been forced to leave behind, according to Winston's figures, 7,000 tons of ammunition, 90,000 rifles and 120,000 vehicles. The huge loss of matériel would take up to nine months to replace. Meanwhile, Germany was massing up to 2,500 bombers and fighters a few miles away across the channel; all that the RAF could muster were a comparatively meager 650 Spitfires and Hurricanes. Day after day the weather was glorious, but many were to look back on the days before the Battle of Britain as the most anxious period of the entire war. Nerves were so frayed, according to Mary, that it was difficult even to "breathe." Winston warned on June 18, "[T]he whole fury and might of the enemy must very soon be turned on us." Yet while he unified his country by painting an all-too-terrifying picture of the imminent perils of a Nazi invasion, he seemed oblivious to the dangers closer to home.

Clementine learned from the unnamed "devoted friend" she met in her drawing room that Winston risked, if not outright "rebellion" from his staff, then a dangerous and hostile "slave mentality." She tore up her first attempt at confronting him—his family knew it was essential to "tidy one's mind" before addressing Winston on something serious. But after further reflection, she felt she could wait no longer. On June 27—just two days after the devastating fall of France, Britain's only major ally—she took to paper again. "I hope you will forgive me if I tell you something that I feel you ought to know," she began. There was a "danger" of his being "disliked" because of his increasingly "rough, sarcastic and overbearing manner," which was so unpleasant that his private secretaries had taken to behaving like "schoolboys" enduring a teacher's beating before escaping as soon as they could "from his presence." Senior colleagues complained that Winston was so "contemptuous" of their ideas that few now dared to venture any, good or bad. "It is for you to give the orders and if they are bungled—except for the King, the Archbishop of Canterbury and the Speaker you can sack anyone and everyone," Clementine advised. "Therefore with this terrific power you must combine urbanity, kindness and if possible Olympic calm. Besides you won't get the best results by irascibility and rudeness. They *will* breed either dislike or a slave mentality (Rebellion in War time being out of the question!) . . . your loving, devoted and watchful Clemmie."[29]

No answer to her letter exists, but Winston did change. While his staff continued to find him on occasion impossible, his "ill-tempered phase," recalled his private secretary Jock Colville, was a "passing one."[30] He quickly learned the conciliatory power of small gestures, once laying his hand on the shoulder of another private secretary after a fraught few hours and saying, "I may seem very fierce, but I am fierce only with one man—Hitler."[31] Living above the shop in Downing Street, Clementine closely monitored his behavior. As Pamela observed, her intervention demonstrated to others "that she was an enormously important component in the whole thing . . . and a very important balance for him." Clementine was "rightly" convinced that "if anything happened to her, Winston might run amok."[32]

Colville, who had already worked for Chamberlain, was just twenty-five when he became Churchill's private secretary. He had dreaded serving under his new boss, with his reputation for boastfulness, recklessness, even instability. The arrival of his "myrmidons"— notably Bracken and the Prof—was equally feared. Yet over time Downing Street became an unusually cohesive if frenzied place to work and Clementine and Winston went to great lengths to treat Colville and others as if they were members of the family. Most of his staff became very fond of them both.

It was not that Winston became any less demanding. He summoned people from their baths with trivial questions and kept them so long they missed all hope of dinner, and despite religiously observing his own midafternoon nap, so that he could keep working until two or three in the morning, he expected his staff to stay on call even though they had worked right through. Colville found that of anyone he had ever known, Winston "was the least liable to be swayed by the views of even his most intimate counsellors."[33] But he now strove to make life entertaining and colorful when he could, and even remembered to show gratitude from time to time. His principal private secretary Eric Seal noted how he had "sobered down, become less violent, less wild, less impetuous."[34] Colville eventually decided that Winston was "lovable"—it was a remarkable turnaround.

It was also clear that there was an alternative authority to appeal to if difficult decisions needed to be made. In June 1940 Winston resolved to fly to France through rough weather to try to convince its leaders to continue fighting. Having exhausted all other avenues in their effort to persuade him it was too risky, the air staff petitioned Clementine. She listened and then asked: "Are the Air Force flying today?" They answered: "Yes, of course—on operations." She replied, "Well, isn't Winston going on an operation?" Her decision was final.[35]

She had, of course, always greatly feared Winston taking off in dangerous conditions—and he himself was no longer a fearless flyer. He had become strangely nervous in the air, disliking going through clouds in case "they contain[ed] mountains."[36] But whereas she had once tried to dissuade him, now she hid her terrors and focused on ensuring everything ran smoothly in his absence. Clementine chose her moments to intervene carefully—and was often present during sensitive discussions with military chiefs, particularly those taking place just before or during meals. Winston would sometimes become "difficult" and start stomping around the room, at which point Clementine might say: "Now, Winston, that's all right, the subject can be let rest for the moment. We are going to have luncheon." General Sir Frederick Pile, chief of Anti-Aircraft Command, witnessed her mediation skills on many such an occasion and recalled that "she bossed him—but in the most delightful way—with great affection and with the deepest understanding of his nature." "I was always amazed," he said, "that this great man could be led along like a sheep by her whenever she thought it necessary." General Pile attributed this quiescence to Winston's admiration of her many qualities, including her judgment and loyalty. "She [had] a first-class brain [and] everything she did was, above all, for his good."[37]

Despite these evident skills, it took Clementine longer than Winston to gain acceptance, let alone affection, in government circles. In 1940, Downing Street—like the rest of Whitehall—was run almost entirely by public-school-educated men with a certain narrow worldview. Few took kindly to the fact that Clementine was no ordinary, biddable political wife, but a force in her own right. She was certainly nothing like the quietly domestic Mrs. Chamberlain. Despite lacking the mandate of the ballot box, Clementine saw it as her duty to help her husband win the war in any way she could, and was often both opinionated and forceful as a result. After discussing "a good deal of politics" with her, the traditionally minded Colville dismissed her admittedly quite radical views with the assessment that they were as "ill-judged" as they were "decisive."[38] He thought it inappropriate for her to be, as he put it, "outspoken," and considered her—not wholly without cause—to be excessively partisan when it came to her husband's interests. In those days he was not unusual in regarding it "a waste of time and exasperating to talk to most women on serious subjects. Sex, the Arts and the Abstract seem[ed] to [him] the only topics to discuss" with them.[39]

It was not an attitude likely to endear him to Clementine, and yet Colville was regularly deployed to accompany her on constituency visits to Epping (on top of her many other duties during the war she acted as surrogate MP) and often made to chaperone her at official engagements. For his part, he seethed at what he saw as a gross indignity for a young but senior Downing Street aide. Eventually, ahead of a visit to Scotland in October 1940, he simply refused to carry out her instructions: "I object to acting as Mrs C.'s private secretary," he railed, choosing instead to delegate responsibility to the considerably more humble Grace Hamblin, the Churchills' long-term family retainer. In return he was treated to one of Clementine's notorious explosions, and firmly "put in his place." "Mrs Churchill was abusive," Colville complained in his diary of October 22, 1940. "She was furious and said I gave myself airs."

Colville was not alone in being slow to recognize the scale and importance of Clementine's unique role. It would take outsiders—notably Americans—to do that. Part of the problem was that Britain's largely unwritten constitution has never defined, or even recognized, the role of the prime minister's unelected spouse. Another was that there were so few women in Whitehall outside the secretarial pool, and virtually none with any real clout. For almost all the war, there were just two female ministers in the whole of government, both of junior rank (whereas in the US the female labor secretary, Frances Perkins, was one of the most powerful members of President Roosevelt's cabinet). Yet here was Clementine giving orders like a man—or worse, like a *senior* minister—and expecting to be treated as such. It was all rather revolutionary for Britain in 1940, even if nothing was known of it in the country at large. Pamela, who had no intention of playing the "ordinary little wife" either, noted that Clementine was "very strong-willed" and "stern." She was "an abnormal woman . . . [who] was very hard on herself, and she was hard on other people." She saw how Clementine was, as the coquettish Pamela put it, "not very feminine."[40]

Clementine recognized from the beginning that this was to be a war fought by men but that victory would depend on the endurance and strength of women. Millions would have to do jobs and act in ways that were "not very feminine." She, like many others, had discovered what she was capable of when called to action in the First World War, only to retreat back into the domestic bubble thereafter. Now, with Britain facing an even greater crisis, women were to be more vital than ever—a point she quickly made clear to Winston.

Not forgetting his earlier treatment at the hands of the suffragettes, he was initially unenthusiastic at the idea of women serving in auxiliary military roles, but Clementine persevered and he became one of the first to appreciate that the country could not win through the sacrifice of its menfolk alone. Even when still at the Admiralty in January 1940 he had delivered a speech in Manchester aimed at drafting a million women to work in the munition and aircraft factories. What she called "Women's Sense" would herald a new social order, in which for the first time mothers and wives would hand over their domestic and childcare duties to others to devote themselves to a national emergency. It had been a historic female call to arms, delivered by Winston but bearing Clementine's fingerprints: "Come then, let us to the task, to the battle, to the toil. Fill the armies, rule the air, pour out the munitions, strangle the U-boats, sweep the mines, plough the land, build the ships, guard the streets, succour the wounded, uplift the downcast, honour the brave . . . There is not a week nor a day, nor an hour to lose."[41]

Clementine took pains to set an example by taking on from July 1941 the highly hazardous work of a fire watcher, her name added to a rota of nighttime shifts. Perched on a prominent rooftop during air raids, surrounded by the deafening clatter of gunfire and choking on the stench of sulfur and gunpowder, she braved all the attendant dangers of being badly burned, cut by shrapnel, or worse. This followed a forthright note she sent to the home secretary—Labour's Herbert Morrison—in May 1941, in response to complaints that the fire-watching service was woefully undermanned. She urged him to ask all "middle-aged women (35–60)" of "independent means" living in the country to register for a few shifts in badly bombed cities like Manchester and Bristol. "I would be glad to have my name associated with the scheme," she added, to force home the point that he could not ignore her request.

Later, she would encourage Mary's decision to join the Auxiliary Territorial Service (ATS) in one of its new "mixed" antiaircraft batteries. To her credit, Mary, like many women, proved particularly adept at handling the intricate mechanisms of the guns and her prowess saw her rise rapidly to the equivalent rank of captain, at which point it was she, not a man, who issued the command "Fire!" During Mary's visits home Clementine reveled in camaraderie with her "soldiering" daughter. They would breakfast in bed together—side by side, trays on their laps, hair in curlers, often giggling like two schoolgirls.

Winston was soon to get his million women civilian workers—and then another million on top. A further half a million signed up for the three services—the WRNS, the WAAF and the ATS. The new American ambassador, Gil Winant, was deeply impressed by the contribution made by so many women. It was a phenomenon he had not expected when he arrived in March 1941 but one that helped convince him, against all the odds, that Britain really might survive.

Clementine was now intimately involved in the direction of the war. She frequently accompanied Winston on visits to garrisons and seaside town defenses. On the cloudless day of September 15, 1940, she descended fifty feet underground with him into the RAF fighter command center at Uxbridge and, in the dark of the Operations Room, watched the direction of what would prove to be the decisive confrontation over British skies. She was gripped by the huge map table before her on which twenty young officers were frantically tracking German bombers and their fighter plane escorts as they stormed over the coastline in massive herringbone formations. On the wall on the other side, red bulbs lit up one by one on a vast blackboard to indicate each RAF squadron as it took to the air for battle. The double-height room, which Winston compared to a theater, was rigid with tension, the "raid-plotters" almost overwhelmed by the reports flooding in of wave after wave of enemy aircraft. The Churchills glanced nervously at the red lights glowing on the other side of the room until Winston asked: "How many more planes have you?" Air Vice Marshal Keith Park, the straight-talking New Zealander in command, quietly replied: "I am putting in my last." The stakes could not have been higher. As the Spitfires and Hurricanes swooped into action above them, Britain's fate was truly in the hands of the famous "Few."

Finally, word came in that after ferocious fighting the depleted and scattered German planes were at last turning for home. Relieved, but as yet unsure of the outcome, the Churchills climbed back up the stairs, blinking as they emerged into the sunlight just as the all-clear was sounded. The tension had been such that on their arrival back at Chequers, the prime minister's country seat, Winston went straight to his room and slept for four hours. Only that evening were they informed that the RAF had won a critical victory. The Battle of Britain was over, but the real bombing campaign had only just started.

The part of supportive companion was Clementine's most visible role in those darkest of days, and its importance to Winston and his ability to conduct the war ought not to be underestimated. But when he had no need for her she used her time to exert an influence elsewhere, taking on causes and problems relating to almost the entire war effort. Winston was so absorbed with the military aspects of the conflict he had little time for the details of the domestic front. It was a gap that Clementine did her best to fill. Her privileged knowledge of the conflict, combined with her memories of the government's failings during the First World War, often helped her identify a need before the "professionals." In June 1940, with air raids starting sporadically outside London, she had dispatched an official note to Winston's principal private secretary requesting details on shelters for people whose homes had been bombed, welfare payments, hospital visits, compensation for injuries and activities to boost morale in hard-hit areas.[42] It showed remarkable foresight and practicality, as well as the compassion for "ordinary" citizens so lacking in 1914–18. Many of her concerns, including those about boosting morale, were acted upon.

Frequently seen smiling alongside her husband, Clementine became the human face of Winston's government and was looked to as someone who could get things done. Her mailbag ballooned, and through the correspondence she received she developed a keen feel for popular opinion—information that fed directly into Winston's speech making, public persona and government policy. The scion of a ducal dynasty relied on the granddaughter of an earl to take the common man's pulse. And yet she did it so effectively that, as Winston's doctor Lord Moran put it in his diaries: "Since 1940 we do not think of the PM as handicapped by living apart from the people. His countrymen have come to feel that he is saying what they would like to say for themselves if they knew how."[43]

Clementine knew that Winston lived his life in "blinkers," and by temperament and background was oblivious to the mind-set of the great majority. She also understood that his authority as a wartime prime minister depended on his popular support. So she sought to be his antennae; she acted as his social conscience as well as his advocate in chief. "From her childhood experiences Clementine never forgot what life was like for working people," explains Jane Portal (now Lady Williams), a onetime personal assistant to Winston and family friend. "She was in no way a snob; that was something very attractive about her. She helped Winston not to be a snob too."[44]

There could be no repeat of the loftiness displayed by Asquith in the last war; Winston's government had to be seen as a genuine coalition of all the classes. The collective spirit of "we can take it"—which was almost all that Britain had going for it in 1940—had to be kept alive. So, with the help of Grace Hamblin, Clementine answered almost every letter personally and championed countless causes. Many concerned the discomforts and distress caused by the war at home, such as the woeful condition of air-raid shelters in London when the Blitz started in September 1940. German bombers attacked the capital for fifty-seven nights without respite, leaving much of the city in smoldering ruins and forcing tens of thousands, young and old, to live sometimes fourteen hours a day in "really horrible conditions of cold, wet, dirt, darkness and stench," often without proper beds, lavatories, lighting, washing facilities or even escape routes in the event of a direct hit or fire. Impetigo and scabies were quickly spreading, and there were fears that typhus and trench fever would follow. Responsibility for the situation lay with no fewer than five competing government agencies, none of which was prepared to use "compulsion where persuasion fail[ed]"[45] to ensure that improvements were made.

Clementine shared no such qualms, particularly not once people began writing to her of their plight. A typical correspondent was a desperate occupant of a shelter in Bethnal Green, East London, who wrote anonymously in pencil: "Madam, I hope you will not be offended by my writing to you as we have all made several complaints to the Council in regards a proper convenient lavatory for ladies and also a heating apparatus (electric) as the shelter where we are is . . . nothing more than an ice box . . . The authorities do not take any notice . . . Madam we shall be very grateful to you if you could do something for us." Clementine immediately wrote to the health minister Malcolm MacDonald, son of the former Labour leader Ramsay, enclosing the letter she had received: "Do you think something can quickly be done to make the people there more comfortable?" Mac-Donald knew, of course, that she enjoyed the full support of the prime minister and that this was not a question but an order. Action was quickly taken, so that when he reported back to her, she was able to reply: "I am so glad that the conditions there are being improved."[46]

It was a scenario she repeated many times. Heaters, full-sized beds, well-lit and clean latrines, disinfected bedding, extra shelters and a host of other improvements were provided as a direct result of

her specific interventions. The more she achieved, the more the letters poured in, some meticulously formal, some addressing her as
"Clementine" as if she were an old friend. Marjorie K. Hopkins of 191
Commercial Road, East London, wrote on July 6, 1941, "I find it very
difficult to thank you adequately for coming to see us at Stepney last
Wednesday . . . I cannot tell you how much it cheered us up to be
able to tell you myself some of my most urgent problems—the men
are giving everything & they only ask that their wives & children
shall have some home. Thank you for giving me such a kindly &
sympathetic hearing—I feel now at last thanks to you something will
be done."

Often Clementine would simply write to the relevant minister—
in this case Minister of Labour and National Service Ernest Bevin—
but on other occasions she would dragoon such an individual into
chaperoning her on an unannounced inspection. It was an "invitation" that even members of the cabinet felt unable to decline, and all
knew that she would monitor their response to any problems discovered. She even recruited her long-term adversary Lord Beaverbrook
(then minister of supply) to deal with the bed crisis, knowing that his
prodigious talents were perfectly suited to solving a "blockage." Sure
enough, within weeks, two million new beds were being manufac-
tured. And, as Clementine had specifically requested, they were all
wide enough for a mother to sleep in alongside her baby.

With a Red Cross representative and more often than not Jock
Colville in tow, she could inspect five different establishments in different parts of London within the space of three hours, leaving others
gasping in her wake. What made her so effective was not only her
practical approach—honed in the canteens of the previous world
war—but also how judiciously she used her position. Winston trusted
her to bother him only when necessary, so if she did convey an issue
to him he almost always took it up. Indeed, he would send word to
her when he had. It is unlikely that any other prime ministerial
spouse in British history has been so involved in government business, or wielded such personal power—albeit almost entirely behind

the scenes. She did not duplicate what Winston was doing, or cross it; she complemented it and he gave her free rein to do so.

Anxious to anticipate and forestall public discontent when she could, she scoured the newspapers for negative stories on subjects as diverse as Bank Holiday railway services (too crowded) or the supply of coal (inadequate). She would send Winston well-argued minutes on how he might deal with the problems (special passes for urgent travelers on the trains and the use of army trucks to distribute winter fuel) and their likely political fallout (such as possible questions in the House of Commons). Almost three decades of private counsel was being put at the service of the nation's struggle for survival. Yet Colville, now an unequivocal supporter of Winston, continued to resent her. When they visited a shelter canteen in a Southwark tube station together, he scoffed at how she was "ridiculously overdressed in a leopard-skin coat."[47]

In fact, she took great care in choosing her wardrobe, conscious of the need to suit either sad or optimistic occasions. She chose strong colors—one favorite was a coral red—and bold styles to suggest a defiant confidence. In a tribute to the women munition workers who wore turbans to keep their hair clean and safely away from machinery or chemicals, she almost always wore one herself, albeit in fine silks, chiffons, or cottons printed with extracts from Winston's speeches; they became her "look." Like the queen, she believed she should dress up to meet the people, just as they would do for her, and that a touch of glamour was welcome amid the shabbiness of war.

This time Clementine's "loudly acclaimed" visit was received with such "universal cheerfulness in squalid conditions" that it impressed even Colville, though he still failed to make the connection with her uplifting choice of clothes. He overlooked the morale-boosting significance of such outward gestures of solidarity. What he should also have appreciated was that despite the very real success of her various works she never sought personal glory, but, as the more observant Pamela commented, only "the very best for Winston" and his desperate battle to win the war. "I don't know that she really wanted anything for herself," Pamela, who watched her closely, later mused.[48]

Colville, like her other detractors, was eventually to come around. As Winston never stopped working, his private secretary spent many weekends en famille at Chequers, where Clementine assiduously drew him into the family orbit. She took the trouble to go for walks with him during his breaks and occasionally shared some harmless gossip or confidences about her youth that she thought might amuse or interest him. He could not fail to be charmed (although when Clementine beat him roundly at croquet and backgammon he claimed ungallantly that "her skill is slight, but [she] talks so much that she wins by force majeure").[49] They even discovered common political ground—namely their joint disapproval of Sir John Anderson, then home secretary and minister of home security.[50]

By April 1941 Colville was noting in his diary that Clementine "looked beautiful" on one of her inspection visits and that she was "followed by an admiring crowd of women and made quite a good speech standing on a chair."[51] (Having caught Winston's fear of extempore speaking, she prepared by laboring over numerous drafts.) Later in 1941, Colville realized that the only way he would overcome Winston's reluctance to let him leave Downing Street to join the RAF was if he won Clementine around first. And sure enough his "release" was granted, largely through "Mrs C's spirited intervention" on his behalf.[52] His hostility finally melted into admiration and affection. When he left in September 1941 to fulfill his dream of becoming a pilot it was with a lump in his throat.

For all her various contributions to the war effort, Clementine remained rigidly focused on Winston; she was, quite literally, always there for him. His staff kept her informed of when his meetings were likely to finish so that she could return home with military precision shortly beforehand, and she was almost unfailingly present at mealtimes. Often he assumed she had been waiting for him all day. It was not until after the war that he became aware of the full extent of her activity in the time they had spent apart.

Whenever possible, she tried to relieve him of avoidable strains, including the incessant demands from friends and relations for special favors. While Clementine went out of her way to help people in genuine difficulty, she could be fierce with those who sought to exploit their personal relationship. Her niece Diana Mitford, a personal friend of Hitler, and her husband, the British Blackshirt leader Sir Oswald Mosley, had been incarcerated as potential security risks. In November 1943 Diana's mother, Sydney Mitford (Lady Redesdale), another Hitler fan, visited Clementine to plead for her daughter's release on compassionate grounds: Diana had a young baby and Mosley was suffering from phlebitis, an inflammation of the veins exacerbated by lack of exercise. Clementine had been a bridesmaid at Sydney's wedding forty years previously and Diana had, of course, been a favorite at Chartwell, but she told Sydney bluntly that the couple were better off in prison as they might otherwise be lynched.

Soon afterward, a Home Office doctor warned that Mosley might die in custody, and so the more forgiving Winston authorized their release. Despite her blood ties to the Mitfords, Clementine felt little sympathy. Her perspective was simple: the Mosleys and Mitfords were fascists and should not be indulged. As Pamela put it, Clementine "was Presbyterian" and "a very *good* woman" who put "morals . . . above any emotion."[53]

There were few outward signs in autumn 1940 of the effects of her immense workload and the interminable pressures she was under. Her growing popular appeal was recognized by the Ministry of Information, which in September commissioned the society photographer Cecil Beaton to take pictures of her at Downing Street. As he waited for her, Beaton inspected the "delightful" reception rooms where the sun streamed in on bowls of sweet peas from Chartwell and the pale-colored walls were covered with Sickert sketches, Nicholson still lifes and family photographs. Particularly appealing was the white-paneled passage room used for dining in small groups. Then Clementine, whom he described as "a bright, unspoilt and girlish woman," appeared and sat on the sofa, elegantly pouring tea in evening dress with her hair glamorously set like Pallas Athene, the Greek goddess of courage. They chatted amiably and even toured the residence together, Beaton admiring the pretty rooftop bedrooms that gave the place the feel of a country manor.

The photographs duly appeared in *Picture Post* in November 1940. However the accompanying profile of the "little known, seldom seen, rarely pictured" prime ministerial spouse implied that the Churchills' marriage was not a love match but had been arranged by Jennie. The unsigned feature, titled "The Lady of No. 10," claimed that Clementine had been "chosen for her son (so it has been estimated) by his mother Lady Randolph Churchill."[54] Then a supposed friend took it upon herself to inform her that the pictures made her look like a "hard-bitten virago" on drugs. When Beaton called in again soon afterward, this time to show Winston some other photographs he had taken of the prime minister and his grandson, it was clear that Clementine had taken the feature as a personal attack. Working herself into a "nervous hysteria," she poured out her frustration: "It isn't as if my life has been too easy. It hasn't but when I married Winston he loved me!" Beaton tried to comfort her, kissing her forehead and holding her hand, but the stopper had been removed. "I don't know why it is, but I suppose my friends are not exactly jealous but they think that other people could do the job better and that I shouldn't have been married to Winston. After all he is one of the most important people in the world."

It was at this point that Beaton's patience ran out: "[T]he moment had come for her to behave with more dignity. She was entirely abandoning herself to a complete stranger. It was really rather reprehensible." Then, as she could so often do after one of these extraordinary lapses, she recovered her composure and snapped back into the collected Clementine most people knew. After he left, Beaton sent her a "bouquet to touch any heartstrings," consisting of dark red and white roses, violets, orchids and carnations, along with an "affectionate" note. Her telegram in response was "ecstatic."[55]

For a rare, cathartic moment she had let slip her private feelings of chronic self-doubt and inadequacy. She was right, however, to think that many still held her in low regard. "The line on Clemmie among all the clever women whom Winston had known was still that she was foolish and not very clever," said her niece Clarissa. Her feelings that she was "inferior in some curious way" never really left her. "But she knuckled down and behaved impeccably all through the war."[56]

After the RAF's victory in the Battle of Britain in the autumn of 1940, the immediate threat of invasion receded, but the Blitz that followed killed forty-four thousand civilians and rendered the centers of the target cities almost unrecognizable. Clementine displayed similar resolve (if not the same physical excitement) during the raids to her notoriously fearless husband, sometimes calmly finishing her cup of tea in the Downing Street garden even while the warning sirens wailed beyond.

Number 10 was, of course, an obvious target and in October a bomb narrowly missed the rickety seventeenth-century building, killing four people nearby. The explosion shattered most of the Downing Street windows (which were fixed up with brown paper), tore doors off their hinges and covered everything with grime. Mercifully the residence did not catch fire, but the Churchills were left without gas or hot water. Now heavily pregnant, Pamela was living with them while Randolph was away at a training camp—although he came back in September 1940 to take the parliamentary seat of Preston in an unopposed by-election. The company suited her, as did the proximity to her doctor, but the bedrooms were particularly exposed to blasts. So at night they traipsed down to the wine cellar, which had been reinforced with steel props. Here one room had been equipped with two bunk beds and another with a single bed. Clementine bagged the single room for herself, leaving Winston to share with his daughter-in-law "and the Baby Dumpling." Pamela quickly discovered why: "I used to fall sound asleep until 1 or 1.30 in the morning when Papa would come down" and climb into the top bunk. "That was the end of my sleep because within two minutes of arriving . . . he started to snore."[57]

After the near miss, the Churchills moved their beds from Downing Street into the Annexe flat, created from the more solidly built government offices around the corner at Storey's Gate. Visitors were greeted by guards in steel helmets and escorted to a tiny lobby where a door opened onto what had once been a utilitarian Air Raid Precautions office. Inside Clementine had the walls painted pastel colors and enlivened the decor with soft lighting, good furniture, a George Romney painting over the fireplace and a George Frederic Watts portrait of a young Lady Blanche. Next door, with the help of chintz hangings, she had softened another office space into her bedroom.

Within these peaceful rooms, the war seemed far away. Unfortunately, the flat's main passage also led to various government offices, including the Home Command HQ, and so officials passing through day and night would regularly bump into Clementine on her way to or from the bathroom, an experience she confessed to finding quite "unnerving."

The Annexe, although protected by thick metal shutters at the windows, was probably not much safer than Downing Street, but it was located directly above the heavily reinforced Central War Rooms thirty-five feet belowground, which were designed to protect the War Cabinet, including Winston (and Clementine), from aerial attack. Even in these cramped underground conditions, however, she insisted on sleeping apart from her husband. Down here her whitewashed bunker room contained little more than a single bed under a pink bedspread and, of course, a chintz armchair. Along the corridor Winston's own, green-covered bed was surrounded by maps and flanked by a basin and a large desk with a telephone. The whole place "looked and smelt like a battleship and one emerged in the morning gasping for fresh air," Jock Colville recalled.[58]

Winston loathed sleeping underground (he did so only three times), preferring to work through the air raids at ground level. As the bombing intensified, this greatly alarmed the cabinet, who alerted Clementine. One lively evening she made Winston promise to go below and, knowing that he rarely broke his word to her, left it at that. When the raid began he gathered his papers and "proceeded to the basement in an exemplary manner." His bodyguard was "mystified by this unusual docility" but a few minutes later, Thompson found him on his feet again in his dressing gown clutching a stash of papers. "A mischievous grin spread all over his face. 'Well Thompson,' said he. 'I have kept my word. I came downstairs to go to bed. Now I am going upstairs to sleep.' "[59]

Winston became what Clementine called "rather naughty" in all sorts of ways. During night raids, while the bombs were still falling and fires raging, he would go out with a flashlight to see the damage for himself. Naturally these excursions provoked alarm among his private secretaries, ministers and the military top brass, but he simply rushed past them all to the front door, stubbornly refusing to stop. General "Pug" Ismay, his dismayed chief of staff, told colleagues "in the language of the barrack room" that anybody "who imagined that he could control the Prime Minister on jaunts of this kind was welcome to try his luck on the next occasion."[60]

Winston had always been attracted to the scent of danger. He also enjoyed being mobbed as soon as he stepped out of his car and was moved to tears by the courage he witnessed amid the unimaginable desolation. Buoyed by the people's cheery resilience, he would walk miles through the debris until well into the night. One bombed-out woman, seeing his eyes brimming with tears, called out, "Look, he really cares," prompting huge cheers.

Clementine was again approached and asked to restrain Winston, so when the urge to go out in a raid took him next, she was ready in coat and scarf to join him. "This time, concerned for *her* safety, he returned home before nightfall," recalled Ismay. "This was her technique. She knew precisely how to handle him." Her presence also made his impromptu visits all the more popular. Women were particularly cheered by her arrival and would surge forward to greet her. She smiled confidently, shook their hands, asked them about the practicalities of their lives and tried to help with food, shelter or clothes wherever officialdom had failed. In response Union flags would be mounted defiantly on piles of rubble, and now both the Churchills were shouted out as heroes.

The trust shown in them on these occasions was overwhelming

and frightening. This was a time when Britain stood alone without major allies, when its "military cupboard" was practically "bare," its cities under the heaviest bombardment in history and the government so short of cash it seriously considered requisitioning wedding rings to melt down for the gold.[61] Winston was often easily moved, and Clementine, despite her normal rigid self-control in public, was also sometimes overcome. On one bomb site visit, with eyes welling up, she was heard to murmur: "Pray God, we don't let them down."[62]

Clementine saw it as her first duty to keep Winston alive. His recklessness spurred her to establish what became known as her "espionage" network: his staff would tip her off if he was planning something unduly dangerous. Winston's refusal to travel in his specially armored car during a raid (he disliked what he called the "iron box" and felt such protection cumbersome, unnecessary and divisive) was one example brought to her attention. She responded, "We've got to look after the Prime Minister. He's being rather naughty," and then issued the "line" to feed the "boss": the next time he planned a trip during an attack—in this case to inspect guns in Richmond Park—all official cars except the armored one were to be hidden and he was to be told that it was the only vehicle available.[63] Outmaneuvered, a furious Winston got into the armored car, which indeed protected him from the shrapnel raining down as he drove across town—but later "naughtily" broke free by commandeering an unarmored army vehicle parked at the side of the road. Clementine reverted to traveling with him on such occasions and he soon took the point.

The stalwart Inches, his valet, was once ordered to hide his boots in another bid to stop him from going out during night raids. Winston was livid, of course, but Inches stuck as long as he could to Clementine's scripted line, claiming the boots were being repaired. On this occasion, the prime minister simply ordered him to fetch them and the poor man finally complied. At other times Winston sought the complicity of his staff by asking them simply not to tell "Mrs C" or "she'll scold me."[64] But Clementine knew his doughty public image belied weaknesses in his health, in particular a susceptibility to colds that had the potential to develop into something more dangerous. As cars were not then heated, she placed rugs on every backseat he might conceivably use and instructed staff to find ever more imaginative ways of ensuring that he wrapped up in cold weather. The fact was that Winston was now in his midsixties and smoked, drank and took no exercise and Clementine fretted that he would not last the war.

Another great danger was the threat of assassination. Hitler knew all too well the incalculable importance of his survival to Britain's chances of victory. It seems incredible now that no one betrayed the whereabouts of the Annexe, although it was on street level, overlooking St. James's Park. But the tight security held. Every member of staff and almost all visitors were investigated by the security services, and any mention of the building's location (or even Winston's sudden absence from it) was forbidden. Even inside, conversations with most friends and relations were stilted. Winston confided everything in Clementine; she was briefed on the most secret military matters, including the Ultra decrypts of Nazi military ciphers by the code-breakers at Bletchley Park (the "golden eggs," as Winston called them). As a result she knew more than the cabinet and found it difficult to relax with outside company, so they entertained less and less and hardly ever went out.

"Outsiders," as the Churchills called friends and relations without the highest security clearance, were grouped together for occasional dinners to minimize the risk of accidental indiscretion. But others with whom they had been close in the past they now avoided completely; so many had expressed pro-German sentiments, or were related to others who held such opinions. Clementine's relations were particularly tricky, and not just the Mitfords. Rosalind, daughter of her cousin and greatest friend, Sylvia Henley, had married George Pitt-Rivers, a prominent eugenicist and open Nazi sympathizer. They had separated in 1937, but Pitt-Rivers was considered such a risk that he too was incarcerated or kept under close surveillance for much of the war, while Sylvia felt that Clementine "pushed her away."[65]

More and more it became natural to spend time with only the "small golden circle of trusted colleagues known to be 'padlock'" and to whom of course that trust was "sacred."[66] Then, at least, conversation flowed freely. But it meant that Clementine became a virtual prisoner, isolated from her own friends and afraid to open her mouth. Goonie, her confidante during the First World War, was away in the country being treated for cancer. (When Goonie died in July 1941 Clementine took in her daughter Clarissa, but despite this and other acts of kindness the two never became close.) Generally the only people Clementine saw were Winston's cronies, such as Bracken and the Prof, whom she invited to join the children and their spouses for Christmas in 1940 at Chequers. It was the last Christmas the family would spend together for four years, but one of the happiest.

One securely "padlocked" relative—albeit a recent addition to the family—was Pamela. She was sufficiently trusted to be present at many highly sensitive discussions—particularly over the dinner table—and became exceptionally well informed as a result. Sadly, her marriage to Randolph had done little to improve his boorish behavior, which—to Clementine's great shame—he frequently exhibited in front of Downing Street staff and guests. "Randolph," Colville wrote, "[was] one of the most objectionable people I had ever met: noisy, self-assertive, whining and rankly unpleasant."[67] At a military dinner in June 1940 at Chequers "he made a scene . . . [about the] inefficiency of the Generals" and Colville "felt ashamed of him for Winston's sake." Yet when Randolph, who had been kept in training for months without seeing action, asked to be allowed to fight, Winston replied that if he were killed "he would not be able to carry on."[68]

With Winston's reputation more important than ever, Clementine lived in fear that any or all of her elder children might dishonor it. "Mary was the child that she adored," recalled Pamela. "Mary never embarrassed Winston; she was too young, and then she was too good . . . the other children were an irritant to her . . . I mean Clemmy really didn't *like* her [other children] . . . because they were . . . very difficult characters."[69]

Clementine's attempts to rein in Randolph continued to meet with little success. "It was always a joke in the family that when she was angry about anything, she would put on her white gloves," Pamela recalled to her biographer. So she knew things must have been bad when, one morning in 1940, Clementine summoned her daughter-in-law to her Downing Street bedroom. There she was, wearing the gloves while eating breakfast from a tray on her bed. "Darling, where was Randolph last night?" Clementine asked. Not having any idea, the heavily pregnant Pamela burst into tears. Clementine had received word that Randolph had arrived "dead drunk" at six that morning and had left secret military maps in his car. She "was in a fury and rightly," as she knew the security breach could be a "terrible scandal" for Winston. She ordered Randolph to leave the house immediately and spend the day at his club.[70] The incident, which largely passed Winston by (as she intended), did nothing to reconcile mother and son.

Pamela and Randolph's only child together, little Winston, was born in the chintzy four-poster bed in his grandfather's bedroom at Chequers (known as Bedroom Two) at 4:40 in the morning on October 10, 1940, not long after a large bomb had exploded nearby. Randolph was in London and could not be contacted—it turned out he was in the arms of someone else's wife—so the event was recorded in the visitors' book by Clementine herself.

Winston was so thrilled by the arrival of a grandson who would carry on the Churchill name that he would sometimes stand and watch Pamela nursing him. It was a rare homely scene in a house that otherwise throbbed with restless activity whenever he was in residence. One observer noted that he "always seemed to be at his Command post on the precarious beachhead and the guns were continually blazing in his conversation; wherever he was, there was the battlefront."[71] He expected Chequers to operate as an alternative headquarters. On a Friday afternoon, private secretaries, phone operators, detectives, chauffeurs and dispatch riders would accompany him down from London in a high-speed convoy, bells ringing as red lights were jumped. Clementine would often go on ahead to help the staff ensure that all was perfect before his arrival.

Gaining access to Chequers, even for Clementine, meant negotiating an ever-changing rigmarole of passwords, codes, identity cards and the nervous challenges of guards. There were spotters on the roof, gun emplacements on a nearby hill, and companies of soldiers billeted in Nissen huts along the Lime Walk. Men from different regiments took turns to guard the house but Clementine socialized only with the most upmarket. "It amused me mildly that Mrs C, who does nothing but profess democratic and radical sentiments, should put off inviting any of the officers to dine until the guard consisted of the Coldstream,"* Colville noted. "The Oxford and Bucks Light Infantry were never invited inside."[72]

Despite all the intrusive security, Clementine and the family were never safe. Chequers's distinctive position close to two areas of high ground made it vulnerable to aerial attack, particularly on moonlit nights. The bomb that fell during Pamela's labor confirmed suspicions that the Luftwaffe was aware of the location of the house. An alternative weekend retreat was needed and the lavishly restored Ditchley Park in Oxfordshire, owned by the Anglo-American Conservative MP Ronald Tree, was selected. Bigger, smarter and better heated than Chequers—and discreetly located down a long single-track road—Ditchley was a bona fide stately home, where prewar standards were maintained courtesy of a family fortune amassed from a Chicago department store. Faced with a request from the prime minister, Tree could hardly refuse, and so the Churchill circus moved there whenever the moon was high (and sometimes when it wasn't).

How Clementine must have relished these brief reprieves from the responsibility of running the prime minister's household. The Trees were spectacular hosts, but the strain—even on a house as grand as Ditchley, with its twenty-nine bedrooms and Velvet Room covered in eighteenth-century Genoese silk—was nonetheless considerable. After just two weekends of accommodating the Churchills,

---

*The Coldstream Guards is the oldest and one of the most distinguished regiments in the British Army, and one of seven regiments in Her Majesty's Household Division, the personal troops of the queen. The "Ox and Bucks" was a relative newcomer and lacked the prestige conferred by such royal connections.

Winston's secretary Kathleen Hill was inquiring if it would be in order to grant extra rations to Nancy Tree's chef.[73]

Clementine knew all too well how challenging it was to produce good food on coupons. Rationing had been introduced in January 1940 and typically limited weekly purchases to two ounces each of butter and tea, one ounce of cheese, eight ounces of sugar, and four ounces each of bacon, ham and margarine per person. She insisted, of course, that the Churchills were issued with the same ration cards as everyone else. Fortunately, this meager fare was regularly topped up by friends and well-wishers, either from their own farms or from abroad, as well as from the extra supplies permitted for government entertaining, so it would be wrong to believe they suffered the same deprivations as others outside their circle. In fact, Clementine put on fourteen pounds during the war as she had little time to exercise or watch her diet. But even in her privileged position it was a struggle to cater for Winston, not least because he liked to conduct much of his business over the dining table. Wartime or no, he would harangue the cook in person if the soup was tasteless. Mercifully for all, Clementine hired Georgina Landemare, who had previously helped out occasionally at Chartwell, to work for her full-time at Downing Street. Mrs. Landemare, who had been married to a French chef, became legendary for what she could do with basic wartime provisions.

Over time, Clementine began to yearn for the odd evening away from the succession of official dinners and the discussion of the war that inevitably dominated them. "She had tailored her whole life . . . totally to Winston," said Pamela, who now saw far more of the Churchills than Randolph, who was mostly away with his regiment.[74] In need of the occasional respite, however brief, Clementine fatefully made Pamela her emissary, periodically sending her daughter-in-law a note on a Saturday afternoon informing her that she would not be down for dinner and that she should act as hostess at the grand Georgian dining table at Chequers in her place. So it was Pamela who became so familiar with the key players in the war and the latest news on the fighting—rather than the Churchill daughters, who were busy elsewhere with their war duties or, in Diana's case, tending her children.

Clementine conserved her energies for the most important occasions, including a tense meeting in midsummer 1940 with the Free French leader General Charles de Gaulle. This took place in the small white dining room at Downing Street—so admired by Cecil Beaton—shortly after Winston had ordered the Royal Navy to open fire on the French fleet anchored at Oran in North Africa to prevent it from falling into enemy hands. It had been a brutal decision, with a resultant death toll of thirteen hundred, but was undeniably necessary. France was now run by a pro-Nazi regime and the battleships might have been commandeered by Germany or its allies. When the conversation over lunch turned to the future of the remaining French fleet, Clementine said she hoped it would support the British effort to defeat the Nazis. De Gaulle caustically replied that it would give the French—whose relationship with so-called Perfidious Albion over the centuries had not always been entirely harmonious—greater satisfaction to turn their guns on their historic rivals, the British.

Clementine found the remark unacceptable. In stately French, she upbraided him for uttering sentiments ill suited to an ally, let alone a guest. Noticing the sudden tension, Winston attempted to placate the general: "You must forgive my wife. *Elle parle trop bien le français.*" Glaring at her husband, Clementine retorted, again in French: "Winston, it's not that at all. There are certain things that a woman can say to a man which a man cannot say, and I am saying them to you, General de Gaulle!" The Frenchman apologized repeatedly to his hostess and the following day he sent her a huge bouquet of flowers.

Pamela, who witnessed the encounter, regarded Clementine as the only person who could say no to Winston "and she did that often, often, often, often . . . She was hard on herself but was also hard on him."[75] In one sitting, however, Clementine had faced down two of the most powerful men in the fragile alliance against Germany. She earned in the process the undying respect of both.

• • •

The winter of 1940–41 appeared to be, in Churchill's own phrase, the "hour of doom."[76] France, Poland, Denmark, Norway, Belgium and Holland had all fallen. Hitler's Luftwaffe bombers were flattening swaths of British cities, his U-boats were sinking vital supply ships in the North Atlantic, and all the while Japan was "glowering on the other side of the globe."[77]

At this stage, America's material contribution to the war amounted to little more than a handful of semi-obsolete destroyers that had arrived late and in a poor state of repair, for which the US had demanded a king's ransom. Churchill tried to keep his tone with the president friendly and patient, and to acknowledge an understanding of the political battles back in Washington. He also for good measure tried to frighten Roosevelt by painting a cataclysmic vision of a strong Europe, united under Hitler's command, ranged against an unprepared America. But while FDR promised military supplies in his "Arsenal of Democracy" speech on December 29, 1940, the US showed no real sign of entering the war and time for Britain was fast running out. Before going any further Roosevelt needed to know whether the old country could really hold out against the Nazis or whether it was simply beyond salvation.

It was at this bleak point in history that the president decided to send a personal emissary to London to find out. He chose an ailing, gambling, wisecracking welfare administrator of humble origins and virulent Anglo-skeptic views.

CHAPTER TEN

Operation Seduction USA

1941–42

Sallow-faced and graying, Harry Hopkins was an incorrigible
workaholic even though cancer had left him with only half a
stomach and thus permanently malnourished. Kept alive by virtue of
a large "personal pharmacy" of pills, he looked as worn out and
frayed as his sagging suits. Divorced from his first wife, left bereft by
the death of his second and now at the mercy of the damp chill of an
English winter, he was in evident need of a comforting female presence. The decidedly unmaternal Clementine instantly took him under her wing.

She had been puzzled by the news that President Roosevelt was
sending as his envoy a diplomatic unknown. The son of a harness
maker and a prime architect of the New Deal, Hopkins bridled at the
very thought of the aristocratic monarchist who had concentrated so
much power in his own hands. He made clear from the start that he
planned to resist the prime minister's legendary persuasive powers.
"I suppose Churchill is convinced he's the greatest man in the world,"[1]
he grumbled to a friend before leaving Washington. Instinctively an
isolationist, he seriously doubted whether Britain was even worth
saving.

Brendan Bracken, who had met him on the croquet power circuit
on Long Island, now informed the Churchills that Hopkins's fact-
finding visit was of incalculable importance. Hopkins might have
been anti-British, but he was closer to Roosevelt than anyone in the
president's inner circle and was regarded on Capitol Hill as the

second-most powerful man in Washington. He lived just down the landing from the president's bedroom in the White House and so endured with Franklin the notoriously unappetizing food served by Eleanor Roosevelt's kitchen.

Hopkins's skepticism was in any case far from uncommon in the US. American opinion—shared by most of Congress and the military— was still largely against involvement in the war. Many feared that supplying armaments to Britain would either leave America unde- fended or ensure that the weaponry would fall into Nazi hands once Britain was defeated. Others believed, wrongly, that the riches of the British Empire were virtually limitless, and they saw no reason to help what they still imagined to be an imperialist nation of murder- ous redcoats. It was clear that the US would only wade in if Roosevelt were personally persuaded to intervene. What Hopkins (and later other key Americans) would report back to the president was, there- fore, vital to Britain's survival.

Fortunately, Bracken had observed that Hopkins combined a Democrat's concern for the many with a taste for hobnobbing with the rich and powerful few. He reveled in the attentions of beautiful highborn women and appreciated fine dining in fancy surroundings. Bombed, blasted but so far unbeaten, the Churchills thus set out to win him over with their particular brand of upper-class elegance, charm and "ambrosial" food. Britain was virtually bankrupt, but no expense was to be spared in making their American guest welcome; everything was to be choreographed for maximum effect. The "half- blind," as Winston later referred to the Americans at this time, were to be made to see. It was Britain's only hope.

Rather than the usual Foreign Office flunky, Bracken himself (at that time the prime minister's parliamentary private secretary) went to meet Hopkins when his flying boat landed at Poole one cold Thursday afternoon in early January 1941. He found the American so exhausted by his lengthy transatlantic journey (a four-lap trip involv- ing up to thirty hours in the air) that he was too weak to unfasten his seat belt. After allowing Hopkins a brief rest, Bracken escorted him to London via a specially scheduled train, which, under Winston's direct orders, was made up of the most luxurious Pullman carriages staffed by conductors in white gloves.

Back at Downing Street, Clementine was already hard at work with Mrs. Landemare planning for a private lunch with Winston the following day. She ensured that the wartime dining room in the basement—one of the few parts of the building still regularly used— looked as appealing as possible, despite the presence of steel shutters at the windows and metal pit props to strengthen the ceiling. The overall effect, enhanced by flowers, chintz curtains and paintings by the French masters Ingres and David, was of a ship's wardroom.

She cannily resorted to another well-tested means of lifting male spirits. Knowing the power Pamela wielded over older men, Clementine prominently placed a particularly flattering photograph of her daughter-in-law with her baby on a fine old antique table. It was one of the first things Hopkins noticed when Bracken escorted him into the room at midday and fixed him a sherry. In a promising start, Hopkins complimented Winston on his daughter-in-law's "delicious" beauty, but it soon became clear he would not be so easy a catch. Deprived of sleep thanks to the Luftwaffe bombing overnight, he challenged his host by suggesting that Winston did "not like America, Americans or Roosevelt." Winston responded with the utmost charm, describing in florid terms his admiration for the president and the nation of which he was leader, and informing his guest that he himself was half American. But even his genial best was not quite enough to win Hopkins around, and they settled down to lunch still at odds.

Hopkins's ill health often made eating a struggle but he relished the menu of tasty clear soup, followed by the tenderest cold beef with green salad, all washed down with one of the finest wines in the government's depleted stocks. Winston insisted he have seconds, including more of what Hopkins called "jelly" with his beef, and the American was only too happy to oblige. The two men discovered they liked each other's wit, pugnacity and irreverence. This was dinner-table diplomacy at its best. By the time a smiling Mrs. Landemare came in with the cheese and the port, followed by coffee, Hopkins was succumbing to Winston's charisma—and Clementine's cuisine. When he eventually emerged onto London's bomb-scarred streets at four o'clock, feeling unusually invigorated, he declared, "I never had such an enjoyable time."[2]

The following day (a Saturday) he was invited for further "enjoyable times" in the historic splendors of Ditchley. There he met Winston and his other guests before and after dinner in the fifty-foot-long library, with its two marble fireplaces, red leather sofas and towering bookcases, and ate in the opulent dining room beneath a huge chandelier and twinkling sconces. He was being treated to the ultimate English country-house weekend—a dramatic contrast to the Roosevelt White House, which was notoriously cluttered and even a little grubby and where the servants ate better than the guests. Here in war-torn England, Clementine ensured Hopkins was waited on hand and foot and that his every need was catered for.

Hopkins pretended his ill health was due to a bug caught on the trip over, but she was not fooled and observed him so attentively that she came to know when he was cold or in pain just "by looking at him." She made sure the fires were banked up and around eleven she urged him to go to bed, saying, "You have a long day tomorrow and you can have a nice talk with Winston in the morning. I've fixed your bed and put a hot water bottle in it." Normally known for "a tongue like a skinning knife and a temper like a Tartar,"[3] Hopkins felt so at ease he even played with Nelson, the scratchy Churchill cat.

The trip was in all respects confounding his expectations. It was, of course, not all pleasure, but it was always purposeful. Both Churchills took their guest on tours of bombing sites during the week, and along with millions of Britons he endured the German air raids by night. Then, on the weekends, he was treated to aristocratic finery. It was a potent mix for a poor boy from Iowa.

Clementine planned virtually every moment of his day with the aim of furthering the British cause, and made a "great fuss" if the staff allowed Hopkins to stray from her carefully chosen itinerary. The message was at all times to be clear and consistent—even if not entirely truthful. The Churchills secretly knew from recent decryption successes at Bletchley Park that the imminent danger of invasion had receded. But Hopkins was to be given the unequivocal impression that it could happen at any time. Although they became genuinely fond of their American guest, with his sardonic humor and personal courage, the national imperative of emphasizing to Roosevelt the scale and immediacy of the Nazi threat trumped everything else.

As the Churchills had hoped, the hard-bitten Hopkins was astonished by the good-humored determination of a people who lived with the constant reality of death and destruction. He was also moved by the enthusiastic welcome he had received as the representative of a nation that had, in truth, been miserly in its support for the last democracy in Europe to hold out against fascism. He reported back to Roosevelt: "The people here are amazing from Churchill down and if courage alone can win—the result will be inevitable."[4] Moreover, he was quickly convinced of Winston's greatness as a leader, exclaiming after one late evening spent with the prime minister: "Jesus Christ! What a man." But for all this, Hopkins had no doubt that "the most charming and entertaining of all the people that he met" on his extended six-week trip "was Mrs Churchill."[5]

"I suppose you wish to know what I am going to say to President Roosevelt on my return," Hopkins remarked to Winston and Clementine at an intimate dinner at the end of January, not long before he left for home on February 10. They sat in agonized suspense, while a blizzard roared outside, until finally he resumed. "Well, I'm going to quote you one verse from that Book of Books. 'Whither thou goest, I will go; and where thou lodgest, I will lodge: thy people shall be my people, and thy God my God.'" He added very quietly: "Even to the end." Tears poured down Winston's face; Clementine too was quietly sobbing. "The words," recalled Winston's doctor Lord Moran, who was present at Clementine's insistence, "seemed like a rope to a drowning man." Their mission had surely succeeded.

Hopkins arrived back in the US "more of a partisan than perhaps might have been expected by anyone who had not been exposed to the Churchillian force."[6] Some even thought he had been bewitched. He told Roosevelt that America must do all it could to help Britain

with guns, ships and planes, and as Britain no longer had the funds
to buy the "cash and carry" armaments it desperately needed, the
president's ideas on financial aid would have to be introduced with
great urgency. Hopkins, already Roosevelt's fixer in chief, now became Churchill's de facto representative in Washington as well. He
even persuaded the once skeptical Roosevelt to describe Winston as
a "brilliant and great leader" in his speech on March 15 at the White
House Correspondents' Association dinner.

Hopkins would return to England just a few months later, but in
the meantime he did not forget his hostess. He sent Clementine parcels of cheese, lipstick, ham, chocolate, bacon, a satin nightdress and
nail polish, knowing how rare all of these were in Britain. "Oh boy,"
she wrote in her thank-you letter, using a signature Americanism in
tribute. "You are a good fairy." She and Mary, she said, had wept with
joy when they opened the parcel and she asked him when he would
be coming back, reminding him to bring plenty of warm clothes
when he did so.[7] Clementine now entered into regular and very
friendly correspondence with Hopkins, telling him just a month later,
for instance, that she was "missing" him.

Enlisting Hopkins's support—even devotion—in Washington
was a decisive coup, but he was not the first influential American to
be won over by the Churchills' joint efforts. On his first night in London Hopkins had dined with Ed Murrow, the resident CBS correspondent, who was then beaming the horror of the Blitz directly into
American homes every night under the radio call sign "*This* is London." Winston had long since identified the debonair Murrow as the
conduit to the hearts and minds of US popular opinion, and through
Clementine's initiative, he had set about drawing the Americans into
the fold. As a result, Murrow was not only well informed—as Hopkins discovered—but also a fervent advocate of Britain's cause.

Although usually reticent in forming new friendships, Clementine had spotted in Murrow's wife, Janet, the opportunity to cultivate
the journalist. A quiet Connecticut Yankee with a dislike of the English class system, Janet was a great influence on her husband but was
largely ignored by the men who dominated the powerful circles in

which he moved. She was known to feel lonely in London, and Clementine had gone to work alongside her distributing American "Bundles for Britain" aid parcels to bombed-out families, during which time she had openly sympathized with many of Janet's radical views. Janet had been surprised and flattered by the attention, writing to her parents in December 1940 that Clementine was "charming, vivacious and attractive."[8]

Clementine rarely issued invitations to Downing Street on her own account, but she made a notable exception for Janet Murrow. And when Ed arrived to collect his wife following one of her earliest lunches with Clementine, Winston seized his moment. Scuttling out from his study right on cue, he waved the American inside with the words "Good to see you. Have you time for several whiskies?"[9] It was an invitation he could hardly refuse. Thereafter the Murrows had joined the select and trusted small band regularly summoned for Downing Street dinners—an intimate circle that excluded many people the Churchills had known for years, and most of the cabinet.

British journalists could only look on with envy at the access granted to the couple, knowing full well that the Americans were "treated as tin gods because they were so useful."[10] Although he greatly admired Roosevelt, Murrow's new understanding of Britain's position had made him, by the time Hopkins arrived, increasingly impatient with America's vacillation in coming to her aid. As Winston admitted, Britain was struggling with an acute shortage of virtually every kind of military hardware, and was "naked before its foes"; only US firepower could save her. "I hope that life goes well for you in America," Murrow wrote in a private letter home at one point, "and that your nostrils are not assailed by the odor of death . . . that permeates the atmosphere over here."[11] His message on air was more tactful but was nevertheless pointed as he hammered in Britain's refusal to surrender. "I saw many flags flying from staffs," he reported after one night of heavy bombing. "No flag up there was white."

Murrow was fortunately close friends with the new American ambassador, Gil Winant, an ex–Republican governor of New Hampshire born to a prosperous New York City family who had worked for FDR on the US Social Security Board in the midthirties before going on to head the International Labour Office in Geneva in 1939. An Abraham Lincoln look-alike with the "rapt gaze of a monk,"[12] Winant had a sense of urgency (no doubt fostered by Murrow even before his arrival in London) and a passionate belief in freedom that were a welcome reversal of the hostile defeatism of his predecessor, Joseph Kennedy. Winant arrived at Bristol on a blustery afternoon in March 1941 to discover a Britain enduring massive casualties from relentless air raids, devastating losses in the fighting overseas and the imminent threat of starvation as Germany's U-boats strangled its naval supply lines. After nine months standing alone, it was evident that the United Kingdom was physically, emotionally and financially bankrupt. "We were hanging on by our eyelids," recalled Alan Brooke, who was shortly to head the British Army.[13] Winant himself would write later, "[Y]ou could not live in London in those early years and not realise how narrow was the margin of survival."[14]

The possibility of defeat was, of course, not to be admitted, but even Clementine allowed herself at one point to wonder aloud to Winston's private secretary, "Jock, do you think we are going to win?" Colville had been well trained and replied "truthfully and unhesitatingly 'Yes.'"[15] All depended, however, on persuading America to intervene.

As they had for Hopkins, the Churchills ensured that Winant's welcome was spectacular. In an unprecedented honor, George VI himself was waiting outside Winant's carriage door when his train stopped at Windsor, and the king even invited the ambassador to stay the night at the castle. The royal offer was refused. Having already witnessed so much suffering, Winant was impatient to get on to London to start work. He told a BBC reporter: "There is no place I'd rather be at this time than in England." Two days later he was treated to an intimate dinner with Winston, and thus was made another recruit to the greater Churchill "family."

Winant soon became a familiar and reassuring figure on the Churchills' visits to bomb-damaged cities. He was struck not only by people's courage but by Clementine's unsung contribution. "The most marked determination and enthusiasm were among middle-aged women," he noted to Roosevelt, observing that such women all showed "great appreciation of Mrs Churchill's coming."[16] Like Hopkins, Winant was a solitary figure, partly estranged from his society wife, Constance, who stayed behind in America. His growing closeness to the Churchills—nurtured by a now-familiar round of dinners, weekends and bomb-site tours—gave him a welcome sense of belonging in a foreign land. He became a fixture of their world, joyfully discovering that even in war it was never dull or drab, but, as one American historian has put it, forever "shot through with color."[17]

Clementine especially loved it when Winant came to visit. Although admired and respected by Winston, he was too much of an idealist for the prime minister's buccaneering taste. By contrast, he and Clementine were kindred spirits. Both were shy and reserved; each was quietly radical, believing in a duty to help the less fortunate. According to Mary, Winant "understood intuitively" her mother's complex nature and her demanding life, and as a result, she confided in him—something she rarely did with anyone else.[18] Clementine also comforted Winant when his pilot son John went missing for five weeks in October 1943.

Going on walks together alone at Chequers or Ditchley, they became instinctive allies. She esteemed his selflessness; he recognized her quiet achievements. He wrote on one occasion to ask her to congratulate Winston on "one of the greatest [speeches] of its kind ever made." He knew that she had played a part in its success: "I especially liked the references to de Gaulle and France and felt that, perhaps you had had something to do with it."[19] Winant held Clementine's courage, resourcefulness, determination and devotion to the British people in the highest regard. Indeed, he could not have admired her more. But it was another Churchill who was to capture his heart.

Glamorous, entertaining and alluring in her WAAF uniform, Sarah was enjoying her contribution to the war effort now that her relationship with Vic Oliver was effectively over. Although strongwilled like her father, at twenty-seven she was feeling emotionally vulnerable and worried about losing her looks. Some elusive quality about her mesmerized the fifty-two-year-old Winant, who relished her rebellious side. His intimate status with her parents—allied to the fact that her London flat in Park Lane was just a five-minute walk from the American embassy in Grosvenor Square—meant that he was frequently thrown into her company, and toward the end of the year they began an affair. As both were still married they kept up appearances, but the relationship was an open secret in Churchill circles.

Years later Sarah, never one to reveal much of herself, would write coyly about a "love affair which my father suspected but about which we did not speak."[20] In truth, this belies her parents' acquiescence: the fraught situation of 1941 meant that almost any consolidation of Britain's "special relationship" with America could be considered an act of patriotism. Though the Churchills may not have talked about it openly, they not only tolerated the affair but gave it plenty of opportunities to flourish. Sarah was, after all, not alone in conducting a "patriotic" relationship. Emotions were heightened by the dangers of war and, as one writer put it, "sex" in those early war years "hung in the air like fog."

Averell Harriman, a rich American lothario with film-star looks, was about to make London even "foggier." He arrived in March, around the same time as Winant, to help set up Roosevelt's new Lend-Lease military aid program. The US would "rent" Britain vital equipment in return for assets rather than hard cash. Although the move stopped short of a declaration of war on Germany, Lend-Lease represented the de facto end to American neutrality and went some way to solving Britain's chronic shortage of currency.

FDR had first conceived of the plan after a desperate plea for help from Churchill back in December 1940, but he always knew it would take a big political push to get it through a skeptical Congress. Hopkins, whose trip to Britain had converted him to the British cause, had worked tirelessly to persuade FDR to proceed with the plan and helped him win the debate in Washington and drive the bill through. Once Lend-Lease was eventually passed by Congress in March 1941, Hopkins became the devoted chief administrator of what was to amount to a $50 billion program. Now Harriman was tasked with actually delivering the essential planes, ships, weapons and equipment that Britain needed to defend herself.

The son of a ruthless railroad tycoon—the man who set private detectives on Butch Cassidy and the Sundance Kid—Harriman was widely considered a power groupie, intent on broadening his own influence at least as much as that of his country. His reputation had suffered when he had chosen not to fight in the First World War only to profit from it through his shipping interests. As a result he was desperate to play a role in this conflict. Many in Washington thought—or rather hoped—that such a hard-nosed businessman would be tougher with the Churchills than Hopkins had been.

Winston and Clementine opted for a swashbuckling reception for his arrival. Harriman was deliberately kept in the dark about where he was going to land until he disembarked at Bristol on the afternoon of March 15. Thereafter Roosevelt's special representative was treated to a meticulously planned "special welcome."[21] "Whoever the President had sent," recalled Mary, however difficult or abrasive his personality, "everybody here was going to bust themselves to get on" with him. "It was immensely important to us how it all went."[22] In a carefully stage-managed maneuver, Winston's naval aide, Commander Thompson, bundled a startled Harriman swiftly past a guard of honor onto a waiting biplane to take him straight to Chequers for dinner. "Dear Mrs Churchill," Harriman wrote ten days later from his suite at the Dorchester hotel. "To be kidnapped on arrival at Bristol, whisked off by plane to Chequers and there find such a warm and friendly welcome from you and Mr Churchill was indeed both a dramatic and delightful beginning of my mission."[23]

The Hollywood-style spectacle had appealed to the adventure-seeking Harriman. So too did his arrival at Chequers, redolent as it was of wood smoke, antiquarian books and the thrill of centuries of history. "I was very excited, feeling like a country boy plopped right into the center of the war," Harriman admitted.[24] He was particularly charmed by what he called Clementine's "unfeigned delight" when he gave her a bag of tangerines he had bought in Lisbon.[25]

Since it was within Harriman's remit to supply the military hardware Britain so desperately needed, Winston focused his attention on him, leaving Clementine to take care of Winant. Within days of his arrival, Harriman was ostentatiously flattered with an office at the Admiralty, access to secret cables and invitations to high-level meetings. "I'm practically a member of the Cabinet," he crowed to a friend back home, W. M. Jeffers, president of the Union Pacific Railroad.[26] Winston told him: "We accept you as a friend. Nothing will be kept from you." He meant, as it turned out, literally nothing.

Harriman's wealth, looks and, most of all, power made him London's latest social catch; he was showered with invitations, often for several engagements a night. One he was advised not to miss was a glamorous dinner at the Dorchester in April, where, seated next to him in a shoulderless gold dress, was twenty-one-year-old Pamela Churchill. Her puppy fat had gone but her curves had not. Her jaw was sculpted and she glowed with the indefinable Churchill allure. Hopkins had already informed Harriman that she was more plugged-in "than anyone in England."[27]

For Pamela, Harriman was the most beautiful man she had ever seen: tanned, dark-haired, six foot one and, unlike the overweight and spotty Randolph, delightfully receptive to her feminine charms. She had been briefed that, as Roosevelt's special emissary, Harriman would be instrumental in deciding whether Britain won the war. So over a lavish dinner of salmon and strawberries—the Dorchester was largely unaffected by rationing—she launched into what friends came to call her "mating dance." She asked him questions, listened raptly to his answers, stroked his arm with her fingertips, and laughed when he attempted a joke.

After dinner, Harriman invited Pamela back to his palatial suite at the Dorchester, where she helped him peel off her dress. They lingered under the sheets throughout the night's heavy bombing, as his ground-floor rooms were deemed capable—thanks to the hotel's modern steel frame and thick concrete floors—of withstanding anything except a direct hit. Randolph was conveniently away overseas with his regiment, and although she continued to spend weekends with the Churchills, Pamela was now spending weekday nights alone in one of the cheap "bilious-coloured" rooms on the exposed top floor of the Dorchester, where the wind whistled in the fireplaces during raids. Her neighbor, Winston's niece Clarissa, remembers being surprised that night not to find Pamela traipsing down to the basement shelters when the bombing started. The building shook and the guns roared, but Pamela was ensconced in bed with the man who might just be able to help bring it all to an end. She no longer felt morally tied to Randolph and was looking for a purpose as well as excitement. It was the first act of her career as the twentieth century's most influential courtesan.

Harriman was entranced. Not only was he entwined with one of the most desirable women in town but as the nerve center of Nazi resistance, London itself was intoxicating. "Blacked out, bombed out, expensive and hard to get around in, it was still magnificent—the Paris of World War II," observed one contemporary.[28] Wealthy, well-connected American civilians, from New York bankers to Hollywood directors, vied to be assigned to the British capital on temporary government duty. Life on the edge was exciting: normal inhibitions were suspended; no one wanted to be alone. Thousands of bombs rained down on London, and thousands sought comfort in one another's arms. But Pamela's seduction of Harriman went beyond consolation; it was a strategic alliance of the highest order. She knew all too well how important the affair could prove to her parents-in-law and to her country.

Word of the relationship spread quickly. Beaverbrook was particularly delighted when he found out. After all, Harriman had only just landed at Bristol and "already he was compromised."[29] Beaverbrook went out of his way to encourage the affair by keeping Pamela's baby, his six-month-old godchild, at his country house in Surrey and by giving her money to spruce up her wardrobe. To do her "job" she needed to be unencumbered and gorgeous. Thus liberated, Pamela quickly set to work, passing on to Beaverbrook, or directly to her father-in-law, anything she gleaned from Harriman about what the Americans were thinking. She also became adept at sifting information in the other direction, to boost Britain's case for more aid. In this way she fast became one of the most important intelligence brokers in the war.

Winston and Clementine could hardly have hoped for more from their campaign to bring Roosevelt's special representative, the very man charged with keeping Britain free, into the "family." America would remain officially uncommitted to the conflict until after Japan's attack on the US naval base at Pearl Harbor eight months later—but now that the man in charge of supplying ships, guns and planes to Britain was sleeping with their daughter-in-law, the Churchills were surely nearer than ever to "dragging" in more American support. Harriman became adroit at translating their most urgent needs into action, persuading Roosevelt, for example, to authorize US ports to repair British warships.

Yet still the questions kept coming back from Washington: Could Britain really hold out? Was America wasting its money on a hopeless cause? Winston's assurances to Roosevelt went only so far, but now Harriman was arguing emphatically that American aid was being put to good use. He became so committed to the struggle that when he returned home he found even close friends regarded him as "unduly pro-British."[30]

No matter that Pamela was still married to Randolph; the national interest took precedence. Far from trying to stop the affair, it appears that Clementine facilitated it, ensuring that Pamela and Harriman were thrust together as often as possible and inviting both to Chequers or Ditchley on weekends. (One small concession to propriety was that Pamela often omitted to sign the Chequers visitors' book if Harriman was present, although most if not all of those invited to these weekends seem to have known about the affair and appreciated its strategic value.) Questions are sometimes posed as to the extent of Clementine's knowledge of the relationship. But few if any in London society were unaware of it (indeed there was some muttering in less well-briefed circles about Pamela's lack of discretion). Even Roosevelt had been informed and would joke about the affair with Hopkins. So while Pamela did not openly discuss the subject with her mother-in-law, she was always convinced that both

Churchills "knew perfectly well." "It was fine and nobody really blamed me," Pamela recalled, "because they understood . . . how difficult Randolph was."[31]

Both Churchills made a point of referring to Pamela's lover as "our dear Averell" but in truth Clementine was never fond of him. He lacked humor, particularly about himself, and treated his staff badly. He also flaunted his wealth and connections, oiling his way from one grand cocktail party to another, and, far from sharing Britain's suffering, maintained a supply of luxuries throughout his stay in London. She thought him yet another coldly ambitious businessman. But whereas in peacetime she had had no qualms about letting self-important people know her opinion of them, now she had to bite her tongue. Harriman was too vital to the war; his ego had to be flattered.

It was for this reason perhaps that Clementine, who generally balked at asking strangers for personal favors, made an exception in May 1941. Eighteen-year-old Mary had recently announced her engagement to the son and heir of her mother's onetime suitor, the Earl of Bessborough, despite having only just met him. Clementine told Harriman that she was convinced Mary was not in love and had simply been swept off her feet with excitement. Mary had refused her mother's pleas to reconsider and ignored her sister Sarah's "frank ridicule."[32] Harriman had daughters, Clementine reminded him, and so must surely understand what young women were like. With Winston so busy running the war, could he perhaps speak to Mary instead?

Harriman was evidently unqualified for the task. He barely knew Mary (and her suitor not at all) and his two daughters had been raised by their mother, who had divorced him while they were young. Most of his recent experiences with young women had been as bedfellows. Nevertheless, he succumbed to Clementine's flattery and agreed. The fact that Clementine had singled him out to play father confessor to Mary was "a source of tremendous gratification . . . He was now at the centre of the action, just as he had always longed to be."[33] Wrapped up against the damp spring weather he took Mary for a walk around the French garden at Ditchley, where he held forth on the need to avoid making hasty decisions. Mary—probably unwittingly—played her part for the war effort. She dutifully wrote to thank Harriman for his worldly "kindness" and credited him for helping her see sense.

Clementine seemed unconcerned that Harriman was cuckolding her son. Pamela had in any case already decided that she would have to make her own way in life. Traveling by sea to a staff job at the British North African command base in Cairo earlier in the year, Randolph had taken to high-stakes gambling with a louche, mon-eyed crowd that included Evelyn Waugh. Thanks to his previous extravagances, money was already extremely tight, but now Randolph cabled Pamela for hundreds of pounds she simply did not have to cover his losses. She begged Beaverbrook for help and (hoping Clementine would not find out) sold the diamond earrings she had been given as wedding gifts, but the debts would even so take years to pay off.

She now carried the Churchill name and had done her bit by providing an heir and no longer had need of the drunken, abusive Randolph and his so-called bachelor rampages. As Clementine had feared, Pamela found him "impossible to be married to" and "his own worst enemy."[34]

When Randolph came home on leave in the spring of 1942 and discovered the affair, he exploded with rage. His anger stemmed not from sexual jealousy, friends said, but a sense of betrayal. He had befriended Harriman on his recent visit to Cairo, made at Winston's request, and had liked and respected him. Even worse was his bitterness toward his parents, whom he accused of condoning adultery "beneath their own roof" and sacrificing his marriage and happiness in order to woo the Americans. "He used terrible language and created a rift that never healed," recalled Alastair Forbes, a friend of Randolph's and Mary's.[35]

To lower the temperature, Pamela agreed "not to see too much of his parents," as Randolph rightly suspected they preferred her company to his own. When he left London at the end of his leave,

Pamela was more discreet. But otherwise her relationships with both Harriman and the Churchills resumed largely unchanged.

Clementine was now expert at preparing official receptions with the military precision necessary to make every one as productive—and as agreeable—as possible. It was a gigantic operation. A typical weekend at Chequers, for instance, would be arranged on a grid system and could easily involve twenty constantly changing guests coming and going, staying variously for lunch, dinner, overnight or all three. Considering the circumstances, her hospitality was legendary. Winston expected no less. The American Treasury secretary Henry Morgenthau (another key target of the Churchillian charm) remembered Winston being in "good form" every time they met during the war—except once: "The night his wife gave him a supper he did not like and so he did not talk all through supper. She said, 'I am sorry, dear, I could not buy any fish. You'll have to eat macaroni.' "[36]

Clementine was not only intent on keeping Winston happily fed within the severe limits of wartime supplies. She also studied their countless visitors' backgrounds, families, interests and tastes in food, and took great care over her seating plans to ensure everyone's compatibility and comfort. Her ministrations were flattering and highly effective. Meals at Downing Street, Chequers and Ditchley were a much-needed, spirit-lifting spectacle, as well as a stage on which Winston could work his magic on his carefully selected guests. He managed to "have his way" over various aspects of the North African campaign in part through his weekly "luncheon conversations in London with General Eisenhower," the American commander of Operation Torch.[37] Having discovered Eisenhower's love of stew, Clementine ensured he was served the finest—with plenty of onions.

The Churchills also made an impression through their eccentric attire. Winston liked to wear a siren suit at dinner—a bizarre onesie-style garment that Clementine had made up for him in a variety of colors and fabrics, including velvet. She, by contrast, presided over more intimate dinners in beautiful flowery silk housecoats with her nightdress underneath.

Despite her hard work few visitors paused to register, let alone admire, her efforts. One rare exception was the Canadian prime minister Mackenzie King, who told Clementine that he "marvelled" at how "you are able to *think* of the many things you do, to say nothing of how you manage to perform them."[38] Very few, apart from Hopkins and Winant, would take the trouble to get to know Clementine herself, in part because Winston disliked sharing her. On one trip to Plymouth, which had been badly bombed, Harriman witnessed a "contest of wills" between the prime minister and the local MP Nancy Astor, who was trying to "carry off Mrs Churchill to a women's political meeting." "In war it is the Prime Minister who must make the vital decisions," Winston declared of his most precious asset. "Clemmie comes with me."[39]

Harriman's daughter Kathleen, who joined her father in London and was also taken under Clementine's wing, noticed how gracious she was in "taking a back seat" to her husband. "But don't get the idea she's mousy, not at all. She's got a mind of her own, only she's a big enough person not to use it unless he wants her to," she wrote to her sister, Mary, after spending a weekend at Chequers in the summer of 1941. She went on to observe that "everyone in the family looks upon him as God and she's rather left out, and when anyone pays any attention to her she's overjoyed."[40] The entire family held the great man in a reverence not far short of worship, hanging on his every word and never missing his speeches. On the occasion of one of his "bolstering" broadcasts to France, they all assembled around the radio, and the knobs were prepared for the right frequency. But then an aunt pressed the wrong one, "the feathers flew" and in desperation Clementine grabbed the radio so hard she broke it. "After an hysterically chaotic scene, everyone rushed upstairs to listen to the remainder of the speech on a servant's set."[41]

The Churchills' outward charm and energy belied the strain of two long years of war. Their frantic dinner-table diplomacy had yet to yield the ultimate prize: despite the collective pressure from the successfully annexed Harriman, Winant and Hopkins, Roosevelt was still refusing to send American troops into combat. Again and again, the president had pulled himself up to the edge of confrontation, only to retreat at the last minute. Even a number of skirmishes between German and American warships in the Atlantic—such as the torpedoing of the destroyer USS *Kearny* in October 1941 and the sinking of another destroyer, the USS *Reuben James*, two weeks later—failed to provoke a declaration of war. What would it take, Winston and Clementine wondered, to propel Roosevelt to lead his country into battle at their side? There was no question that saving Britain was a moral imperative, but while America stepped up its aid under Harriman, it would not fight. One critical historian has concluded: "If Munich had been Great Britain's least glorious hour, mid-1941 was surely America's."[42]

A strategic error by Hitler was, however, about to present Britain with another, rather different ally, one that also proved decisive to its survival. In June 1941, Hitler had launched a bloody invasion of the Soviet Union, catching Stalin by surprise despite repeated warnings from the British, who had been alerted to the imminent Operation Barbarossa through Bletchley Park decrypts, and marking the beginning of four years of war on the Eastern Front. Until the Panzers swept across the Soviet border, Stalin had been providing Hitler with huge material assistance under the terms of the Nazi-Soviet pact of 1939. Yet those same Russians, who had previously stood by during Britain's darkest hours and even negotiated with Hitler for a share of the spoils of British defeat, now demanded urgent aid and assistance. The Soviet ambassador, Ivan Maisky, dashed down to Chequers to deliver a note to Churchill from Stalin requesting the immediate deployment of British troops in northern France to take the pressure off the Russian front, where casualties were horrendous. Although he certainly welcomed the Soviet Union into the war against Hitler (which military chiefs thought likely further to delay a German invasion of home shores), Winston believed the plan to be unworkable; Britain had been fighting alone for so long it could spare neither men nor matériel. When Maisky protested at his refusal, Churchill quickly moved away, so the Russian was left alone by the fireplace with Hopkins. When the two began discussing the Soviet idea of a new front in Winston's absence, the ever-vigilant Clementine sensed the potential danger to the British position. She quickly approached the pair with a broad smile and the offer of tea. Maisky realized that with Clementine on the prowl the occasion was "unsuitable" for lobbying the Americans and left; no damage was done.[43]

Exhausted by her relentless workload and family worries, and plagued by bouts of bronchitis, Clementine had not taken a break, apart from the occasional weekend, since the summer of 1939. Nor was she alone in this. The Prof was showing "signs of breaking up under the strain," Beaverbrook's asthma was becoming more severe, Commander Thompson had lost over thirty pounds, and more than a smattering of military commanders and civil servants kept themselves going with an arsenal of pills and booze, while others had found themselves simply incapable of carrying on. Even the notoriously tough Alan Brooke later admitted that as the war dragged on he came perilously close to a nervous breakdown. So when Winston finally received an invitation from FDR to discuss the war at a secret summit in Placentia Bay, in Newfoundland, in August 1941, Clementine was jubilant and threw herself into the preparations. By contrast, Roosevelt kept his wife, Eleanor, in the dark, telling her, along with the rest of the nation, that he was going fishing.

With Winston out of the country from August 4, Clementine seized her chance for a respite. She checked into a "Nature Cure" clinic known colloquially among England's upper classes as the "mad-house." Today, Champneys in Tring, Hertfordshire, is more of a beauty clinic and spa offering some conventional medical services, but in the 1940s, Dr. Lief's establishment had a reputation for strange "electrical" appliances and putting its patients into padded cells where they were "starved and hosed and worse."[44] Fortunately, Clementine's treatment appears to have been of a milder sort: "The 'mad-house' is comfortable and well run," she related on her fourth day. "I have massage, osteopathy, hot and cold showers etc etc, but nothing to eat so far but tomatoe [sic] juice and pineapple juice." She was looking forward to being allowed some milk the following day, and then to "work up" to solid food. "The idea is to give the digestion a complete rest."[45]

Dr. Lief was undoubtedly concerned about his VIP patient, who even now never stopped monitoring events. Upon her return home, he advised her to take a day off from her duties every week, but though "rest days" were duly marked in her diary for the next couple of months it became obvious the idea was unsustainable. Neither the Nazis nor her husband observed a six-day week. Even so, when she went to greet Winston at King's Cross station on the morning of August 19, she felt much revived, and the news from his summit gave cause for optimism. He and Roosevelt had signed the Atlantic Charter—outlining their joint hopes for the postwar world and affirming the principles of self-determination and free trade—and had developed what appeared to be a genuine and warm relationship. The president had resisted making any promise that the US would enter the war, but surely it could not now be long in coming?

Four long months later, on the night of Sunday, December 7, the closest of the Churchills' circle gathered for dinner at Chequers—"Pug" Ismay, Winant, Harriman and his daughter Kathleen, Pamela, Winston's private secretary John Martin and naval aide Commander Thompson. The mood was glum: news from the front was relentlessly bad and yet America was still stalling. Under Lend-Lease, it was stepping up supplies, but still it would not join the actual fighting. Clementine, too exhausted to join them, had taken to her bed. Winston was so down he silently held his head in his hands. Around nine, his butler Sawyers carried in a little flip-top radio and switched it on for the BBC news, just in time to catch a momentous announcement: "Japanese aircraft have raided Pearl Harbor, the American naval base in Hawaii."

What happened next is a little unclear. Some reports suggest Winston danced a celebratory jig with Winant, others that in the

confusion of the moment the prime minister simply asked the ambassador what he should do first. It is known that the two men soon
put in an urgent call to Roosevelt, who talked of being "in the same
boat now." The new certainty that America would soon be at war
(Roosevelt declared war on Japan the following day and three days
later Japan's allies Germany and Italy declared war on the US) was
obviously an untrammeled relief for the British. But the Americans
present joined in the palpable excitement. "The inevitable had finally
arrived," Harriman recalled. "We all knew the grim future that it
held, but at least there was a future now."[46]

Once he had discussed the news and its repercussions with Clementine, Winston retired to bed and in his own words "slept the sleep
of the saved and the thankful." He had long compared America to a
woman who had to be wooed; now she was, as he put it, finally "in
the harem." Across the Atlantic, no one thought to inform the president's wife. Eleanor had been her husband's political partner during
the New Deal social reforms of the thirties, but as Franklin's attentions had shifted from welfare to weapons she had found herself increasingly excluded. Now she was left to deduce that America had
joined the fighting from the frantic traffic in and out of her husband's
office.

The next day Churchill began making plans to visit Roosevelt in
Washington. Clementine wished him luck with his momentous
mission—"May God keep you and inspire you to make good plans
with the President"—while excoriating, in an uncommonly bellicose
tone, those "Nazi hogs" and "yellow Japanese lice."[47] After crossing
the Atlantic through a series of terrific gales, Winston stayed at the
White House over Christmas, leaving Clementine behind with her
cousin Maryott Whyte (who was still serving the Churchills), as
Mary was on active duty with her guns at Enfield, North London.

Lacking Clementine's loving patience, the White House staff
found Winston a trying guest and misinterpreted the glass constantly
to be found by his side as an indication that he "drank like a fish." (In
fact, he disliked the president's American martinis so much he would
excuse himself and pour them down the lavatory, refilling the glass

with water.)[48] During his visit, he was given the Rose Suite within the family quarters on the second floor, only a few doors down from the president. Taking advantage of this proximity, the two leaders often talked long into the night.

It was not just the staff who were disturbed by his nocturnal habits and supposed drinking habits. Eleanor Roosevelt, a near-teetotaler whose family was riddled with alcoholism, loathed Winston's night-owl lifestyle and railed at the effect of his visit on the health of her husband, who had been partially paralyzed by polio since 1921 and needed regular sleep. She also disliked the way Churchill, in her view, romanticized war. Unwilling to play the part of adoring listener to the great man, she was forthright in her own opinions; they were never likely to get on.

Eleanor's discovery in 1918 of Franklin's adulterous relationship with her beautiful social secretary, Lucy Mercer, had made her fiercely independent. Roosevelt's illness—and his desire to avoid a career-wrecking divorce—may have brought them back together, but the resulting partnership was professional rather than intimate. When Franklin could not attend speeches or rallies in the 1920s because of his condition, Eleanor stood in for him, becoming as a result one of the first great female voices of the Democratic Party. She had also acted as the president's eyes and ears during his administration's battle to implement the New Deal welfare plan in response to the depression of the thirties. But their marriage, according to one of their five surviving children, remained in a state of "armed truce" throughout.

Unlike Winston, Franklin was not a one-woman man. He chose to surround himself with adoring and undemanding admirers, referred to by Eleanor as his "handmaidens." During the war these included the exiled Princess Märtha of Norway—who was striking, flirtatious and at his request called him "dear godfather"—his private secretary Missy LeHand and also, unbeknown to his wife, a woman with a voice like seductive "dark velvet," the very one whom he had promised to forsake to save his marriage: Lucy Mercer (now married to a society figure twenty years her senior).

Eleanor retaliated by building her own fiefdom at Hyde Park, two miles from the main house, a collection of stone buildings known as Val-Kill. Here, in her loneliness, she established a rival court, and attempted to build several intense relationships with both women and men. But nothing could quite assuage her feeling of disappointment and betrayal. By the time America entered the war, she was fifty-seven and age had not been kind to her. Her wavy brown hair was flecked with gray and her buckteeth and receding chin detracted from her dazzling blue eyes. Nearly six foot tall, she dominated a room but did not conform to Winston's ideas of an "attractive" woman. Uninterested as she was in fripperies such as good food, decor or even her own dress, he felt there was something unusually masculine about her. Churchill may not have been convinced, but the American people appreciated the energy she expended on their behalf, and her unfailingly sharp-minded and wholesome public image; she often enjoyed higher approval ratings than her husband. Her "My Day" syndicated column, highly paid lecture tours, press conferences, speeches to party conventions and solo visits to slums, mines and factories had in time made her one of the most visible figures in American life, and a potent political force in her own right.

Winston appears to have been unfamiliar with the role Eleanor had pursued during her nine years as First Lady. Or, more likely, he willfully failed to appreciate her work for the poor in order to make a point. Such activism smacked of a form of female emancipation that was more characteristic of American women, a phenomenon he was not eager to see spread to British shores (and especially to his own home). When Eleanor asked him over lunch what Clementine was doing for the war effort he mischievously expressed his delight that his wife did not engage in any public activities, saying that she stayed at home. A strained silence fell on the table as all eyes turned toward Mrs. Roosevelt, but she never "batted an eyelash."[49] It was fortunate for Winston that Clementine had remained in England.

No doubt he compared Eleanor unfavorably to Clementine—as had Harry Hopkins—when it came to the food served at her table. Ernest Hemingway once claimed the cooking at the Roosevelt White

House to be "the worst [he had] ever eaten" and the president himself remarked that it "would do justice to the automat." Eleanor's cook, Henrietta Nesbitt, was not yet restricted by wartime rationing as Mrs. Landemare was in Britain but the US First Lady's puritan streak blinded her to the sensory—and diplomatic—shortfalls of her dreary and repetitive cuisine. Mrs. Nesbitt's signature salads, for instance, were composed of "a mountain of mayonnaise, slice of canned pineapple [and] carved radishes."[50] Roosevelt never touched them, murmuring sadly, "No thank you," when offered one, although guests felt obliged to peck at one out of politeness. Winston was horrified to be presented with the sort of creamy soup he particularly detested not once but several times during his stay, including on Christmas Day. Evidently, Eleanor had failed to research her guest's particular likes and dislikes, as her British counterpart would have done.

Occasionally the president would rebel, refusing to eat any more liver, string beans or broccoli, all of which he particularly loathed, and once turning away salt fish after it had been served for lunch four days in a row. By contrast, the undercooked quail and pheasant he loved were kept off the menu. Eleanor herself took an "almost grim satisfaction in the austerity"[51] but Roosevelt half-jokingly warned her that his unappetizing diet did not "help" his "relations with foreign powers," saying, "I bit two of them today."[52] Some observers said her stubborn attitude was a form of drawn-out culinary revenge for Franklin's affair.

Whatever the case, Eleanor was clearly a determined woman who did not see it as her duty to pamper and indulge her husband, or to run a house with Clementine's attention to detail. Visitors to the White House came away astonished to find their white gloves blackened by the dust, filthy threadbare carpets and curtains in the process of rotting away.

Winston seems to have been too busy discussing strategy with Roosevelt to write home much during his trip, apart from one lengthy letter sent from the ship on his way over. He added a quick postscript on arrival, noting, "All is very good indeed . . . The Americans are magnificent in their breadth of view."[53] He did, however, telephone from the White House to establish Clementine's foot size so that he could buy her some much-desired new stockings. She in turn mostly reported on domestic news, except for a gentle reminder that the American declaration of war was only the beginning: "I have been thinking constantly of you & trying to picture & realise the drama in which you are playing the principal—or rather it seems—the only part—I pray that when you leave, that the fervour you have aroused may not die down but will consolidate into practical & far-reaching action."[54]

It was during Churchill's time with the Roosevelts—twenty-eight months into the war, beyond Clementine's watchful gaze—that the pressures of his position finally caught up with him. During a ceremony in front of a large crowd on Christmas Eve at which he helped Roosevelt light the Christmas tree on the White House's South Lawn and delivered a moving speech, he began to feel palpitations. Then, on Boxing Day night, after addressing Congress for the first time, as he leaned out to close a stubborn bedroom window he was gripped by an acute pain in his chest and found himself struggling to breathe.

His doctor, Lord Moran, suspected he had suffered a minor heart attack but decided not to tell anyone, especially not his sixty-seven-year-old patient. America had only just entered the war and there was "no one but Winston to hold her by the hand."[55] Nothing could be allowed to impede the success of the so-called Arcadia summit in drawing up a joint strategy—although the episode was an ominous harbinger of things to come.

When Winston finally left Washington on January 14, Hopkins handed him an affectionate note for Clementine. "You would have been quite proud of your husband on this trip because he was ever so good natured . . ." She had been given a welcome respite from the grueling task of looking after her husband. In her absence, Hopkins had discovered the immensity of managing two men he referred to as the "prima donnas."[56] No wonder he was admitted to the Navy Hospital shortly after the prime minister's departure, where he collapsed from exhaustion. The war was exacting a heavy price on everyone.

• • •

America's entry into the war, however heartening, did nothing immediately to stem mounting discontent at home. In January 1942 criticism of the government's prosecution of the war—not least the recent loss of two great battleships, reverses in the African desert and almost unchecked Japanese advances through British territories in Southeast Asia—led to a vote of confidence in the Commons. Winston won by 464 to 1, but that success failed to silence the critics and the doubters. Even his once infallible rhetoric was losing its potency, and his ministers—some of whom were jealous at Winston's trips away from the drabness of wartime London to the bright lights of Washington—began to grumble about drift and detachment at the top. It is significant that Winston now appointed the Labour leader Clement Attlee as his deputy prime minister, the first person in Britain to hold such a role, to take the reins in his absence. Winston, convinced that the "bulk of the Tories" hated him, began to wonder whether his time in power had run its course. Victory in battle still seemed determined to elude him. And worse was yet to come.

On February 15, 1942, the Japanese took Singapore after the surrender of sixty thousand British troops—a defeat Winston himself described as the worst disaster and largest capitulation in British history. Clementine fretted about the effect this latest ignominy would have on his already battered morale. "Oh how glad I am that you are back once more to encourage, to cheer, to charm us," she wrote to Hopkins when he visited again in April 1942. "You can't think what a difference it makes to Winston. He is carrying a very heavy load and I can't bear his dear round face not to look cheerful and cherubic in the mornings . . . What with Singapore . . . we are indeed walking through the Valley of Humiliation."[57]

Winston's woes were exacerbated, in Clementine's view, by Beaverbrook, who was destabilizing the government with periodic threats to resign as minister of supply or by demanding vastly greater powers to carry on. In her desire to protect Winston, she sometimes overreacted. Her view of her longtime enemy had recently softened, in part because of his pride in his gallant pilot son Max, and also because of his generosity to her numerous causes. But now she believed his impetuous behavior was harming her husband; she even suspected he might have his sights set on toppling him. During a heated row with Winston in mid-February 1942 she unleashed an angry tirade against Beaverbrook, whom she feared would turn out to be another Fisher—then rapidly regretted it. "My Own Darling, I am ashamed that by my violent attitude I should just now have added to your agonising anxieties—Please forgive me," she wrote in a little note. But she refused to suppress her suspicions of Beaverbrook completely: "Try ridding yourself of this microbe which some people fear is in your blood. Exorcise this bottle Imp & see if the air is not clearer & purer."[58]

In the event, Beaverbrook was persuaded to become minister of production, only to resign a fortnight later, blaming his asthma. Pamela, despite being both Beaverbrook's protégée and his intimate, backed Clementine's judgment. Clementine knew "probably quite rightly . . . that Max would use Winston to the maximum but also throw him to the wolves if he felt inclined."[59] Ironically, Beaverbrook professed to be a great fan of Clementine, and of the "home life" she created. Winston's "relationship with Mrs Churchill," he told a friend, "might be told in story form as a life-time of domestic content."[60]

The military situation took a further dire turn in June 1942, while Winston was again staying at the White House. Devastating news came through of the fall of the strategically important port of Tobruk in North Africa and the surrender of thirty thousand British and Empire troops to a German force half the size. Hopkins knew from experience how Clementine, intimately involved in the war as ever, would be deeply concerned at this latest bitter setback and wrote to her immediately to stress that Winston was trying to put on a brave face. "No one knows better than you that Tobruk was a great shock to him." He nevertheless conceded, "There was nothing any of us could do or say that could temper the blow."[61] The jibe from the Labour MP Aneurin Bevan, a long-term critic of the coalition government, that Winston "won debate after debate, but lost battle after battle" wounded him deeply.[62] But all those months of wooing the Americans had paid off, as Roosevelt offered support in place of criticism, diverting vital Sherman tanks and guns from the US military to help the beleaguered British recapture lost ground.

On his return to Britain Churchill defiantly won another confidence vote in early July 1942 (this time by 477 votes to 25), but in his speech to the Commons he offered a rare glimpse of his own suffering—an admission that bore all the signs of Clementine's gift for reading the public mood: "Some people assume too readily that, because a Government keeps cool and has steady nerves under reverses, its members do not feel the public misfortunes as keenly as its independent critics," he said. "On the contrary, I doubt whether anyone feels greater sorrow or pain than those who are responsible for the general conduct of our affairs."

Family grievances also weighed heavily on the Churchills at this time—not least Randolph's bitterness toward them. One night in spring 1942, father and son rowed so violently about "condoning" Pamela's affair with Harriman that Clementine feared Winston might have a seizure; she banned Randolph from Downing Street for the rest of the war. "I think the greatest misfortune in R's life is that he is Papa's son," Mary recorded in her diary of the time. "Papa has spoilt and indulged him & is very responsible."[63] Nevertheless, Mary and her sisters were outraged at Pamela's adultery and never really forgave her.

Not long after this distressing confrontation, a humiliated Randolph volunteered to leave a safe staff job in Cairo to join the Special Air Service (SAS) and operate behind enemy lines. It seemed as if he could do no right; Clementine was furious with him for what she perceived as gross selfishness at a time when Winston was "bearing not only the burden of his own country but, for the moment, of an un-prepared America." She raged at Randolph's decision, saying he should simply have "quietly and sensibly" rejoined his old regiment rather than choosing a highly risky operation that would cause his father "agony of mind." Pondering whether she should send Randolph an "affectionate" cable begging him, for his father's sake, to rejoin his old regiment, she concluded plaintively: "He might listen to me, as though he does not care for me, I know he respects me."[64] Wisely, she did not cable him and Randolph went on to sign up with the SAS as he had desired. It was an occasion when her concern for her husband perhaps blinded her, as her daughter Mary reflected, to the interests of her son.

Not that she was unwilling to confront Winston when she had to. One instance was his order, in early November 1942, for the church bells to be rung to celebrate the British Army's first major victory, at El Alamein in Egypt, where Lieutenant-General Montgomery's troops had irreversibly broken the German line and secured the Suez Canal. She shared his joy at for once receiving good news—made possible in large part by those Sherman tanks Roosevelt had delivered after the fall of Tobruk—but the bells had remained silent since the outbreak of war in case they were needed to signal an invasion and Clementine feared that ringing them now, to mark a single triumph, would be both premature and hubristic. Mary, who was at home on leave, remembered her mother being "violent" in her argument and in her view "quite rightly."[65] In the face of such formidable opposition, Winston backed down—at least until British forces had triumphantly reentered Tobruk (scene of their previous humiliation) a few days later.

It was natural for him to be ebullient, even overbearing, in victory. Perhaps Clementine also reminded him to treat his staff well. One of his secretaries in those weeks, when the war finally seemed to be turning in Britain's favor, recalled how "once he began to bark he quickly stopped himself."[66]

Clementine took particular pains to ensure Winston was on his best behavior when they welcomed Eleanor Roosevelt to Britain at the end of October 1942 for a three-week trip to find out more about women's experience of the war and to visit American troops. Once again, they pulled out all the stops: after spending her first few days at Buckingham Palace with the king and queen, Eleanor was to join Winston and Clementine for a weekend at Chequers. "I confide my Missus to the care of you and Mrs Churchill," wrote Roosevelt, who had encouraged the trip as a way of soothing Eleanor's obvious discontent at her reduced political role. (She now felt so distanced from him that she had just rejected a rare request to come back and live with him again as his wife.) "I know our better halves will get on beautifully," he had written to Winston in parting. He sent as a gift a Virginia ham, prompting the diplomatic response from Clementine (who was now accustomed to receiving one from almost every visiting American): "I so *love* Virginia hams."

It was the first time these redoubtable women had met, and both were curious. They certainly looked different: Clementine beautiful and immaculately presented, Eleanor a little horsey and often rather windswept. More significantly, their public personas stood in marked contrast: Clementine avoided voicing her views publicly and remained at her husband's side almost throughout the war, whereas Eleanor maximized her own status, traveled widely without the president (to the point that the *Washington Star* once ran the ironic headline MRS. ROOSEVELT SPENDS NIGHT AT WHITE HOUSE) and confidently aired her own opinions in newspaper columns, even when they were at odds with her husband's policies. Eleanor had learned to use her position as America's First Lady to further causes she believed in and was frequently credited with having become the "most influential woman of her age."[67] She was even sometimes referred to, half-jokingly, as "Madam President." Clementine was merely (if incorrectly) viewed as *just* Winston's wife.

These apparent differences masked an astonishing number of parallels in their lives. They were of a similar age and upper-class background; they shared a concern for the poor and a dislike of gambling and extravagance that led some to consider them "crashing bores." (Roosevelt in particular felt the constraints of "living with a saint.") Both had also been schooled in England—in Eleanor's case after the early deaths of her parents—and each had been taken in hand by an inspirational headmistress. They had endured difficult and fearful childhoods, and as girls had been considered plain (Eleanor's mother had called her "granny"). Their lives had been touched by family tragedy and left them plagued by self-doubt, sometimes even depression. Neither was conventionally "feminine" (one of Clementine's former employees thought she "would have made a very good man"). Like Clementine, Eleanor thought herself an inadequate mother and had lost an infant child, and like Winston, Franklin was unwilling to impose discipline on his children. Their respective broods were often unhappy and sometimes unpleasant: the four Roosevelt sons who reached adulthood were to rack up eighteen marriages between them; Clementine's offspring would blunder through eight (although Mary was successfully happy in hers).

They also shared the chronic loneliness and isolation that often afflicts the wives of ambitious men. Their husbands had dealt with huge personal crises—the humiliation of the Dardanelles had brought Winston to his lowest ebb; polio had crippled Roosevelt—and bounced back stronger. Winston and Franklin were implacable optimists who, in some ways, had never entirely grown up. Now fate had chosen them to carry the immense burden of saving the world, and neither man's spouse found her supporting role easy, although in divergent ways each "shattered the ceremonial mould"[68] and went far beyond what political wives had achieved before. Eleanor had never wanted to be First Lady; there was much in Clementine that *did* want to be married to the prime minister, but this desire was tempered by her insecurity. The two women were keepers of their husbands' consciences, safeguarding the "ordinary" citizen's interests; both were brave and stoical. On occasion, they shored up the Anglo-American alliance when Roosevelt and Winston fell out. Ultimately, however, one was to prove considerably more influential during the war than the other, although not the one observers at the time might have guessed.

Eleanor arrived in London at Paddington station on the evening of October 23, 1942. A large crowd had gathered to greet her. People were grateful to the Americans for entering the war and impressed by stories of Eleanor Roosevelt's commitment to the poor. The king and queen were there too, to "welcome [her] with all [their] hearts." At Buckingham Palace she was put in an enormous suite, specially restored after a bombing raid. She was also given her own ration card and assigned a bed in the converted cellar that served as a royal air-raid shelter. A five-inch mark had been drawn in the bath to show the maximum depth of water permitted and she was told there would be no heating, whatever the weather, until November 1. Though First Lady of the most powerful country on Earth, Eleanor felt intimidated by the grandeur of her surroundings, and on her first night she stumbled around in the dark because she could not find the light switches.[69] Uncharacteristically, she even fretted about her wardrobe and her hair.

British women struggling with severe clothing rations warmed to Eleanor's lack of ostentatious glamour; some were taken with the idea that her hat and coat looked as if they had been made over. She came across as more homely than Clementine—more believably of the people—and she was refreshingly informal. She instantly called Clementine's secretary Grace Hamblin by her first name—an unimaginable familiarity in the Churchill household until that point—and thereafter Clementine (but not Winston) followed suit. She drowned her insecurities in a punishing work schedule that included touring the capital with the queen, dozens of trips up and down the country, and—like a surrogate mother—a promise to sort out the unsuitable thin cotton socks issued to American soldiers stationed in Britain (the first had arrived back in January 1942). She made sure American commanders ordered 2.5 million woolen replacements.

Like her compatriots, Clementine was bowled over by Eleanor's boundless energy, as well as her flattering curiosity about every detail of life on the home front. Her enthusiasm never seemed to flag, and she soon outpaced not only the posse of "saggy-kneed" reporters who trailed her every move but also Clementine. On one visit Clementine was left to sit and rest on a marble staircase while Eleanor ran up four flights to chat with more workers. The American First Lady went out of her way through mud and rain to meet the former hairdressers, typists and housewives who were now digging ditches, servicing planes and driving tractors. She was also impressed by the legions of female volunteers who had stepped up to staff hostels, mobile libraries and canteens, or to spruce up shelters and distribute the thousands of tons of clothing and other supplies collected from America and the Commonwealth. The huge and unconventional role of British women in wartime had become the norm through necessity, but Eleanor's praise lent it dignity, even glamour. She talked enthusiastically about transplanting many of the ideas she saw in action in Britain back to the US. (On her return home, she hired a dancer to develop a program for entertaining children in case bombing raids started in America, explaining that she had seen "similar activities" in the shelters Clementine had shown her in Britain.)[70] It was all enormously gratifying for her British counterpart, who had done so much to bring women into the war both by organization and by her own example; almost the entire female population was now taking part in the struggle in some way.

Their contribution, in a country whose attitudes had previously seemed so conservative, appears to have struck many Americans—and helped to convince them that Britain really might prevail. "It was not just the occasional woman who was operating a machine or scrubbing a floor," Winant noted. "It was all the women. And it wasn't just the women who were used to hard work, but frequently those who lived lives of comparative leisure."[71] Harriman wrote to a friend: "It is the spirit of the women that is carrying this country through the frightful experience of the bombing."[72] He told his wife, "[T]he women are the mainstay of England."

Harriman's assistant Robert Meiklejohn was similarly "astonished by the absence of fear or panic" during even the most ferocious bombing raids. When, as a result of one attack, the department store Selfridges caught fire, his female neighbors "acted as if the bombing were like a thunder storm . . . A couple of women came up on the roof about three-thirty AM in their bathrobes and weren't at all frightened."[73] The US Treasury secretary Henry Morgenthau noted in his diary: "What the women in England were doing was just unbelievable . . . If it were not for the women, England would cave in today."[74]

Apart from that early call to arms in Manchester, however, Winston rarely acknowledged the part being played by women. His doctor later recalled that in all the years he had spent by Winston's side he had only heard him mention women in conversation once, concluding: "He is not interested in them."[75]

Winston was thus blind to Eleanor's popular appeal, whereas Clementine observed how Madam President was a celebrity in her own right, prompting spontaneous outbursts of cheering wherever she went. In Oxford, Cambridge, Bristol, Birmingham, Manchester, Liverpool, Glasgow, Belfast and Edinburgh, she received standing ovations. In London, people loitered around the American embassy just to catch a glimpse of her. She was no silent shadow to her husband but a fully fledged public figure; someone who used her fame and popularity to aid others or to raise morale. In what was probably her first direct letter to the president, Clementine described in gushing terms the effect his wife's presence was having "on [Britain's] women and girls," saying, "When she appears their faces light up with gladness and welcome."[76] She paid tribute to Eleanor's handling of the press: "I was struck by the ease, friendliness and dignity with which she talked with the reporters, and by the esteem and affection with which they evidently regard her." Even the enemy took note of the sensational coverage she received: the Nazi propaganda chief Joseph Goebbels issued an order to German journalists to play it all down.

Eleanor meanwhile found Clementine attractive, youthful and charming but constrained by her husband's notion that women should stay in the background. "She has had to assume a role because of being in public life," Eleanor noted in her diary; "the role is now part of her, but one wonders what she is like underneath."[77] She saw that Clementine worked diligently to support relief efforts for Russia and China, but also observed that she was "very careful not to voice any opinions publicly or to associate with any political organizations."[78] They enjoyed each other's company and talked together a great deal, but Clementine was so guarded that Eleanor found it a challenge to discern what she really believed.

By contrast, the First Lady's vocalism sometimes risked undermining her husband. In July 1940 she had appeared to argue in her newspaper column against the military draft—which Roosevelt had just unequivocally endorsed. The very next day, after a forthright memorandum from Franklin, she had been forced to write that her comments had been misunderstood and that she was not, in fact, an opponent of the draft after all.[79]

Yet there is no doubt that a bond formed between the two women over the course of the visit, especially after a poignant trip via Canterbury to the port at Dover, where they could see the German-occupied French coastline across the channel. As ever, crowds of excited women and children surged forward to see Eleanor, who beamed warmly back at them and talked to as many as she could. The next day, Canterbury was heavily bombed by daylight. As Clementine wrote to Roosevelt, it was more than likely that some of those who had so happily greeted them were among the casualties. A clearly shaken Eleanor wrote to her husband that "the spirit of the English people is something to bow down to."[80]

Though it is possible she was simply displaying good manners in front of such an important guest, there were occasional flashes of tension between Winston and Clementine during the visit that might suggest she welcomed Eleanor's willingness to challenge him. At a small dinner party held in Eleanor's honor, attended by Brendan Bracken and Henry Morgenthau, the prime minister brought up the subject of Spain. Eleanor asked why it had not been possible to help the antifascists. Winston replied that those around the table would have been "the first to lose [their] heads" if the Spanish republicans had won. Eleanor, who recalled his being "quite annoyed"[81] by her intervention, countered that she did not care if she lost her head. Incensed by the public confrontation, Winston fired back: "I don't want you to lose your head and neither do I want to lose mine!" At this point, Clementine leaned across the table and said pointedly, "I think perhaps Mrs Roosevelt is right." An astonished Winston rose abruptly from the table, signaling that dinner was over.

"I do not think Mrs Roosevelt ever really got my father," Mary said in an interview much later. "She was very suspicious of him. He loved jokes and stories and was never earnest—not her sort at all."[82]

Sensing the antipathy between Eleanor and her husband, Clementine took pains to be her most charming and emollient with the president himself, writing: "On each occasion that Winston has been to America he has told me of your great goodness and hospitality to him & I only wish that I could do something adequate to show you how I feel about this. I hope one day to meet you in person & tell you." It was perhaps the first time she felt the need to paper over cracks in the Churchill-Roosevelt alliance. It would not be the last.

Shortly after Eleanor returned to America, a Gallup poll revealed that she was probably "the target of more adverse criticism and the object of more praise than any other woman in American history."[83] Nearly half of the country thought it brilliant she did not stay at home and spoke her mind, but two in five thought it terrible, wanting her to remain indoors, "where a wife belongs." It proved that attitudes were still conservative, but in the US at least, things were changing fast. FDR was intensely proud of what she had achieved in cementing relations between the two powers at this crucial moment in the war and she herself was on a high. The trip had been met with unalloyed enthusiasm in the British and American press—one *Newsweek* reporter gushed that she had received "the greatest ovation ever paid any American touring Britain." Meanwhile, Clementine had watched and learned. For the rest of the war she was to push herself forward in a way that would have been unthinkable before.

The influence was not entirely one-sided. When Eleanor got home, she did something completely out of character: she took an hour and a half out of her frenetic work schedule to have her hair and nails done.

CHAPTER ELEVEN

From FDR to Stalin

1943–45

It was an almost intolerable burden to bear alone. Winston's doctor had met Clementine privately sometime in January 1943, and what he had told her was devastating. Winston's worsening heart condition meant he might suffer a critical coronary thrombosis at any moment. Flying long distances or at very high altitudes, Lord Moran explained, not only made such an occurrence more likely, it would also make it more severe. Knowing what this might mean for Winston's capacity to continue conducting the war, Moran had decided he must seek instruction from Clementine: should the prime minister be informed of the seriousness of his condition, or should he deliberately be kept in the dark?

After talking it over with Mary,[1] Clementine took the decision that Winston must be allowed to carry on unencumbered by fears for his own life. Throughout 1943, he was to be almost perpetually in the air, shuttling between conferences in Europe, America, the Middle East and Africa, often flying over the most hostile terrain. When someone once spoke of the leaders of America, Britain and the Soviet Union as the Holy Trinity, Stalin quipped: "If that is so, Churchill must be the Holy Ghost. He flies around so much."[2] Yet Clementine did not attempt to dissuade her husband from these travels. Often, indeed (provided Moran accompanied him) she applauded them. She thought first and foremost of what was best for her country; she redoubled her efforts to care for her husband but kept the awful truth of his condition to herself. It was arguably her most decisive—and courageous—act of the war.

Apart from the particular risks to his health and the danger of enemy attack, air travel at the time was generally far riskier than it is today. Transatlantic flights were made in converted bombers or flying boats often at an altitude of only eight thousand feet, at which turbulence was frequently severe. Bombed-out runways, technical faults and primitive navigation systems meant that accidents were frequent. Virtually every conference Winston attended was marked by the death of one or more of the participants in a plane crash, and back home there was often an agonizing wait before Clementine knew whether he had been on board.

Once upon a time, her horror at the thought of his flying had threatened to drive her to hysteria, but in the thirty years since she had learned to maintain a cheerful façade. She would watch his plane take off and would keep her eyes fixed on it until it disappeared into the "blackness." The sheer willpower required for a woman of her fearful disposition was exhausting. "The effect she so often conveyed of serenity was an artifact of self-control," Mary explained, "and she paid a high price for it in nervous strain."[3]

Nor was sea travel without worry: ships were vulnerable to U-boat or aerial attack, and often a radio blackout was imposed to prevent the Germans from finding out where he was, meaning that Clementine was cut off too. On one crossing to America, notices in Dutch were posted around the ship with the aim of starting a rumor that Queen Wilhelmina of the Netherlands was aboard. In wartime, Winston had come to hate the sea almost as much as the air, fearing drowning or, worse, being captured. Clementine slipped books into his luggage—classic novels or a biography of Napoleon—to take his mind off the danger. Not that he sought to avoid it: even at home he would put himself at risk, insisting that the cars in which he traveled should jump red lights and go the wrong way around roundabouts to save time. It was all a bit much for Clementine, who preferred a stately pace.

Winston kicked off 1943 by flying thirteen hundred miles in an unheated bomber to meet Roosevelt in Casablanca. Clementine, perhaps unsurprisingly given what she now knew, was especially affectionate during his absence. On January 14, two days after his departure, she wrote: "My darling the Annexe and No 10 are dead & empty without you." Smoky, the Annexe cat, "wander[ed] around disconsolate." She reassured him that there had been no leaks about the meeting: "So far at this end 'the secret' is water-tight."[4] Winston was equally solicitous—particularly after bombing resumed over London on January 18. Using his code name "Air Commodore Frankland," he cabled his private office (somewhat hypocritically): "Air Cde Frankland wishes you to ensure that Mrs Frankland and the servants go down to the shelter in event of air raids warning."[5]

Afterward, when he flew on to meetings in Cairo, Turkey, Cyprus and Algiers, Clementine tried to keep his spirits high with wordplay, punning on his next code name, "Mr. Bullfinch." "I am following your movements with intense interest," she wrote. "The cage is swept and garnished, fresh water and hemp seed are temptingly displayed, the door is open and it is hoped that soon Mr Bullfinch will fly home." An amused Winston replied: "Keep cage open for Saturday or Sunday. Much love."[6]

The Roosevelts' correspondence was meanwhile concerned almost entirely with practicalities.[7] Indeed, Winston's thoughts about FDR were markedly more emotional than the First Lady's. When the president's plane took off at the end of the conference, he remarked: "If anything happened to that man, I couldn't stand it. He is the truest friend . . . [and] the greatest man I've ever known."[8]

Clementine made a point of waiting, beautifully dressed and smiling, to welcome Winston whenever he arrived home from his travels, and his return from North Africa on February 7 was no exception. Even while he was still in transit, she had been unable to conceal from him that her "anxiety & tension" were "severe." Yet she praised his decision to extend the trip: "What an inspiration was the visit to Turkey," she cabled him. "And how glad I am you did not allow yourself to be deviated from that extra lap of your journey. I'm thinking of you flying thro' the tenebrous dark & pray you make a good land-fall."

She was then informed of the dreaded news that his plane had developed a technical fault. "Thank God engine trouble discovered *before* you started. I shall come to station to meet you. Please let me get into train before you come out—I like to kiss my Bull-finch privately & not be photographed doing it!"[9]

Their reunion did little to quell her unease. Winston returned unwell—with a nagging cold and a look of utter weariness—and less than a fortnight later, on one of the rare occasions when they ate alone together during the war, he became seriously sick. The next day he was diagnosed with pneumonia, which, for an exhausted man in his late sixties, was a life-threatening illness. Clementine kept a brave face, but that Sunday she prayed at the Royal Military Chapel in Wellington Barracks, a gilded refuge across St. James's Park from Downing Street. In under a week Winston was feeling better; only then did Clementine tell Mary, now her most trusted confidante, how worried she had been.

The doctors packed them both off for ten days' convalescence at Chequers, but it was not much of a "rest cure." The Churchills received the king in the White Parlour (as Winston was not yet strong enough for his weekly audience at the palace), and Anthony Eden, the foreign secretary, and a variety of other ministers—often with their wives and children in tow—also descended on the house. In between, Clementine rushed off to fulfill her own official duties.

Two years earlier she had become president of the YWCA's Wartime Appeal, her introduction to large-scale fund-raising. The Young Women's Christian Association provided hotels, clubs and canteens for women war workers and the rising numbers of servicewomen. Clementine had started making broadcast appeals for donations on the BBC, at first sticking rigidly to someone else's script but over time gaining in confidence and putting more of herself into the message. In pursuit of her cause, she now found herself holding forth in such intimidating all-male bastions as the stock exchange, prompting a remark from the queen in 1943 that she was a "brave woman." "Don't be shocked," she felt obliged to tell Winston, "I didn't force my way in. I was invited by the Chairman . . . I was terrified, but I think it all went off very well . . . I wore my best hat and made myself up to the best advantage I hope!"[10]

Following Eleanor Roosevelt's dictum that "you must do the thing you cannot do," Clementine was at last defying her instinctive reserve. Her onetime critic Jock Colville (now returned to the Churchills' staff) marveled at her newly confident popular touch. In March 1944 he accompanied her to a "Back to Work" exhibition for disabled servicemen, and was "impressed" by the way she "talked to all the men there and did the whole thing with real thoroughness."[11]

It was, however, her appeal for the Red Cross Aid to Russia Fund—originally launched back in October 1941—that was to become her greatest work. By Christmas she had already raised £1 million, and buoyed by this success she increasingly pushed herself forward to maintain the momentum over the difficult long haul. She recruited factory workers, millionaires and widows; she organized auctions, flag days and galas and persuaded celebrity musicians to give concerts. In 1943, she appealed directly to schoolgirls to knit gloves, scarves and hats for the Russian forces and rewarded them with effusive letters of thanks. Dorothy Southon—who had been evacuated from Folkestone to a school in south Wales—and her two friends sent "a large number" of knitted items to Downing Street "for Mrs Churchill." They were thrilled by her hand-signed response:

> Dear Gladys, Pamela, and Dorothy,
>   Thank you very much for your gift which I have just received. I am most grateful to you for the trouble you have taken to help the heroic Russians in their terrible but victorious struggle against the wicked invaders of their country.
>
> Your sincere friend,
>
> Clementine S. Churchill[12]

She also presided over home nations football matches (internationals were otherwise suspended during the war) in aid of her fund. At the England v. Scotland game in January 1942 at Wembley, she was forced to excuse herself to the sixty-four-thousand-strong crowd, explaining that she had to hurry away to see "[her] husband," who had just arrived back from his first trip to the White House. Standing on that hallowed turf in fur-trimmed hat and coat, while protective fighter planes soared overhead, she smiled gratefully as the spectators cheered. The next fixture, in February 1943, saw England triumph 5–3 over Wales and raised the bar for charity fund-raising events to a new height, bringing in £12,500 in a single day. In all, the donations eventually totaled £8 million (some £300 million in today's money).

Clementine's success demonstrated both people's trust in her and their sympathy for the Russians. By late 1941, government polling had revealed a striking increase in admiration for the Soviet Union—inspired by its resistance to the Nazi forces then surging eastward over the steppes and the stoic suffering of the Russian people in the face of appalling bloodshed. (Millions of Russians had already died; by the end of the war, the total would rise to an estimated twenty-seven million, compared to fewer than four hundred fifty thousand Britons.) Clementine reported back to Winston from her street tours, as well as her mailbag, that many in Britain were "disturbed and distressed" at their inability to do more to help the Soviets militarily. She suggested—and he agreed—that her fund might help assuage these feelings and head off potential trouble.

The lack of British assistance was clearly a bone of contention with Stalin, who still bore a grudge toward Winston over the latter's attempts to "strangle Bolshevism at birth" by intervening on the side of the White Russians following the 1918 armistice. It was vital to defuse this history of antagonism and keep a suspicious Kremlin as an ally. It would be disastrous if Moscow swapped sides again and sought peace with Germany, or became too close to Washington and moved to shut Britain out. So Clementine's Aid to Russia Fund served yet another purpose—as both Churchill and Eden saw clearly: it represented a critical show of solidarity at a time when Britain's meager military resources simply could not afford to be "bled white" by the Soviet clamor for support.

Soon hundreds of thousands of tons of medical supplies were on their way to Russia from a country itself struggling desperately with shortages. Meanwhile, Clementine worked closely with Agnes Maisky, the imperious wife of the Soviet ambassador, to resolve "conflicts of interest." It was a meeting of two volatile and patriotic women and produced plenty of fireworks, but ultimately a useful strategic friendship was forged. In a show of solidarity, Madame Maisky gave Clementine a copy of *War and Peace* inscribed "1812–1942. We destroyed our enemy then, we shall destroy our enemy also today." A year later, in February 1943, Clementine matched the gesture by (rather curiously) presenting Madame Maisky with another copy of the same work: "Here is a book for those who would penetrate the vastness and mystery of Russia." "Evidently," Ambassador Maisky noted with satisfaction, "Tolstoy's novel made a great impression on Mrs Churchill, leading her to see our people in a new way."[13] When the Maiskys were recalled to Moscow in September 1943 (Stalin deemed them to have become too pro-Churchill), Agnes thanked Clementine for her kindness.[14]

In March 1943, thanks to the strain of Winston's illnesses and her own onerous workload, Clementine developed a painful boil. Her doctors, as so often, prescribed respite from her husband, on this occasion at the seaside. Unusually she obliged, guiltily deserting Winston and taking his brother, Jack, as company for ten days at the Royal Hotel in Weymouth. She found it "curious" and "delicious" to be out of the thick of it, but it was not merely the helpings of Bird's custard at every meal that quickly bored her. Life with Winston, at the center of world events, may have stretched her to the breaking point—she was fond of quoting a line of Swinburne's poetry: "even the weariest river winds somewhere safe to sea"—but theirs was a colorful and thrilling existence. The Weymouth trip reminded her again that the alternative was insufferably "dull."

Arriving back in London in early May she found Winston preparing for another trip to Washington to plan the Allies' next move.

Tidings from North Africa, as he steamed across the Atlantic, were cheerier than the previous year, with General Alexander reporting that British forces were now "masters" of the coast. Clementine told Winston she wished she could be with him "in this hour of Victory . . . so that we could rejoice together & so that I could tell you what I feel about *your* North African Campaign."[15] She understood his craving for adulation and was assiduous in applauding his every success. This time the king also sent his congratulations, prompting Clementine to write to Queen Elizabeth—a rare royalist sally—that she had "cried with joy" at Winston's receipt of such recognition. Yet she did not allow her happiness (or her brief exile in Weymouth) to blind her to her concerns about the forthcoming meeting with Roosevelt. "I'm so afraid the Americans will think that a Pacific slant is to be given to the next phase of the War," she warned. "Do re-assure me that the European Front will take 1st place all the time."[16]

Upon arriving in Washington, Winston observed that the First Lady was not on hand to attend to the president but was "away practically all the time." Even when she was around, it became clear that Roosevelt was less than forthcoming with his wife, failing to inform her, for instance, that Winston and his entourage would be staying at the White House until shortly before they arrived. Though Eleanor was "offended" she rallied herself admirably, leading Winston to comment that "no-one could have been more friendly than she was during the two or three nights she turned up."[17] But she could not help venting her exasperation at her husband in her column, bemoaning the fact that "it had not occurred" to him that she needed time to prepare the rooms. "Before all orders were finally given, it was 10 am and I was half an hour late for my press conference," she told the world.[18] Roosevelt was thoroughly displeased at her indiscretion. By contrast Clementine never even hinted publicly about her private disagreements with Winston. But then he kept nothing from her.

Roosevelt had been closing parts of his life to Eleanor ever since his affair with Lucy Mercer more than twenty years previously. But his increased reticence after the war broke out became such that she often had little real inkling of what was going on, referring to her

newly reduced role as that of "plain citizen."[19] This feeling of redun-
dancy depressed her. "What you think or feel seems of no use or
value so I would rather be away," she wrote to her daughter Anna;
she preferred to "allow the important people" to take the decisions.
Winston was aghast at this lack of trust. "You know I tell Clemmie
everything," he told FDR over drinks at the White House one evening. Roosevelt replied: "Well, I don't do that with Eleanor because
she writes a column and she might confuse what should be said and
what shouldn't be."[20]

Curiously, for all her formidable intelligence, Eleanor considered
herself in any case unqualified to advise her husband. "One can never
be certain that one's advice is correct," she once explained, being
circumspect about the entire concept of what she called "petticoat
government."[21] This left her in what she felt to be the lesser role of
agitator, most productively on behalf of black servicemen, who at the
time were segregated, with few senior black officers (only two in the
whole US Army in 1940), and received little if any combat training.
She also lobbied—albeit often with little success—on behalf of European Jews seeking asylum in the United States and against Roosevelt's internment of Japanese Americans. According to her friend
Joseph Lash, her semi-exclusion was the consequence of Eleanor's
being "too independent, too strong, ethically too unrelenting to provide him with the kind of relaxed, unjudging company he wanted."[22]

There was something of Violet Asquith in Eleanor Roosevelt.
Both were of immense intelligence but with a propensity to pursue
an argument so vehemently that, in Violet's case, "she would advance
on her prey unrelentingly and drive him back into the fireplace."
(Jock Colville was just one victim who had the back of his trouser
legs "badly singed" as a result.)[23] Such unleavened bluntness would
not have suited Churchill at all; nor did it suit the equally egotistical
Roosevelt.

Despite their candid conversation about their respective wives,
Winston came away from Washington a reduced figure in FDR's
eyes. Now that American money, forces and firepower were flooding
into the war, the president saw himself as the senior partner in the

alliance and expected to have his way. Some of Roosevelt's closest aides recognized that he was "jealous" of Winston's legendary status and thought it not "just" that Winston should take "all the credit as leader of the Free World." He no longer looked forward to the prime minister's visits to the White House,[24] and neither did he share Winston's conviction that the future of the world depended on a "fraternal association"[25] of the English-speaking peoples.

Like many Americans of the time, Roosevelt tended to be more suspicious of British imperialism than of Russian totalitarianism. Moreover, the Red Army was no longer in disarray, as it had been until autumn 1942; after "astounding" victories in the Caucasus and Stalingrad, it was now seen as a mighty military force, particularly in comparison to the British. So while he was pouring on the charm for Winston at Shangri-La (the presidential retreat now known as Camp David) in May, Roosevelt was simultaneously petitioning Stalin for a secret meeting in July that would specifically exclude him. To Winston, word of this attempted deception came as a bitter personal blow.

Nonetheless, after a month in the US he arrived back in London on June 5 feeling revitalized. With the victory in North Africa, a lull in the bombing and his concept of an invasion of Sicily gaining American support, overall the war was moving in Britain's favor. The consequent lifting of the strain, however slight, permitted the Churchills a little time for entertainment. They played bezique, at which the strategically minded Clementine roundly beat him, and they went to the theater, taking in two new plays by Noël Coward: *This Happy Breed* and *Present Laughter*. As soon as the couple were spotted, the audiences erupted in applause, while the playwright received them in his box after the first act. Later Noël Coward would make occasional visits to Chequers, sometimes finding Clementine alone while Winston was shut up in meetings. During these precious hours, they played croquet, gossiping deliciously about the theater and high politics.

A couple of months later, in August 1943, Winston set off to Quebec for yet another conference with Roosevelt. By now the Allies had successfully invaded Sicily, causing panic among the Italian fascists and precipitating, on July 25, the ousting and imprisonment of Mussolini himself. With the Axis powers seemingly in retreat, Churchill and Roosevelt were to discuss the imminent landings on mainland Italy, and to plan what would become the D-day invasion of northern France. This time, there was to be a novel addition to the two-hundred-strong British entourage. Hoping to impress Roosevelt and thus enhance Anglo-American relations, Clementine broke with the all-male tradition at such events by accompanying her husband. Indeed, the summit became something of a family affair, as Mary was given special leave to act as the prime minister's confidential assistant, or aide-de-camp (ADC), during the trip.

Upon receiving word from Winston that Clementine and her daughter would be attending, the president cabled back, "I am perfectly delighted,"[26] although, in truth, the news raised awkward questions regarding Eleanor's possible involvement. Roosevelt answered such questions by dispatching his wife to visit US troops in the Pacific and asking his cousin Daisy Suckley—who could be relied on to proffer uncritical "smiling homage"—to act as hostess in her stead. Sensing his influence over Roosevelt was waning, Winston hoped that Clementine would charm the president just as she had previously made supporters of Winant, Hopkins and Harriman.

On August 10 the Churchills arrived in Canada on board the *Queen Mary* and were taken to the Citadelle, the fortified royal residence on the cliffs above the Saint Lawrence River. That evening Clementine gazed out across Quebec and, after four years of blackout, marveled at the sight of twinkling lights, although she felt too dog-tired to enjoy it for long. As even Colville now observed, being married to Winston Churchill was exhausting in the extreme: "The claims on her energies were incessant" and the "trials imposed"[27] gargantuan in scale.

Physically and mentally drained by the journey, she feared she would let her husband down. She had counted on a sea voyage to give her a boost but had found sleeping on board a busy ship difficult, arriving in Canada in a crumpled state and desperately in need of time alone. So she turned down Roosevelt's invitation to spend a few days before the conference at Hyde Park, his country estate, staying behind at the Citadelle instead under the concerned eye of the Canadian prime minister, Mackenzie King. Winston was bitterly disappointed, but Clementine judged that if she was to be of use during the conference proper, she would have to conserve her energy. Mercifully, by the time he and Mary returned to Quebec from their visit to Hyde Park, she appeared to be back in form. Not even General Hastings "Pug" Ismay, Winston's devoted chief of staff, guessed at her condition, writing in his memoirs that her mere presence "was a great comfort" in case the "PM got ill or was too naughty." Mary was also a boon. "What other member of his staff could march into the PM's bedroom and make him get up in time for his appointments?"[28]

Roosevelt seems not to have noticed anything remiss when he finally met her on August 17, 1943. For her part, Clementine was disappointed by the man whom her husband so adored. His easy charm usually won over detractors but it had the opposite effect on her. His greatest crime appears to have been that he took the "liberty" of addressing her as "Clemmie," a privilege normally reserved for the most deserving and long-serving friends. She was incensed at his "cheek." Mary thought it amusing (after all, Winston referred to her as "Clemmie" to the president), but it colored Clementine's opinion of Roosevelt for good. She treated him to a frosty stare. "My mother could be very critical and, at the same time, admire somebody very much," Mary explained. "That's how she was with the President. She respected him enormously but she was also a sharp spotter of clay feet, and she thought he could be very vain."[29]

Over dinner one night Roosevelt was to transgress again when the names of Sarah Churchill and the president's son Elliott cropped up in conversation. He leaned over to Clementine and whispered conspiratorially: "Wouldn't it be wonderful if something happened between those two?" Bristling with rage (and somewhat hypocritically, considering the blind eye she had turned to Sarah's affair with Winant), she drew herself up and retorted: "Mr President, I have to point out to you that they are both married to other people!" "He met his match all right," was Mary's conclusion.[30] But Daisy Suckley, a close confidante of FDR's, wrote in her diary: "With all her charm of manner, Mrs C is so very English & reserved."[31]

This moralistic version of "Clemmie" was never likely to appeal to Roosevelt. Far from her own turf and feeling overstretched, Clementine was losing her touch. It was in any case made abundantly clear that the Americans generally were in the driving seat and that for all the Churchills' efforts, Britain's leading role was transparently over.

After this most frustrating conference, the Churchill entourage decided to rest for a few days in the Laurentian Mountains. Having enjoyed a spot of trout fishing on Snow Lake, in canoes paddled by French Canadians, they repaired for the evening to luxurious log houses, with fires blazing and hot baths at the ready. "This quiet life is doing [Winston] good but he feels like he is playing truant," noted his doctor, Lord Moran.[32] In truth, nothing could dispel their general unease; no one could shake off persistent colds and lingering fatigue, especially not Clementine, who returned to Quebec early, frightening Mary with her excessive anxiety.

The party eventually rejoined Roosevelt and his entourage on September 1 at the White House, where, despite his increasingly fragile health, nothing could prevent Harry Hopkins from rising from his sickbed to greet them. The Churchills were delighted to see their trusted old ally on his feet—no doubt aware that his doctors believed that even his iron-willed commitment to waging the war could not reverse what was now a fast-approaching death sentence from cancer. But they were alarmed at how his influence over Roosevelt was ebbing away—in part because he was widely seen as their "lapdog."[33]

Fortunately, Clementine was more successful in winning over the American people than she had been in charming their president. On September 2, she attracted generous notices for her first-ever press conference. Drawing on her observations of Eleanor at work, "Mrs Winnie" joked with reporters like an old hand. The *Washington Times Herald* was gushing: "A prettier piece of English womanhood you could not find . . . [with] engaging dimples." Hailed as "Winston's greatest asset," she was described as "witty, daring and direct" and a "brilliant platform speaker." Was England becoming dowdy in the war? she was asked. Dressed in shimmering black silk, she had not thought so, she replied, "until [she] came to America!"

A few days later, Roosevelt, exhausted by Winston's late-night discussions, left the Churchills in temporary occupation of the White House and fled to Hyde Park for a rest. Winston summoned generals and politicians to the presidential residence, while Clementine threw a party for the wives of British and Commonwealth officials in the grandeur of Edwin Lutyens's British embassy; the event was so elegant and convivial it remained a talking point for months. Field Marshal Dill of the British Joint Staff Mission, who was, of course, not invited but heard all the chatter afterward, wrote her what he called a "serious FAN letter," reporting that she had given "infinite pleasure."[34]

Clementine was proving herself a public triumph in Washington. But she had always been accident-prone when stretched, and this was no exception. On her last day in town, she fell down some steps in a bookshop and cracked her elbow. She left the capital with her arm in a sling and in considerable pain. It seemed little on this trip was destined to go their way.

On September 12, the couple traveled on to Hyde Park for their thirty-fifth wedding anniversary, before returning to England. Winston infuriated her by not being ready when their train pulled in at the station; Roosevelt, who had come down to greet them in person, was kept waiting as a result. Eventually a humiliated Clementine accompanied FDR up to the house alone, although he returned to the station to resume his long vigil for her husband.[35]

Winston made amends later when he told Clementine how much he loved her. His spirits had been lifted by being back at the Roosevelt family home. Springwood, the Hyde Park mansion, was a gentleman's house, enlarged piecemeal over the years, and with thirty-five rooms it was of comparable size to Chartwell. Somehow, in its antiques, military memorabilia and rambling passageways, it also created a similar ambience. The president mixed cocktails by the fireplace in the large paneled library, and the two parties dined together, but the Churchills did not stay the night. Instead they were to board another train to take them to their waiting battle cruiser, HMS *Renown*.

There were high emotions on both sides during the farewells, with Roosevelt promising to visit Britain the following year and Clementine eager to get away. On the train, Winston thanked his ally in another rhapsodic letter: "I cannot tell you what a pleasure it has been to me, to Clemmie and to Mary to receive your charming hospitality . . . You know how I treasure the friendship with which you have honoured me."[36] The president replied less effusively some time later, sending his "best to all three of [them]." Suckley wrote in her diary that she had detected something new in the president's manner toward the Churchills: the "first very definite chill of autumn."[37]

A brisk departure from the harbor at Halifax was crucial for security reasons, but there was a problem: Winston was "running amok" and refusing to board. He had received news that British forces landing at Salerno, at the head of his personally planned assault on southern Italy, were meeting unexpectedly savage resistance from the Germans. His reaction was as irrational as it was explosive: he had to be flown to Italy at once to see the fighting for himself. The sudden arrival of the prime minister would no doubt have proven a disastrous distraction, but nothing General Ismay or the other generals and officials said could deter him. So they enlisted Clementine. "Leave it to me, Pug," she said, smiling.

"I hear you've changed your plans," she said to Winston soon afterward. "Yes," he replied. "You and Mary will be quite all right on the *Renown*." "Oh no, we won't," she answered; she would not have it said that a whole battleship had been put at the beck and call of the prime minister's wife and daughter. Refusing to board, she declared that she and Mary would return by convoy—a highly vulnerable mode of travel regularly picked off by U-boats. "We will be all right," she insisted, knowing full well the impact this standoff would have on him. An hour later Winston sent for Ismay and told him the expedition to Italy was canceled.[38]

Having been shut out of the Quebec conference, Eleanor made an early bid to accompany Roosevelt to the next meeting in November 1943, at the Soviet legation in Tehran. (This was the first of the so-called Big Three gatherings with Stalin.) Roosevelt dodged her request by claiming that women were not allowed aboard warships. But then she discovered that Winston was bringing Sarah and was livid.

Clementine also seems to have had regrets about missing the first Big Three, telling Winston: "I'm more lonely this time than ever before, because I have tasted of the excitement & interest of travel in War Time in your company."[39] Winston pined back: "How I wish you were out here with me."[40] But it was perhaps fortunate she had stayed behind, for she was busy putting out fires in the cabinet. Among those most in need of soothing was the Labour Party home secretary, Herbert Morrison, who felt "battered" by demonstrations over his decision—on compassionate grounds and with the prime minister's approval—to release the still unrepentant Mosleys. Clementine invited him to lunch and "comforted him as well as [she] could," saying, "I think is he shewing political courage." She similarly tried to placate Ernest Bevin, the minister of labor and national service, "who seemed in a bit of a temper" with Morrison.[41] All the while, she reviewed reports on parliamentary debates, read the most secret telegrams, kept Clement Attlee informed of the prime minister's progress, dealt with constituency matters, and sent back to Winston digests of public reaction to the war. Now that he was so frequently absent, her contribution on the home front was more vital than ever. And though she was not present at the conference, this did not prevent her from exerting an influence there too.

No less distrustful of Roosevelt than before, she counseled her husband to be wary of how he handled the president. In particular, she tried to assuage his fury over Roosevelt's refusal to back a British operation on the Greek island of Leros (which had capitulated to the Germans just before the summit). The disagreement was yet another sign of growing American resistance to his strategic ideas. Winston's health was sliding again, too. "Your cold must have made you miserable & . . . I know Leros must cause you deep unhappiness," she wrote. "But never forget that when History looks back . . . your patience & magnanimity will all be part of your greatness. So don't allow yourself to be made angry—I often think of your saying, that the only thing worse than Allies is *not* having Allies!"[42]

Winston continued to devote his time and attention to Roosevelt, much in the manner of a love-struck suitor. On their way to Tehran they met in Cairo, where he took enormous trouble (including conducting a reconnaissance trip himself) to arrange for the disabled president to visit the Pyramids. "I love that man,"[43] he told Sarah with tears in his eyes, and wrote to Roosevelt: "Anything like a serious difference between you and me would break my heart."[44] Winston was of course accustomed to casual cruelty from the previous object of his adoration, his father, and Roosevelt was eminently capable of perplexing caprice. As Mary later characterized the relationship: "In love there is always one who kisses, and one who offers the cheek."[45] Indeed, the next occupant of the White House, Harry Truman, was to describe his predecessor as the "coldest man [he] ever met" but said "he was a great president."

Clementine understood the strategic imperative of befriending Roosevelt (Britain depended on the US for food as well as military muscle, and would be financially sunk if the Lend-Lease aid program were curtailed, let alone closed) but she thought Winston sentimental and emotionally transparent. She had warned him to be more guarded. Now he was to discover the real nature of his "friendship" with the president. The Big Three conference felt in fact more like the Big Two. Tehran was the moment when Roosevelt clearly chose Stalin over Winston, finding it "amusing" when the Russian leader bullied his British ally. The president even joined in the taunting, laughing at Winston for his "John Bull" habits. The leaders Winston referred to as the Soviet bear and the American buffalo—in effect the new superpowers—enjoyed showing their indifference, even antipathy, to the poor little British donkey. Winston reddened and scowled (he told Clementine he found such behavior "grim" and "baffling"), but Stalin narrowed his eyes and guffawed. "My father was awfully wounded," said Mary. "For reasons of state, it seems to me, President Roosevelt was out to charm Stalin, and my father was the odd man out."[46]

After six weeks with a heavy cold in Tehran Winston asked his doctor: "Do you think my strength will last out the war? I fancy sometimes that I am nearly spent."[47] Yet despite the ordeal of the conference, he insisted on returning to Cairo afterward for further talks with Roosevelt. By now Winston was also suffering from a "gyppie tummy"; Clementine pleaded with him not to fly anymore but to come home on a "perfectly good cruiser."[48]

Moran also tried—and failed—to persuade him to abandon a subsequent flight to Tunis to see the American commander General Eisenhower. By the time Winston reached Eisenhower's white, cube-shaped villa near ancient Carthage, the sixty-nine-year-old prime minister was feeling so ill he went straight to bed. The next morning he was diagnosed with pneumonia again, and a seriously fibrillating heart. A terrified Moran urgently sent for a specialist backup team. "We were at last," he realized, "right up against things."[49]

Alarmed that Winston might die any moment, the cabinet secretly requested Clementine to fly out to be by his side. Winston put it more meekly in a cable to her: "If you could come it would be lovely."[50] She packed to leave at once, knowing full well that the crisis she had so feared since January was finally upon them. But the London airfields were closed by thick fog, so she had to endure the agony of waiting as aides frantically phoned around to find an alternative way out. Eventually she, Grace Hamblin and Jock Colville made the tortuous drive through the blackout and swirling mist to RAF Lyneham in Wiltshire, only to discover that their designated plane had developed a fault. Nothing else airworthy was available except an unheated Liberator bomber, but with the news from Carthage still worsening Clementine could wait no longer. Fortunately the bomb racks had already been removed, so a few RAF rugs were hastily spread on the floor while Clementine (rarely seen in trousers) was zipped into a flight suit ready for takeoff. Colville remembered her seeming "gay and apparently unconcerned"; she later admitted to Mary, however, that she had been so frightened her knees had been knocking together.

Though Clementine was exhausted once they were in the air, the fears inside her head made sleep impossible; no doubt she revisited many times her decision not to tell Winston about his heart condition. But her only option was courage: she dug into her luggage and produced a backgammon board. Draped in blankets to keep the perishing cold at bay and sustained by black coffee, Clementine and Colville played at least thirty games during that long, slow flight. Normally a fiercely competitive player, she struggled to focus and lost a total of two pounds and ten shillings.[51] Meanwhile, Sarah was at her father's side counting down the hours and trying to sustain his morale by reading aloud from *Pride and Prejudice* until Clementine could reach them. Fortunately, Winston was enthralled, observing to his daughter that her mother was "so like" Elizabeth Bennet, Jane Austen's sharp-witted heroine.[52] Even so, his condition was deteriorating and privately his doctors wondered whether his wife would arrive in time.

The bomber finally reached Carthage, after refueling in Gibraltar, on the afternoon of December 17. Winston "received the news of her arrival with considerable emotion," Moran noted, "but when [Moran] told her later how pleased he had been, she smiled whimsically: 'Oh yes,' she said, 'he's very glad I've come, but in five minutes he'll forget I'm here.' "[53] Her presence had an extraordinary effect, however, and Winston was soon able to send Mary a soothing message: "Your Mother is here. All is joyful. No need to worry. Tender love. Papa."[54]

For her part, Clementine was shaken by Winston's forlorn appearance, even though his doctor reassured her that he looked much better than he had two days previously. She tended to him at his bedside for a couple of hours before retiring herself.

Later that evening they dined in his bedroom. Winston was reluctant to allow her to leave him and in the night he asked for her again. She returned to his side, sitting with him until he fell asleep once more. Breaking with a lifetime's habit, she even breakfasted with him the following morning, when Moran informed her that Winston had suffered another, milder attack of fibrillation in the small hours. He was ordered to avoid excitement—and cigars—and Clementine set to work on a treatment she knew would make an instant difference. The meals being supplied by Eisenhower's staff were, as she put it, "vurry American." "Your poor father literally cannot eat the food," she wrote in horror to the family back home. "Last night we had a partridge for dinner which Sawyers informed us was cooked for an hour and a half! The result was concrete!"[55]

With Clementine now on hand, Winston was soon able to work in bed, summoning assistants and giving orders almost as normal. Sir John Martin, one of his private secretaries, observed just how important she was to his ability to go on. "Above all, Churchill was sustained in storm and stress," he judged, "because his life was rooted in such a happy marriage."[56] He did not, however, respond well to being told to take things easy and there was a lot of shouting. "He is very difficult," grumbled Moran. "On two occasions he got quite out of hand."[57]

In this he was not alone. After being all but absent for two years, Randolph had flown in from Cairo and was "causing considerable strife in the family and entourage."[58] Winston enjoyed playing bezique with his son, so he was allowed to stay, but there was a palpable tension in the air. Although Randolph's lack of consideration for his mother was evident to many of those present, Clementine smiled reassuringly and tolerated his misbehavior for Winston's sake. But privately her nerves had been stretched to the breaking point. Convinced that her husband's decline was irreversible, she told Lady Diana Cooper, who joined the party shortly afterward, that even if he survived this time his days were running out. "I never think of after the war," she revealed. "I think Winston will die when it's over . . . He's seventy and I'm sixty." The war, she told her friend, "will take all we have."[59]

On Christmas Day, she attended a service in an ammunition shed, arranged by the Coldstream Guards. There was a "dramatic culmination," Colville recalled, "when, as the Padre said the Gloria in excelsis Deo, the bells of Carthage Cathedral pealed loudly from the hill above and a white dove . . . fluttered down in front of the congregation."[60] Winston finally appeared to be out of danger and they soon left for a period of convalescence at Villa Taylor, near the Mamounia hotel in Marrakech, described by Clementine as a "mixture of Arabian Nights and Hollywood." Considerate as ever, she had made sure they delayed their departure until after Christmas so that the staff could celebrate all together.[61]

Meanwhile, she resorted to every conceivable ploy to boost Winston's strength, even enlisting her old foe Beaverbrook to entertain him. They went on picnics in the Atlas foothills, and during the eighth and last of these trips, Winston felt sufficiently strong to climb up a large boulder. Diana Cooper observed that Clementine said nothing, "but watched him with [her] like a lenient mother who does not wish to spoil her child's fun nor yet his daring."[62] She also invited General Montgomery to join the party for New Year's Eve, although she objected to his typically imperious manner. "Mrs Churchill was the only person I knew who always succeeded in subduing General Montgomery," noted Colville. On this occasion, she asked Montgomery's aide-de-camp, Noel Chavasse, to join them for dinner. "'My ADCs don't dine with the Prime Minister,' objected Monty, tartly. Mrs Churchill gave him a withering look. 'In my house General Montgomery, I invite who I wish . . .' Noel Chavasse dined."[63]

Montgomery's boastful swagger could cow even the most rugged army officers but not Clementine. Nor was she awed by any of Winston's other generals—even toughies like the chief of the imperial general staff Alan Brooke, who at Chequers used to accompany her to church on Sundays. She happily spent time alone with them, on walks or over lunch, and encouraged them to speak candidly about their troubles. After a decent interval, usually around two years, some were even allowed to address her as "Clemmie."

She noticed how many of them were unmarried, with no one to

help them bear the immense strain of fighting the war. These lonely men drew comfort from the companionship and fine food given so freely at Churchill family dinners. She was also solicitous of the wives of those who were married, sending them her "love and thoughts" when their husbands were about to embark on great battles. According to the cabinet secretary, Sir Edward Bridges, relations between the prime minister and the military "were infinitely better in the Second War than in the First"[64]—and this was in no small measure a result of Clementine's efforts. Sir Leslie Rowan, another private secretary, said the "most precious gift of all" was the friendship extended by both Churchills.[65] Whether such kindness was motivated by the strategic companionship of war, rather than by genuine affection, is unclear. Pamela, for one, found herself wondering who Clementine "really, really liked"[66] for herself rather than for duty.

While Winston lay gravely ill in Morocco, a crisis had been brewing among his fellow leaders. Roosevelt had demonstrated his readiness to tread roughshod over his closest ally, and Stalin's hostility to Britain and her prime minister had been evident from the start. As ever, the Free French leader General de Gaulle—whom Winston had the previous year considered placing under house arrest for "insubordination"—was also playing up, arranging and canceling visits on a whim. Winston loved France "like a woman"[67] and had done so much to fight her corner, despite Roosevelt's obvious "loathing" of de Gaulle and the Soviet leader's indifference to the French as a whole. France for both Winston and Clementine was of special emotional significance; their shared love of l'Hexagone had helped to bring them together. But the prickly de Gaulle had caused Winston apoplexy by cabling out a "boorish" message that was clearly unappreciative of all the prime minister had done for him. Now the Frenchman announced he was *definitely* on his way for what threatened to be a stormy encounter to discuss sensitive military plans. "I am trying to smooth Papa down," Clementine anxiously reported to the family, although she was also lecturing him to avoid antagonizing de Gaulle unnecessarily. "I hope there will be no explosions!"[68]

When the French leader arrived, Clementine was waiting for him. She quickly diverted him away from his aides and into the garden, where she could speak frankly. Sarah overheard part of the conversation, during which Clementine remarked pointedly: "Mon Général, you must take care not to hate your allies more than your enemies."[69] The subsequent lunch and discussions with Winston played out more amicably than expected, with de Gaulle most unusually insistent on speaking English.

By January 18, 1944, Winston was fit enough to return to England and resume his prime ministerial duties. Clementine's appearance in the House of Commons gallery reflected a degree of concern about the reception he might receive after being out of the country for more than two months. There was a growing feeling that he was spending too much of his time bestriding the international stage and not enough overseeing events at home. She smiled down at him as he entered the chamber and saw the House rise to cheer him, but the MP Henry "Chips" Channon found the welcome, for a man who had cheated death, merely "courteous," even "curiously cold." He thought Winston looked "disappointed," observing that he was "not loved" by MPs. The next day Winston complained of more pains around his heart, although he ascribed them to indigestion.[70]

Despite a halfhearted attempt at reconciliation in May 1943, there was never any real hope for Pamela's marriage with Randolph. She was enjoying her freedom—and doing too important a job for her country. "She was honey drawing flies," noted a CBS correspondent.[71] The so-called flies were mostly American.

She had moved out of the Dorchester and, after sharing a flat in Grosvenor Square with Harriman and his daughter Kathleen for a few months in 1942, had made a new home in November that year opposite the Connaught Hotel. Three-year-old Winston had his own room, but he and the accoutrements of infant life were rarely in evidence. Her softly lit drawing room was painted a flattering peach and furnished, Clementine-style, with antiques, silver-framed photographs and fresh flowers. Here on most evenings she presided over small groups of American generals, diplomats and journalists, interspersed with the odd infatuated Brit whom she ignored (as they were obviously of little use). Sometimes a call would come in to her number—Mayfair 5975—from Downing Street and she would say to her guests: "I have to go. He's calling me now." Over a game of late-night bezique she would then pass on to Winston whatever she had gleaned.[72]

Pamela's flat was a rationing-free zone and her male guests treasured their invitations to five-course dinners of oysters, salmon, beef and whisky. Much of the food came courtesy of the American military; one general from the Eighth Bomber Command routinely dropped off cartons of prime juicy steaks. Ed Murrow's wife, Janet, recalled feeling out of place: "Unless you were important in some way, you weren't very welcome."[73] Few other women were invited, and those who were gazed at Pamela's couture dresses and wondered how she paid for it all. Most thought Harriman was picking up the bill—her biographer has suggested he also provided her with a car, petrol and a £3,000 yearly allowance—but by then he was not the only American seeking her favors. Some suspected the real paymaster was Beaverbrook, and that he was buying information, either for his own benefit or the Churchills'.[74]

Along with others in their circle, the Duff Coopers, long-term intimates of the Churchills, thought that Winston and Clementine themselves were behind the arrangement. "They set Pam up in a very luxurious flat . . . where her job was to give dinner parties to the top American brass and if necessary go to bed with them afterwards," says their son John Julius Norwich, who remembers his parents discussing the matter. "Winston wanted her to do pillow talk. He wanted her to get messages to them and from them, but not through the Ministry of Defence and his own generals. He also wanted to get to know more about their characters . . . Pamela was absolutely superb at doing this. I've no idea how many generals she took to her bed. I should think probably several."[75] The likelihood is that Pamela had more than one source of income. Whatever the degree of their actual involvement, what is certain is that Winston, who never kept anything from Clementine, directly benefited from her "work."

When Harriman was reluctantly posted to Moscow late in 1943, Clementine acknowledged the impact of the move on her daughter-in-law. It was still unusual to use the phone casually but Clementine called her immediately and "was very sweet and said [she] must be very sad," Pamela later recalled.[76] On that and another occasion when the two women discussed Harriman's departure, Randolph was never mentioned. Yet Pamela was not "very sad" for long. She "sort of cried" on handsome Ed Murrow's shoulder, and hypnotized by her sexiness and the aura that came with being close to the prime minister, Murrow fell hopelessly in love.

At the behest of Brendan Bracken, Winston's most loyal lieutenant, Pamela had signed up in the autumn of 1943 to work at the Churchill Club, a gathering place for Americans arriving in London based in Ashburnham House, a stately old mansion behind Westminster Abbey. She had no assigned role beyond representing the Churchill family, but she laughed with the officers, put them at their ease, and her come-hither style made her appear available even when she was not—"Often though she was," as one biographer would have it.[77] She made the best of the liberties of wartime, simultaneously enjoying herself and aiding the British cause. As she was to put it later: "It was a terrible war, but if you were the right age, [at] the right time and in the right place, it was spectacular."[78]

Pamela's sources on both sides were unparalleled. One of her conquests was General Frederick Anderson, the young head of the US Eighth Bomber Command. According to the writer and Washington player Bill Walton, a good friend of Pamela's, the Churchills knew about this affair as well and "would question her on . . . [Anderson's] position on certain key bombing strategies."[79] The American historian Lynne Olson notes that "rarely—before or since—has diplomacy been so personal,"[80] or, indeed, so sexual. Harriman, Winant, Anderson, Murrow and many others had all become involved in love affairs with Churchills. There can be little doubt that Winston and Clementine knew about these relationships, and there is good reason to believe they condoned them. What underlay this acceptance was not moral permissiveness but strategic necessity. When confronted with wartime adultery that was of no use to the British cause, the Clementine of the Second World War was no less disapproving than that of the First. She once reportedly refused to sit next to the writer Clare Boothe Luce, the wife of *Time* magazine owner Henry Luce, at dinner because of an alleged affair she had conducted "with one of [Britain's] best generals."[81]

Randolph had in any case formally left Pamela in the autumn of 1942, and she went to see Winston in the Cabinet Room in Downing Street to tell her father-in-law of their plans to divorce. He was upset but also understanding and gave her his permission to go ahead with the proceedings. The divorce was eventually granted in December 1945 on the grounds of Randolph's desertion, leaving her with custody of young Winston. She concluded that Randolph "needed someone like his own mother, who lived entirely for her husband."[82] Sadly there was no one else quite like Clementine, and long ago she had chosen father over son. But by then the war was over and so was the great "business transaction," although the grateful Churchills gave Pamela £500 a year for the rest of their lives.

Winston had misgivings about D-day at every moment until its success was assured. He was haunted by the possibility that tens of thousands of British, American and Canadian lives might be sacrificed on a hastily conceived European incursion merely to meet Stalin's incessant demands for a second front that would divide the Wehrmacht's resources and so alleviate Russia's suffering. It was a fear shared by Commonwealth leaders, who assembled to discuss the progress of the war in London in May 1944; all were intent on avoiding a repeat of the Dardanelles. But it was equally clear that the conflict was moving into a new phase and that Operation Overlord—as the invasion of northern France was code-named—was the inescapable next move. The US was scoring significant victories against the Japanese in the Pacific, the RAF and the American Eighth Bomber Command had joined forces to flatten German cities, and Allied troops were continuing their grueling northward slog through the Italian peninsula. By 1944 Winston had run out of excuses to delay the Allied landings in Normandy and had devoted much of the early part of the year to planning the armada of seven thousand vessels and eleven thousand aircraft that would transport the first wave of one hundred and fifty thousand men.

By the spring, the whole of Britain was in a state of febrile alert, but the supreme lockdown on their timing and location ensured the key details were kept secret. After the commanders were informed of the planned date—June 5—the camps holding the assault troops and the ports of departure were sealed. Telephone calls were forbidden, mail impounded, foreign embassies cut off from their home countries. The tension was unprecedented and Clementine witnessed its emotional and physical toll not only on Winston but also on General Eisenhower, the American supreme commander, who was smoking and drinking too much and began to suffer from headaches, recurring throat infections, skyrocketing blood pressure and low spirits. When he came to dine with Winston, Clementine fussed over Eisenhower and made sure to feed him his favorite dishes. She saw the agonies of command intensify still further when the operation had to be postponed until June 6 because of bad weather.

Whereas Roosevelt waited until the evening before the invasion, just as Eleanor was going to bed, to brief her on the plan, Winston had shared the details—and the dangers—of Operation Overlord with Clementine from the beginning. At one point he had expressed an intention to watch the battle unfold from the bridge of the cruiser HMS *Belfast*. Fortunately, the king had joined her in opposing the plan, forcing his prime minister to count down the final hours back in London. On the day itself, Winston lunched with His Majesty while Clementine ate with the head of the army, Alan Brooke. News throughout the day remained for the most part positive. That evening, Churchill was able to give a fairly confident report on progress to the House of Commons.

By the time he finally reached the beachhead of liberated France, on June 12, it was becoming clear that the operation—although not yet complete—had been a success, and with fewer Allied deaths than feared (around four thousand on D-day itself). Here, at last, was the pivotal strike against the Nazis that he had so fervently longed for. But it also signaled a sea change within the Alliance: now that the Americans were out in force, and so firmly in charge, Churchill's role was to diminish—and with it his spirit. His appetite for action remained undimmed, but as the Allies rolled back the German occupation he became ever more certain he was living out his last days. In Downing Street it was becoming noticeable that urgent papers were being ignored and decisions delayed while he frittered away his time on lengthy reminiscences, often late at night. Clementine disapproved of these reveries and would absent herself from them in protest, not least because they detained the staff. Worse, lack of sleep meant that Winston was often unable or unwilling to give his attention to complex matters, or perform well in the Commons. "Result: chaos" was how Colville characterized Downing Street toward the end of 1944.[83]

Winston had survived years of crushing dismay, dashed hopes, disastrous losses and even national humiliation. He had been forced to make unspeakable decisions—such as the bombardment of the French fleet at Oran, or giving the command for a small force to fight to the death at Calais so that their compatriots might get away—that made him physically sick and would leave him tormented for the rest of his life. Time and again he had stared into the abyss and kept himself and his country going, but "the anguish of the hour" always cut him deeply. Since 1941, he had been receiving reports of cold-blooded and systematic extermination of Jews—although it was not until July 1944 that Churchill became aware of Polish camps such as Auschwitz. He had worked 110-hour weeks, his sleep constantly broken by air raids as well as his knowledge of the sheer horror of events; even the thought of a holiday had been a luxury. His regime as war leader would have destroyed a man of less titanic strength and ability. At his lowest points, Clementine had been there to find a way of chivying him along. So when, one evening at Chequers in June 1944, just after the successful landings in Normandy, Winston announced despondently that he was "an old and weary man," she responded brightly: "But think what Hitler and Mussolini feel like!" No doubt with Vic Oliver in mind, he replied: "Ah, but at least Mussolini has had the satisfaction of murdering his son-in-law" (a reference to Count Ciano, whom Mussolini, under pressure from the Nazis, had had shot by firing squad for treason). His own witticism cheered him a great deal, albeit temporarily.[84]

From the fall of France in June 1940 until December 1941, when America entered the war, Winston had carried the fate of Europe and the British Empire on his shoulders. By summer 1944 he had allies to share the burden and Britain's survival was no longer in doubt, but as his doctor noted, he was "less certain of things now than he was in 1940, when the world was tumbling round his ears."[85] Not only was he no longer at the peak of his powers, but Roosevelt was largely deaf to his point of view. This increasingly obvious presidential indifference stoked what Moran called "the fires that seem[ed] to be consuming him."[86] The doctor helped Clementine to keep her husband going—he gave him barbiturates known as "reds" every night to help him sleep—but "it was plain that he was nearly burnt out."[87]

Winston was snippy and disagreeable and his government was similarly ill at ease. With renewed bombing from June 13, London had lost its strange wartime luster and was now deserted. Schools and theaters were closed. No one bothered any longer to dress for dinner. Even with victory in sight, it was difficult to keep up morale as the V-1 flying bombs known as doodlebugs fell on the capital day and night. All those concerned with directing the war were exhausted. "It's not the hard work, it's the hard worry," explained one.[88]

Instinctive understanding of the masses had long eluded Winston, but so engrossed was he in the liberation of Europe—and so fatigued by it—that he had become oblivious to discontent on the home front. Many industrial workers felt the monotonous grind of their labor was overlooked and unappreciated, and the country had suffered a rash of unhelpful strikes. Winston appeared to offer little recognition of those not actually engaged in the fighting, nor much hope for a better life after the war. Upon visiting Britain in August 1944, Roosevelt's Treasury secretary Henry Morgenthau was struck by how "pent-up frustration was vented by angry attacks on government leaders," noting that Winston himself "had been publicly jeered."

When Morgenthau asked to take a tour of air-raid shelters, no one could think of a single senior government figure sufficiently popular to escort him without inciting protests. Eventually, Clementine emerged as the obvious and only choice.[89] Morgenthau, whose wife, Elinor, was Eleanor Roosevelt's best friend, watched her in action: smiling, listening, raising spirits and providing practical help. Her easy, personable, almost motherly style was now suddenly familiar. "The dame is unbelievable . . . She is like Mrs Roosevelt!"[90]

August 1944 brought the liberation of Paris. Winston was away in Italy, so Jock Colville accompanied Clementine on the twenty-seventh to a service at St. Paul's Cathedral to give thanks. It was a moving occasion—virtually everyone went "red with emotion when the Irish Guards played the Marseillaise"[91]—and she felt Winston's absence keenly. Two days later she was at Northolt air base to greet him on his return, but when the plane landed a frantic Moran emerged, yelling that his patient had a raging temperature of 103 degrees with another patch on his lung. Clementine was once again "sick with fright."

Rushed home to bed, Winston was treated with a rudimentary forerunner of antibiotics known as M & Bs (or May & Baker's, after the name of their manufacturers). This fresh bout of pneumonia was hushed up, however, and he carried on almost as normal. In just six days he was due to depart for the second Quebec conference with Roosevelt, a last-hope opportunity to resurrect himself in the president's eyes and advance British military priorities. The two leaders had recently indulged in an unprecedentedly acrimonious exchange about future strategy. Churchill was deeply opposed to the American-backed idea of an invasion of the south of France. He feared the consequent and potentially disastrous weakening of British forces in Italy and was convinced that diverting some of them to France would impede their ability to sweep into Vienna as quickly as possible to contain Russian ambitions in Central Europe. He had already briefed Clementine on what he felt he needed to achieve—namely preventing large numbers of British troops from being "mis-employed for American convenience"—and made it clear that her presence would be a "pleasure" but also a "help" in achieving this goal.[92] Knowing the matter to be delicate, he had informed Roosevelt of her attendance in advance. The president had cabled back: "Perfectly delighted . . . Eleanor will go with me." Earlier the same day he had lunched with Lucy Mercer.

Eleanor arrived in Quebec intent on more than the observation of diplomatic niceties. As a leader's wife, she may have been barred from the negotiations themselves, but there was still much she could achieve, particularly in tandem with Clementine. A couple of days after she and Roosevelt greeted the Churchills at Quebec City station on September 11, she announced her intention to broadcast to the Canadian people. Intent on pulling Clementine into the spotlight with her, Eleanor made clear that she was expecting her to do the same.

Clementine initially refused, writing in her diary that she felt "hounded."[93] Yet she was now an international celebrity; it was time to put her fame to good use. So eventually she agreed. Before that, however, they were both due to attend an official lunch hosted by the wife of the lieutenant governor of Quebec, Lady Fiset. Although anxious to plan her radio address, Clementine had to endure seven courses, four wines, several liqueurs and introductions to sixty-five guests. "I am sorry to confess that I was in a filthy temper," she wrote later.

Her mood deteriorated even further when Lady Fiset announced that Eleanor had a few words to say. Sure of what was coming next, Clementine darted behind a potted palm, only to be "fished" out from her hiding spot when her turn inevitably came. "I won't repeat . . . what I said because I have forgotten, being under the in-

fluence of the luncheon," she recorded. Nevertheless, her later broadcast (in which she thanked the Canadians for supporting her various
causes) went surprisingly well. Harriman, who was also in Quebec,
said that it was "beautifully delivered in both English and French."
Winston, already cheered by how Mary was proving "natural and
amusing with the President,"[94] was ecstatic when he heard about her
success.

Determined to avoid the mistakes of the previous Quebec conference, Clementine stayed on her best behavior and made a strenuous
effort to ensure that Winston was on his. There were new stresses at
this summit caused by Roosevelt's fading health. His doctors were
especially keen to deter him from taking part in late-night drinking
sessions, and even the Americans realized the best way of achieving
this was by enlisting Clementine's help. One evening, after the two
parties watched a movie together, she duly took her husband firmly
by the arm and steered him to bed. It was ten thirty p.m. "Aren't I a
good boy," a biddable Winston muttered.[95]

On September 17 the Churchills left to spend a few days in Hyde
Park, where Clementine was introduced to the "high-spirited" Anna
(the only Roosevelt daughter, whom she decreed to be "much the
nicest" of the brood). Judging that Franklin's frailty meant his mind
was no longer "pinpointed" on the war for more than four hours a
day, and hoping to reintroduce some sparkle to the Anglo-American
relationship, Clementine made sure to spend as much time with
Anna and Eleanor as possible. Yet for all the "blaze of friendship"
described by Winston the second Quebec conference achieved little.
On September 20, their main strategic differences with the US still
unaddressed, the Churchills boarded the Queen Mary for home. The
Americans' success on D-day, and their greatly superior forces (three
million in Europe by the end of the war compared to Britain's one
million), confirmed that they were now top dog. Roosevelt put on his
old charm for Winston but proceeded blithely to ignore his fears
about the Soviets' expansionist advances.

Two days later, from her cabin on board ship, Clementine sent
Eleanor a letter that was quite out of character in its gushing famil-

iarity, one that demonstrated her diplomatic sensibilities and hopes of reaching FDR through his good wife. "I shall always remember my delightful visit to Hyde Park," she wrote, "the picnics, sitting near the president, & my two long walks with you through your woods." She also made sure to praise Anna, whom she described as a "wonderful combination of [Eleanor] & the President," saying, "Please (though the acquaintance is short!) give her my love." She closed by forecasting that in the forthcoming election, which she knew Roosevelt feared he was going to lose, the United States would "honour itself by yet again returning its great leader—great in Peace & great in War."[96] Now was not the time for any further cooling of relations; Britain had become dependent on her former colony, not only to help bring the war to an end but to help her survive economically in the peace thereafter.

When the Churchills arrived back in Britain on September 26, they had a tremendous row. The subject is not recorded but Winston seems to have made the error of contradicting Clementine in public. His apology was fulsome: "My darling One, I have been fretting over our interchange at luncheon yesterday . . . forgive me for anything that seemed disrespectful to you."[97] Upon his departure shortly afterward for Moscow, Clementine grabbed the opportunity to spend two whole days in bed. "My mother always seemed calm and serene, as if she were coping with everything," Mary remembered. "But she was a bomb waiting to go off."[98] Even in wartime, Winston was tolerant of her outbursts. Once when she flounced off, Winston declared: "I am the unhappiest of men." The statement was so patently untrue that staff who witnessed the incident burst out laughing.

On November 10, at the invitation of Charles de Gaulle, Winston and Clementine flew to Paris to celebrate the city's liberation. The scenes were unforgettable: crowds on pavements, balconies and rooftops cheered their heroes, the general and *Church-eel*, under a dazzling blue sky and a protective umbrella of Spitfires. Unfortunately, as Winston and de Gaulle toured the streets in an open-top car, Clementine got caught up in the melee and was not at first allowed to enter the Quai d'Orsay, where the Churchills were staying in great splendor. The wife of one of the most famous men in the world was not recognized; the guards refused to believe this unassuming woman was who she claimed to be.

The joy of Paris was not to last. Winston had largely stopped talking about Hitler and was becoming obsessed instead with the dangers of Communism; the impending peace worried him as much as, if not more than, the war. He believed the Red Army was spreading across Eastern Europe like a "cancer." Of particular concern to him was Greece, where the guerrilla group ELAS was intent on establishing a Communist one-party regime. Angered by reports from British troops of atrocities (including the butchering of "bourgeois" elements) committed by these so-called freedom fighters, he saw it as imperative to prevent Greece from falling under Soviet influence at a time when it was already too late to save much of Eastern Europe from the same fate. Clementine saw all too clearly, however, the dangers of Winston's intemperate assault on ELAS in favor of the exiled and unpopular Greek king; many regarded the guerrillas as a heroic liberation army and the US needed little excuse to dismiss Winston as a monarchist reactionary.

On December 4, 1944, Clementine made one of her bluntest interventions in a note hand-delivered by a trusted servant: "Please do not—before ascertaining full facts repeat to anyone you meet to-day what you said to me this morning i.e. that the Communists in Athens had shewn their usual cowardice in putting the women & children in front to be shot at—Because altho' Communists are dangerous, indeed perhaps sinister people, they seem in this War . . . to have shewn personal courage . . . I am anxious (perhaps over-anxious)."[99]

She observed that some of the more liberal American newspapers were already tarring Britain with the same brush as Russia: both were imperial powers seeking to impose their will on other nations. Her fears were borne out the very next day when the new US secretary of state, Edward Stettinius, publicly attacked Winston's policy of deploying British troops to impose an all-party provisional government in Athens. Furious, Winston forgot Clementine's counsel and dashed off an angry telegram direct to Roosevelt, probably "the most violent outburst of rage in all their historic correspondence."[100] Even his staff doubted his judgment at this point; certainly the gulf with Roosevelt was now wider than ever.

When he took questions on Greece in the Commons on December 8, the super-loyal Colville judged Winston's performance "very bad." Some say Winston's consumption of alcohol increased at this time, among them Alan Brooke, who wrote in his diary that the prime minister "was very tired" and had "tried to recuperate with drink . . . As a result he was in a maudlin, bad tempered, drunken mood . . . so vindictive [against the Americans] that his whole outlook on strategy was warped."[101] Brooke saw his own relationship with Winston as essentially one of playing "nanny to an infantile tyrant," a tyrant he thought—perhaps even *hoped*—would not make it through to the end of the war.

Clementine, meanwhile, had been busy with elaborate plans for a "cosy" family Christmas, one that would finally bring all the Churchills together after four long years. Following the success of D-day and the liberation of Paris, there was much to celebrate. Late on Christmas Eve, however, Winston was to be seen sitting in the Great Hall at Chequers, reviewing secret telegrams and talking to Nellie, who was "most outrageously"[102] reading the messages with him. Clementine, meanwhile, was upstairs in tears—all her hopes dashed, even if she was, as always, "resigned to the inevitable." Winston was preparing to leave for Northolt, taking Sawyers, his two most attractive typists and Anthony Eden on a highly perilous mission to Athens. With only lukewarm backing from the cabinet, and virtually none from the Allies, his audacious gambit was to attempt to broker a democratic settlement in Greece, and somehow prevent the dual threats of a Communist takeover and civil war.

The negotiations were played out over Christmas in the freezing, semiderelict Greek foreign ministry, punctuated by gunfire and shell explosions. Only supportive cables from Clementine—composure rapidly restored—prevented seventy-year-old Winston from feeling "lonely."[103] Some progress was made, however, and he also found himself surprisingly well disposed toward the Communist represen- tatives, describing them as "presentable figures in British battle dress." Although his Santa Claus diplomacy was by no means an in- stant success, the civil war subsided not long after, and his presence certainly cheered the British troops in Athens, who were successfully able to hold the city. Winston's engagement with the Communists, together with his distancing from the exiled king, served him well in terms of public opinion. We may never know for sure whether Clem- entine's words of caution had any direct bearing on the talks but she certainly approved of his attempts at conciliation, writing on Decem- ber 28 that she had been "moved and thrilled to read of all that has happened while [Winston was] in Athens."

Even before the Greek adventure, the days preceding Christmas had been far from free of anxieties. Clementine felt her estrangement from Randolph keenly, and desperately wanted him to be there. There had been a slight rapprochement in July 1944, when he had fi- nally cooled down after a series of explosive rows with his parents over their encouragement of Pamela's infidelities. "I know how diffi- cult things have been for you," he had written to her, "and I do know that you have tried to understand my point of view." At that time Randolph was recovering from knee and spine injuries sustained when his military transport plane crashed on landing in Yugoslavia, and Winston had sensed that the thaw in relations was a fragile one. He had therefore decided against giving Randolph, whom he visited while he was recovering in Algeria, a forthright letter from Clemen- tine because he did "not have the heart." "He is a lonely figure by no means recovered," Winston argued, desperately hoping to keep the peace. "I am sure he would have been profoundly upset & all his pent up feelings would have found a vent on me. Please forgive me for not doing as you wished."[104]

Clementine's response was unusually stern and shows how fam- ily feuds can dominate even in the midst of war. She insisted that her letter had been "very mild & moderate" and that she particularly "minded" that Randolph had not allowed his son, young Winston, to stay on with them at Chequers while Pamela was in quarantine with scarlet fever.[105] Winston eventually relented, and sent the letter on to Randolph as she had suggested.

Perhaps Clementine's instincts on this occasion were right, as the child and his nanny subsequently returned to Chequers. Unfortunately, she reignited the fire by inviting him and his mother to the Christmas celebrations, prompting an outburst from Mary, not normally Randolph's staunchest defender. Disapproving of Pamela's American liaisons, Mary argued that the invitation was disrespectful and Winston was convinced to withdraw the offer, which he did in a tactful note: "Some of the family are worried about the effect on Randolph . . . Clemmie & I therefore with great regret suggest to you we fix another date for you to come."

Notwithstanding this hiccup, Grandpapa had already won the boy's adoration.[106] Young Winston wrote years later that his grandfather's kindness during the war was "remarkable"; he cited as an example Winston's gift to him of *Aesop's Fables* that ill-fated Christmas. By contrast, he barely mentions Clementine, although it is almost certain that she chose and purchased the book. (It was she, too, who scoured London for a much-longed-for model steam train set.) Perhaps what Pamela described as Clementine's occasionally "rather austere" demeanor was to blame for the lack of juvenile appreciation. Taking young Winston to see her "was a production" as "Clemmy was never cosy"[107] and expected the best of manners.

Whether in private or in public, it was not Clementine's lot to attract recognition for her deeds on Winston's behalf. When heavy snowfall resulted in a fuel shortage in January 1945, she came up with the solution. "The radio announced this morning that coal distribution by Army lorries begins to-day!" she told Winston. "It didn't mention who thought of this."[108] This intervention in the coal crisis—and others—reflected Winston's perennial lack of interest in the home front. Ministers complained that he did not read his briefs and was indulging himself by "talking on and on."[109] Part of the problem was his preoccupation with developments overseas. But in exercising greater powers than any other British leader of modern times, he had also become accustomed to unquestioning obedience. In early 1944 he had even entertained the idea of becoming foreign secretary as well as prime minister and minister of defense—until it rapidly became clear that Clementine was implacably opposed to the idea. Mackenzie King disapproved of the way he nevertheless bullied the capable and obliging Attlee, and likened his other ministers to "a lot of schoolboys frightened by the headmaster."[110]

As the war entered its final months, the Labour leader's patience ran out. On a snowy Saturday in January 1945, with Winston restricted to Downing Street by a heavy cold, Attlee wrote him a two-thousand-word letter, typing it himself—poorly—so that none of his staff should see it (although Winston's did). He protested the prime minister's "lengthy disquisitions" in cabinet on papers that he had not read and subjects that he had "not taken the trouble to master." He railed about Winston's "undue attentiveness" to Bracken and Beaverbrook, whose views—"often entirely ignorant"—were given more weight than the "considered opinion" of cabinet committees. "Greatly as I love and admire the PM I am afraid there is much in what Attlee says and I rather admire his courage in saying it," Colville, by no means a Labour man, noted in his diary.[111] Winston exploded when he read Attlee's missive, drafting a viciously sarcastic reply in which Attlee's intervention was denounced as a "socialist conspiracy." His staff was instructed "not to bother about Atler or Hitlee."[112]

In high dudgeon, Winston brought Attlee's letter to Clementine expecting her comforting support. He was greatly surprised to find that she took Attlee's side and thought the deputy prime minister's message "true and wholesome." It speaks volumes of the weight Winston attached to her opinion that the previous brutal response was discarded, and he sat down to write "a short, polite acknowledgement."[113]

At the time of Attlee's protest, Winston was preparing for yet another conference of the Big Three and was fretting, somewhat ironically, that Roosevelt had not been reading the papers he sent him. The ailing president had also taken, rather dismissively, to calling Churchill "Winnie." On their way to Yalta on the Black Sea—the spot of maximum inconvenience Stalin had chosen for the summit—Winston and Roosevelt arranged to meet beforehand on the Mediterranean island of Malta. By the time he landed on January 30, the prime minister had already suffered another "serious alarm" (now an almost habitual occurrence when he traveled by plane) and was "restless." One morning on Malta, even though she was back in London, he just turned "his face to the wall . . . [and] called for Clemmie."[114]

Roosevelt's own physical decline prompted Moran to wonder whether the president was well enough to hold office at all. The First Lady was now so infrequent a companion that she had failed to register his persistent cough or the gradual draining of color from his face. But Anna, who accompanied her father to the conference, noticed his hands were shaking.

At Yalta itself, a few days later, Winston, Roosevelt and Stalin agreed on a joint communiqué proclaiming the Allies' intention to strive for a peace in which "all the men in all the lands may live out their lives in freedom from fear and want." "I hope you will like communiqué published tomorrow morning," Winston wrote to Clementine on February 12, 1945, although he knew full well that Stalin was acting out a lie. The Soviet leader had already installed a puppet government in Warsaw and the Red Army had occupied most of Poland, the very country for which Britain had so reluctantly gone to war in 1939. Winston told Clementine despondently that "the misery of the whole world appalls me" and that he feared "new struggles may arise out of those we are successfully ending." Although he had Sarah for company, he badly wanted his wife: "I miss you much . . . I am lonely amid this throng."[115]

Clementine advised him to "grapple close to the President" as it had cheered him in the past. But in truth that was no longer possible. The Americans had made Stalin their main focus; it was clear that if the proposed highly secret plans for an atom bomb for Japan did not work Russian military support would be needed to end the fighting in the Pacific.

Post-Yalta, Winston's mood sank lower still: the better the news from the Allied forces in Europe, the darker his fears for the future. He found the prospect of the end of the war, and all the challenges that would come with it, profoundly depressing. Nor was he the only Churchill to feel this way. On April 1, 1945, Pamela sent a letter to Harriman in the same spirit: "[Peace] is something one has looked forward to for so long that when it happens, I know I am going to be frightened."

Winston's pessimism was affecting his work. Even the dedicated Colville was infuriated by constantly finding the prime minister's ministerial boxes full of unread papers. Conversely, his opinion of Clementine never ceased to rise. He accompanied her on a tour of YWCA clubs in Brussels in March 1945 and pronounced, "Never can the welfare of the troops have been so lavishly and painstakingly cared for . . . Mrs C could not have done her job better or spoken more effectively . . . She looked ravishing, was always interested and never condescending."[116]

Indeed, Clementine's star was rising fast—and she was about to embark on her most independent and exciting venture yet. Invited by the Soviet Red Cross to visit Russia in April to see the results of her fund-raising, it transpired that Stalin (who had so belittled her husband) wanted to honor her by thanking her in person for her work. But with relations between Britain and the Soviet Union—over Poland in particular—becoming increasingly icy, Winston hesitated to let her go. Some biographers of Churchill, such as Roy Jenkins, have criticized her for accepting the invitation, but this was a singular and rare personal honor, and the trip might also reap diplomatic dividends. In any case she had already learned some Russian and had a Red Cross uniform altered so that it did not make her "look like an elephant."

The queen invited her to tea beforehand, and Clementine shared her excitement with the Downing Street staff and a few personal friends by throwing a small party. She even invited Beaverbrook. Yet she could not entirely conquer her anxiety about leaving Winston by himself for so long, or her trepidation at flying so far. Before leaving she wrote to Mary: "Darling supposing anything happened to me (e.g. air crash) Do you think you could be released from the ATS on Compassionate grounds to look after Papa?"[117] She also wrote to Sarah: "[S]ay a little prayer now & then for your devoted Mother who altho' she keeps up a brave front sometimes feels like a nervous old lady."[118]

Knowing she would be spending her sixtieth birthday (like her fiftieth) away from him, Winston gave her a diamond-encrusted heart-shaped brooch. After just one day, she wrote about the "long separation" and implored him to "think of [his] Pussy now & then with indulgence & love."[119] Winston made sure the British ambassador in Cairo, where she was grounded for several days by storms, gave her his birthday note on April 1. "Your lovely Birthday telegram was handed to me in Church this morning," she told him.[120]

More bad weather during the final stage of her flight forced the plane down to an altitude of just two hundred feet for the last hundred miles, but it made a perfect landing, and she was able to disembark pristine in her blue uniform. "I was there at the Moscow aerodrome, gay with the Union Jack and Red flag," Radio Newsreel's man in Moscow reported. Presented with a large bouquet of roses by the reception party, which included Foreign Minister Molotov as well as Ivan and Agnes Maisky and Averell Harriman, she thanked everyone in "well-chosen and well-practised" Russian.

As she toured hospitals from Leningrad to Stalingrad (all equipped courtesy of her Red Cross fund) and received a Soviet Red Cross Distinguished Service Medal for her "exceptional" contribution to the Russian war effort, Clementine delighted in being the center of attention. Cheering crowds greeted her everywhere, dancers at the ballet applauded her, many onlookers threw bunches of violets at her feet. Such an effusive welcome rivaled that given to Eleanor Roosevelt on her tour of Britain back in 1942. She cuddled children, posed for photographs and chatted in snippets of English and Russian with as many as she could. She even gave a press conference. Back home, reports of her astonishing popularity made Winston burst with pride. "My darling one . . . Your personality reaches the gt masses & touches their heart." He told her of the "lovely accounts" from British and American officials of the good she was doing: "At the moment you are the one bright spot in Anglo-Russian relations."[121] He also made sure she was kept in the geopolitical loop by asking the British ambassador, Sir Archibald Clark Kerr, to show her secret Foreign Office telegrams—including those on how Russia was already breaching agreements made at Yalta on the independence of Poland and Romania. At one point he even sent senior military officials to brief her. She was there, as Winston sternly reminded her, to be his eyes and ears: "Please telegraph to me freely every day about your doings and political outlook," he cabled on April 5.[122] Shoring up the alliance at a time of heightened tensions remained her paramount duty, however: "Please always speak of my earnest desire," he instructed her, "for continuing friendship of British and Russian peoples."[123]

Two days later, she received an invitation to meet Stalin himself at the Kremlin—or the "Ogre in his Den,"[124] as she had previously described him. Clementine, her Red Cross secretary Mabel Johnson and Grace Hamblin were led by their Red Army escort down "long impressive corridors" until finally they came to a great double door. The guards "indicated, in no light terms, by placing their guns across the entrance,"[125] that Grace (who had received no express invitation) would not be permitted to enter, and so the other two women went through without her. Once inside, Clementine and Johnson could see the stocky figure of Stalin, flanked by Molotov, behind a writing desk at the far end of a vast and imposing room (most likely his study in the neoclassical splendor of the Kremlin Senate). They walked the distance to his desk, where, speaking through an interpreter, Stalin thanked Clementine for the work done by her fund. She knew that Winston was hoping for a great deal from this meeting; having taken advice from the ambassador, she presented Stalin with a gold fountain pen, saying: "My husband wishes me to express the hope that you will write him many friendly messages with it." Stalin was not to be won so easily. He put the pen to one side, muttering that he wrote only with a pencil.

Clementine initially attributed this ungracious response to what she and her companions referred to as Russian "dourness." But Stalin later added the vaguely ominous "I will repay him," and one of Clementine's interpreters, Hugh Lunghi, who was stationed at the British military mission in Moscow, subsequently explained that the marshal had been making a point. He was deliberately denying the British government the satisfaction of having him publicly acknowledge the gift (or giving one in return). Nor did he wish to raise her stature still further by allowing his name to become attached to Clementine's tour. *Pravda*, the official newspaper of the Soviet Communist Party, carried just two, purely factual sentences on this extraordinary meeting, citing the date and the names of those present. Her very success and strength of character were making her a potential threat, one that was becoming difficult to control. "The Soviet authorities didn't want her to steal too much of the limelight," Lunghi explained. "The Cold War was already starting."[126]

Lunghi was monitoring the reaction to Clementine's visit of the Soviet news agency TASS and the Russian press in general, and he noted: "On the whole they were trying to be complimentary and nice but then [as relations worsened] they left her out of the picture and became increasingly rude." Meanwhile, Winston "was very annoyed [Clementine] had not given him a full account of her talks with Stalin." As Lunghi recounted, "The alliance [with Russia] was about to break up so it was important to get every little clue as to what Stalin was thinking." Yet all she said in her message following the meeting was: "Miss Johnson and I received by Marshal Stalin. Pen gracefully received."

Ten days later Winston's patience for news ran out and he cabled with a terse: "You have not yet sent me the account of your talk with Stalin." Her lack of response—at least in writing—might suggest she was concerned about Soviet surveillance; most likely, though, her reluctance was simply due to Stalin's conduct, which had left so little of cheer to report. The encounter was surely the highlight of her six-week tour, but the growing crisis between Moscow and London—which Winston described to her as "dynamite"[127]—meant it was kept curiously quiet. The *Times*'s Moscow correspondent seems to have been unaware it had even taken place.

Despite the souring of intergovernmental relations, Clementine continued to receive a rapturous welcome from the Russian people. In one military hospital equipped by her fund, the stoic Clementine was "visibly moved" when wounded men lined the stairways and corridors to bid her farewell. Winston was not alone in being disturbed by the "inconsistency" between the apparent warmth of her reception and the growing chill emanating from the Kremlin. For all her outward charm, Clementine was determined to act on the growing evidence of the Soviets' brutality and treachery. Eleanor Rathbone, an independent MP with a keen interest in Poland, had written to her in Moscow about the large number of Poles being deported to the horrors of the Soviet labor camps. Thus briefed, Clementine "rather flew at" Maisky, who was reduced to beating a "diplomatic retreat." Indeed, even while she was still in Moscow, she was more in favor of adopting a tough stance with Stalin than was her husband. Upon her return to London in May, she wrote back to Rathbone and made plain her view that the West should "break off Diplomatic relations" with Moscow if "they do not mend their ways." In a handwritten annotation to this line, she told the MP, "Winston would disapprove!"[128] She appreciated the difference between the enveloping friendliness of the Russian people and what she viewed as their "sinister" Soviet government and thought only a tough stance would pay dividends.

During her stay, Lunghi came to appreciate that Clementine was no ordinary emissary. He recalled how she constantly exploited her position to glean useful information for her husband and country. One such occasion was when she used the Soviet guesthouse provided for her in Moscow to invite the immaculately attired Josip Tito, the Communist leader of the Yugoslav partisans, to afternoon tea. "Tito was trying to grab Trieste," recalled Lunghi, referring to the ambitious Communist's designs on the Italian city on the Yugoslav border, and Clementine was "sounding him out" on an increasingly alarmed Winston's behalf. Perhaps aware of Tito's fondness for the finer things in life, she had intended to serve him an "English vicarage tea," even remarking that she would teach the Russian staff to cut the crusts off the sandwiches. She was somewhat surprised, therefore, when a servant wheeled in two trolleys laden with bottles of vodka. "She was obviously horrified and rather angry," Lunghi said. "But in the end all was merry" and her intelligence mission went to plan.

Outside Moscow, she particularly enjoyed the spontaneous post-dinner singing in Leningrad, during which her hosts were surprised to discover that she knew "Song of the Volga Boatmen." It was here that she learned Stalin was to award her the prestigious Order of the Red Banner of Labor. But her travels beyond the capital left Clementine cut off from the extraordinary events unfolding further west. Away from the relative security of the British embassy, she no longer had access to secret official telegrams. She therefore had no inkling why Molotov was on the platform to greet her when she returned to Moscow on her private train (specially provided by the Soviets with a butler, maids and guards) on April 13. Molotov informed her of the shocking news that Roosevelt was dead. Needing time to think, she suggested he join her in her private carriage for a few moments of silent reflection. She then alighted and immediately proceeded to the British embassy to phone Winston and discuss her next move.

The cable she later sent to Eleanor (via the British ambassador in Washington) is surprisingly flat, as if in her shock she resorted to the safest option: "I am deeply grieved and send my respectful sympathy and my thoughts. Clementine Churchill." Eleanor replied a few days later, with equal formality: "I am grateful for your thought of us . . . We are grateful that the President suffered no pain and had no long illness . . . Very cordially yours, Eleanor Roosevelt." It was Winston who, despite his differences with the First Lady, immediately struck the right note: "Accept my most profound sympathy in your grievous loss which is also the loss of the British Nation and of the cause of freedom in every land . . . I trust you may find consolation in the magnitude of his work and the glory of his name." A grateful Eleanor replied: "Your beautiful message has given me comfort and renewed courage."

"No one fought more valiantly than he to save the world," Clementine hastily wrote to Averell Harriman. "It is cruel that he will not see the Victory which he did so much to achieve." It was indeed cruel. Franklin had told Eleanor to acquire some "fine" clothes for their long-awaited trip to Britain together in May—which suggested just a glimmer of a brighter future together. Yet when he keeled over with a cerebral hemorrhage at lunchtime on April 12, during a short break at his house at Warm Springs, Georgia, none of the four women in attendance was his wife. He was, instead, with Lucy Mercer, who within an hour had packed up and left.

Surely aware of his own ever-growing reliance on Clementine, Winston paid a sensitive tribute to Eleanor in the Commons. "In this extraordinary effort of the spirit over the flesh, of will-power over physical infirmity," he told MPs, "he was inspired and sustained by that noble woman his devoted wife." At the last moment, he decided not to attend the funeral of the man he had once hailed as his greatest friend—"on account," he cabled Clementine, "of much" that was "going on [in Britain]."[129] He appears to hint in the shorthand of an encrypted cable that this decision (made while his plane was waiting for him at the aerodrome) had been calculated to improve Britain's standing in Washington. Perhaps after all that he had endured at Roosevelt's hands, he was using his absence to signal his (and Britain's) rediscovered independence. In any case, he was able to report to his wife that he had received a "very nice telegram from President Truman opening our relations on the best conditions."

For two days running in April, a clearly shocked Winston cabled Clementine in Rostov-on-Don in Russia about the "intense horror" of "German brutalities" being discovered by Allied troops as they liberated the Nazi concentration camps. "They did not have time to cover their traces," he told her on April 21, suggesting that until now even Churchill, one of the first to warn of Nazi persecution of the Jews back in the 1930s, had no idea of the sheer scale of what would become known as the Holocaust.[130]

Clementine was undoubtedly aware of the tireless campaigning on behalf of the Jews by Eleanor Rathbone, the MP who urged her on her visit to Russia to speak out about the atrocities in Poland. The two women knew, trusted and admired each other, and Clementine would have been aware of Rathbone's National Committee for Rescue from Nazi Terror, which she had set up in 1943, as well as her frequent interventions in Parliament. Rathbone's persistent pressure on the government may indeed have led to Churchill's reference a year earlier to what he called a "bestial policy of cold-blooded extremism." Controversy still rages as to the exact extent of the Allies' knowledge of Hitler's murder camps and whether Churchill or Roosevelt could have done more earlier to save the Jews. During the war itself, Churchill's aim above all was to save Britain from invasion and the world in general from tyranny, rather than specifically to halt the Nazi genocide. Many of those in power at the time believed that throwing everything at defeating Hitler represented the Jews' best chance of survival.

On April 30, Hitler shot himself in his bunker in Berlin. A week later Germany surrendered. In London, Winston was making urgent inquiries into whether the capital would be ready to celebrate the designated Victory in Europe Day, on May 8, and receiving "assurances" from Scotland Yard that there was "no shortage of beer."[131]

In Moscow, Clementine longed to be home with her husband. Before her departure, however, there was a mild panic at the British embassy because no one could be found to conduct a VE service until she had what was widely credited as a "brainwave."[132] Dr. Hewlett Johnson, known as the "Red Dean" of Canterbury for his Communist sympathies, was due to arrive in town at midnight on the seventh. He had previously accused her Red Cross fund of "poaching" public support from alternative, more politically motivated campaigns, such as his own Joint Aid to Russia Committee. Now she grabbed the opportunity to recruit a critic as an ally, by asking him to preach. Dr. Johnson was delighted and sat up until dawn composing his address.

"All my thoughts are with you on this supreme day my darling," she cabled Winston on May 8 itself. "It could not have happened without you."[133] From a balcony overlooking Whitehall, he told the jubilant crowds that it was not a victory of any class or any party: "My dear friends, this is your hour." Clementine personally arranged a simultaneous party at the embassy in Moscow. She grabbed a glass of champagne and climbed onto a chair, declaring, "We will drink to victory!"

She also found time to think of Eleanor, writing to her the following day in more affectionate terms: "All yesterday I was thinking of you and your husband to whom we owe so great a part of the victory. Love from Clementine Churchill."[134] This elicited a warmer response, although not "love." "I am deeply appreciative of your thinking of me," Eleanor replied "affectionately," although she found it "impossible to rejoice" until Japan was also defeated.

Winston too was far from jubilant. Moran noticed he did "not seem at all excited about the end of the war."[135] A few days earlier, he had ordered his ambassador to show Clementine more secret cables on Russian atrocities, and on May 5 had warned her, "I need scarcely tell you that beneath these triumphs lie poisonous politics and deadly international rivalries." He instructed her to come back urgently. "Do not delay beyond the 7th or 8th except for weather. On no account leave in bad weather."[136] "I long to be with you," she replied, "but have some necessary engagements to fulfil . . . after which I shall joyfully fly home."

Those last few days were packed with more concerts, hospital tours and receptions staged in her honor. Most important was her award ceremony at the Kremlin on May 7.[137] It seems likely from the Churchills' correspondence that she was hoping to have another crack at extracting useful intelligence from Stalin, whom she was expecting to award her the honor. No doubt it was a crushing disappointment then that the marshal chose not to come and a deputy, Mr. Shvernik, officiated: "I heartily congratulate you," he told her with great pomp. "You have accomplished tremendous work . . . for our heroic Red Army."

Clementine's "eyes open" tour had been, in personal terms, a triumph. After six weeks apart, Winston wanted to be there to greet her in person when she arrived at Northolt on May 12, but as usual he was running late. Her plane circled the airfield several times to allow his speeding red Napier to reach the side of the runway just as it landed. Clementine emerged, still wearing her Red Cross uniform, smiling with joy as she walked proudly down the steps to meet her husband, the great victor.

CHAPTER TWELVE

A Private Line

1945–65

At any other time Clementine would have relished the palatial appointments of an elegant penthouse in her favorite London hotel. Although maintaining a proud façade, she was in truth despondent at finding herself in the Brook Penthouse at Claridge's, for all the streams of visitors whisked up in a special lift to see them. Winston simply pointed tearfully to the seventh-floor balcony and declared a dislike of "sleeping near a precipice."[1] But, having been turfed out of Downing Street by an ungrateful electorate, they simply had nowhere else to go.

When Winston had called a general election two weeks after VE Day, Beaverbrook had predicted he would be voted back to power with a hundred-seat majority. Winston had believed him. After all, cheering crowds turned out to line the route wherever he went; another term was surely his due. But Clementine had been more doubtful. Having dutifully dealt with her mailbag during the war and toured the country listening to people's woes, she had known that there was a yearning among the populace for social reform, and that many saw Labour as the only party to offer credible policies on housing, jobs and social security. Winston, she believed, could no longer rely on his personality, or even his war record. He had to paint a rival vision of a fairer Britain all his own.

Instead, he had opened his campaign with a patently absurd warning that a Labour government would result in a tyranny enforced by a home-grown "Gestapo." Clementine had begged him to drop the words from his speech, but it was as if, under Beaverbrook's influence, his reason had once again deserted him. To turn on his wartime coalition colleagues so provocatively, with what the *Economist* dubbed "pernicious nonsense," seemed unstatesmanlike. It helped to revive searing memories of the unemployment under the Tory-led governments of the "hungry thirties"; indeed, many still felt cheated by Lloyd George's promise to build "a country fit for heroes" after the First World War.

Neither had Winston been physically fit for the election. During the campaign, he had finally returned to his constituency (formerly Epping, but now redrawn and renamed Woodford), but as he was touring the streets Clementine had realized he was on the point of collapse and had to rush him into a church to rest. On other occasions she had campaigned successfully without him, addressing six hustings on the eve of polling day alone while he traveled up and down the country. This was not the aloof prewar Clementine with that distinctive glare, but a formidable and skilled politician. Warm and spontaneous, she tried to make amends for Winston's Gestapo gaffe by insisting that he *would* introduce "great reforms" and *would* work "harmoniously" with the other parties. Dressed in a striking flame-red chiffon turban, she beseeched the crowd to reward their wartime hero with "a great solid magnificent vote!"[2] But despite garnering cheers aplenty she came away unconvinced they would translate into support for Winston in the ballot box.

Polling day had been set for July 5 but the results were delayed for three weeks to allow for the arrival of postal votes from troops overseas. "I hear the women are for me, but that the men have turned against me," Winston remarked with surprise during the long wait. Clementine quickly reminded him how bitterly he had once opposed female suffrage. "Quite true," he conceded.[3] After a brief holiday at Hendaye in southwest France, he set off for the final Big Three conference at Potsdam. He had pleaded with Clementine to accompany him to meet Stalin again, as well as the new American president, Harry Truman, but she had refused. She took refuge, implausibly, in the need to report on her Russian trip to the Women's British Soviet

Committee and said she wanted to press on with plans to reopen Chartwell. More likely she wished to conserve her energies for the electoral verdict she now privately dreaded—having seen signs of widespread discontent on her tours of shelters and from her mailbag; Attlee was emerging as a much better campaigner than anyone had expected and she feared that Winston's cronies were wildly overconfident and that he himself had "lost his touch." So Mary went in her place. On July 25 father and daughter flew back, midsummer, in time for the result the following day.

By the time Clementine arrived in Woodford to attend the count, on the morning of the twenty-sixth, Winston's only opponent (a "crack-pot" independent, as Mary dubbed him) had already amassed surprisingly large piles of votes. As news began to come in that Labour was taking Tory seats by the dozen, Clementine deserted her post and fled back to the Annexe to find Winston staring blankly at the wall of the map room, where the results were being posted on a special chart. His seat was safe but every minute brought word of fresh reverses elsewhere—Sandys *out*, Randolph *out*, Bracken *out*.[4] At six o'clock that evening he ordered drinks and cigars for the staff and set off to Buckingham Palace to resign. By then Winston knew he had fallen victim to one of the greatest landslides in British electoral history. His belittled deputy, Clement Attlee, had become his prime minister.

After retreating to bed for an afternoon rest, Clementine returned in the evening and was "riding the storm with unflinching demeanour,"[5] while others tried and failed to hide their tears. She even suggested that the result might prove a "blessing in disguise," although Winston clearly did not think so. Mary and Sarah attempted to lift the gloom by donning their smartest evening dresses for a special dinner prepared by a crestfallen Mrs. Landemare. But within hours, wearing a previously unseen look of exhaustion and despair, Clementine was already packing up. "My mother was out of Downing Street quicker than lightning," recalled Sarah.[6] Number 10 and the Annexe had already become "hateful."[7]

The result could not have been more painful, but it did not change

the respect Clementine felt for Attlee. To her great credit, she now
went out of her way to help Violet Attlee move into Downing Street,[8]
while the Labour leader made sure to return her kindness. He most
unusually offered the Churchills a last weekend at Chequers, and
later temporarily released Jock Colville from his private office to
work at Claridge's on tying up their affairs. Having spent a weekend
with the Attlees by this time, Colville inevitably found himself making comparisons. He judged Clement and Violet to be charming, but
their food nowhere near as good and their lifestyle more formal. Mrs.
Attlee was welcoming, a onetime beauty, but, Colville sighed, Clementine's "sometimes caustic comments and unflagging perfectionism
were missing."[9] No one could match how she looked and acted the
part of First Lady. At a grand dinner three years later, Clementine's
mere presence, even out of power, was considered by Chips Channon
so "distinguished" that she made other women present seem "almost
naked."[10]

The shock at the election result was felt around the world. From
Potsdam, the British ambassador to the USSR, Sir Archibald Clark
Kerr, reported to Clementine that the Russian delegation was left
"gibbering and bewildered" at the news. Molotov, whom she had got
to know well in Moscow, was "grey in the face and clearly much upset, throwing up his fat hands and asking why? Why?"[11] "The leader in
the *Times* today summed it up best when they said 'Gratitude belongs
to history & not to politics,'" Pamela explained to an equally astonished Harriman. She believed Winston was taking the news "wonder-
fully" but added: "Poor Clemmie I feel very deeply for her."

She was not the only one to worry about Clementine's reaction;
Field Marshal Montgomery was also concerned and offered to release
Mary from her military duties to look after her. Many others, including Clark Kerr, wrote specifically to Clementine to thank her "for
being so uniformly kind." Winston's chief of staff, Pug Ismay, wrote
emotionally to both of them to say how much their "kindness" had
meant to him, describing himself as their "devoted servant." Members of the public sent messages stating how much the "nation" was
in her debt, saying that Winston could not have achieved "a quarter"

of what he had done without her. Field Marshal Alexander (now supreme Allied commander in the Mediterranean) had already written to the board of Clementine's maternity hospital, Fulmer Chase, to say that it had made a "direct contribution to the winning of the war"[12] by significantly raising officer morale.

The president of the *Toronto Star* newspaper, meanwhile, compared the shock at the election result in Canada and the US to the reaction after Roosevelt's death. Eleanor Roosevelt, who had been relieved to relinquish her position as First Lady after her husband's death, struggled to imagine the Churchills' state of mind. She suggested that they were "probably very happy and look[ing] forward to a few years of less strenuous life." She did concede, though, that "to those who lay down the burdens of great responsibility, there must come for a while a sense of being rudderless."[13]

In truth, neither Clementine nor Winston felt there was much to live for anymore—no enemy to overcome, no government to lead, no people to inspire. "It would have been better," Winston told Moran in all seriousness, "to have been killed in an aeroplane or to have died like Roosevelt."[14]

Believing he lacked the strength to fight on in politics and that his health would soon fail for the last time, Clementine had fervently hoped to persuade Winston to retire in glory but only once the war was won. Earlier in the year she had taken the precaution of some quiet house-hunting and had found a suitable "little" place at 28 Hyde Park Gate, Kensington. Now that Winston had been forcibly "retired," she sent in the builders. Unfortunately, the press managed to snatch a glimpse of the beautiful double-aspect drawing room, with its hundreds of leather-bound books and oil paintings of the Duke of Marlborough, and in the now less deferential climate the Churchills came under fire for redecorating to a level unthinkable for "lesser folk" struggling with the legacy of six years of war and shortages of everything from paint to builders.[15] The rumpus merely added to their feelings of rejection.

With Chartwell also being reconfigured, they were left to brood in their suite at Claridge's. Clementine told Mary, "[T]ime crawls wearily along . . . since your Father was hurled from power." Even creating a "comfortable & happy" home—her great forte—seemed beyond her: mice and moths had munched through the loose covers and curtains at Chartwell, and without the luxury of her old "diplomatic rations" she could not replace them. Aware that so many were in a far less fortunate position, she felt ashamed—particularly when offers of cottages, curtains and help of all sorts started flooding in from the public. The sudden bump to earth had left her "dropping to pieces." When she attempted to help the devoted Moppet and her other staff scrub and polish Chartwell, she was sent away: "I am too old & inefficient," she continued.[16] "I blush to think that I who organised the Russian Fund, . . . Fulmer . . . & who complained about the organisation of the YWCA am stumped by my own private life."

When Japan surrendered on August 14 after the bombing of Hiroshima and Nagasaki, she rushed over to Parliament the next day to watch the House of Lords express its congratulations to the king.[17] Alas, she never arrived. She could not push her way through the crowds to the gallery and was left forlorn and disappointed in the lobby outside. "How are the mighty fallen!" noted Chips Channon.[18]

A few days later she pleaded with Mary to return home from her unit near Hamburg, in Germany, saying, "I am very unhappy & need your help with Papa . . . in our misery we seem, instead of clinging to each other, to be always having scenes." Clementine blamed herself, telling Mary, "I'm finding life more than I can bear"—in large part because Winston was being "very difficult," not least over his food. Now restricted to standard rations, he was being served tiny portions of meat and vented his fury at the staff, as well as at Clementine. "I can't see any future," she told her terrified daughter. "We are learning how rough & stony the World is."[19]

Nor could she face accompanying Winston on what she feared would be an explosively bad-tempered painting holiday in Italy in early September. It was a relief that Sarah agreed to go instead, traveling in the prime ministerial aircraft that Attlee had put at their disposal. From a commandeered marble palace on the shores of Lake Como, where he was royally fussed over, Winston frequently regretted out loud that Clementine had declined to join him. He recognized the blame was mainly his and wanted her to know he was behaving himself. "He says I'm to say—he's good. He really is!" Sarah reported back, adding that she had been "so distressed" to see her mother "so unhappy and tired" back in London. "Six years is a long time to live at such a high tempo, knowing as fully as you did all the . . . decisions. You are bound to feel a reaction."[20]

When Winston returned in early October, Hyde Park Gate was ready. The rearrangement of Chartwell to cut housekeeping costs was nearly finished too. But with the Churchills' wartime reprieve now over, even Clementine's economies were not enough to forestall the inevitable financial reckoning and Winston was once again forced to consider selling. It was this prospect that prompted an old friend, Lord Camrose, to marshal other wealthy admirers to buy Chartwell from the Churchills for £50,000 and present it to the National Trust, on condition that Winston and Clementine could go on living there for the rest of their lives. This generosity, and Winston's lucrative return to writing, meant that for the first time in years the Churchills were to become satisfactorily well-off.

In July 1947 Clementine organized a thank-you lunch for their benefactors (in a characteristic touch, she sent cards entitling their chauffeurs to a free meal at the Wolfe Café in Westerham). Winston celebrated by buying the farms adjoining Chartwell, amounting to some five hundred acres. He was now a country landowner of stature, leader of His Majesty's Most Loyal Opposition, a hugely successful author, and a worldwide war hero and celebrity. His attendance in the House of Commons was only fitful—although he did turn up to make his now-famous intervention condemning the splitting of India and Pakistan into two separate states under the Indian Independence Act of 1947, and rightly predicting appalling sectarian violence between Hindus and Muslims. But his devotion to writing *The Second World War* was considerably more constant, as if he were hell-bent on writing his account of the conflict before anyone else did. In this way, he threw himself into his new life and tried to put the hurt of July 1945 behind him.

From helping to run the war Clementine was reduced once more to running houses. Feeling redundant and ignored, she longed for Winston to retire from politics altogether and for the ceaseless whirl around him to stop. She wanted to share a quieter, calmer life with him. But he pursued his own interests in the same old self-absorbed way, simply expecting her to be on tap whenever he needed her for comfort. Late 1945 was marred by more bitter rows, and she began to doubt whether he had ever valued her at all. It did not help her low spirits that he could be dismissive of her in public. "Please don't interrupt, Clemmie," Cecil Beaton heard him growl at a society dinner in December 1945, where Winston was enjoying being the star turn. And yet at the end of the evening she lovingly wrapped him up in coats and scarves before they headed off into the cold night. "I realised to what a degree," the fascinated Beaton observed, "all in his family circle must pay him due deference."[21]

Many marriages, strained by the traumas of war, fell apart around this time. Worried that her parents' partnership might suffer the same fate, Mary tried to shore her mother up, writing to her that "despite all his difficultness—his overbearing—exhausting temperament—he *does* love you and *needs* you so much." She acknowledged Clementine's occasional yearning for "the quieter more banal happiness of being married to an ordinary man" rather than the "splendours and miseries of a meteor's train" and alluded to what she described as the "equality of [their] temperaments," saying, "You are both 'noble beasts.' Your triumph is that you really have been and are—everything to Papa . . . without surrendering your own soul or mind."[22] Clementine had continued to attend her Red Cross and other meetings, but now took doctors' advice to cancel her forthcoming engagements. She spent time instead replying to the many letters of sympathy she received from friends, former staff and members of the public.

Throughout 1946, Winston was festooned with honors from allies and liberated countries around the world. Early in the year Clementine joined him on a trip to America, where he was showered with honorary degrees and given a civic welcome in New York while he also held talks with President Truman. In March he dominated the news with his thunderous speech at Westminster College, in Fulton, Missouri, in which he spoke of an ominous "iron curtain" behind which the ancient capitals of Central and Eastern Europe now lay under Soviet servitude. Although only a year, it seemed a long time since Clementine had been so fêted in Soviet Russia; all her hopes of friendliness between Moscow and the West appeared to have been dashed.

Typically, she hovered in the background as Winston lapped up the attention. She was genuinely surprised if anyone noticed her at all. But in June 1946, two months after her sixty-first birthday and in the last round of honors awarded for wartime achievement, Attlee made her a dame for her work on the Aid to Russia Fund and the "many other services which made so marked and brave a contribution." She was thrilled that he thought she had been "able to help a little"[23] (although she would never style herself according to the title she had received). Other awards were to follow. That same month the University of Glasgow granted her an honorary degree for her "womanly grace and . . . wisdom, a power to achieve, a faith to persevere, and a full measure of . . . courage."[24] And, later in the summer, Winston watched her receive a doctorate of civil law at Oxford University for being "the very Soul of Persuasion [and] Guardian Angel of our country's guardian."[25] It was, however, another two years before she received the recognition that mattered most.

On their fortieth wedding anniversary in September 1948, while they were staying at Cap d'Antibes in the south of France, Winston finally put his thoughts and feelings down in writing. Perhaps only now that others had honored her did he appreciate how vital she had been during the war. Maybe only once he believed his own place in history was assured could he finally take stock of the sacrifices made by those around him. Arguably, he was also realizing that it was thanks to her continued devotion that he was able to carry on in front-line politics in his seventy-fourth year. To Sarah, he proudly remarked, "At her best, no one can beat her."[26] In a note to Clementine pushed under her bedroom door he wrote: "I send this token, but how little can it express my gratitude to you for making my life & any work I have done possible."[27]

Feeling appreciated at last, Clementine reverted to her old role of saving Winston from himself. At a dinner in the late 1940s, the economist John Kenneth Galbraith observed her reaching out to restrain him from drinking too much of the Connaught Hotel's fine wines.[28] On another tour of America in March 1949—where Winston was again celebrated by everyone from the president downward—he decided he was disinclined to bother with a mere university banquet that had been arranged in his honor in Boston. Clementine was quick to tell him to go, sternly saying, "[T]he country has been combed for the finest food and wines, and . . . many of the faculty did not have dinner jackets, or their wives long dresses, and they have bought them specially because you are coming." Winston did as he was told.[29]

The war had undoubtedly changed the Churchills' approach to others as well as to each other. Clementine had taken on some American customs: no longer outraged by the use of first names, she tolerated even "fringe friends" calling her Clemmie. They were both friendlier to their neighbors and staff, and longtime employees such as Grace Hamblin were no longer expected to use the back door. Moppet, Mary's stalwart nanny, continued to work for the Churchills in other ways after the war (including supervising a flock of chickens that came as a gift) and, even when she retired, continued to be a close companion to the family. With financial worries finally a thing of the past, and plenty of help to run their lives, Clementine became reconciled to living at Chartwell and was ironically more enthusiastic than Winston about improving the grounds.

Feeling equally secure in her marriage, she even encouraged Winston to flirt with old flames such as Violet Asquith or Pamela Lytton—as well as with new admirers, including the beautiful Odette Pol-Roger, the grande dame of his favorite champagne house. Tactfully she would leave him alone with such women for dinner, taking the chance to go to the theater with an assistant. "During the course of the evening," recalled one secretary, Heather White-Smith (then Wood), "she would whisper with a twinkle 'I wonder what is going on?' "[30] The once-jealous Clementine recognized that such harmless old-age dalliances stopped Winston from getting bored and made him more pliable. They also provided her with welcome free time.

The war had left Clementine with a taste for public duty but in want of a role. She could be forgiven for being envious of Eleanor Roosevelt, who, at the age of sixty-one, had only just begun her substantive career. Far from sinking into gloomy obscurity following her husband's death, Eleanor relished her independence, refusing to be seen merely as Franklin's widow. In December 1945, President Truman had approached her about becoming a delegate to the United Nations, an organization she viewed as her husband's greatest legacy. During her stint at the UN, Eleanor would chair the commission charged with drawing up an international bill of rights and in 1952 she was even touted as a possible Democratic candidate for the presidency. "Her real life's work began after FDR's death," confirms her grandson David Roosevelt. "The Universal Declaration [of Human Rights] was her crowning achievement."[31]

This success did not greatly endear her to Winston. He constantly dodged her requests for meetings or to appear with her on television in America. Clementine was more forthcoming, especially following Eleanor's trip to London in 1948 for the unveiling of a statue of her husband outside the American embassy. "Your visit has given me joy as it has to so many," she cabled afterward, signing off with "Love."[32] Mostly it was Eleanor who kept the relationship alive, however. She was assiduous in sending the Churchills her good wishes at Christmas and agreed to appear as Sarah's first guest on the younger Churchill's American television chat show in 1951, providing her with a gratifying scoop.[33]

Eleanor's globe-trotting was a far cry from her counterpart's largely domestic existence. Clementine was therefore pleased in 1949 to be invited to chair the YWCA's National Hostels Committee. It was hardly the UN but it gave her the chance to exercise her talent for organization, and she soon became an effective scourge of hard mattresses and inadequate bathrooms. Nearly a decade later she would involve herself in an appeal for World Refugee Year, and another for the building of New Hall, Cambridge, the university's third college for women. Never forgetting how her old headmistress Miss Harris had wanted her to go on to university, she maintained a keen interest in women's education even though none of her own daughters had taken degrees. She argued strongly that the new Cambridge college founded in Winston's honor in 1960 should be coeducational. Contrary to some reports she initially lost that battle, but Churchill College was one of the first all-male colleges to vote to admit women a few years later.

While she lacked a prominent public role of her own, she at least found a new and perhaps unexpected purpose in her grandchildren. In February 1947, Mary married Christopher Soames, an ebullient young diplomat. Although Clementine was initially untrusting of this new arrival (and perhaps a little jealous), over time she grew to like and rely on him. Fearful of losing Mary as a companion, she suggested the young couple move into the house at Chartwell Farm, which Winston had just bought. Until it was ready, they could stay at the big house. The couple's noisy lovemaking[34] was soon to be heard by everyone, amusing Clementine but driving to distraction the noise-averse Winston—who marched down from his study to order the embarrassed couple to keep quiet. Although never a diaper-changer, Clementine doted on the grandchildren who soon followed, enjoying nursery teas in a way unthinkable with her own brood. Mary recalled how at one family picnic her mother remarked, "You have so much fun with your children that I now realise how I missed out."[35]

Making up for lost time, she enjoyed taking her eventual tally of ten grandchildren to Christmas pantomimes in London. And when Edwina Sandys, her eldest granddaughter, made her society debut in 1957, Clementine arranged a dance for her at Claridge's. (She and

Winston even tapped their feet in time to Chubby Checker's "The Twist" when it was younger sister Celia's turn a few years later.) But even the diplomatic Mary admitted that she had learned from Clementine's mistakes. "I made a conscious decision to put my children first because I did feel something had been . . . yes, missing at home."[36]

Diana and her husband, Duncan Sandys, with their three children, were also frequent visitors to Chartwell and both got on well with Winston. Clementine disliked Duncan, however, and there remained "an atmosphere of watchfulness"[37] whenever she spent time with Diana. Nor had relations with Randolph improved. He continued to upset Winston with his drunken scenes. Clementine found the arguments impossible to bear and would either erupt angrily or withdraw into a chilly silence. Underlying the tension was Randolph's bitterness at his parents' collusion in Pamela's infidelity. Clementine nevertheless insisted on continuing to see her former daughter-in-law. She felt that Pamela had suffered unfairly since the war, in part as a result of outsiders' jealousy. There were those who accused her of having lived "high on the hog," and from certain quarters came ridiculous suggestions that she had in some way collaborated with the enemy. Nothing could have been further from the truth.

Clementine sympathized when Pamela was abandoned by Ed Murrow—who decided he could not bear to leave Janet (who had long since known about the affair) after she became pregnant with his child during a holiday reconciliation back in the US. Later Clementine was uneasy when Pamela took up with the Italian Gianni Agnelli, heir to the car manufacturer Fiat, and was even more perturbed when Agnelli—followed by a series of other wealthy lovers—showered Pamela with gemstones and couture but also omitted to marry her. "One has to remember that Clementine was very Scottish," said a younger member of the family. "I remember going with Pamela to lunch with Clementine, and going up in the lift she took off all her jewellery and put it in her handbag. She didn't want Clementine to see what she had as she thought it would upset her."[38]

Only in his rare reflective moments did Randolph concede that his mother had gone out of her way to help him. As chairwoman of a trust Winston had set up at the end of the war to look after his children and grandchildren, she quietly bailed out his extravagances. Randolph married again in November 1948, and Clementine bought the newlyweds a house. A year later his new wife, June Osborne, gave birth to a daughter, Arabella. But by then June was also already finding her husband's bullying, drinking and temper unbearable.

Sarah returned to acting after the war, and in the autumn of 1946 signed up with an Italian film company in Rome. Still hell-bent on stardom, she excitedly sent a synopsis of her latest movie to all her family but "the only person who really took trouble to read it was [her] father."[39] Gil Winant, who had been "let go" by the less appreciative Truman administration, was still devotedly in love and planning to divorce his wife to be with her. She knew him to be a good man but recoiled from the idea of entering into wedlock again so soon. "It seems that I must always hurt the person who loves me," she wrote in despair to her father.[40] On November 3, 1947, a distraught Winant took a pistol out of his dressing-gown pocket at his home in Concord, Massachusetts, and shot himself. Clementine sent four dozen yellow roses to his funeral and made Winston accompany her to Winant's London memorial service at St. Paul's. She was consumed by grief at the loss of her friend; Sarah was riven with guilt.

Sarah returned to America to work in theater and television and later hitched up with the handsome British photographer Antony Beauchamp. Winston took an instant dislike to Beauchamp when they met in Monte Carlo in January 1949. Clementine also had her doubts after hearing him shout at Sarah in her hotel room and gently tried to persuade her daughter against committing herself. But in October Sarah and Beauchamp took a holiday together in Sea Island, Georgia, and they decided to marry there and then. Sarah cabled her parents but by the time her message arrived they had already read about it in the newspapers.

Despairing at her daughter's stubborn folly over another ill-advised marriage, Clementine ignored Sarah's pleading letters or replied with brief, businesslike telegrams. Eventually, Beauchamp wrote angrily to Clementine that her disapproval was making Sarah ill. Urgently apologizing, Clementine begged Sarah, "[F]orgive me and believe in my love . . . for you."[41] Mother and daughter were joyfully reunited in England in May 1950 and the following year she bought a London "nest" for the couple in Pimlico. Sarah understood that Clementine was trying to "crush" her doubts about Beauchamp and doing "everything she could to make [them] happy."[42] Clementine could not, however, conceal her fears about the union, or about Sarah's increasing dependence on alcohol to get her through.

Needing to escape the troubles of family life and restore their strength, in the years immediately after the war Winston and Clementine resumed their enthusiastic holiday-making. As so often before, many of their trips were taken separately, and frequently Winston would be hard at work on the six volumes of the highly successful (and lucrative) *The Second World War* while he was away. In August 1949, Winston went to stay at Beaverbrook's cliff-top villa, La Capponcina, near Monte Carlo. While playing cards late one night with friends he suffered a stroke. When informed, Clementine chose to stay at home, in the apparent belief that the media storm her sudden appearance would provoke might be worse than her absence. Fortunately, the stroke was mild and Winston flew home a week later. Even so, it was a sign of things to come.

The next general election, in February 1950, saw Labour returned to power by the narrowest of margins. Voters had grown tired of living in a gray world of housing shortages and continued rationing while defeated countries seemed to be recovering from the war more swiftly. Despite his stroke, growing deafness and a hernia operation, Winston's health appeared surprisingly robust and his attacks on Labour's record were beginning to be heard. Clementine too was feeling better about life, until May 1951, when she endured the first of a series of invasive operations after being admitted to the hospital for a major gynecological "repair." This time she could afford not to stint on her convalescence and spent weeks resting at Chartwell before embarking on extensive holidays in southwest France, Paris, the Alps and Venice. A snap election was called on her return in early October and now the Tories, after waging an upbeat campaign, came home with a majority of seventeen seats. Just short of his seventy-seventh birthday, Winston was once again prime minister.

Of course there was satisfaction that he had been restored to power after the ignominy of 1945, but she thought him too old and his health too compromised for high office, and she could muster little enthusiasm for an all-Conservative administration—even if it avoided rolling back many of the Attlee reforms. Being in the thick of things again no doubt offered some compensation, though. Winston consulted her, as usual, on appointments—including his plan to offer the prestigious role of war secretary to Duncan Sandys. She quickly warned that he would be exposing himself to allegations of nepotism and Sandys was duly downgraded to the more junior post of minister of supply. This intervention aside, Clementine struggled to summon her old enthusiasm for government. The mold she had broken in 1940, becoming Britain's first active First Lady, contracted back into a more conventional (and perhaps constitutionally correct) shape during Winston's second term. She involved herself more with hospitality and ceremony than with helping to run the country. Her hands-on tours in February 1953 of the East Anglian coast—where floods had killed hundreds and made thousands more homeless—were a rare public reminder of her wartime role.

Clementine rented out Hyde Park Gate to the Cuban ambassador so that she could move back into a Downing Street that had also physically changed since her previous residency. The staterooms on the first floor—largely abandoned by the Attlees and used only for the occasional large official function—were now looking drab. The imitation silk curtains installed by the dreaded Ministry of Works had shrunk five inches from the floor and the sofas had been reupholstered in unflattering greens and browns. Clementine knew better than to spend public money on a lavish redecoration, but she somehow worked wonders on the fine Georgian rooms. The Bristol glass chandeliers were scrubbed to sparkling perfection and the addition of simple bunches of flowers, family photographs and William Nicholson paintings in muted colors, displayed in beveled frames, banished the austerity-era dreariness.[43] She planned to live in the modest self-contained flat in the attics that the Attlees had created for their own use, but it was not an arrangement that commended itself to Winston, and despite her initial objections about convenience and staffing, she eventually gave way. Citing the need to entertain foreign dignitaries before, during and after the coronation of the new queen (George VI died on February 6, 1952), the Churchills soon moved back downstairs into their customary grandeur, with Clementine compensating as far as possible for what the aesthete Cecil Beaton described as the "puky" new color scheme.

A couple of weeks after the king passed away, Winston suffered from a spasm of the cerebral arteries that caused temporary confusion in his speech. The condition was kept secret outside a small inner circle but it raised questions as to how long he could carry on. Clementine was also weakening. Suffering from an overwhelming sensation of fatigue, she canceled her public engagements that summer and resorted to her old pattern of taking "cures." This escape from the grind of tending to Winston perked her up—as did another holiday afterward with Sarah and Antony on the island of Capri. When her niece Clarissa announced she was to marry Anthony Eden, the foreign secretary, she immediately offered to return from Italy to host the wedding at Downing Street only a week later.

Large-scale entertaining became the dominant chore of Clementine's second term at Number 10, particularly in the lead-up to the coronation of Queen Elizabeth on June 2, 1953. There was a succession of state visits, a Commonwealth conference, a banquet for the heads of state and government attending the coronation, and a whirl of other lunches, dinners and receptions. On the great day itself Clementine draped herself in the satin robe of the Order of the British Empire and borrowed a tiara from a friend. Riding beside Winston in a coach during the procession she looked radiant, but the strain of the preparations had taken its toll. Though barely noticeable, her arm was encased in a sling because of neuritis, a painful inflammation of the nerves that would in time drive her once again to near collapse.

Three weeks later Clementine hosted a dinner for thirty-eight at Downing Street in honor of the Italian prime minister, Alcide De Gasperi. She presided over the event with her usual élan. As the guests were leaving the first-floor Pillared Room, however, she glanced back only to see Winston struggling to rise from his chair. Christopher Soames quickly informed De Gasperi that the prime minister was overtired, and others present apparently attributed the slur in his speech to the wine. Winston seemed to improve a little once he was helped to bed, but it was confirmed in the morning that he had suffered another stroke. Incredibly, he still held a cabinet meeting, at which his colleagues noticed little untoward, and it took all Clementine's strength to persuade him not to take questions in Parliament that afternoon. Some excuse would have to be found, as his illness was to be kept utterly secret; Winston wanted nothing to get in the way of an impending conference in Bermuda with US president Eisenhower (he still believed in a very personal style of diplomacy with American presidents as the surest way of influencing them, in this case over the issue of the "Western alliance" approach to Russia at a pivotal point in the Cold War following the death of Stalin earlier in the year). But the next day he was much worse and had to be bundled out of town to the seclusion of Chartwell, and the conference, which had already been announced and attracted worldwide interest, would have to be canceled. Now the queen and the cabinet were informed of the true nature of his illness, but Lords Beaverbrook, Bracken and Camrose took it upon themselves to gag the press about its being a stroke.

In reality, Churchill was losing the use of his left leg and arm and needed constant nursing. Moran feared he would not last the weekend and the family, including a subdued Randolph, swiftly gathered around him. For once Randolph marveled at his mother's capacity to deal with a crisis, not least because she had herself had a fall and had broken several ribs. "I thought you were magnificent on Saturday & doing everything possible to maintain Papa's morale," he wrote to her soon afterward. "So long as that persists no miracle is impossible."[44] Winston did start to improve, albeit slowly, but he was still far from capable of running the country, let alone traveling to Bermuda. Unavoidable decisions were being made by Colville and Soames on the basis of what they thought he would have done, and it is more than probable—for she was in constant attendance—that they did so after occasional consultation with Clementine. The blanket of secrecy about his condition was so carefully maintained by the small, makeshift (and certainly undemocratic) band running the country that only carefully selected visitors, such as Violet (Asquith) Bonham Carter, were permitted. These the ever-alert Clementine waylaid beforehand, making them promise not to offer him unrealistic hopes of staying at Number 10.

"Clemmie said that she *felt sure* he ought to retire in the autumn & begged me not to urge him to stay on," Violet noted in her diary.[45] She also observed how difficult Winston was to handle, having become prone to sudden and unreasonable rages "like a violent child." Later Violet wrote to her old rival, with what sounds like genuine praise: "I must tell you darling, what *intense* admiration I felt for your courage, wisdom & dispassionate judgment."[46] She was right: Clementine was taking an unsentimental view—understanding more clearly than others that her ailing husband could no longer command the same authority, either at home or abroad. The problem was that everyone else was either too scared or did not appreciate the need to suggest to him directly that he should step down, and Clementine was reluctant to make herself a lone voice on this most sensitive of subjects. The unresolved question of his future was to overshadow their lives for the next two years.

As Winston gradually recuperated, so did his impatience rapidly increase. Clementine thought him rashly intent on projecting himself as indestructible. They argued bitterly over whether he should accept an invitation from the queen to attend a horse race in September and then stay with her at Balmoral. True to form, Winston quickly apologized for losing his temper, although he also got his way. He and Clementine duly joined the royals at the St. Leger Stakes at Doncaster, where their forty-fifth wedding anniversary was celebrated joyfully, and then took the train up to Scotland. Perhaps Clementine had been unreasonably pessimistic; after the strain of the past couple of months, Balmoral proved to be an uplifting break.

Shortly afterward Winston flew to the south of France for another holiday at Beaverbrook's villa. Clementine took the opportunity to spend a few quiet days with Nellie at the theater in Stratford. Rather than begrudging her this brief respite, he acknowledged he was more dependent on her than ever. In private he begged: *"Please continue to love me* or I shall be very unhappy."

When Winston resumed his full duties as prime minister in October 1953, a disapproving Clementine fled from him yet again. Although he was stronger—and rescheduled the Bermuda conference with Eisenhower for December—he found her absence troubling. During a short flit to Paris, he wrote to her about his loneliness three times: "One night I had dinner in bed as I did not want anyone but you for company," he pined.[47]

Even news that he had won the Nobel Prize for Literature for *The Second World War*, the many other books written over his lifetime and, of course, his famous wartime speeches, failed to lift his mood. In any case, he was prevented from receiving the award in person, as the ceremony in December clashed with the rearranged conference. So Clementine flew to Stockholm in his place, staying with the king and queen of Sweden at the royal palace. She was welcomed not as a mere substitute for her husband but as an honored guest in her own right—Queen Louise described her presence as nothing short of "queenly."[48] The Swedish press followed her closely, writing enthusiastically about everything she wore, said and did. At a banquet for nine hundred people, she was "quite overcome"[49] when the band suddenly struck up "Oh My Darling, Clementine."

Winston's other great honor that year came when Queen Elizabeth made him a Knight of the Garter, the highest order of chivalry, which is restricted to just twenty-four living recipients at any one time. Some, such as his private secretary Anthony Montague Browne, thought he should have declined the title, going down in history as

"the Great Commoner" like Pitt the Elder (at least until he unexpectedly accepted an earldom). Clementine, though now styling herself
Lady Churchill, was widely thought to share this view.

Clementine still loved attending big occasions; it was *organizing* them
that she found so draining. She'd had her fill of playing hostess during
the war. But she continued to drive herself and those around her extremely hard; adamant that every event should be flawless, she exploded at staff for the most trifling lapses in standards. Sometimes
before yet another Downing Street dinner she would work herself up
into a state of near hysteria, only to reappear shortly afterward, immaculate in jewels and finery and smiling gracefully at the guests as
if she had not a worry in the world.

   Winston remained difficult, of course, and could be brusque and
petulant with his entourage. But his sense of fun and loyalty on other
occasions made him easier to forgive. When he went to greet the
queen on board the royal yacht *Britannia* upon her return from Australia in 1954, one of his servants was "overcome by the splendor" of
the celebrations and became "incapacitated." Although cross at this
indiscretion, Winston worried that if Clementine found out she
would insist on instantly sacking the poor man. The evening ended
with the prime minister "surreptitiously undressing the servant . . .
and . . . tucking him up with many admonitory remarks. Nothing
was heard of the incident . . . again."[50]

   It was not only the staff of whom Clementine could be intolerant.
She was becoming increasingly "aggressive" with Winston. Mary
thought he indulged her outbursts only because he realized he had
imposed another term of office on her against her wishes. Clementine would sometimes fret afterward that she had been unkind or too
touchy. Usually, though, it was Winston who would be first to sue for
peace, asking for absolution for imagined slights or, as Clementine
put it, sweeping her "into the waste paper basket."[51] There is a sense
that during his second stint as prime minister Winston took ever
greater pains to placate Clementine. As he weakened, she became

more dictatorial. During dinner at Chartwell one evening in July 1953, not long after his stroke, he leaned toward her with: "You will not be angry with me, dear, but you ought not to say 'very delicious.' 'Delicious' alone expresses everything you wish to say." Eyes blazing, she rounded on him "with a discourse on manners in which," Moran observed, "Clemmie did all the talking and Winston took in every word."[52]

She refused to accept his failing health as an excuse for rudeness. When on one occasion he slumped in a chair, yawned widely and made no effort to talk to a visiting relative, Clementine rebuked him by administering a sharp tap on the knuckles with a fork.[53] Her mood was not eased by her neuritis. By the spring of 1954 she was wearing a surgical collar (she hated being seen in it). The treatment favored by her doctors—and by Clementine herself—seems as before to have been to escape from Downing Street, and so in May she packed her bags for a three-week "cure" at Aix-les-Bains. Her health improved—as it invariably did once away from Winston and the family—but the condition would not subside entirely for the rest of her husband's time in office.

Even without the neuritis she would have had reason to seek solace. Sadness tinged virtually every aspect of Clementine's life in the 1950s. Devastated by her husband's flamboyant womanizing, Diana had suffered a nervous breakdown around the same time as Winston's stroke. Clementine was dismayed to see her daughter in such agony, but their relationship had never been strong and at this point it appears to have collapsed altogether. There were several harrowing scenes when wounding accusations were made on both sides. Randolph later recounted that he had once found Diana armed with a carving knife threatening to kill her mother.[54] Clementine's secretary Chips Gemmell remembers Diana coming to visit when she was "off her head." "It was terrifying," she says. "I was asked to make sure she got into a taxi safely afterwards."[55] Diana, by Sarah's account, nursed a sense of being "greatly wronged" (although by no one specifically) and complained of a "lack of recognition."[56] She found some comfort in her father, who talked to her about Black Dog, but such was Winston's own health, and the demands on him as prime minister, that this was as much as he could offer.

Sarah tried to help, but her own marriage was in trouble, as Antony had taken to bedding a series of actresses. From 1955 they lived apart and by August 1957 she was on the brink of filing for divorce when Clementine phoned her with tragic news: Antony had taken his life with an overdose of sleeping pills. Yet again a man Sarah had loved had committed suicide—and all the self-recrimination that had attended Winant's death came flooding back. In January 1958 she was in the US working on a television program and renting what she described as a "rickety cabin" in Malibu. It was outside her home one evening that she was arrested and charged with drunkenness. Humiliating pictures of her were splashed across the newspapers, followed by accounts that she had behaved so violently in her police cell that it had been necessary to restrain her with a straitjacket.

Clementine quickly arranged for Sarah to fly to the south of France, away from the press pack. She joined her for a few days, and during her long, nonjudgmental talks with her daughter the two women drew much closer. Sarah then went on to a Swiss clinic, of which her only memory was being probed about whether her drinking was linked to her loving her father more than her mother. Upon her return to Britain there were more tussles with the police and court appearances for her public drunkenness (Clementine once questioned Sarah's wisdom in wearing a leopard-skin coat in the dock and remonstrated on another occasion against the police's forcibly carrying her daughter into the proceedings). There was even a ten-day spell in Holloway Prison. Clementine largely bore the burden of instructing solicitors, dealing with the newspapers and trying to persuade Sarah to undergo more treatment. Inevitably, Sarah's beloved career suffered. Clementine was relieved when she found her daughter sober enough to be "pleasant," but there was now a persistent fear that Sarah would succumb to a breakdown, or even kill herself with booze.

Clementine had few confidantes to turn to. She had lost her sole surviving sibling to cancer in February 1955. Nellie was sixty-six when she died, little more than six months after her diagnosis. Clementine's staff at that time remember her nursing her sister in her final days and being utterly bereft at her death. "There was an even greater loneliness about her now," recalled her assistant of the time, Heather White-Smith. One of Nellie's last outings had been to Winston's eightieth birthday party in November 1954, which was not the joyful occasion Clementine had hoped. Parliament had decided to mark the occasion by presenting him with a portrait by the fashionable artist Graham Sutherland. Clementine took immediately to the debonair and charming painter, describing him as a "wow" (the highest Churchill accolade) even though she thought many of his modernist paintings "savage" and "cruel." Winston agreed to several sittings, and a fortnight before the big day he was shown the final work. Clementine was initially intrigued by the untraditional treatment, but Winston's reaction was instant loathing—and she too came to resent how it presented an ancient, grumpy figure in depressing grays and browns, colors he detested. "She thought it made him hideous," Grace Hamblin recalled.

This was not the heroic legacy either had envisioned, but Clementine spent the next two weeks reminding him that the hated gift had been born out of the affection and respect of his colleagues. The twenty-three thousand birthday telegrams and cards that poured in from around the world helped to lift both their spirits so that by November 30 itself, they were able to receive the painting in good grace. As Parliament welcomed them in Westminster Hall with a deafening ovation, Clementine glowed.

Afterward the portrait was hidden away in the basement at Chartwell, until one day Clementine asked Grace for her help. "Lady Churchill was very much exercised. [She asked,] 'So now, what do you suggest?' " Grace offered to destroy it, and with the help of her brother sneaked it out of Chartwell "in the dead of night" and took it by van to his home several miles away, where they lit a bonfire in the back garden out of the sight of passersby. "It was a huge thing so I couldn't lift it alone,"[57] Grace revealed in an extract of a taped interview closed to the public for twenty years. She threw the painting on the fire and watched it burn, telling Clementine the next morning what she had done.

For years, rumors circulated about the portrait's fate, and various theories were expounded as to the circumstances of its disappearance. "I destroyed it," Grace confessed on the secret tape before her death, "but Lady C and I decided we would not tell anyone. She was thinking of me."

The birthday applause had been genuine, but so were the growing concerns about Winston's "twilight" powers. While he chose to remain in office Clementine never hinted beyond their inner circle at her own feelings and treated sniping in the press with contempt; she had no desire to "hound" him into resigning and was implacably opposed to others' forcing him out, which she feared would literally kill him. But there were signs of brewing unrest in the cabinet that could be ignored no longer, and given her unique influence over the prime minister, it was inevitable she would be somehow drawn in. One morning in July 1954, Harold Macmillan, then minister of housing, visited her alone in Downing Street. He told her Winston no longer commanded the support of all his cabinet colleagues and would have to step down. She listened and agreed to convey his arguments to her husband.[58] But then, most unusually, her courage failed her. Clearly shaken, she sent for Colville as soon as Macmillan had left the room and arranged for him to join her and Winston at lunch.

Clementine was still agitated when the three met shortly afterward in the white-paneled dining room; however, she finally summoned up the resolve to relate the morning's events. Winston reacted surprisingly well, merely summoning Macmillan that afternoon to inform him that he intended to "soldier on." Clementine never forgave the man she now considered the leader of an anti-Winston cabal. Still, it was now clear that politically the prime minister was living on borrowed time. In the New Year, after four years of Tory government, thoughts inevitably turned to the next general election and he at last conceded that he could no longer postpone setting a date for his departure. Early April was chosen but Clementine's relief was tempered by fears for his morale. Her neuritis returned with a "vengeance"[59] and in March she spent two weeks at Chequers. Winston joined her on weekends but during the week he was alone, with only dark thoughts for company. This time his majestic career at the top table of politics was really at an end. "It's the first death—& for him, a death in life,"[60] Clementine told Mary.

Before stepping down, however, they were to hold one of their famously good parties. The first day of April had been dominated by gossip about Guy Burgess and Donald Maclean, two Foreign Office officials who had disappeared four years previously and were now suspected of having passed secrets to the Russians. The mood quickly lifted as guests climbed the Downing Street stairs for after-dinner drinks—or rather the forty-six magnums of Pol Roger champagne ordered by Grace. The invitation cards stated merely that Sir Winston was "At Home" to celebrate Lady Churchill's seventieth birthday, yet there were distinct undertones that the event marked the end of an era. Clementine's Labour friends were present among the convivial crowd, and she made a point of greeting Mrs. Attlee with a kiss. Winston's old loves Violet Bonham Carter and Pamela Lytton were also in attendance, mixing with Sylvia Henley and the surviving Romillys and Mitfords. Clementine's secretary Heather Wood and the other staff mingled amiably, wearing specially bought evening dresses. (Anthony and Clarissa Eden were absent, however, and his subsequent distancing of himself from the Churchills hurt both deeply.)

In the throng, Cecil Beaton noticed that for once all eyes were on Clementine rather than Winston. For most people her face was almost as familiar as his—"her Grecian profile, the deep-set pale-blue eyes . . . These two faces [had] together travelled through many epochs in [the British people's] personal history. Tonight was a private goodbye." She was dressed in black lace with embroidered orchids at the waist; "her eyes were focused to other distances." Beaton heard that she was in agony (as she confessed to Violet, she was "doped" up to ensure she was "gay as a lark") but he also noted that there was still "fire and dash in the consort of the old warrior."[61]

With the newspapers on strike, the reaction was surprisingly muted when Winston resigned a few days later on the afternoon of April 5. The following day the Churchills hosted a good-bye tea party for the Downing Street staff and Winston departed for Chartwell, cheers ringing in his ears as he walked the long corridor from the Cabinet Room to the front door for the last time. Clementine stayed in London to orchestrate the move, joining him a few days later for Easter but spending most of the time in bed. Shortly afterward, they set off with Colville and the Prof for a holiday in Sicily. Sadly they decided to come back early—the weather was cold and gray and Clementine was in constant pain.

So began the Churchills' final stretch outside the magic circle of power—for the first time without hope of rejoining it. Winston descended into a "state of apathy and indifference."[62] Only when a furor over the queen's sister, Princess Margaret, and her hopes of marrying the divorced Group Captain Peter Townsend threatened to spark another royal constitutional crisis in the autumn of 1955 was a flicker of interest sparked. Initially, Winston thought the princess should be allowed to have her way, and may have intended to make his position clear. But, recalling how he had so nearly torpedoed his career by supporting Edward VIII's plans to marry Wallis Simpson, Clementine responded bluntly: "If you are going to begin the abdication all over again, I'm going to leave [you]."[63]

Clementine's daughters agreed that the adjustment to civilian life was worse for her than for their father. He was still showered with admiring attention, and he had his cronies, his painting and writing, and, above all, Chartwell. By contrast, she had hoped to enjoy their liberation from high office by socializing in London and going to the theater, but decades of devotion had left her with few friends, and Nellie's death had robbed her of one of her few remaining sources of female companionship. Sometimes she became so desperate to talk that she unburdened herself to less-than-discreet or -loyal acquaintances. On more than one occasion she had long heart-to-hearts at crowded parties with the notorious gossip Noël Coward—once she was "extremely trenchant" about Randolph, for instance, and on another occasion she poured out her feelings about Diana's illness.[64] In 1958 she tried to contact some old Berkhamsted school friends,[65] and often she immersed herself in the light escapism of a Barbara Cartland novel. But mostly, in her loneliness, she turned to the young women she employed as secretaries. She took them to the royal box at Wimbledon, to the theater, cinema and art galleries, and invited them for lunch, drinks or even just to watch television.

One of these women was Shelagh Montague Browne (Anthony's second wife), who before she married lived in the flat above the Churchills' Hyde Park Gate offices. She remembered how Clementine would "ring up and say 'I see you're in, dear, would you like to come and watch *Emergency Ward Ten* with me?'" Clementine would then encourage her to stay for supper, although Montague Browne sometimes tried to plead a prior engagement. On other occasions, when Clementine spotted friends arriving at her flat, she would telephone to say, "They look interesting." "So I would invite her over for a drink and she would arrive in an instant. I thought how vulnerable she was and how she needed girlfriends."[66] Chips Gemmell remembers one poignant lunch with Clementine, saying, "I saw her hand coming towards me very slowly so I took it. I think it was a sweet gesture."[67] In August 1955, she invited one of her favorites, eighteen-year-old Heather Wood, to accompany her to St. Moritz for a month. Heather found herself listening to Mrs. Winston Churchill's "most intimate" secrets[68] and, for a time at least, became almost a surrogate daughter. Early one morning, there was a gentle knock on Heather's hotel room door, and Clementine was standing outside "like a small, shy girl." "I do hope you are not being worn out dear by this tiresome old woman," she said.[69]

Winston worried about her deeply but was either too miserable himself or too immersed in his own pursuits—he was still writing and painting into the early 1960s—to help her. Although he was lonely and increasingly relied on his private secretary Montague Browne for companionship he rarely accompanied his wife on her chosen jaunts. It was another man, a friendly American widower called Lewis Einstein, who provided her with male company in St. Moritz—as well as a large chauffeured car to take her on scenic drives through the mountains.

Clementine returned to Chartwell from St. Moritz in September 1955 in good spirits, only for her neuritis to flare up again within a couple of months. Regular self-administered injections of pethidine, a highly addictive opiate, brought only partial relief and added insomnia to her troubles. Her evident anguish was starting to frighten those close to her, prompting a Roman Catholic friend to give her a rosary. Worried that her mother was becoming desperate, Sarah wrote: "I wish all was better for you—When you hold your rosary at night—do not wish for sad things . . . pray we can all yet be happy— I am powerless & incapable in front of your despair—but I thank you for sharing it with me—it makes me feel closer to you."[70]

A Chartwell family Christmas saw a brief improvement in her condition, but in January 1956 Clementine was admitted to the hospital for three weeks. Winston had already returned to the south of France to stay at La Pausa, a luxurious stone villa built in 1927 by Coco Chanel and now owned by his literary agent, Emery Reves. He wrote to her every couple of days and at one point planned to return. Clementine preferred him to stay put and, upon finally being discharged, ignored his entreaties to convalesce with him at La Pausa and set off instead on an eight-week cruise to Ceylon. In need of undemanding company, she had planned to take the sweet-natured Heather Wood, but Wood had decided to leave to create a life of her own. (Winston tried personally to persuade her to stay, to no avail, although she felt the "parting" from her "second mother" "very deeply"; Clementine gave her a gift of a V for Victory lapel brooch in rubies, diamonds and sapphires.) Since Heather would not come to Ceylon she took Sylvia Henley. The two cousins enjoyed themselves but Winston became irritated when Clementine failed to write for long periods. Every time he tried to persuade her to stop at La Pausa on her way home she countered with an unconvincing excuse, such as not having the right clothes. Montague Browne interpreted Clementine's avoidance of her husband as her way of enduring a life lived "on the brink of a nervous breakdown." Yes, she "shied away" from the enormous "stress of [Winston's] gradual but perceptible physical and mental decline . . . It was never neglect; it was exhaustion."[71]

She returned to Britain in better spirits on April 12 but departed after only a month to stay with Lewis Einstein in Paris. In August she again hooked up with her attentive "crony"—as her family began to refer to him—back in St. Moritz. If Winston felt any jealousy toward this innocent liaison there is no evidence of it in his letters or behavior. In fact, the Churchills had reestablished a mutually viable pattern: short periods together in London or Chartwell, between often lengthy trips apart.

For his part, Winston was now back in France with Reves and his Texan girlfriend, the former model Wendy Russell. Clementine's dislike of Reves and Russell was clear, and was another reason she dodged La Pausa. She suspected them of parading Winston as a trophy and disapproved of how they indulged him. On returning home after one of his trips there, he made the mistake of ordering sauce with his fish. Clementine flared up immediately. "This is not the South of France!" she declared pointedly. "We are not vulgar, rich people!"[72]

Reves and Russell would invite selected guests for Winston's entertainment. One such was Noël Coward, who visited La Pausa for lunch in June 1956. Coward certainly amused Winston but he also observed that the former war leader was "absolutely obsessed with a senile passion for Wendy Russell. He followed her about the room with his brimming eyes and wobbled after her across the terrace."[73] There are indications that Clementine herself suspected Winston had a crush on Russell (although she feared for his dignity rather than for his fidelity). In any case she finally persuaded Winston to spend some time away from Reves, in the Hôtel de Paris in Monte Carlo, by promising to visit if he did. But it was not until he took up with the Greek ship owner Aristotle Onassis that Clementine extended her stays. Onassis was a charismatic charmer and his wife, Tina, was kind and engaging; here was a couple that appealed to them both.

The Onassis yacht, the *Christina*, was itself a wonder and at the

end of September 1958 Winston and Clementine were invited to join
a Mediterranean cruise. They boarded on a high, having just celebrated their golden wedding anniversary together at Beaverbrook's
Riviera villa, La Capponcina. In one of his rare flashes of generosity,
Randolph had arranged for an avenue of golden roses to be planted
in the walled garden at Chartwell to commemorate the occasion, and
engaged a number of well-known artist friends, including Augustus
John and Cecil Beaton, to paint pictures of the flowers for a leather-
bound album to be presented to his parents on the day. For once
Clementine was simultaneously astonished and delighted by her son.

Reves and Russell were now out of the picture and peeved. Clementine had vetoed them from the *Christina* guest list, declaring she
would bail out if they came on board. Onassis indulged her and subsequently invited the Churchills on four more cruises. He proved
himself a perfect host, gathering agreeable guests and choosing
routes around the Greek islands and the West Indies that he knew
would appeal to them. Clementine had adored sea journeys ever
since her cruises on the *Rosaura* in the 1930s, and life aboard the *Christina* brought out the best in her; now it was Clementine, rather than
Winston, who held court over dinner.

The happy setup changed, however, when Onassis began an affair with the opera singer Maria Callas. Celia Sandys joined her
grandparents on the *Christina* in July 1959 when Callas was also there
and remembers, "[W]e watched events unfolding, and met each evening in my grandmother's cabin to gossip."[74] Onassis and Tina separated soon afterward and divorced in 1962. Winston traveled with
Onassis on three more occasions, but Clementine, out of loyalty to
Tina, never did so again.

Winston's final cruise with Onassis, in 1963, took him to the Adri-
atic. By his side were his faithful secretary Anthony Montague
Browne; young Winston, now a twenty-two-year-old journalist; and
Jock Colville and his wife. Against his better judgment, he had also
been persuaded to include his son. Over dinner one evening Randolph attacked his father verbally in front of other guests, making
"violent reproaches" about how Winston and Clementine had en-

couraged Pamela to seduce Americans during the war. "What he said was unseemly in any circumstances," Montague Browne related, "but in front of comparative strangers it was ghastly."[75] Twenty years on, Randolph still could not forgive or forget.

Back home the ever-fragile Diana was in torment. Three years earlier her twenty-five-year marriage to Duncan Sandys had ended in divorce, breaking her heart. In early 1963 he brought her fresh pain and humiliation when he became embroiled in a notorious sex scandal. During the Duchess of Argyll's divorce case, photographs were released in which the duchess was shown wearing nothing but pearls while fellating someone whose face is out of view; it was widely speculated that Sandys was the "headless man" in question. While Clementine never became close to Diana, she was sympathetic about this latest ordeal and mother and daughter now at least spent more time together.

A bright spot in the gloom was offered by Sarah, who had managed finally to put unhappiness behind her when she married again in April 1962. Even Clementine took to Baron (Henry) Audley, a sensitive and engaging fifty-year-old man of weak health. Now in her late forties, Sarah could barely believe her luck. They settled happily in Spain, until fifteen months later, in July 1963, Henry suffered a cerebral hemorrhage and died. The bishop of Gibraltar conducted the funeral at the British naval cemetery in Málaga, but beforehand he visited her privately to seek reassurances about her behavior and sobriety during the ceremony: "You won't let me down will you?" he asked. Two days later she returned to England for a time and went to Chartwell for lunch, where her father met her at the door. "We stared silently at each other; then he took my hand and said simply, 'We must close ranks and march on.'"[76]

Not even the most luxurious existence could protect the Churchills from the depredations of old age. Since mid-1958 Winston had employed a male nurse, Roy Howells, and as he entered his late eighties he suffered further bouts of pneumonia. Especially troubling was his descent into deafness. Clementine badgered him to wear a hearing aid, but he resisted what he felt to be a fiddly imposition; he talked less and less, leaving her to fill the lulls in conversation. So far as she was able, she tried to keep his chin up, but Clementine was now carrying the burden of a husband who quite openly wanted to die.

Nor was she in fine fettle herself. After at last conquering her neuritis in the summer of 1958 she had developed shingles, which left her with a drooping eyelid and in need of yet more surgery. Recurrent flu dogged her winters, and she continued to suffer from periodic lows. In 1961, with Winston due to embark on a cruise with Onassis, she agreed to be admitted to the hospital for a complete rest and checkup. There was no obvious physical cause of her severe fatigue but she was formally diagnosed with depression.

After Winston's resignation as prime minister, he rarely spoke in the Commons and even less in his constituency. And yet his responsibilities as a member of Parliament continued. Once again, Clementine was obliged to act as his proxy. Her diligence minimized the mutterings among younger party members, but she herself remonstrated with her husband for relying on her too often to stand in for him. He hated constituency glad-handing and did nothing to hide it, so she strove to keep him out of trouble by making "every visit . . . seem a great pleasure."[77] She was anxious lest the voters guess (correctly) that his excuses were mere covers for a lack of interest.

Nevertheless, in the election year of 1959 he returned to Woodford to make it clear he would be standing again. That October, at the age of seventy-four, Clementine joined Winston on the trail to fight their fifteenth election together. Weary as she was, she understood that this was the sole remnant of a once magnificent public life. That did not stop her from thinking it was high time he gave up, and when Winston won back his seat with a reduced majority, it was apparent that others thought so too.

Three years later, in the summer of 1962, Winston broke his hip at the Hôtel de Paris in a fall. He needed two operations and a lengthy period of recuperation. Clementine rarely felt able to leave his side as he was an obstreperous patient and a danger to himself when left unattended. He refused to stop smoking cigars in bed and appeared oblivious when on one occasion he set fire to a napkin, valance and carpet. Even his professional nurse, Howells, found him exhausting. "He drained the people around him of every last drop of energy," he recalled. "Apart from the physical strain, the mental wear and tear was tremendous."[78] After one especially unproductive visit to her onetime idol, Violet finally conceded she would never have done as Winston's wife. "It is as though you alone could reach him with comfort & amusement," she wrote to Clementine. "Your 'private line' with him has remained intact . . . You have had so many years of . . . anxiety & strain with never a let-up—& now W needs you & claims more from you than ever before."[79]

Virtually unable to walk, he wanted merely to sit silently gazing into the fire or, when at Chartwell, at the view. He got muddled when playing cards, he rarely picked up his paintbrushes and, partly as a result of his deafness, he would descend into long periods of complete silence. Even mealtimes passed with barely a flicker of the old Winston. Clementine now had to shout to make herself heard. Sometimes he lay in bed all day doing nothing. He told Diana, "My life is over, but not yet ended."[80] A troupe of nurses tended him around the clock and the expense of it all frightened Clementine. To save money she started taking buses instead of the car, until Winston found out and made her promise to stop.

They began to feel as if they were practically the only survivors from a former age. Roosevelt and Stalin (although both younger) were long since dead and Clementine was troubled to hear, in October 1962, that Eleanor Roosevelt had fallen ill with a virulent strain of tuberculosis. She cabled the former First Lady with best wishes from them both and Eleanor wrote back, with a visibly shaky signature, to thank Clementine for her kindness. "The bug is still with me but I hope to win the battle shortly. With warm good wishes to both of you and hoping that you are both enjoying good health."[81] She died just three weeks later.

Finally, in May 1963, Winston accepted the realities of his own position. With great sadness he announced he would not be standing again as an MP and the Commons prepared to pay him a special tribute. But when Clementine received a copy of the proposed wording the following year, she reacted with cold fury, denouncing it as "mangy."[82] It was duly rewritten to her liking to include a reference to the "unbounded admiration and gratitude" of the House of Commons for Winston's services to the nation and the world, and above all his "inspiration of the British people when they stood alone." Clementine was at Winston's side when the reworded resolution, printed on vellum, was delivered by a delegation led by the prime minister, Sir Alec Douglas-Home. After a brief private ceremony in the downstairs dining room at Hyde Park Gate, the politicians hurried back to the Commons and the present day.

Winston's health appeared to rally over the summer, but by the autumn of 1963 it was clear that Clementine's was deteriorating. David Montgomery, the field marshal's son, remembers even his notoriously unemotional father remarking that "he was worried about the toll the strain . . . was taking from her." "She struggled to be jolly . . . and to keep her equilibrium," recalls her assistant Shelagh Montague Browne. "She was very courageous." Sadly she became so overwrought that in early October she had to be sedated and admitted to Westminster Hospital, where her now severe depression was treated with electroconvulsive therapy (ECT). Montague Browne remembers being told that the shock treatment was for "a chemical imbalance in her brain."[83]

Clementine was still in the hospital when, during the night of October 19–20, Diana, who had also been receiving ECT,[84] took a huge overdose of sleeping pills and was found dead on the bedroom floor of her Belgravia flat by her housekeeper. She had recently been a great help and support to both her parents as well as Sarah in her grief over Henry's death. She had also found fulfillment in her work helping many others through the Samaritans, a fast-growing charity set up ten years previously by a London vicar to help the desperate and the suicidal. She had lunched with her daughter Edwina that very day in seemingly good spirits and had also made plans to visit her mother in the hospital and to dine with her father the following evening. Her death was therefore both "unexpected" and "inexplicable." Mary had to rush to the hospital, while still reeling from the shock, to break the news to her mother before she heard it on the radio. One small mercy was that Clementine was already heavily sedated, cushioning the blow. As both Sarah and Randolph were abroad, Mary had similarly to inform Winston. "He sat the whole day without speaking or moving, in tears," recalls his former secretary Jane Portal. "I think he felt—I don't know about Clementine, but I'm sure any parent would—what had he done to make this happen?" Mary then had to phone the newly widowed Sarah at her home in Spain. Clementine was released from the hospital only the day before Diana's funeral and neither she nor Winston was well enough to attend—although they were both present at the memorial service the following week, which was held at St. Stephen Walbrook, the City of London church where the Samaritans had been founded. An air of immeasurable sadness now hung over the Churchill family.

In November 1964 Winston turned ninety. Clementine took great care over his birthday celebrations, beginning by singing him "Happy Birthday" in his bedroom in the morning. "That was lovely," he said, smiling.[85] Later she gave him a small gold heart for his watch chain, engraved with "90," and gathered the clan for a candlelit feast of all his favorite dishes. He beamed at everyone but was obviously frail and somehow detached.

In the new year, on January 12, he suffered another stroke, and over the following days slid into a coma. Clementine brought in a priest to pray at his bedside, but mostly she just sat serenely, holding his right hand, his beloved marmalade cat asleep at his feet. He was deeply unconscious but clasped her fingers so tightly the nurses were convinced he was aware of her presence. It was as if he simply could not let her go. Slipping quietly into his softly lit bedroom, the family came to see these two great figures together for one last time. As

Winston took his final breaths the cold winter morning of January 24, they instinctively sank to their knees.

Later Clementine invited Violet—the woman who had loved but lost him—to say her good-byes. She went into his room to spend ten minutes with him alone. Two days afterward, Winston's body was taken to Westminster Hall to lie in state until the burial on January 30. Every day, often after dark, Clementine slipped in through a side door to watch the mournful but dignified queues of people coming to pay their last respects.

Churchill had long ago declared that he wanted to be buried like a soldier and would not make do with what he scornfully dubbed the 1945 "farm-cart funeral" of Lloyd George. Clementine was consulted on numerous aspects of the occasion to ensure that his wishes were carried out (he wanted military bands, for instance, of which he was given nine), but in any case the queen had previously made it clear that he would be granted the honor of a full state funeral. Thus, with imperial ceremony, his coffin was drawn slowly through London's streets from Westminster to St. Paul's Cathedral by one hundred and four ratings and officers of the Royal Navy. Hundreds of thousands lined the route on that bitterly cold day, while men and women from wartime resistance movements in France, Denmark and Norway raised a hundred flags in salute.

Clementine followed in silence with Sarah and Mary in the queen's horse-drawn town coach, equipped with lap rugs and hot-water bottles against the penetrating chill. Sarah, although drunk at the time, remembered the creaking of the carriage, the sounds of the horses' hooves, the distant ninety-gun salute and the drums "beating out the relentless precision of the slow march."[86] When they arrived at St. Paul's Cathedral, Her Majesty was already in her pew—an exceptional suspension of protocol on the part of the monarch—and the Churchills were told there was no need to curtsy. A gallant Randolph lent his arm to his mother and escorted her inside, where fifteen past and present heads of state including Presidents de Gaulle and Eisenhower were among the thousands waiting.

Another mourner, Cecil Beaton, thought age and grief made

Clementine look more beautiful than ever. He found himself unutterably moved by "the face of Lady Churchill asking for instructions as to procedure, with small jerky little steps, yet marvellously dignified, a face in a crowd, another sample of selflessness and pure feeling."[87] Yet she still frowned upon "crying on parade" and remained dry-eyed all through the day.

After the service Churchill's coffin was loaded onto a motor launch and borne down the Thames to a special train waiting at Waterloo station. The booms of the dockside cranes were lowered as he passed and fighter jets dipped their wings as they roared overhead. Yet more silent crowds lined the tracks as the train made its way to Oxfordshire. Clarissa Eden told Beaton that the "family all felt touched" by the groups of people gathered at "country stations and footballers standing to attention" as "Churchills galore" raced by in their carriages "all eating, and drinking Medoc."[88] She described turning to look at her aunt and feeling "deeply touched by Clemmie who looked frightened, muttering 'How kind you all are. Where do you want me to go next?'"

At the brief private burial at Bladon, the Blenheim parish church, Clementine's greatest wish was that the press should stay away. So, with just the family and a few close friends around her, she laid a wreath of roses, tulips and carnations, and bade her private farewell with the words: "I will soon be with you again."[89]

Epilogue

Clementine never slept a night at Chartwell again. Within weeks of Winston's death she had sold both London properties and let go many of the staff. It was as if she needed to shed these symbols (and expenses) of her marriage before she could begin the final chapter of her life alone. Not that her devotion to Winston diminished; henceforth, her work was to guard his reputation and legacy. To that end she immediately handed Chartwell over to the National Trust and asked for it to be returned to the appearance and layout of its 1930s heyday. With the public soon to be permitted to troop around the house, all traces of Winston's struggles and indignities as an old man were to be expunged. He was to be remembered as a great statesman and warrior rather than a frail human being, and so his bedroom had to be specifically shut off from view. Clementine would remain until her death intimately involved in decisions about how to present Chartwell to best effect, without having to shoulder the ultimate responsibility. Mary believed that as a consequence her mother derived more genuine satisfaction from the house in the last twelve years of her life than in the forty she had lived there with Winston.

Home was now an elegant five-bedroom flat at 7 Prince's Gate, a stone's throw from Hyde Park. Diana's daughter Celia Sandys visited often and remembered that her grandmother continued to live in considerable style, with a cook, two maids, a secretary and "a driver and car purring at the door."[1] Inflation and nursing costs eventually began to stretch her finances, though, and toward the end of her life she began to fret about money again. In February 1977 it was announced that she had chosen to sell some of her paintings, and the following month an auction of five works fetched £86,300. The sale prompted an outcry—LADY CHURCHILL OBLIGED TO SELL HEIRLOOMS was how the *Times* reported the story on its front page. Thousands of people sent her donations from their savings, which her secretary dutifully returned. Others began a campaign to persuade the government to grant her an allowance. In the end, she had to put out a statement: "I greatly deplore any idea that either special legislation or an appeal should be initiated." "It was completely ridiculous, she lived very comfortably," recalls Celia. "But there was a panic that she was going to run out of money. Maybe she didn't have a lot in the bank but it was embarrassing that pensioners were sending her teabags."

Clementine had drawn Celia closer to her since Diana's suicide in 1963. After Winston's death she also softened her attitude to Randolph, and mother and son at last found some enjoyment in each other. She went to stay with him on several occasions at his house at East Bergholt in Suffolk, and he would go to noticeable lengths to make her visits "enchanting," picking vast bunches of scented flowers from the garden, and on one occasion placing a copy of Francis Bacon's *Essays* by her bed. He was still prone to drunken rages—one year she bought a cheap new dinner service from the Reject Shop for his birthday to replace the finer ones that had been smashed[2]—but she had been touched by his tenderness following Winston's death, when he had told her, "I know what a terrible time you have had in the last ten or fifteen years . . . When you have had a good holiday and rest you must try to create a new life for yourself."[3]

The Labour prime minister, Harold Wilson, seems to have reached a similar conclusion. Four months after Winston's funeral he made her a life peer as Baroness Spencer-Churchill of Chartwell. Wilson's thinking was said to be that it would please the people to know that Clementine had been persuaded to rejoin public life. For her part, she was thrilled at entering Parliament on her own account and derived great pleasure from taking her seat in the House of Lords on the crossbenches, independent of any particular party. She intended to become very active and in July 1965, no doubt remembering Winston's agonies over the death penalty during his time as home secretary, voted in favor of the bill proposing that capital punishment be abolished. That first year she made thirteen appearances, but in 1966 she attended just seven times and did not vote or make a speech. In the past she had shown time and again a flair for politics, as well as a capacity to shine on big occasions, but at the age of eighty, with her hearing and sight fading, her body if not her mind was no longer up to the task. The tragedy is that it was all twenty years too late. If Winston, like Roosevelt, had died in 1945, as she had feared at the time, she might have secured her own great political reputation. Yet this was not to be, as she had dared to imagine all those years ago, her "reincarnation" into politics in her own right.

There was, however, release. An almost ethereal calm seems to have descended on Clementine during her nearly thirteen years as a widow. All those nervous complaints largely disappeared, even if the harsh challenges of her life did not. The sudden if not entirely unexpected death of Randolph from a heart attack at the age of fifty-seven in June 1968 hit her cruelly, of course, but there was no emotional collapse as of old, merely a controlled silence. She had now outlived three of her five offspring, and Sarah was still drinking herself to her grave by slow stages. Only on days when she knew her mother was coming to take her out to lunch would she try particularly hard to stay sober; she was to survive Clementine by just five years. By contrast Mary was always the perfect daughter, living a rich and full life until 2014.

Contemporaries "took a very dim view of the Churchill children," David Montgomery, son of the field marshal, recalls. "Apart from Mary they were seen as disastrous."[4] Now established as the great matriarch of the Churchill clan, Clementine responded by seeking to protect the family's good name wherever she could. She took a stern line with Randolph's daughter, Arabella, in the 1970s over the "unfortunate" publicity when the girl joined a group of people occupying empty buildings. Even Winston's greatness was dealt

the occasional punch by newly published diaries or revisionist histo-
ries, though such "gusts of controversy" usually blew themselves out.
His towering reputation across the globe was secure, and if her light
was fading, so be it. At least she was still remembered among the
Churchills' surviving wartime allies. The only letter she received on
the first anniversary of Winston's death was a warm, handwritten
expression of solidarity from Charles de Gaulle.[5]

She enjoyed the winter of her life as she had always hoped: living
in London and visiting theaters and galleries. Her new secretary,
Nonie Chapman, proved to be a faithful companion, while other former members of staff, such as Doreen Pugh and Heather Wood,
would sometimes stop by for lunch in her beautiful dining room. "I
always came from one to two thirty exactly as she got tired," remembered Pugh. "She liked these one-to-ones." Violet was a regular caller,
until her death in 1969, and Pamela remained loyal too, sending
Clementine presents and visiting from time to time—as in 1971, when
she finally got engaged to her wartime lover Averell Harriman. "My
dear," Clementine said, smiling knowingly, "it's an old flame rekin-
dled!"[6] As Winston's former secretary Jane Portal, who also stayed in
touch, put it: "Perhaps at the end she was, while treasuring her memories, able finally to be herself." On good days she was still capable of
tilting her head back to emit a youthful laugh. She was also at last
able to cultivate her own friendships, old (such as Field Marshal
Montgomery) and new, developing a great affection for Lady Gladys
d'Erlanger, whom she called by her nickname "Smut," the mother of
young Winston's wife, Minnie.

In Winston's final years life had clung to him, not he to life, and
Clementine could surely be forgiven for feeling a sense of relief immediately after his death; no doubt her existence without him was
more restful. But as she grew older his absence pained her more and
more. "What I miss most about Winston is his company, his affectionate nature, his wit and his longing to kindle passions. His imagination was boundless," she told the *Times* on her birthday in 1974.

Immaculately dressed as always, Clementine was lunching at
home on December 12, 1977, when Nonie noticed a sudden change in

her breathing. She died a few minutes later from a heart attack, aged ninety-two, proud and unbowed until the end. Her funeral, attended only by family and close friends, was held a few days afterward at Holy Trinity Brompton, the fashionable Anglican church in South Kensington where she had worshiped in her latter years. She was buried quietly with Winston at Bladon, as she had always planned. On January 24, 1978, thirteen years to the day since his death, a memorial service was held for her at Westminster Abbey. The Labour prime minister James Callaghan attended, as did the leaders of the Conservative and Liberal parties, Margaret Thatcher and David Steel. Her grandson Winston read an extract from the sermon spoken at her wedding, including these prescient lines: "There must be in the statesman's life many times when he depends upon the love, the insight, the penetrating sympathy and devotion of his wife."

Clementine was not cut out from birth for the part history handed her. Adversity, combined with sheer willpower, burnished a timorous, self-doubting bundle of nerves and emotion into a wartime consort of unparalleled composure, wisdom and courage. The flames of many hardships in early life forged the inner core of steel she needed for her biggest test of all. By the Second World War the young child terrified of her father, as she then believed him to be, had transmogrified into a woman cowed by no one.

Just as Winston forever sought to impress his late father and redeem his failings, so was she fired by her need to prove her critics wrong—and herself worthy of her brilliant and volatile husband. This private struggle to fashion a public persona of such determination and elegance cost Clementine her health and her happiness. In her search for perfection it was she, rather than Winston as has long been supposed, who succumbed to full-blown depression and the miseries of its treatment. But it should never be forgotten how she overcame prejudice, even ridicule, to do much that a woman had never done before. Although she had no political status of her own, Winston's unfailing trust in and dependence on her meant that she was able to command civil servants, dress down generals, chivy cabinet ministers and face up to presidents on his behalf. Her power and influence—and the results she achieved—would be unthinkable for a prime ministerial spouse today. Britain does not have an official role for the consort of her premier. Even so, whoever occupies that uncertain position is subject to the unforgiving eye of the modern media—a trial that Clementine was mostly spared thanks to the greater deference of her time. It is no accident that her most significant contribution came at a moment of extraordinary crisis, when normal constitutional conventions were bent out of shape by the desperation of the hour. The fact is that she saw what had to be done to help her country survive—and did it.

She had her faults, not least her shortcomings as a mother and perhaps a dash of hypochondria. But she was the lodestar for one of the greatest men of the twentieth century and he loved her without question for nearly sixty years. He claimed marrying her had been his most brilliant achievement: "For what," he asked, "can be more glorious than to be united with a being incapable of an ignoble thought?" As she inspired and sustained Winston, so did she help lead her country through its darkest hour, yet neither has served her memory well. She has been largely forgotten in the annals of history. Winston, whose tome *The Second World War* has influenced many scholars' subsequent understanding of that conflict, must shoulder some of the blame. He refers to her in volume 2 just once, and we find her in the index only as "Churchill, Mrs." Of all the influences in his life she was the most woefully unappreciated—but in truth she was the strongest.

The Great Man view of history—subscribed to by Winston himself, unsurprisingly—has always tended to ignore or devalue the significance of marriage. Winston Churchill could be reckless, blindly loyal, self-absorbed, oversentimental, prejudiced, devoid of empathy and vainglorious. He wanted absolute devotion from the people closest to him and would sometimes reject out of pique those who refused to give it. These flaws were inextricably bound up with his sense of destiny and his own all-consuming commitment to the British Empire. Without them he could not have been the supreme statesman he became, but they were also sometimes his undoing, and without a countervailing force in his life, one prepared to stand up to him when necessary, he would probably have been wrecked by them.

Clementine was certainly more to him than that. Winston's chief of staff General "Pug" Ismay, who observed both Churchills at the closest of quarters, saw how her continuing confidence in Winston throughout their lives was his "mainstay." He firmly believed that without her the "history of Winston Churchill and of the world would have been a very different story." Winston Churchill, the embodiment of British courage and resolve, receptacle of the nation's fire and brimstone, took his strength, Ismay witnessed, "from Clemmie."[7]

Ultimately he did recognize that his greatest achievements would have eluded him but for his wife's unflinching belief and guidance. She boosted and never betrayed him; she counseled but also challenged; she chided as well as consoled. She shored up his inadequacies, moderated his extremes and stopped him from making countless mistakes. She was in a way his ultimate authority, his conscience and the nearest he had to a direct line to the people. Without her by his side sharing the burden, it is difficult if not impossible to imagine his becoming the single-minded giant who led Britain, against almost impossible odds, to victory over tyranny. The way she managed a character described by Attlee as "fifty per cent genius, fifty per cent bloody fool"[8] was itself a type of genius.

Clementine could not have invested more in a partnership that was almost certainly the most important of its time. Theirs was the ultimate coalition. Nothing has been seen like it to this day. As Sarah was wont to say, she was born of not one but two great, strong people, who were inextricably tied to each other to the enduring benefit of us all. When in 1940 he became prime minister of a country fighting alone for its survival, Churchill declared he had nothing to offer but blood, toil, tears and sweat. In truth, he should have added to this now legendary list.

Last, but not least, he had Clemmie.

Acknowledgments

There are so many people and organizations I wish to thank, but I would like to start with the Winston Churchill Memorial Trust for granting me a fellowship in 2014. The trust's support and generosity made it possible for me to conduct invaluable research in the US and I am truly grateful to them.

Others in the US made my time there both productive and enjoyable. I am so grateful for the kindness shown by David and Manuela Roosevelt, who gave me such a wonderful insight into Eleanor Roosevelt and the family as a whole; to Henry Morgenthau III for his reminiscences and his daughter, Sarah, for her hospitality; to Fritzy and Jack Goodman for their hospitality and introductions; to Lee Pollock, the executive director of the US Churchill Center, for his enthusiasm, energy and resourcefulness; to James Kariuki of the British embassy in Washington, DC, for his time and assistance; and to June Hopkins (Harry's granddaughter) for giving me some helpful pointers. The staff of the Library of Congress could not have been more helpful or friendly, nor could Robert Clark and the team at the Franklin D. Roosevelt Presidential Library in Hyde Park, New York. I am also grateful for the assistance given me by the staff at the John F. Kennedy library in Boston.

I would like to express my sincere thanks to Gina Lynn and family in DC, David Taylor and Helen Nowicka, Zoe and Phyllis Waldron, and David Wighton and Charis Gresser for all their encouragement, support and hospitality. Thanks too to the Hay-Adams hotel in DC and the Waldorf Astoria Hotel in New York.

While in the US I had the great good fortune to meet the distinguished historian Lynne Olson, whose books I greatly admire. I thank her for her invaluable help and encouragement and for reading these pages for me.

In the UK the incomparable Allen Packwood, director of the Churchill Archives in Cambridge, has been a tower of strength and has put up with countless queries from me. I am indebted to him for his wise words and guidance and believe he does us all a great service as a custodian of our national heritage. His staff are unfailingly patient, helpful and friendly.

Terry Charman at the Imperial War Museum in London is another great asset to his country; his knowledge and enthusiasm are magnificent and inspiring and I thank him too for his vital and numerous contributions. In addition I must express my sincere thanks to Phil Reed and Tom Wright for their help, including a thrilling private tour of the Churchill War Rooms. Thank you to Claridge's for allowing me a glimpse of the Churchills' penthouse suite.

Of course a special word of thanks must go to members of the Churchill family for their thoughts, recollections and encouragement. I am so grateful to Celia Sandys and Edwina Sandys for sharing what were sometimes obviously painful memories and pay tribute to their courage. I was equally fortunate to talk to Randolph Churchill, Emma Soames and Minnie Churchill, and wish to express my sincerest gratitude to them all. Minnie kindly allowed me to view her mother's correspondence with Clementine.

Many former members of the Churchills' staff were supremely helpful in painting a picture of Clementine and I loved meeting them. I would like to express my warmest thanks to Heather White-Smith, Lady Williams, Doreen Pugh, Jill Burridge, Chips Gemmell and Shelagh Montague Browne for their fond and insightful memories. The Countess of Avon, John Julius Norwich and David Montgomery were also thrilling to interview.

I am indebted to Lord Stanley of Alderley and his family, not least for the chance to peruse the family photograph album for hitherto unpublished pictures of Clementine; to Lady Bonham Carter for her time and permission to quote extracts from her family papers held at the Bodleian Library in Oxford; and to the librarians for pointing me in the right direction.

Thanks must also go to John Forster, archivist at Blenheim Palace; Alan Brown at Lloyd's of London; and the volunteers and staff at Chartwell, who have all gone out of their way to be helpful. I am also grateful to Nvard Chalikyan for her translation from the Russian.

The author Michael Shelden was very generous in allowing me to draw on his excellent account of the lead-up to the Great War in his commendable book on Winston Churchill, entitled *Young Titan*.

Lesley Koulouris at Berkhamsted School was a wonderful guide through the school archives and I am grateful to the headmaster and staff at Summer Fields. Kevin Gordon of the Seaford Historical Society and Anthony Woodhead from Winston Churchill's former constituency of Woodford were both extremely generous with their knowledge and time and I thank them both profusely.

Joe Cooper and Briony Peters provided timely and important help in researching and checking and I wish them all the success in their future careers. My heartfelt thanks too to Frances Goodhart, Alison Ramsey, Neil Sherlock, Tom Barry, Anthony Marks, Sally Barnes, Jean Purnell, Sue Purnell, Eve Waldron, Paul Larcey, Richard Courtain and David Savva for support of various sorts, and to Paul Marston and British Airways for their help with my flights.

I have been fortunate indeed to have had Sam Harrison as my wise and erudite UK editor and Heather Holden Brown has once again proved herself a redoubtable agent. My warmest thanks also go to Melissa Smith, Jessica Axe, Liz Somers, Lucy Warburton and Charlotte Coulthard at Aurum Press for all their patience, commitment and help and Steve Gove for his tireless copyediting. Joy de Menil at Viking is an inspiring US editor, and Grainne Fox an equally vital support and source of encouragement. I thank them both and all the team at Viking and Fletcher & Co.

Back in the UK, the wonderful London Library has been very accommodating.

For the many more who have helped me on my way to understanding a great and complex figure, I pass on my thanks. My family most of all.

Notes

Much of the background material for this book was taken from original sources held by the Churchill Archives in Cambridge. "CSCT" refers to papers belonging to the Clementine Spencer Churchill Trust collection, while "CHAR" denotes the Chartwell Papers, belonging to the Winston Spencer Churchill collection, and "CHOH" denotes the Churchill Oral History Collection. When no dates are given for CSCT files, a file number is provided instead.

I also found much of interest in the Library of Congress in Washington, DC, particularly in the as yet unformatted Pamela Harriman papers, abbreviated here as "PHP." Many of the quotations in the text are taken from taped but unused interviews she gave to her biographer Christopher Ogden. The Averell Harriman Papers too were very useful.

The Roosevelt and other invaluable papers are held by the Franklin D. Roosevelt Presidential Library at Hyde Park, New York, denoted here as "FDRL."

The Asquith, Bonham Carter and Montagu Papers are held at the Bodleian Library, Oxford University.

Introduction

1. Pawle, *War and Colonel Warden*, 302. In the end, there were about four thousand British, American and Canadian deaths on D-day itself.
2. Moran, *Struggle for Survival*, 244.
3. Bonham Carter, *Churchill as I Knew Him*, 18.
4. Nel, *Mr. Churchill's Secretary*, 187.
5. CSCT, August 10, 1921.
6. CSCT, August 6, 1928.
7. In fact, they were pale blue.
8. It was a dark reddish gold, turning to silver in middle age.
9. Booth and Haste, *Goldfish Bowl*, 15.
10. Harris, *Attlee*, 412.
11. Diana Farr, *Five at Ten: Prime Ministers' Consorts Since 1957* (Andre Deutsch, 1985), 104–105, quoted in Booth and Haste, *Goldfish Bowl*, 121.
12. Booth and Haste, *Goldfish Bowl*, 263.
13. Winant, *Letter from Grosvenor Square*, 46.

1. The Level of Events

1. CSCT, Clementine's notes for "My Early Life."
2. Gibb (a member of Lloyd's), *Lloyd's of London*.

3. Soames, *Clementine Churchill*, 9.
4. Ibid.
5. CSCT, "My Early Life."
6. Ibid.
7. Ibid.
8. Ibid.
9. Ibid.
10. CSCT 3/1, essays by Blanche, Countess of Airlie.
11. CSCT, "My Early Life."
12. Ibid.
13. Beaton, *Restless Years: Diaries 1955–63*, 146.
14. Soames, *Clementine Churchill*, 39.
15. Letter from Beatrice Harris to WSC, March 19, 1941, Berkhamsted School.
16. CSCT 3/8.
17. Author's interview with Shelagh Montague Browne, March 29, 2014.
18. Ibid.
19. Ibid.
20. Asquith, *Diaries*, 494.
21. Hassall, *Edward Marsh*, 131.
22. Randolph S. Churchill, *WSC* I:2, 989.
23. Winston Churchill, *Savrola*, 42.
24. Ibid., 19.
25. Birkenhead, *Churchill*, 112.
26. Shelden, *Young Titan*, 104.
27. Lee, "A Good Innings," 97.
28. Fishman, *My Darling Clementine*, 24.
29. CSCT 2/1.
30. Ibid.
31. Ibid.
32. Former secretary Nonie Chapman, recorded in CHOH 3.
33. CSCT 2/1.
34. Fishman, *My Darling Clementine*, 26.
35. CSCT, undated.
36. Ibid.
37. Airlie, *Thatched with Gold*, 125.
38. Fishman, *My Darling Clementine*, 28.
39. Leslie, *Jennie*, 280.
40. Bonham Carter, *Lantern Slides*, August 16, 1908, 163.
41. Asquith Papers, MS Bonham Carter, 153.

2. More Than Meets the Eye

1. Soames, *Clementine Churchill*, 56.
2. CHAR, September 20, 1908.
3. Bonham Carter, *Champion Redoubtable*, xxviii.
4. Asquith Papers, Diary of Margot Asquith, MS Eng. d.3206.
5. Bonham Carter, *Lantern Slides*, 171.
6. Author's interview with Shelagh Montague Browne.
7. CHAR, August 31, 1895, quoted in Sebba, *American Jennie*, 208.
8. Quoted in Sebba, *American Jennie*, 289.

9. Sandys, *Young Churchill*, 160.
10. Ibid., 107.
11. Jackson, *Churchill*, 33.
12. Sandys, *From Winston with Love and Kisses*, 178.
13. Buczacki, *Churchill and Chartwell*, 41.
14. CSCT, May 3, 1913.
15. Gilbert, *WSC*, vol. 4, 893–94.
16. CSCT, May 30–31, 1909.
17. CSCT, June 1, 1909.
18. Asquith Papers, MS Bonham Carter, 165.
19. Bonham Carter, *Churchill as I Knew Him*, 260.
20. Ibid., 235.
21. Soames, *Clementine Churchill*, 65.
22. CSCT, September 6, 1909.
23. CSCT, September 11, 1909.
24. CSCT, July 27, 1914.
25. CSCT, September 12, 1909.
26. CSCT 1/5, August 7, 1911.
27. CSCT, November 3, 1909.
28. CSCT, November 10, 1909.
29. Vanderbilt Balsan, *Glitter and the Gold*, 132.
30. Sebba, *American Jennie*, 212.
31. CSCT, January 30, 1913.
32. CSCT, January 31, 1913.
33. Shelden, *Young Titan*, 218.
34. Scawen Blunt, *My Diaries*, September 5, 1909, 267–71.
35. Esher, *Journals and Letters*, December 1, 1909.
36. Hassall, *Edward Marsh*, 346.
37. Soames, *Clementine Churchill*, 100.
38. CSCT, October 18, 1909.
39. Gilbert, *WSC*, vol. 2, 120.
40. Lord George Riddell, *More Pages from My Diary, 1908–1914* (Country Life, 1934), quoted in Morgan, *Churchill: Young Man in a Hurry*, 317.
41. Addison, *Churchill: The Unexpected Hero*, 48.
42. Gilbert, *WSC*, vol. 4, 800.
43. CSCT, September 18, 1909.
44. CSCT, July 14, 1912.
45. Soames, *Clementine Churchill*, 72.
46. Wilfrid Scawen Blunt Collection, Fitzwilliam Museum 11/1975, January 30, 1911.
47. Manchester, *Last Lion*, vol. 1, 411.
48. Soames, *Clementine Churchill*, 78.
49. CSCT, December 19, 1910.
50. CSCT, undated, but probably June 3, 1911.
51. Asquith Papers, MS Bonham Carter, 154, Letters to Venetia, October 2, 1911.
52. CHAR, February 10, 1910.
53. CSCT, April 18, 1912.
54. CSCT, March 25, 1912.
55. H. H. Asquith to WSC, quoted in Gilbert, *WSC*, vol. 2, 1483.
56. Asquith Papers, MS Bonham Carter, 155.

57. Asquith Papers, Diary of Margot Asquith, MS Eng. d.3206.
58. Morgan, *Churchill: Young Man in a Hurry*, 332.
59. CSCT, July 23, 1913.
60. CSCT 1/8.
61. Fishman, *My Darling Clementine*, 37.
62. CSCT, June 29, 1911.
63. CSCT, April 29, 1914.
64. CSCT, April 23, 1914.
65. CSCT, April 27, 1914.
66. CSCT 1/8.
67. I am grateful for this summary to Michael Shelden in *Young Titan*.

3. The Pain and the Pride

1. CSCT, August 14, 1914.
2. CHAR, January 12, 1916.
3. Manchester, *Last Lion*, vol. 3, 484; Gilbert, *WSC*, vol. 3, 59.
4. Asquith, *Letters to Venetia Stanley*, November 2, 1914, 305.
5. Gilbert, *WSC*, vol. 3, 824–25.
6. CSCT, September 19, 1914.
7. Asquith Papers, Diary of Margot Asquith, MS Eng. d.3210, fols. 97–113.
8. CSCT, September 26, 1914.
9. Asquith, *Letters to Venetia Stanley*, October 5, 1914, 263.
10. CSCT 3/16.
11. Bedell Smith, *Reflected Glory*, 67.
12. Manchester, *Last Lion*, vol. 3, 440; Gilbert, *WSC*, vol. 2, 565.
13. Asquith, *Letters to Venetia Stanley*, February 26, 1915, 450.
14. Soames, *Clementine Churchill*, 137.
15. Jenkins, *Churchill*, 270–71.
16. Bonham Carter, *Churchill as I Knew Him*, 21.
17. Gilbert, *WSC*, vol. 7, 1070.
18. Asquith Papers, MS Eng. 27, May 20, 1915.
19. Gilbert, *WSC*, vol. 3, 459, quoted in Morgan, *Churchill*, 525–26.
20. Asquith Papers, Diary of Margot Asquith, MS Eng. d.3198–3218, May 20, 1915.
21. Ibid.
22. Asquith Papers, MS Eng. lett. c.542/1, fols. 89–92.
23. Montagu Papers, April 27, 1915.
24. Asquith, *Letters to Venetia Stanley*, January 10, 1915, 368. For a fuller version of these letters, consult the Asquith Papers, Bodleian Library, Oxford University.
25. Ibid., January 26, 1915, 396.
26. Ibid., February 1, 1915, 410.
27. Keith-Lytton to Margot Asquith, May 15, 1915, Asquith Papers, MS Eng. c.6678.
28. Asquith, *Letters to Venetia Stanley*, 116, referring to letter 342, 479.
29. Fishman, *My Darling Clementine*, 57.
30. Hassall, *Edward Marsh*, 479.
31. Fishman, *My Darling Clementine*, 57.
32. Author's interview with Edwina Sandys, April 25, 2014.
33. Shelden, *Young Titan*, 321.

4. I Believe in Your Star

1. CSCT, November 19, 1915.
2. CSCT, November 21, 1915.
3. Ibid.
4. CSCT, November 19, 1915.
5. CSCT, November 23, 1915.
6. Ibid.
7. CSCT, November 27, 1915.
8. CSCT, November 21, 1915.
9. CSCT, March 21, 1916.
10. CHAR, March 15, 1916.
11. Riddell, *War Diary*, March 1916, 66.
12. CSCT, August 12, 1923.
13. CSCT, November 25, 1915.
14. Jenkins, *Churchill*, 396.
15. Bonham Carter, *Churchill as I Knew Him*, 132.
16. Soames, ed., *Speaking for Themselves*, xiv.
17. CSCT, December 4, 1915.
18. CSCT, December 6, 1915.
19. CSCT, December 17, 1915.
20. CSCT, December 18, 1915.
21. CSCT, December 20, 1915.
22. CSCT, January 7, 1916.
23. CSCT, December 1, 1915.
24. CSCT, December 28, 1915.
25. CHAR, December 30, 1915.
26. CSCT, January 3, 1916.
27. CHAR, January 7, 1916.
28. CHAR, January 9, 1916.
29. CHAR, January 11, 1916.
30. CHAR, January 16, 1916.
31. Bonham Carter, *Churchill as I Knew Him*, 445.
32. CHAR, February 16, 1916.
33. CSCT, December 17, 1915.
34. CSCT, March 16, 1916.
35. Manchester, *Last Lion*, vol. 1, 591.
36. CHAR, January 29, 1916.
37. CHAR, January 31, 1916.
38. CHAR, January 24, 1916.
39. CSCT, January 27, 1916.
40. CHAR, February 4, 1916.
41. Bonham Carter, *Churchill as I Knew Him*, 384.
42. CSCT, December 1, 1915.
43. CSCT, December 6, 1915.
44. CSCT, November 28, 1915.
45. CHAR, January 30, 1916.
46. CHAR, February 23, 1916.
47. CHAR, February 27, 1916.
48. CHAR, February 16, 1916.

49. Bonham Carter, *Churchill as I Knew Him*, 449.
50. *Hansard*, seventh series, vol. 80, col. 1430, quoted in Jenkins, *Churchill*, 306.
51. CHAR, March 13, 1916.
52. CSCT, March 13, 1916.
53. CHAR, March 24, 1916.
54. CSCT, March 21, 1916.
55. CHAR, April 6, 1916.
56. CHAR, March 25, 1916.
57. CSCT, March 28, 1916.

5. Married Love

1. Bonham Carter, *Churchill as I Knew Him*, 466.
2. Ibid., 22.
3. Hough, *Winston and Clementine*, 365.
4. Beaverbrook, *Politicians and the War*, 82.
5. CSCT, September 8, 1918.
6. CSCT, September 10, 1918.
7. CSCT, September 15, 1918.
8. CSCT, October 29, 1918.
9. Soames, *Clementine Churchill*, 213.
10. CHAR, August 11, 1918.
11. Lady Jean Hamilton's diaries, August 10, 1919, Hamilton Papers, Liddell Hart Centre for Military Archives, King's College, London.
12. Lady Jean Hamilton's diaries, June 21, 1918, quoted in Lee, *Jean, Lady Hamilton*, 198–99.
13. CSCT, October 29, 1918.
14. CSCT, September 12, 1918.
15. Olson, *Troublesome Young Men*, 163.

6. Loss Unimaginable

1. CSCT, March 9, 1919.
2. Montague Browne, *Long Sunset*, 124; Colville, *Fringes of Power*, 677.
3. CSCT, September 14, 1919.
4. Jackson, *Churchill*, 171.
5. For more details on the Churchills' homes, see Buczacki, *Churchill and Chartwell*.
6. Buczacki, *Churchill and Chartwell*, 91.
7. Ibid., 91–92.
8. Jenkins, *Churchill*, 187.
9. CSCT, January 27, 1921.
10. CSCT, February 7, 1922.
11. Soames, *Clementine Churchill*, 223.
12. CHAR, February 21, 1921.
13. Thompson, *Assignment: Churchill*, 7.
14. Ibid., 13.
15. Ibid., 15.
16. McKenna Papers, Churchill College, Cambridge; Morgan, *Churchill*, 282.
17. Leslie, *Jennie*, 305.
18. CSCT, March 22, 1925.
19. Pearson, *Citadel of the Heart*, 88.

20. CHAR, January 4, 1922.
21. CSCT, January 22, 1922.
22. CSCT, August 10, 1922.

7. A Country Basket

1. Sarah Churchill, *Thread in the Tapestry*, 22.
2. Gilbert, *WSC*, vol. 4, 878.
3. CHAR, November 9, 1922.
4. Buczacki, *Churchill and Chartwell*, 129.
5. Author's interviews with Heather White-Smith during 2013–2015.
6. CSCT, February 17, 1924.
7. CSCT, March 15, 1925.
8. Thompson, *Assignment: Churchill*, 45.
9. Pearson, *Citadel of the Heart*, 205.
10. Howells, *Simply Churchill*, 40.
11. Author's interviews with former members of staff during 2013–2015.
12. Soames, *Clementine Churchill*, 283.
13. Author's interview with Lady Williams, née Jane Portal, June 26, 2013.
14. Buczacki, *Churchill and Chartwell*, 134.
15. Ibid., 145.
16. Author's interview with Shelagh Montague Browne, March 29, 2014.
17. CSCT, January 29, 1927.
18. Sarah Churchill, *Keep On Dancing*, 18.
19. Book inscription to Chips Gemmell (one of Clementine's former personal assistants).
20. Riddell, *Lord Riddell's War Diary*, 66.
21. CSCT, September 25, 1928.
22. Author's interview with Lady Avon, Clarissa Eden, née Churchill, May 15, 2013.
23. CSCT 3/24.
24. Jackson, *Churchill*, 185.
25. Colville, *Inner Circle*, 34.
26. Pearson, *Citadel of the Heart*, 234.
27. Soames, *Clementine Churchill*, 97.
28. Bonham Carter, *Churchill as I Knew Him*, 218.
29. CHAR, January 28, 1922.
30. CSCT, February 24, 1924.
31. Author's interview with Shelagh Montague Browne, March 29, 2014.
32. Thomas, *Churchill*, 24.
33. Manchester, *Last Lion*, vol. 2, 784.
34. Soames, *Clementine Churchill*, 238.
35. CHAR, March 31, 1920.
36. CHAR, September 10, 1926.
37. Arthur Ponsonby, quoted in Gilbert, *WSC*, vol. 5, 118.
38. Stelzer, *Dinner with Churchill*, 159.
39. Author's interview with Chips Gemmell, April 23, 2014.
40. Author's interviews with Heather White-Smith during 2013–2015.
41. *Illustrated London News*, March 1981.
42. Author's interview with Shelagh Montague Browne, March 29, 2014.
43. CSCT, February 18, 1932.
44. Author's interview with Chips Gemmell, April 23, 2014.

45. Ibid.

46. Soames, *Clementine Churchill*, 266.

47. Ibid.

48. *Daily Telegraph*, August 16, 2002.

49. Best, *Churchill*, 29.

50. Soames, *Clementine Churchill*, 267.

51. Sarah Churchill, *Keep On Dancing*, 67.

52. Author's interview with Celia Sandys, October 1, 2013.

53. CSCT, September 12, 1909.

54. CSCT, July 23, 1913.

55. Sarah Churchill, *Keep On Dancing*, 10.

56. PHP, box 4.

57. Soames, *Clementine Churchill*, 267.

58. CSCT, April 8, 1928.

59. John S. Churchill, *Crowded Canvas*, 56.

60. Evelyn Waugh to Ann Fleming, January 27, 1965, in Waugh, *Letters of Evelyn Waugh*, 630.

61. Sarah Churchill, *Keep On Dancing*, 5.

62. Ibid., 15.

63. Ibid., 6.

64. Author's interview with Lady Avon, May 15, 2013.

65. CSCT, March 22, 1925.

8. Temptation and Redemption

1. Jackson, *Churchill*, 185.

2. CSCT, March 20, 1928.

3. Author's interview with Lady Avon, May 15, 2013.

4. Ogden, *Life of the Party*, 93.

5. PHP, box 3.

6. Moran, *Struggle for Survival*, 180.

7. Soames, *Clementine Churchill*, 284.

8. Soames, ed., *Speaking for Themselves*, 277.

9. Bonham Carter, *Churchill as I Knew Him*, 218.

10. Lysaght, *Brendan Bracken*, 68.

11. CSCT, January 18, 1931.

12. Cowles, *Winston Churchill*, 253.

13. James, *Bob Boothby*, 36.

14. Colville, *Fringes of Power*, 196.

15. CSCT 1/26.

16. Winston S. Churchill, ed., *Never Give In!*, 101.

17. Jackson, *Churchill*, 217.

18. Winston S. Churchill, ed., *Never Give In!*, 108.

19. CSCT, August 22, 1934.

20. Winston S. Churchill, *His Father's Son*, 65.

21. Pearson, *Citadel of the Heart*, 217.

22. CSCT, April 15, 1935.

23. Author's interview with John Julius Norwich, June 6, 2013.

24. Winston S. Churchill, *His Father's Son*, 75.

25. CSCT, February 17, 1931.

26. CSCT, March 5, 1931.

27. CSCT, November 14, 1928.

28. CSCT, November 12, 1928.

29. CSCT 3/25, Clementine's diaries, February to March 1931.

30. CSCT, July 25, 1937.

31. Pearson, *Citadel of the Heart*, 221.

32. Winston S. Churchill, *His Father's Son*, 44.

33. Leslie, *Cousin Randolph*, 8.

34. Sarah Churchill, *Keep On Dancing*, 15.

35. Leslie, *Cousin Randolph*, 13.

36. Sarah Churchill, *Keep On Dancing*, 16.

37. Soames, *Clementine Churchill*, 275.

38. CSCT, January 1, 1935.

39. CSCT, January 23, 1935.

40. CSCT, December 29, 1934.

41. CSCT, February 22, 1935.

42. CSCT, February 26, 1935.

43. Soames, *Clementine Churchill*, 295.

44. Ibid., 266.

45. CSCT, April 11, 1935.

46. Soames, *Clementine Churchill*, 301.

47. Ibid., 278.

48. Author's interview with Lady Avon, May 15, 2013.

49. *Illustrated London News*, March 1981.

50. CSCT, February 21, 1936.

51. *Illustrated London News*, March 1981.

52. Author's interviews with Heather White-Smith during 2013–2015.

53. Sarah Churchill, *Keep On Dancing*, 56.

54. Duff Cooper, *Old Men Forget*, 171.

55. Soames, *Clementine Churchill*, 306.

56. Pearson, *Citadel of the Heart*, 271.

57. CSCT, January 7, 1936.

58. CSCT, September 5, 1936.

59. Winston Churchill, *Gathering Storm*, 155.

60. Pearson, *Citadel of the Heart*, 213.

61. Best, *Churchill*, 150.

62. CSCT, February 2, 1937.

63. Manchester, *Caged Lion*, 373.

64. CSCT, December 19, 1938.

65. CHAR, January 19, 1939.

66. CHAR, December 13, 1938.

67. Gilbert, *WSC*, vol. 5, 1316.

68. CSCT, July 27, 1939.

9. A World of Accident and Storm

1. Duff Cooper, *Diaries*, 275.

2. Winston Churchill, *Gathering Storm*, 320.

3. Ibid., 319.

4. Manchester, *Caged Lion*, 537.

5. Thompson, *Assignment: Churchill*, 127.
6. Soames, *Clementine Churchill*, 316.
7. Diana Cooper, *Trumpets from the Steep*, 37.
8. Ibid.
9. *Midwife*, December 21 1942.
10. Ogden, *Life of the Party*, 75.
11. Ibid., 69.
12. Ibid., 85.
13. Ibid., 87.
14. Ibid., 121.
15. PHP, box 4.
16. Olson, *Citizens of London*, 241.
17. Ibid., 243.
18. Colville, *Fringes of Power*, 36.
19. Ibid., 39.
20. Moran, *Struggle for Survival*, 371.
21. Colville, *Fringes of Power*, 38.
22. Gilbert, *WSC*, vol. 6, 358.
23. Fishman, *My Darling Clementine*, 139.
24. Gilbert, *WSC*, vol. 6, 358.
25. Tree, *When the Moon Was High*, 116–17.
26. Cowles, *Era and the Man*, 318.
27. Moran, *Struggle for Survival*, 330.
28. PHP, box 3.
29. CSCT, June 27, 1940.
30. Colville, *Fringes of Power*, 281.
31. Wheeler-Bennett, ed., *Action This Day*, 140.
32. PHP, box 3.
33. Colville, *Fringes of Power*, 125.
34. Ibid., 170.
35. Fishman, *My Darling Clementine*, 151.
36. Moran, *Struggle for Survival*, 167.
37. Fishman, *My Darling Clementine*, 147.
38. Colville, *Fringes of Power*, 173.
39. Ibid., 251.
40. PHP, box 3.
41. Fishman, *My Darling Clementine*, 145.
42. CSCT 3/33.
43. Moran, *Struggle for Survival*, 15.
44. Author's interview with Lady Williams, June 26, 2013.
45. CSCT 3/33, Clementine's undated notes on plans for tackling problems in the shelters.
46. CSCT 3/33.
47. Colville, *Fringes of Power*, 276.
48. PHP, box 3.
49. Colville, *Fringes of Power*, 195.
50. Ibid., 201.
51. Ibid., 379.
52. Ibid., 413.

53. PHP, box 3.
54. "Lady of No. 10."
55. Beaton, *Years Between*, 51.
56. Author's interview with Lady Avon, May 15, 2013.
57. Winston S. Churchill, *His Father's Son*, 180.
58. Colville, *Fringes of Power*, 375.
59. Thompson, *Sixty Minutes*, 50.
60. Fishman, *My Darling Clementine*, 153.
61. Colville, *Fringes of Power*, 229.
62. Fishman, *My Darling Clementine*, 154.
63. Ibid., 158.
64. Author's interviews with former staff during 2013–2015.
65. Soames, *Clementine Churchill*, 330.
66. Ibid., 317.
67. Colville, *Fringes of Power*, 177.
68. Ibid., 178.
69. PHP, box 3.
70. Ibid.
71. Meacham, *Franklin and Weston*, 87.
72. Colville, *Fringes of Power*, 238.
73. Buczacki, *Churchill and Chartwell*, 220.
74. PHP, box 3.
75. Ibid.
76. Winston Churchill, *Second World War*, vol. 2, 226.
77. Ibid., 4.

10. Operation Seduction USA

1. Parrish, *To Keep the British Isles Afloat*, 125.
2. Lash, *Roosevelt and Churchill*, 277, quoted in Meacham, *Franklin and Winston*, 87.
3. Sherwood, *Roosevelt and Hopkins*, 80.
4. Ibid., 243.
5. Ibid., 241.
6. Parrish, *To Keep the British Isles Afloat*, 192.
7. Hopkins Papers, July 18, 1941, 1 B4F1, Georgetown University, Washington, DC.
8. Murrow Papers, Tufts University, Medford, Mass., December 7, 1940.
9. Alexander Kendrick, *Prime Time: The Life of Edward R. Murrow* (Little, Brown, 1969), 231, quoted in Olson, *Citizens of London*, 31–32.
10. Olson, *Citizens of London*, 31.
11. Ibid., 33.
12. Moran, *Struggle for Survival*, 134.
13. Brooke, *War Diaries*, 248.
14. Winant, *Letter from Grosvenor Square*, 3–4.
15. Colville, *Fringes of Power*, 382.
16. Winant, *Letter from Grosvenor Square*, 46.
17. Parrish, *To Keep the British Isles Afloat*, 146.
18. Soames, *Clementine Churchill*, 390.
19. CSCT 3/43, dated August 2 but no year.
20. Sarah Churchill, *Keep On Dancing*, 159.
21. Parrish, *To Keep the British Isles Afloat*, 211.

22. Ibid.
23. CSCT, March 26, 1941.
24. Parrish, *To Keep the British Isles Afloat*, 210.
25. Harriman and Abel, *Special Envoy*, 21.
26. Averell Harriman Papers, May 30, 1941, box 159.
27. Parrish, *To Keep the British Isles Afloat*, 173.
28. Olson, *Citizens of London*, xvii.
29. Ogden, *Life of the Party*, 122.
30. Ibid., 167.
31. PHP, box 3.
32. Colville, *Fringes of Power*, 382.
33. Olson, *Citizens of London*, 97.
34. Ibid.
35. Bedell Smith, *Reflected Glory*, 106.
36. Morgenthau, *Roosevelt and Morgenthau*, 482.
37. Harriman, *Special Envoy*, 172.
38. CSCT, Mackenzie King to Clementine, June 4, 1944.
39. Harriman, *Special Envoy*, 29.
40. Averell Harriman Papers, box 159.
41. Beaton, *Years Between*, 54.
42. Olson, *Citizens of London*, 117.
43. Maisky, *Memoirs of a Soviet Ambassador*, 179.
44. Evelyn Waugh to Nancy Mitford, December 1950 (exact date unknown), in Waugh, *Letters of Evelyn Waugh*, 342.
45. CSCT, August 7, 1941.
46. Harriman, *Special Envoy*, 112.
47. CSCT, December 19, 1941.
48. Meacham, *Franklin and Winston*, 145.
49. Rosenman, *Working with Roosevelt*, 296.
50. Sherwood, *Roosevelt and Hopkins*, 214.
51. Parrish, *To Keep the British Isles Afloat*, 205.
52. Anna Roosevelt Halsted Papers, box 75, April 1942, FDRl.
53. CSCT, December 21, 1941.
54. CSCT, December 29, 1941.
55. Moran, *Struggle for Survival*, 17.
56. Sherwood, *Roosevelt and Hopkins*, 478.
57. George McJimsey, *Harry Hopkins: Ally of the Poor and Defender of Democracy* (Harvard University Press, 1987), 247–48, cited in Goodwin, *No Ordinary Time*, 343.
58. CSCT, February 12, 1942.
59. PHP, box 3.
60. Lord Beaverbrook Papers, March 3, 1943, cited in Hough, *Winston and Clementine*, 509.
61. Hopkins Papers, June 24, 1942, 1 B4F1, Georgetown University, Washington, DC.
62. Jenkins, *Churchill*, 697.
63. Winston S. Churchill, *His Father's Son*, 203.
64. CSCT, April 11, 1942.
65. Soames, *Clementine Churchill*, 356.
66. Gilbert, *WSC*, vol. 7, 252.
67. Goodwin, *No Ordinary Time*, 11.

68. Ibid., 10.
69. Morgenthau, *Diaries*, 483.
70. Eleanor Roosevelt, *This I Remember*, 185.
71. Winant, *Letter from Grosvenor Square*, 171.
72. Averell Harriman Papers, box 159.
73. Robert Meiklejohn Papers, box 211, Library of Congress.
74. Morgenthau, *Diaries*, September 23, 1944.
75. Moran, *Struggle for Survival*, 201.
76. Clementine Churchill to Franklin D. Roosevelt, November 1, 1942, FDRL.
77. Diary of Eleanor Roosevelt, October 20, 1942, FDRL.
78. Lash, *Eleanor and Franklin*, 664.
79. Goodwin, *No Ordinary Time*, 140.
80. Lash, *Eleanor and Franklin*, 662.
81. Diary of Eleanor Roosevelt's trip to London, box 1364, FDRL.
82. Meacham, *Franklin and Winston*, 197.
83. Goodwin, *No Ordinary Time*, 397.

11. From FDR to Stalin

1. Soames, *Clementine Churchill*, 366.
2. Harriman, *Special Envoy*, 362.
3. Mary Soames, *Sunday Times*, December 18, 1977.
4. CSCT, January 14, 1943.
5. CSCT, John Martin to private office, undated.
6. National Archives, Kew, PREM 4/72/1.
7. Meacham, *Franklin and Winston*, 204.
8. Kenneth Pendar, *Adventure in Diplomacy: Our French Dilemma* (Simon Publications, 2003), 151–52, quoted in Meacham, *Franklin and Winston*, 213.
9. CSCT, February 5–6, 1943.
10. CSCT, December 10, 1943.
11. Colville, *Fringes of Power*, 476.
12. BBC Southern Counties Radio, "Letter from Mrs. Churchill."
13. Maisky, *Memoirs of a Soviet Ambassador*, 208–9.
14. CSCT, September 13, 1943.
15. CSCT, May 13, 1943.
16. Ibid.
17. CSCT, May 28, 1943.
18. Swift, *Roosevelts and Royals*, 180.
19. Goodwin, *No Ordinary Time*, 82.
20. Interview with Mary Soames, in Meacham, *Franklin and Winston*, 21.
21. Goodwin, *No Ordinary Time*, 109.
22. Lash, *Eleanor and Franklin*, 699–700.
23. Colville, *Churchillians*, 112.
24. Moran, *Struggle for Survival*, 837.
25. Cowles, *Era and the Man*, 338.
26. Meacham, *Franklin and Winston*, 228.
27. Colville, *Churchillians*, 22.
28. Ismay, August 26, 1943, *Memoirs*, 304.
29. Interview with Mary Soames, in Meacham, *Franklin and Winston*, 233.
30. Ibid., 236–37.

31. Ward, *Closest Companion*, 238.

32. Moran, *Struggle for Survival*, 122–23.

33. *Philadelphia Record*, August 6, 1943.

34. CSCT, September 23, 1943.

35. Hassett, *Off the Record with FDR*, 201.

36. Kimball, *Churchill and Roosevelt*, 447.

37. Ward, *Closest Companion*, 238.

38. Wingate, *Lord Ismay*, 100.

39. CSCT, November 23, 1943.

40. CSCT, November 26, 1943.

41. Ibid.

42. CSCT, November 23, 1943.

43. Sarah Churchill, *Thread in the Tapestry*, 62–63.

44. Gilbert, *WSC*, vol. 7, 89.

45. Meacham, *Franklin and Winston*, xiii.

46. Ibid., 265.

47. Moran, *Struggle for Survival*, 151.

48. CSCT, December 2, 1943.

49. Moran, *Struggle for Survival*, 162.

50. National Archives, previously unlisted but quoted in Soames, ed., *Speaking for Themselves*, December 16, 1943, 494.

51. Colville, *Footprints in Time*, 134.

52. National Archives, Cabinet Papers, CAB 120/120, quoted in Soames, *Clementine Churchill*, 381.

53. Moran, *Struggle for Survival*, 164.

54. Soames, *Clementine Churchill*, 379.

55. Ibid., 380.

56. Wheeler-Bennett, ed., *Action This Day*, 157.

57. Moran, *Struggle for Survival*, 165.

58. Colville, *Fringes of Power*, 456.

59. Diana Cooper, *Trumpets from the Steep*, 182.

60. Colville, *Fringes of Power*, 457.

61. CSCT, December 24, 1943.

62. Diana Cooper, *Trumpets from the Steep*, 181.

63. Colville, *Fringes of Power*, 459.

64. Wheeler-Bennett, ed., *Action This Day*, 235.

65. Ibid., 263.

66. PHP, box 3.

67. Moran, *Struggle for Survival*, 241.

68. Soames, *Clementine Churchill*, 385.

69. Ibid., 386.

70. Colville, *Fringes of Power*, 467.

71. Parrish, *To Keep the British Isles Afloat*, 240.

72. Ogden, *Life of the Party*, 125.

73. Ibid., 173.

74. These include suggestions in Parrish, *To Keep the British Isles Afloat*, 241.

75. Author's interview with John Julius Norwich, June 6, 2013.

76. PHP, box 1.

77. Ogden, *Life of the Party*, 145.

78. PHP, box 3.

79. Bedell Smith, *Reflected Glory*, 113.

80. Olson, *Citizens of London*, xv.

81. Testimony from a nurse at Bernard Baruch's South Carolina estate in *New York Times*, January 31, 1988, quoted in Parrish, *To Keep the British Isles Afloat*, 6.

82. *Sunday Times*, October 31, 1982.

83. Colville, *Fringes of Power*, 530.

84. Robert Bruce Lockhart, director of the Political Warfare Executive (in charge of propaganda), quoted in Macmillan, *War Diaries*, 474.

85. Moran, *Struggle for Survival*, 173.

86. Ibid., 35.

87. Ibid., ix.

88. Dalton, *War Diary*, 714.

89. Morgenthau, *Mostly Morgenthaus*, 361.

90. Morgenthau, *Diaries: Years of War*, 336.

91. Colville, *Fringes of Power*, 506.

92. CSCT, August 17, 1944.

93. CSCT, Clementine's private diary, September 14, 1944.

94. PHP, box 164.

95. Meacham, *Franklin and Winston*, 299.

96. Kimball, *Churchill and Roosevelt*, vol. 3, 332.

97. CSCT, October 8, 1944.

98. Lovell, *Churchills*, 473.

99. CSCT, December 4, 1944.

100. Sherwood, *Roosevelt and Hopkins*, 837.

101. Brooke, *War Diaries*, July 6, 1944, 566.

102. Colville, *Fringes of Power*, 538.

103. CSCT, December 29, 1944.

104. CSCT, August 12, 1944.

105. CSCT, August 15, 1944.

106. Winston S. Churchill, *Memories and Adventures*, passim.

107. PHP, box 3.

108. CSCT, January 30, 1945.

109. Colville, *Fringes of Power*, 537.

110. Moran, *Struggle for Survival*, 194.

111. Colville, *Fringes of Power*, January 20, 1945, 554. The quotations are taken from Colville's more pithy but accurate summary of the letter rather than the less concise words of Attlee himself.

112. Ibid., 554.

113. Ibid., 555.

114. Moran, *Struggle for Survival*, 232–33.

115. CSCT, February 1, 1945.

116. Colville, *Fringes of Power*, 568.

117. Soames, *Clementine Churchill*, 404.

118. Ibid., 404.

119. CSCT, March 29, 1945.

120. CSCT, April 1, 1945.

121. CSCT, April 2, 1945.

122. CSCT 3/49.

123. CSCT, April 6, 1945.
124. CSCT, August 4, 1942.
125. Grace Hamblin Files 1/4, Churchill College, Cambridge.
126. CHOH.
127. CSCT, April 6, 1945.
128. CSCT 3/37.
129. CSCT, April 14, 1945.
130. CSCT, April 21, 1945.
131. Gilbert, *WSC*, vol. 7, 1341.
132. Pawle, *War and Colonel Warden*, 373–74.
133. CSCT, May 8, 1945.
134. Eleanor Roosevelt Files, FDRL.
135. Moran, *Struggle for Survival*, 168.
136. CSCT, May 5, 1945.
137. Clementine's honor, to be worn on the left breast, gave her the right to free travel on trams, trains and ships on soft seats and in first-class carriages, as well as advantageous accommodation, pension and tax rights in Russia, plus a monthly allowance of twenty rubles.

12. A Private Line

1. Moran, *Struggle for Survival*, 309.
2. Thomas, *Member for Woodford*, 130–31.
3. Moran, *Struggle for Survival*, 279.
4. Pawle, *War and Colonel Warden*, 399.
5. Mary Soames's diary, July 26, 1945, quoted in Soames, *Daughter's Tale*, 460.
6. Sarah Churchill, *Thread in the Tapestry*, 88.
7. Soames, *Clementine Churchill*, 426.
8. Harris, *Attlee*, 412.
9. Colville, *Fringes of Power*, 613.
10. James, ed., *Chips*, 429.
11. CSCT 3/56, July 27, 1945.
12. CSCT, June 1, 1945.
13. Leonard C. Schlup and Donald W. Whisenhunt, eds., *It Seems to Me* (University Press of Kentucky, 2001), 62, quoted in Meacham, *Franklin and Winston*, 361.
14. Moran, *Struggle for Survival*, 310.
15. Ibid., 325.
16. Soames, *Clementine Churchill*, 428.
17. Addison, "Japanese Surrender."
18. James, ed., *Chips*, 411.
19. Soames, *Clementine Churchill*, 429.
20. Sarah Churchill, *Keep On Dancing*, 78.
21. Beaton, *Happy Years*, 53.
22. Soames, *Clementine Churchill*, 439.
23. Ibid., 443.
24. Ibid.
25. Ibid., 444.
26. Sarah Churchill, *Thread in the Tapestry*, 94.
27. CSCT, September 12, 1948.
28. Meacham, *Franklin and Winston*, 366.

29. Gilbert, *WSC,* vol. 8, 466, quoted in Sandys, *Chasing Churchill,* 201.
30. White-Smith, *My Years with the Churchills,* 34.
31. Author's interview with David Roosevelt, April 19, 2014.
32. FDRL, box 1542.
33. FDRL, box 1683.
34. Author's interview with Chips Gemmell, April 23, 2014.
35. *W* magazine, November 9–16, 1979.
36. *Illustrated London News,* March 1981.
37. Soames, *Clementine Churchill,* 452.
38. Author's interview, April 29, 2014.
39. Sarah Churchill, *Keep On Dancing,* 97.
40. Ibid., 95.
41. Soames, *Clementine Churchill,* 458.
42. Sarah Churchill, *Keep On Dancing,* 139.
43. Beaton, *Strenuous Years,* various pages.
44. Soames, *Clementine Churchill,* 475.
45. Bonham Carter, *Daring to Hope,* 127.
46. Bonham Carter Papers, August 13, 1953.
47. CSCT, October 16, 1953.
48. White-Smith, *My Years with the Churchills,* 24.
49. Soames, *Clementine Churchill,* 481.
50. Colville, *Churchillians,* 64–65.
51. Moran, *Struggle for Survival,* 741.
52. Ibid., 454.
53. Ibid., 494.
54. Pearson, *Citadel of the Heart,* 368.
55. Author's interview with Chips Gemmell, April 23, 2014.
56. Sarah Churchill, *Keep On Dancing,* 207.
57. CHOH 24/4.
58. Horne, *Macmillan,* various pages.
59. Bonham Carter Papers, 165.
60. Soames, *Clementine Churchill,* 493.
61. Beaton and Vickers, *Beaton in the Sixties,* 226.
62. Moran, *Struggle for Survival,* xii.
63. Longford, *Queen Mother,* 130.
64. Noël Coward, *Diaries,* 207.
65. Letter from Clementine to the school, May 24, 1958, Berkhamsted School archives.
66. Author's interview with Shelagh Montague Browne, March 29, 2014.
67. Author's interview with Chips Gemmell, April 23, 2014.
68. Author's interviews with Heather White-Smith during 2013–2015.
69. White-Smith, *My Years with the Churchills,* 54.
70. Soames, *Clementine Churchill,* 499.
71. Montague Browne, *Long Sunset,* 148.
72. PHP, box 3.
73. Coward, *Diaries,* 322.
74. Sandys, *Chasing Churchill,* 11.
75. Montague Browne, *Long Sunset,* 299.
76. Sarah Churchill, *Keep On Dancing,* 204.
77. Thomas, *Member for Woodford,* 181.

78. Howells, *Simply Churchill*, 19.
79. CSCT, October 27, 1962.
80. Gilbert, *In Search of Churchill*, 316.
81. CSCT, October 16, 1962.
82. Soames, *Clementine Churchill*, 528.
83. Author's interview with Shelagh Montague Browne, March 29, 2014.
84. Sarah Churchill, *Keep On Dancing*, 206.
85. Howells, *Simply Churchill*, 168.
86. Sarah Churchill, *Thread in the Tapestry*, 15.
87. Beaton and Vickers, *Beaton in the Sixties*, 17.
88. Ibid., 19.
89. Author's interview with Edwina Sandys, April 25, 2014.

Epilogue

1. Author's interview with Celia Sandys, October 1, 2013.
2. Author's interview with Doreen Pugh, September 9, 2013.
3. Winston S. Churchill, *His Father's Son*, 462.
4. Author's interview with David Montgomery, November 28, 2013.
5. Colville, *Churchillians*, 210.
6. PHP, box 3.
7. Fishman, *My Darling Clementine*, 464.
8. Moran, *Struggle for Survival*, 828.

Bibliography

Addison, Christopher. "The Japanese Surrender: Address to the King." *Hansard* 137, August 15, 1945. http://hansard.millbanksystems.com/lords/1945/aug/15/the -japanese-surrender-address-to-the.

Addison, Paul. *Churchill: The Unexpected Hero.* Oxford University Press, 2005.

Airlie, Mabell. *Thatched with Gold: The Memoirs of Mabell, Countess of Airlie.* Edited by Jennifer Ellis. Hutchinson, 1962.

Asquith, Lady Cynthia, and L. P. Hartley. *The Diaries of Lady Cynthia Asquith 1915–18.* Century, 1987.

Asquith, H. H. *Letters to Venetia Stanley.* Edited by Michael Brock and Eleanor Brock. Oxford University Press, 1988.

Barrymore, Ethel. *Memories.* Hulton Press, 1956.

BBC Southern Counties Radio. "A Letter from Mrs. Churchill." September 23, 2005, *WW2 People's War.* http://www.bbc.co.uk/history/ww2peopleswar/stories/04/ a5878704.shtml.

Beaton, Cecil. *Diaries 1922–39: The Wandering Years.* Weidenfeld & Nicolson, 1961.

———. *Diaries 1939–44: The Years Between.* Weidenfeld & Nicolson, 1965.

———. *Diaries 1944–48: The Happy Years.* Weidenfeld & Nicolson, 1972.

———. *Diaries 1948–55: The Strenuous Years.* Weidenfeld & Nicolson, 1973.

———. *Diaries 1955–63: The Restless Years.* Weidenfeld & Nicolson, 1976.

———. *Diaries 1963–74: The Parting Years.* Weidenfeld & Nicolson, 1978.

———. *Self Portrait with Friends: The Selected Diaries of Cecil Beaton 1926–1974.* Weidenfeld & Nicolson, 1979.

Beaton, Cecil, and Hugo Vickers. *Beaton in the Sixties: The Cecil Beaton Diaries as He Wrote Them, 1965–1969.* Weidenfeld & Nicolson, 2003.

Beaverbrook, William Maxwell Aitken. *Politicians and the War 1914–1916.* Lane Publications, 1932.

Bedell Smith, Sally. *Reflected Glory: The Life of Pamela Churchill Harriman.* Simon & Schuster, 1997.

Best, Geoffrey. *Churchill: A Study in Greatness.* Oxford University Press, 2003.

Birkenhead, 1st Earl of (Frederick Edwin Smith). *Churchill 1874–1922.* W. H. Allen, 1989.

———. *The Prof in Two Worlds.* Collins, 1964.

Bonham Carter, Violet. *Champion Redoubtable.* Weidenfeld & Nicolson, 1999.

———. *Daring to Hope.* Orion, 2000.

———. *Lantern Slides: The Diaries and Letters of Violet Bonham Carter 1904–1914*. Weidenfeld & Nicolson, 1996.

———. *Winston Churchill as I Knew Him*. The Reprint Society, 1965.

Booth, Cherie, and Cate Haste. *The Goldfish Bowl: Married to the Prime Minister, 1955–1997*. Vintage, 2005.

Boyle, Andrew. *Poor, Dear Brendan*. Hutchinson, 1974.

Brooke, Alan, 1st Viscount Alanbrooke. *War Diaries 1939–45*. Weidenfeld & Nicolson, 2002.

Buczacki, Stefan. *Churchill and Chartwell: The Untold Story of Churchill's Houses and Gardens*. Frances Lincoln, 2007.

Churchill, Clementine. *My Visit to Russia*. Hutchinson, 1945.

Churchill, John S. *Crowded Canvas*. Odhams Press, 1961.

Churchill, Randolph S. *Twenty-One Years*. Houghton Mifflin, 1965.

Churchill, Sarah. *A Thread in the Tapestry*. Deutsch, 1967.

———. *Keep On Dancing*. Weidenfeld & Nicolson, 1981.

Churchill, Winston. *My Early Life*. The Reprint Society, 1944.

———. *Painting as a Pastime*. Odhams Press, 1948.

———. *Savrola*. Longmans Green, 1900.

———. *The Second World War*. Vol. 1, *The Gathering Storm*. Cassell, 1948.

———. *The Second World War*. Vol. 2, *Their Finest Hour*. Cassell, 1949.

———. *The Second World War*. Vol. 3, *The Grand Alliance*. Cassell, 1950.

Churchill, Winston S. *His Father's Son: The Life of Randolph S. Churchill*. Weidenfeld & Nicolson, 1996.

———. *Memories and Adventures*. Weidenfeld & Nicolson, 1989.

———, ed. *Never Give In!: The Best of Winston Churchill's Speeches*. Hyperion, 2004.

Clark, Alan. *The Donkeys*. Pimlico, 1998.

Cockett, Richard. *My Dear Max: The Letters of Brendan Bracken to Lord Beaverbrook, 1925–58*. Historians' Press, 1990.

Colville, John. *The Churchillians*. Weidenfeld & Nicolson, 1981.

———. *Footprints in Time*. Collins, 1976.

———. *The Fringes of Power: 10 Downing Street Diaries 1939–1955*. W. W. Norton & Company, 1986.

———. *Winston Churchill and His Inner Circle*. Simon & Schuster, 1981.

Cooper, Lady Diana. *The Light of Common Day*. Houghton Mifflin, 1959.

———. *Trumpets from the Steep*. Hart-Davis, 1960.

Cooper, Duff. *Diaries 1915–51*. Edited by John Julius Norwich. Weidenfeld & Nicolson, 2006.

———. *Old Men Forget: The Autobiography of Duff Cooper*. Rupert Hart-Davis, 1953.

Cornwallis-West, Mrs. George. *The Reminiscences of Lady Randolph Churchill*. Edward Arnold, 1908.

Coward, Noël. *The Noël Coward Diaries*. Edited by Graham Payn and Sheridan Morley. Little, Brown, 1982.

Cowles, Virginia. *Looking for Trouble*. Hamish Hamilton, 1941.

———. *Winston Churchill: The Era and the Man*. Hamish Hamilton, 1953.

Dalton, Hugh. *The Second World War Diary of Hugh Dalton, 1940–45*. Edited by Ben Pimlott. Jonathan Cape, 1986.

Eden, Anthony. *The Memoirs of Anthony Eden, Full Circle*. Cassell, 1960.

Esher, Reginald Viscount. *Journals and Letters of Reginald Viscount Esher*. Nicholson and Watson, 1934.

Fedden, Robin. *Churchill and Chartwell*. National Trust, Pergamon Press, 1968.

Fishman, Jack. *My Darling Clementine*. W. H. Allen, 1974.

Gibb, D. E. W. *Lloyd's of London: A Study in Individualism*. Macmillan, 1957.

Gilbert, Martin. *In Search of Churchill*. HarperCollins, 1995.

———. *Winston S. Churchill*. Vol. 3, *The Challenge of War 1914–1916*. Heinemann, 1971.

———. *Winston S. Churchill*. Vol. 4, *World in Torment 1916–1922*. Heinemann, 1975.

———. *Winston S. Churchill*. Vol. 5, *The Coming of War 1936–1939*. Heinemann, 1982.

———. *Winston S. Churchill*. Vol. 6, *Finest Hour 1939–1941*. Heinemann, 1983.

———. *Winston S. Churchill*. Vol. 7, *Road to Victory 1941–1945*. Heinemann, 1986.

Gilbert, Martin, and Randolph S. Churchill. *Winston S. Churchill*. Vol. 2, *Young Statesman 1901–1914*. Heinemann, 1988.

Goodwin, Doris Kearns. *No Ordinary Time: Franklin & Eleanor Roosevelt: The Home Front in World War II*. Touchstone, 1995.

Harriman, William Averell, and Elie Abel. *Special Envoy to Churchill and Stalin, 1941–1946*. Random House, 1972.

Harris, Kenneth. *Attlee*. Orion, 1995.

Hart-Davis, Duff, ed. *End of an Era: Letters and Journals of Sir Alan Lascelles from 1887 to 1920*. Hamish Hamilton, 1986.

Hassall, Christopher. *Edward Marsh: A Biography*. Longmans, 1959.

Hassett, William. *Off the Record with FDR*. George Allen & Unwin, 1960.

Hastings, Max. *Finest Years: Churchill as Warlord 1940–45*. Harper Press, 2009.

Holmes, Richard. *Churchill's Bunker: The Secret Headquarters at the Heart of Britain's Victory*. Profile Books, 2009.

Horne, Alistair, *Macmillan: 1894–1956*. Macmillan, 1988.

Hough, Richard. *Winston and Clementine: The Triumphs and Tragedies of the Churchills*. Bantam Books, 1991.

Howells, Roy. *Simply Churchill*. Robert Hale, 1965.

Ismay, Lord Hastings. *The Memoirs of Lord Ismay*. Heinemann, 1960.

Jackson, Ashley. *Churchill*. Quercus, 2012.

James, Robert Rhodes. *Bob Boothby: A Portrait*. Hodder & Stoughton, 1991.

———, ed. *Chips: The Diaries of Sir Henry Channon*. Weidenfeld & Nicolson, 1967.

Jenkins, Roy. *Asquith*. Collins, 1964.

———. *Churchill*. Pan Macmillan, 2001.

Kimball, Warren F., ed. *Churchill and Roosevelt: The Complete Correspondence*. Vol. 2, *Alliance Forged*. Princeton University Press, 1964.

———. *Churchill and Roosevelt: The Complete Correspondence*. Vol. 3, *Alliance Declining*. Princeton University Press, 1984.

"The Lady of No. 10." *Picture Post*, November 23, 1940.

Lash, Joseph. *Eleanor and Franklin*. Deutsch, 1972.

———. *Roosevelt and Churchill*. Deutsch, 1977.

Lee, Arthur Hamilton. *"A Good Innings": The Private Papers of Viscount Lee of Fareham*. Edited by Alan Clark. John Murray, 1974.

Lee, Celia. *Jean, Lady Hamilton 1861–1941: A Soldier's Wife*. Celia Lee, 2001.

Lees-Milne, James. *Caves of Ice*. Faber and Faber, 1983.

Leslie, Anita. *Cousin Randolph: The Life of Randolph Churchill*. Hutchinson, 1985.

———. *Jennie: The Life of Lady Randolph Churchill*. Hutchinson, 1971.

Lockhart, Sir Robert Bruce. *The Diaries of Sir Robert Bruce Lockhart*. Vol. 1, *1915–1938*. Macmillan, 1973.

———. *The Diaries of Sir Robert Bruce Lockhart*. Vol. 2, *1939–1965*. Macmillan, 1980.

Longford, Elizabeth. *A Pilgrimage of Passion: The Life of Wilfrid Scawen Blunt*. Weidenfeld & Nicolson, 1979.

———. *The Queen Mother*. HarperCollins, 1981.

Longford, Ruth. *Frances, Countess Lloyd-George: More Than a Mistress*. Gracewing, 1996.

Lovell, Mary S. *The Churchills: In Love and War*. W. W. Norton, 2011.

———. *The Mitford Girls: The Biography of an Extraordinary Family*. Abacus, 2003.

Lysaght, Charles Edward. *Brendan Bracken*. Allen Lane, 1979.

Maisky, Ivan. *Memoirs of a Soviet Ambassador*. Hutchinson, 1967.

Manchester, William. *The Caged Lion: Winston Spencer Churchill, 1932–1940*. Michael Joseph, 1988.

———. *The Last Lion: Winston Spencer Churchill*. Vol. 1, *Visions of Glory: 1874–1932*. Michael Joseph, 1983.

———. *The Last Lion: Winston Spencer Churchill*. Vol. 2, *Alone: 1932–1940*. Little, Brown, 1988.

———. *The Last Lion: Winston Spencer Churchill*. Vol. 3, *Defender of the Realm: 1940–1965*. Little, Brown, 2012.

Marsh, Edward. *A Number of People: A Book of Reminiscences*. Heinemann, 1939.

Martin, Sir John. *Downing Street: The War Years*. Bloomsbury, 1991.

McGowan, Norman. *My Years with Churchill*. Souvenir Press, 1958.

Meacham, Jon. *Franklin and Winston: An Intimate Portrait of an Epic Friendship*. Random House, 2004.

Minney, R. J. *No. 10 Downing Street*. Cassell, 1963.

Mitford, Nancy. *The Stanleys of Alderley: Their Letters Between the Years 1851–1865*. Hamish Hamilton, 1939.

Montague Browne, Anthony. *Long Sunset: Memoirs of Winston Churchill's Last Private Secretary*. Podkin Press, 2009.

Montgomery, Bernard Law. *The Memoirs of Field Marshal the Viscount Montgomery of Alamein*. Collins, 1950.

Moran, Lord Charles. *Churchill: Taken from the Diaries of Lord Moran*. Houghton Mifflin Company, 1966.

———. *Winston Churchill: The Struggle for Survival 1940–1965*. Simon & Schuster, 1982.

Morgan, Ted. *Churchill: Young Man in a Hurry, 1874–1915*. Simon & Schuster, 1984.

Morgenthau, Henry. *Diaries: Years of War, 1941–1945*. Houghton Mifflin, 1967.

———. *Mostly Morgenthaus: A Family History*. Ticknor & Fields, 1991.

———. *Roosevelt and Morgenthau: A Revision and Condensation of the Morgenthau Diaries*. Edited by John Martin Blum. Houghton Mifflin, 1970.

Nel, Elizabeth. *Mr. Churchill's Secretary*. Hodder & Stoughton, 1958.

Ogden, Christopher. *Life of the Party: The Biography of Pamela Digby Churchill Hayward Harriman*. Little, Brown, 1994.

Olson, Lynne. *Citizens of London: The Americans Who Stood with Britain in Its Darkest, Finest Hour*. Random House, 2010.

———. *Troublesome Young Men: The Rebels Who Brought Churchill to Power and Helped Save England*. Farrar Straus Giroux, 2007.

Parrish, Thomas. *To Keep the British Isles Afloat: FDR's Men in Churchill's London, 1941*. Smithsonian, 2009.

Pawle, Gerald. *The War and Colonel Warden*. G. G. Harrap, 1963.

Pearson, John. *Citadel of the Heart*. Macmillan, 1991.

Reynolds, David. *In Command of History: Churchill Fighting and Writing the Second World War*. Penguin, 2004.

Riddell, Lord George. *Lord Riddell's War Diary 1914–1918.* Nicholson & Watson, 1933.

Roosevelt, Eleanor. *This I Remember.* Hutchinson, 1950.

Roosevelt, Elliott, ed. *The Roosevelt Letters.* Harrap, 1952.

Rosenman, Samuel. *Working with Roosevelt.* Hart-Davis, 1952.

Sandys, Celia. *Chasing Churchill: The Travels of Winston Churchill.* Unicorn Press, 2014.

———. *From Winston with Love and Kisses: The Young Churchill.* Texas A&M University Press, 2013.

———. *The Young Churchill.* E. P. Dutton, 1995.

Scawen Blunt, Wilfrid. *My Diaries.* Vol. 2, *1900–1914.* Alfred. A. Knopf, 1921.

Sebba, Anne. *American Jennie: The Remarkable Life of Lady Randolph Churchill.* W. W. Norton, 2007.

Shelden, Michael. *Young Titan: The Making of Winston Churchill.* Simon & Schuster, 2013.

Sherwood, Robert E. *Roosevelt and Hopkins: An Intimate History.* Harper & Brothers, 1948.

Soames, Mary. *A Daughter's Tale: The Memoir of Winston and Clementine Churchill's Youngest Child.* Black Swan, 2011.

———. *Clementine Churchill.* Doubleday, 2002.

———, ed. *Speaking for Themselves: The Personal Letters of Winston and Clementine Churchill.* Black Swan, 1999.

Stanley, Thomas, Eighth Lord Stanley of Alderley. *A Politically Incorrect Story: The Stanley of Alderley Family 1927–2001.* Privately printed, 2002.

Stelzer, Cita. *Dinner with Churchill: Policy-Making at the Dinner Table.* Short Books, 2011.

Swift, Will. *The Roosevelts and the Royals.* John Wiley, 2004.

Taylor, A. J. P. *English History 1914–1945.* Penguin, 1982.

Thomas, David. *Churchill: The Member for Woodford.* Frank Cass, 1995.

Thompson, Walter H. *Assignment: Churchill.* Farrar, Straus & Young, 1955.

———. *Sixty Minutes.* Christopher Johnson, 1957.

Tilden, Philip. *True Remembrances of an Architect.* Country Life, 1954.

Tree, Ronald. *When the Moon Was High.* Macmillan, 1975.

Vanderbilt Balsan, Consuelo. *The Glitter and the Gold.* Harper, 1952.

Vickers, Hugo. *Cecil Beaton: The Authorised Biography.* Weidenfeld & Nicolson, 1985.

Ward, Geoffrey. *Closest Companion: The Unknown Story of the Intimate Friendship Between Franklin Roosevelt and Margaret Suckley.* Houghton Mifflin, 1996.

Waugh, Evelyn. *The Letters of Evelyn Waugh.* Edited by Mark Amory. Phoenix, 1980.

Webb, Beatrice. *Our Partnership.* Longmans, Green, 1948.

Wheeler-Bennett, Sir John, ed. *Action This Day: Working with Churchill.* Macmillan, 1968.

White-Smith, Heather. *My Years with the Churchills: A Young Girl's Memories.* Cotesworth Publishing, 2011.

Winant, John Gilbert. *A Letter from Grosvenor Square.* Houghton Mifflin, 1947.

Wingate, Sir Ronald. *Lord Ismay: A Biography.* Hutchinson, 1970.

Index